WEAPON OF PEACE

How Religious Liberty Combats Terrorism

Religious terrorism poses a significant challenge for many countries around the world. Extremists who justify violence in God's name can be found in every religious tradition, and attacks perpetrated by faith-based militants have increased dramatically over the past three decades. Given the reality of religious terrorism today, it would seem counter-intuitive that the best weapon against violent religious extremism would be for countries and societies to allow for the free practice of religion; yet this is precisely what this book argues. *Weapon of Peace* investigates the link between terrorism and the repression of religion, both from a historical perspective and against contemporary developments in the Middle East and elsewhere. Drawing upon a range of different case studies and quantitative data, Saiya makes the case that the suppression and not the expression of religion leads to violence and extremism and that safeguarding religious freedom is both a moral and strategic imperative.

Nilay Saiya is assistant professor of public policy and global affairs at Nanyang Technological University.

T0381691

Weapon of Peace

HOW RELIGIOUS LIBERTY COMBATS TERRORISM

NILAY SAIYA

Nanyang Technological University

CAMBRIDGE
UNIVERSITY PRESS

University Printing House, Cambridge CB2 8BS, United Kingdom

One Liberty Plaza, 20th Floor, New York, NY 10006, USA

477 Williamstown Road, Port Melbourne, VIC 3207, Australia

314-321, 3rd Floor, Plot 3, Splendor Forum, Jasola District Centre, New Delhi - 110025, India

79 Anson Road, #06-04/06, Singapore 079906

Cambridge University Press is part of the University of Cambridge.

It furthers the University's mission by disseminating knowledge in the pursuit of education, learning and research at the highest international levels of excellence.

www.cambridge.org
Information on this title: www.cambridge.org/9781108464116
DOI: 10.1017/9781108565127

First published 2018
First paperback edition 2019

A catalogue record for this publication is available from the British Library

ISBN 978-1-108-47431-3 Hardback
ISBN 978-1-108-46411-6 Paperback

For Jessica, Cristiano and Sanjay

Contents

Figures and Tables

Figures

Tables

Acknowledgments

This book would not have been possible without the encouragement and advice of many individuals, more than can possibly be recognized in this brief space. I will nevertheless attempt to acknowledge those to whom I am most greatly indebted. This project builds on the work of several giants in the field of religion and global politics. These individuals include Robert Dowd, Thomas Farr, Jonathan Fox, Anthony Gill, Brian Grim, Allen Hertzke, William Inboden, Ahmet Kuru, Eric Patterson, Timothy Samuel Shah and Monica Duffy Toft, several of whom were kind enough to comment on portions of this manuscript. Foremost among these giants is my mentor and friend Daniel Philpott, without whose support and encouragement this book would not have been written. His thorough reading of numerous draft chapters, thoughtful feedback and constant encouragement helped keep me focused and motivated throughout the writing process. I owe him a profound debt of gratitude.

I am grateful for the helpful feedback offered by several others, including Robert Bosco, Michael Boyle, David Campbell, Kevin Den Dulk, Michael Desch, Robert Joustra, Kathryn Lambert, Paul Lenze, Andres Martinez, Bryan McGraw, Ashlyn Webb and Joshua Su Ya Wu. I am most grateful for the advice, comments and critiques raised in the thoughtful, substantive and thorough reviews offered by the reviewers for Cambridge University Press.

Over the years, I have had the good fortune of working with several excellent student research assistants at the University of Notre Dame and the State University of New York. These students include Sean Callan, Michael Kavanagh, Colin Kerr, Sean Kipybida, Rebekah Klingensmith, Christopher Licata, Samantha Schifano and Jaqueline Shine. I am especially indebted to my assistant of four years, Joshua Fidler, whose work on this book can only be described as virtuoso. Special thanks also to Cassandra Persons who helped me overcome the technical challenges in completing this book.

I thank those at the Berkley Center for Religion, Peace, and World Affairs at Georgetown University – and the Religious Freedom Project in particular – for inviting me to present my work on religious freedom and violent religious extremism at the summit "International Religious Freedom: Towards a Model of Transatlantic Cooperation" in 2015. I am also grateful to the leadership of the Religious Freedom Institute – especially Thomas Farr and Timothy Samuel Shah – for arranging for me to present my findings on religious repression and terrorism to the National Security Council of the United States and the US Department of State in 2017. The feedback I received at these events, both from scholars and from policymakers, helped strengthen the arguments and evidence in the pages that follow.

This project draws, in part, on the quantitative data on religion–state arrangements and international religious freedom painstakingly compiled by Roger Finke, Jonathan Fox, Brian Grim and those at the Pew Research Center. The quantitative, cross-national study of religion has made rapid progress thanks to the hard work of these individuals.

My editor at Cambridge University Press, John Berger, did an outstanding job editing this book. I thank John for so enthusiastically believing in this project and for his patience in seeing it through. I am grateful to John's team at Cambridge University Press who managed the day-to-day operations of this project, especially Danielle Menz and Rebecca Jackaman. Special thanks also to my copyeditor, Ami Naramor, for so assiduously reading this manuscript.

Generous research support for this book was made possible through grants from the Andrew W. Mellon Foundation, the Research Office of the State University of New York and the University of Notre Dame.

Finally, I thank my wife, Jessica, and my children, Cristiano and Sanjay, who were a constant source of moral support throughout. It is to them I dedicate this book.

Introduction: Religious Resurgence, Repression and Resistance

A beautiful, seemingly ordinary late summer morning witnessed one of the most barbarous atrocities in recent history. On that day, nineteen religious zealots hijacked four civilian airliners and skillfully guided them into two of the most recognizable buildings in the world: the World Trade Center in New York City and the Pentagon in Washington, DC, taking the lives of 3,000 civilians. The strikes of September 11, 2001 were the most spectacular and devastating attacks by a terrorist group against a state in world history and a catalyst for jihadi movements around the world. Many believe that the 9/11 attacks, carried out by an extremist Islamist organization known as al Qaeda, ushered in a new era of terrorism qualitatively different from previous periods of terrorist activity, distinguished by its overtly religious character, uncompromising worldview and relative lethality. The strikes also led to a fundamental rethinking of domestic and international security policy as decision makers took the unique threat posed by the "new terrorism" seriously. Americans quickly saw an overhaul and reorganization of their government bureaucracies and the implementation of broad-ranging security measures. Internationally, the United States embarked on a campaign known as the "Global War on Terrorism" to eliminate al Qaeda and related groups. This war witnessed the toppling of the Taliban regime in Afghanistan one month after the 9/11 attacks, the invasion of Iraq in 2003 and subsequent ten-year occupation of that country, drone wars in Pakistan and Yemen and special operations in dozens of other states.

Since those attacks at the turn of the century, the world has experienced a sharp increase in violent religious extremism. Today, religious terrorism poses a significant challenge for many countries around the world. Data derived and coded from the Global Terrorism Database reveal that in the year preceding the 9/11 attacks, the world witnessed only 255 identifiable religious terrorist attacks. By the year 2014, that number had risen nearly tenfold to 2,237.[1] The number of religious terrorist groups has proliferated as well. In 2001, the US Department of State designated only seven religious groups as "foreign terrorist organizations," which it deemed posed a

---

[1] This number itself underestimates the number of religious terrorist attacks since it takes into account only "identifiable" religious terrorist incidents.

national security threat to the United States. By the year 2016, the number had reached forty-five.[2] During the same time that religious terrorism has been rising, terrorism rooted in secular concerns has seen a relative decline.

Religion-related terrorism has now become a daily occurrence. Anyone who opens a newspaper or watches cable news on a regular basis is bound to be inundated by stories of religious violence: the atrocities of the Islamic State in Iraq and Syria (ISIS), the conflict between Muslims and Christians in Central Africa, attacks by Buddhists against Muslims in Burma and Hindus in Sri Lanka, the kidnapping of schoolgirls in Nigeria by Boko Haram or recent lone-wolf attacks in Europe and the Americas. Hardly a day goes by without news headlines reporting religiously based beheadings, crucifixions, assassinations, bombings or attacks on holy sites. Episodes such as these testify to a world where religion exerts a consistent and deadly influence on patterns of violence. What lies behind this surge in religiously moti-vated terrorism?

To answer this question, we must consider three global trends related to religion. The first is the so-called global resurgence of religion.[3] Recent scholarship has shown that religion is gaining in strength worldwide and is more politically engaged today than it has ever been. Owing to processes like modernization, globalization and democratization – the very developments that the secularization thesis (the idea born of the Enlightenment that religion would eventually disappear as societies modernized) predicted would kill off religion – coupled with the evident failures of secular projects and ideologies in developing countries, the major world religions have experienced a newfound relevance in the modern world. Even today, nearly 85 percent of the global population subscribes to some form of religious belief.[4] The realization that the world is becoming more and not less religious led eminent sociologist Peter Berger, once an ardent supporter of the secularization thesis, to remark in 1999 that the world is "as furiously religious as it ever was, and in some places more so than ever."[5]

The second trend involves the concurrent attempts to restrict religious practice in the face of this resurgence. Successive reports by the nonpartisan Pew Research Center have revealed that approximately three-quarters of people in the world live in countries characterized by "high" or "very high" religious restrictions. Incredibly,

[2] US Department of State, "Country Reports on Terrorism, 2000–2016," last modified 2016, www .state.gov/j/ct/rls/crt/.
[3] See Josè Casanova, *Public Religions in the Modern World* (Chicago, IL: University of Chicago Press, 1994); Gilles Kepel, *The Revenge of God: The Resurgence of Islam, Christianity, and Judaism in the Modern World* (University Park, PA: Pennsylvania State University Press, 1994); Peter L. Berger, *The Desecularization of the World: Resurgent Religion and World Politics* (Grand Rapids, MI: William B. Eerdmans Publishing Company, 1999); Monica Duffy Toft and Timothy Samuel Shah, "Why God Is Winning," *Foreign Policy* 155 (2006): 39–43; Monica Duffy Toft, Daniel Philpott and Timothy Samuel Shah, *God's Century: Resurgent Religion and Global Politics* (New York, NY: W. W. Norton, 2011).
[4] Pew Research Center, "The Global Religious Landscape," last modified December 18, 2012, www .pewforum.org/2012/12/18/global-religious-landscape-exec/.
[5] Berger, *Desecularization of the World*, 2.

the reports also find that only 1 percent of the world's population lives in countries where religious liberty is increasing.[6] These findings are confirmed by the work of the director of the Religion and State Project, Jonathan Fox. His research shows that of thirty specific types of religious limitations, twenty-eight are more common today than they were in 1990.[7] High restrictions on religious belief and practice can be found in every region of the world and within every faith tradition. Religiously repressive regimes can be found in Christian Russia and Eritria, Buddhist Burma and Laos, Hindu India and Nepal, Muslim Pakistan and Saudi Arabia, and Jewish Israel.

The convergence of these two antithetical trends – religion's revival and simulta- neous regulation – has given rise to a third development: resistance. Religious believers who find the practice of their faith stifled are likely to resist those efforts or support those who do. Sometimes this resistance takes the form of nonviolent protest as in Eastern Europe following the collapse of the Soviet Union. At other times, the reaction to repression can turn violent, even to the point of tearing countries apart and threatening the stability of their neighbors.

This book contends that these three trends are inextricably intertwined. The argument put forward in these pages is a simple one: attempts by states and societies to repress assertive religion produce the very fanaticism and terrorism that they seek to avoid. It is no coincidence that the vast majority of countries in the world from which the most serious threats to domestic and international peace and security arise are the very ones in which religious persecution is a significant problem. Not only do militant groups believe that their religions' teachings, rituals and scriptures justify violence, they must also engage in a battle for hearts and minds, attempting to convince the larger population that their ideas are justified. The greater the level of suppression, the more likely that the wider populace will take these claims seriously.

Because religion remains a primary identity of people (especially in highly religious countries), religious freedom is inevitably connected to peace, stability and successful political orders. Where religious liberty does not exist, the potential for domestic and international peace and stability will be greatly weakened. The compromising of religious liberty is particularly dangerous because of religion's proven ability to inspire deadly conflicts against those who hold different faith beliefs. While not necessarily always the direct proximate cause of conflict, restric- tions that inhibit religious belief and practice can contribute to extremist theologies that result in aggression toward specific religious communities, the government or

---

6 Pew Research Center, "Rising Tide of Restrictions on Religion," last modified August 9, 2011, www.pewforum.org/2011/08/09/rising-restrictions-on-religion2/; Pew Research Center, "Religious Hostilities Reach Six-Year High," last modified January 1, 2014, www.pewforum.org/2014/01/14/ religious-hostilities-reach-six-year-high/.

7 Jonathan Fox, "Equal Opportunity Oppression: Religious Persecution Is a Global Problem," *Foreign Affairs*, last modified August 31, 2015, www.foreignaffairs.com/articles/2015–08-31/equal-opportunity- oppression.

even other countries. It is this overlooked dimension of terrorism on which this book hopes to shine light.

The relationship between religious freedom and religious terrorism is not necessarily self-evident. There is also a competing perspective. This position holds that unrestrained religious liberty opens the floodgates to religious extremism, especially in an interconnected world where radical ideas can spread like wildfire. According to this line of reasoning, religious extremists benefit from environments of religious freedom to create a world where they can ultimately impose their view of religion upon everyone else.[8] Conversely, increasing repression of religious groups can raise the costs of rebellion and deter potential terrorists.[9] This logic rests on the assumption that liberalism shackles governments from using all of the weapons in their arsenal to optimize their counterterrorism strategies. In countries where this thinking prevails, the result is a perceived zero-sum game: religious restrictions, as morally problematic as they might be, are seen as necessary to curtail religious terrorism.

Many state leaders around the world have bought into this logic, contending that effectively averting terrorism may require their governments to limit or suspend freedoms like religious liberty in the name of national security. In the Middle East and North Africa, leaders have resorted to sham trials, severe sentences for nonviolent dissidents and the widespread use of force in the name of combating terrorism.[10] In Central Asia, thousands of men of faith have reported being detained and forced to shave their beards by authorities keen on battling radicalism and foreign religious influences. In 2015, the Tajik parliament voted to ban Arabic-sounding foreign names, while the Supreme Court voted to outlaw the Islamic Renaissance Party of Tajikistan, the country's only Islamic political party, and sentenced several of its members to prison terms the following year.[11] In neighboring Uzbekistan, the state has engaged in a campaign of systematic persecution of religious groups, targeting nonviolent believers who preach or study religion outside of officially sanctioned state institutions. The Uzbek government has justified the repression of religion as a necessary step to prevent terrorism.[12] In China, the state has passed a series of laws targeted against religious groups, ranging from bans on fasting during Ramadan to prohibitions on the wearing of religious garb, ostensibly

---

[8]   Katerina Dalacoura, *Islamist Terrorism and Democracy in the Middle East* (New York, NY: Cambridge University Press, 2011).

[9]   Shadi Hamid, *Temptations of Power: Islamists and Liberal Democracy in a New Middle East* (Oxford: Oxford University Press, 2014).

[10] Luke Lagon and Arch Puddington, "Exploiting Terrorism as a Pretext for Repression," *Wall Street Journal*, January 28, 2015, A15.

[11] Hardeep Matharu, "Tajikistan Police Shave Beards of 13,000 Men to 'Tackle Radicalism,'" *Independent*, last modified January 21, 2016, www.independent.co.uk/news/world/asia/tajikistan-police-shave-beards-of-13000-men-to-tackle-radicalism-a6825581.html.

[12] Human Rights Watch, *Creating Enemies of the State: Religious Persecution in Uzbekistan*, last modified March 29, 2004, www.hrw.org/report/2004/03/29/creating-enemies-state/religious-persecution-uzbekistan.

for the purpose of nipping religious extremism in the bud.[13] In Europe, far-right parties like France's National Front, Germany's Alternative Party, Hungary's Jobbik, Austria's Freedom Party and Greece's Golden Dawn have been surging in popularity, owing, in large part, to their hostility to Muslim immigration – a stance spurred by the Syrian refugee crisis. In the wake of separate terrorist attacks in Paris in 2015, some French politicians called for the official institutionalization of mosques and for banning the Arabic language during Muslim ceremonies. Likewise, across the Atlantic, in his quest to become America's forty-fifth president, Donald Trump persistently scorned refugees, embraced the idea of a mandatory Muslim registry and the policing of predominately Muslim neighborhoods, proposed torturing the family members of suspected terrorists and vowed to ban Muslims from entering the country. During his first week in office, Trump signed an executive order temporarily banning citizens of seven Muslim countries from entering the United States for a period of ninety days and refugees from Syria indefinitely. The president justified these unprecedented measures on national security grounds.

Given the reality of religious terrorism today, political leaders in these countries might be forgiven for believing that measures like these are the best weapon against violent religious extremism. This book directly challenges this view, arguing that repressive environments like these that choke religious liberty and independent thinking serve as a natural breeding ground for terrorism. In addition to suppressing the positive contributions that religion can make to society, repression also silences the voices of liberalism and moderation and empowers the narrative of extremists who claim that the state is acting unjustly toward people of faith.[14] Violence occurs because religious restrictions both create grievances on the part of targeted groups and sometimes encourage dominant religious groups to undertake violence themselves against other religious communities. Thus, regimes that repress religion invite the very belligerency they seek to thwart through such restrictions.

Conversely, religiously free countries allow for the development of a wide range of diverse perspectives, religious practices and cross-cutting cleavages.[15] The freedom of thought and exchange of ideas that is part and parcel of religious liberty serves to create a marketplace of views that can empower liberal and moderate voices who challenge the claims made by religious extremists, thus diminishing the appeal of extremism and prospects for religious strife. In such countries, individuals belonging to different religious communities tend to see each other as legitimate, even if they disagree on matters of faith and

---

[13] Li Ya, "China Bans Many Muslims from Ramadan Fast," *Voice of America News*, last modified July 8, 2014, www.voanews.com/a/china-bans-many-uighur-muslims-from-ramadan-fast/1952829.html.

[14] Lisa Anderson, "Fulfilling Prophecies: State Policy and Islamist Radicalism," in *Political Islam: Revolution, Radicalism, or Reform?*, ed. John L. Esposito (London: Lynne Rienner Publishers), 17–31.

[15] Chris Seiple and Dennis R. Hoover, "Religious Liberty and Global Security," in *The Future of Religious Liberty: Global Challenges*, ed. Allen D. Hertzke (New York, NY: Oxford University Press, 2013), 315–330.

practice.[16] Freedom thus has the effect of leveling the playing field among the different religious groups in society. Furthermore, the political openness attendant to religious liberty allows potential extremists to work through alternative and legitimate channels – electoral participation, grassroots activism and civic engagement – by which they can seek to shape religion, politics and society.[17] Finally, regimes tolerant of religion promote stability through the civic activities in which they allow religious bodies to engage: running schools, hospitals, orphanages and charities; reducing poverty; and promoting faith-based reconciliation practices. Illiberal religious groups holding radical theologies may well exist in religiously free countries, but the environment of freedom can serve to deprive fringe groups of the legitimacy they need to thrive.[18]

FIVE QUALIFICATIONS

Before proceeding, it is necessary to underscore five qualifications about the nature of the argument. First, this book in no way suggests that religiously free countries *never* experience religious terrorism or that countries with high levels of religious restrictions *always* do. Much depends on the nature of the repression and the political opportunities present. In fact, a good case can be made that the most brutally authoritarian states like Nazi Germany, Stalinist Russia or contemporary North Korea are best at suppressing terrorist impulses because they effectively block all collective action avenues for terrorists to organize around their cause.[19] In these cases, the degree of religious persecution is so intense and pervasive that religious groups cannot carry out *any* practices central to their faith, let alone engage in violence.[20] This extreme and exceedingly rare form of repression notwithstanding, however, the basic correlation between religious repression and religious terrorism still holds as most states lack the ability or the desire to regulate religious life to such an extent. Indiscriminate and widespread repression of religion generally raises the costs of *remaining peaceful* for ordinary citizens, insofar as armed resistance presents the possibility of changing the status quo, thus decreasing the costs of collective

[16] Anthony Gill, *The Political Origins of Religious Liberty* (New York, NY: Cambridge University Press, 2008).
[17] Alfred C. Stepan, "Religion, Democracy, and the 'Twin Tolerations,'" *Journal of Democracy* 11, no. 4 (2000): 37–57.
[18] Thomas F. Farr, *World of Faith and Freedom: Why International Religious Liberty Is Vital to American National Security* (New York, NY: Oxford University Press, 2008), 243–272.
[19] Mayer N. Zald and John D. McCarthy, *The Dynamics of Social Movements: Resource Mobilization, Social Control and Tactics* (Cambridge, MA: Winthrop Publishers, 1979); Doug McAdam, John D. McCarty and Mayer N. Zald, *Comparative Perspectives on Social Movements: Political Opportunities, Mobilizing Structures, and Cultural Framings* (Cambridge: Cambridge University Press, 1996).
[20] Although, at least in the case of the Soviet Union, a good argument can be made that decades of brutal repression by Vladimir Lenin and Joseph Stalin and more recently Vladimir Putin against the tiny Chechen enclave gave rise to an extreme Islamist secessionist movement and cycles of violence and extremism.

action.[21] Furthermore, while terrorism in religiously free settings may occur, it tends not to be widespread and is often perpetrated by "lone wolf" terrorists who lack broad-based societal support for their violent actions. While terrorism indeed poses a threat to both religiously free and religiously restrictive societies alike, it is apparently able to flourish only in the latter. When faith-based terrorism does occur in religiously free countries, it can usually be linked in some way to a religiously restrictive state.

Second, this book focuses on one particular manifestation of religious repression: the manner in which governments restrict religion. There are other ways in which religion can be repressed, however. Most important apart from government restrictions are restrictions on religion that arise at the societal level. Often, the most vocal advocates for religious restrictions are those of dominant religious groups. As explained by sociologists Brian Grim and Roger Finke, established or dominant religious groups frequently call not only on political leaders but also their own followers to deny religious freedoms to others in order to advance their own religious agenda, shut out religious competitors or protect the culture and society as a whole.[22] Such restrictions can include harassment or intimidation of religious groups, detention or displacement of individuals, forced conversions and the imposition of religious dress. The reason I do not examine the ways in which these social religious restrictions foment terrorism is a methodological one. Such restrictions are often carried out by extremist organizations (including terrorist groups), and including them in the present analysis risks conflating the explanation – religious repression – and the outcome – terrorism. I thus leave it to future work to disentangle the relationship between social religious regulation and terrorism.

Third, I in no way discount the importance of ideas in explaining religious terrorism. Indeed, political theology – the ideas a religious group holds about political authority – matters a great deal in explaining religious terrorism.[23] Theological explanations for religious terrorism rightly note that how religious militants interpret their faiths' foundational claims, key sacred texts, historical doctrines and contemporary contexts can inspire them to take up the gun.[24] Such theologies can also exist in any country and at times operate independently of a

---

[21] Nilay Saiya, "Explaining Religious Violence across Countries: An Institutional Perspective," in *Mediating Religion and Government: Political Institutions and the Policy Process*, ed. Kevin R. den Dulk and Elizabeth Oldmixon (New York, NY: Palgrave, 2014), 209–240; Nilay Saiya and Anthony Scime, "Explaining Religious Terrorism: A Data-Mined Analysis," *Conflict Management and Peace Science* 32, no. 5 (2015): 487–512; Nilay Saiya, "Religion, State and Terrorism: A Global Analysis," *Terrorism and Political Violence*. doi: 10.1080/09546553.2016.1211525.

[22] Brian J. Grim and Roger Finke, *The Price of Freedom Denied: Religious Persecution and Conflict in the 21st Century* (New York, NY: Cambridge University Press, 2011), 202–213.

[23] Daniel Philpott, "Explaining the Political Ambivalence of Religion," *American Political Science Review* 101, no. 3 (2007): 505–525.

[24] Bruce Hoffman, "'Holy Terror': The Implications of Terrorism Motivated By a Religious Imperative,'" *Studies in Conflict & Terrorism* 18, no. 4 (1995): 271–284; Mark Juergensmeyer, *Terror in the Mind of God: The Global Rise of Religious Violence* (Berkeley, CA: University of California

country's level of religious freedom. That said, in general, such beliefs tend to become radicalized and more widespread under conditions of repression for the reasons outlined earlier. When religious actors are denied autonomy and freedom to carry out their faith-based practices and these actors subscribe to a political theology that sees violence as an acceptable means to an end, the turn to the gun becomes far more likely.[25]

Fourth, I do not claim here that repression of religion explains *all* aspects of religious terrorism. As a multifaceted and complex phenomenon, terrorism cannot be reduced to a single cause. Indeed many factors – economic dislocation, foreign occupation, a sense of victimhood and threats to traditional ways of life – can certainly exacerbate religious tensions and function as catalyzing agents. Sometimes these forces combine with the denial of religious liberty to fuel grievances and perpetuate conflict. That said, while religious factors may not be the only ones that matter, religious terrorism cannot be properly understood absent their consideration. It is my argument that religious freedom is among the most important but also overlooked of these religious considerations.

Finally, it is possible that countries might become more repressive in *response* to terrorist attacks, thus explaining part of the correlation between religious restrictions and terrorism.[26] Indeed, the need to effectively respond to terrorism can prompt governments to adopt measures that curb a range of freedoms, including religious liberty. For this reason, the relationship between repression of religion and terrorism is best understood as a dynamic, interactive and ongoing cycle: states repress religion; faith-based groups resist and strike back; repression of these groups intensifies as terrorism is used as a pretext for cracking down further on religion.[27] While a spiral of violence is common in religiously repressive countries, a careful examination of the historical record shows that widespread terrorism usually follows rather than precedes repressive policies. Governments might then use the realized threat of terrorism as a justification for further repression.

Press, 2003); Magnus Ranstorp, "Terrorism in the Name of Religion," *Journal of International Affairs* 50 (1996): 41–62; Jessica Stern, *Terror in the Name of God: Why Religious Militants Kill* (New York, NY: Harper Perennial, 2003); Assaf Moghadam, *The Globalization of Martyrdom: Al Qaeda, Salafi Jihad, and the Diffusion of Suicide Attacks* (Baltimore, MD: Johns Hopkins University Press, 2008).

[25] Philpott, "Explaining the Political Ambivalence of Religion," 518–521; Farr, *World of Faith and Freedom*, 243–272; Roger Finke and Jaime D. Harris, "Wars and Rumors of Wars: Explaining Religiously Motivated Violence," in *Religion, Politics, Society, and the State*, ed. Jonathan Fox (New York, NY: Oxford University Press, 2012), 53–71.

[26] Peter S. Henne and Jason Klocek, "Taming the Gods: How Religious Conflict Shapes State Repression," *Journal of Conflict Resolution*. doi: 10.1177/0022002717728104.

[27] Brian J. Grim and Roger Finke, "Religious Persecution in Cross-National Context: Clashing Civilizations or Regulated Religious Economies?" *American Sociological Review* 72, no. 4 (2007): 633–658.

WHAT IS RELIGIOUS TERRORISM?

Some might take issue with the topic under investigation in this book – religious terrorism, the form of violence most likely to result from religious repression. These scholars might argue that because religion is an inherently nebulous concept with imprecise boundaries, the religious–secular dichotomy is best avoided altogether. They would also point out that any attempt to define religion would either leave behind particular belief systems that are generally recognized as religions or include certain systems that most would classify as nonreligious. Religion, in their view, is nothing more than a social and modern construction, and, therefore, it is impossible to distinguish religious from secular violence.[28] Theologian William Cavanaugh, for example, maintains that "the very distinction between secular and religious violence is unhelpful, misleading, and mystifying."[29]

It is indeed difficult to develop a definition of religion that is narrow enough to encompass everything people generally think of as "religious," but that does not include other systems of thought that share certain commonalities with religion and that is also broad enough to include both theistic and nontheistic religions. That religion is notoriously difficult to define should not, however, prevent scholars from studying this subject of importance as a unique class of phenomena. After all, one would be hard-pressed to point to *any* concept of interest to social scientists on which scholars are unanimous in their understanding – i.e., power, politics, democracy, peace, etc. Yet the fact that these ideas are difficult to assign a precise definition has not prevented social scientists from using them effectively and furthering knowledge on these issues. The same logic can be applied to religion.

Following scholar of religion Ivan Strenski, I attempt to use the term "religion" within a specific bounded context such that it is clear what does and does not constitute religion in the pages that follow.[30] I conceive of religion in terms of the core components common to most of the world's faith traditions: (1) a separation of the sacred and profane; (2) a belief in a supernatural being or beings with whom communication is possible; (3) a belief in transcendent realities or an afterlife; and (4) the use of rituals and symbols to attain "knowledge of and harmony with the widest reaches of transcendent reality."[31] I therefore define "religion" as the inter-connected set of beliefs, rituals and practices that form around transcendent, all-encompassing and supernatural answers to ultimate questions related to the purpose of existence. Some might criticize this definition as "essentialist." Nevertheless,

---

[28] Terry Nardin, "Review: Terror in the Mind of God," *Journal of Politics* 63, no. 2 (2001): 683–684; Alexander Spencer, "Questioning the Concept of 'New Terrorism,'" *Peace, Conflict & Development* 8 (2006): 1–33; William T. Cavanaugh, *The Myth of Religious Violence: Secular Ideology and the Roots of Modern Conflict* (Oxford: Oxford University Press, 2009); Jeroen Gunning and Richard Jackson, "What's so 'Religious' about 'Religious Terrorism'?" *Critical Studies on Terrorism* 4, no. 3 (2011): 369–388.

[29] Cavanaugh, *Myth of Religious Violence*, 7.

[30] Ivan Strenski, *Why Politics Can't Be Freed from Religion* (Chichester: Wiley-Blackwell, 2011).

[31] Toft, Philpott and Shah, *God's Century*, 21.

focusing on beliefs and practices rooted in supernatural assumptions has the benefit of allowing for the differentiation of religious and secular frameworks and avoiding debates as to whether ideologies like Marxism or nationalism constitute religions. Another benefit is that a focus on transcendence allows for the separation of terrorist groups driven by a professed religious ideology from groups that may coalesce around a common religious identity but do not have religious goals or motivations as in the cases of the Tamil Tigers, the Irish Republican Army and the Greek Orthodox National Organisation of Cypriot Fighters (EOKA).

Like religion, terrorism has proven a notoriously difficult concept to define. Some estimates put the number of definitions at more than 100.[32] Still, as with defining religion, it is possible to delineate certain features of terrorism that recur in these various definitions. In general, terrorism (1) involves violence and destruction, (2) has political objectives, (3) is premeditated, (4) attempts to instill fear in members of society and (5) primarily targets civilians. For the purposes of this book, then, religious terrorism is defined as premeditated violence, political in nature, which is perpetrated against noncombatants by subnational actors who are driven by a discernible religious motivation or ideology and whose attacks have the intention of instilling fear in members of society.[33]

Much of the quantitative work on terrorism does not attempt to disaggregate terrorism with respect to ideology, motivations or tactics. The majority of these studies tends to lump terrorist groups together without taking into account the guiding ideologies of different organizations. There are good reasons, however, to disaggregate religious and secular terrorism. First, scholarship has shown that religious terrorism constitutes a distinct form of political violence, inherently different from other manifestations of violence. Religious terrorists look to their faith as a source of inspiration, legitimation and worldview, resulting in a totally different incentive structure than exists for their secular counterparts.[34] The belief that they have divine sanction to wage a spiritual war plausibly influences the nature and scope of the demands religious militants make and the violence they undertake. Second, even though religious terrorism is a subset of terrorism in general, only about half of all identifiable terrorist attacks were carried out by religious actors since the end of the Cold War, leading to the possibility that the traits that characterize terrorism in general may not apply to religious terrorists specifically. A general category of "terrorism" runs the risk of being an overly aggregate outcome variable. For this reason, it might be a better idea to differentiate terrorist incidents based on who the perpetrators are and their long-term objectives.

The fact that religious terrorists are motivated by faith beliefs does not preclude the possibility of them seeking religiously informed *material* goals. Studies on

[32] Walter Laqueur, *The New Terrorism: Fanaticism and the Arms of Mass Destruction* (New York, NY: Oxford University Press, 1999), 6.
[33] Bruce Hoffman, *Inside Terrorism* (New York, NY: Columbia University Press, 2006), 81–131.
[34] Juergensmeyer, *Terror in the Mind of God*, 125–126.

religious conflict, for example, seem to concur that, while religious conflicts, including terror campaigns, must have a religious dimension, they do not necessarily have to be *solely* over theological issues. Religious terrorists almost always seek terrestrial objectives like national liberation, regime change, territorial change, policy change, social control, economic concessions or status quo maintenance, though they are always motivated by a religious imperative in seeking these goals.[35] For example, competing claims over sacred land are an enduring feature of many religious terrorist campaigns, which, to an outsider, may appear as mere squabbles over territorial demarcation. One of the reasons al Qaeda so vociferously opposes the United States owes to the latter's perceived defiling of the Muslim holy cities of Mecca and Medina by the presence of American troops in the Arabian Peninsula after the First Persian Gulf War. Similarly, in Iraq, a host of radical Islamist organizations took up the gun in an unrelenting terrorist campaign against the United States and its coalition partners after the 2003 invasion. Driven primarily by religion, these groups sought the withdrawal of Western troops from the country, showing how material ambitions and religious ideology can work in conjunction with one another. In short, religious terrorist groups always have political objectives, but these goals derive from religious belief.

Because religious terrorists make fundamentally religious demands or have overtly religious objectives that are motivated by a theological imperative, religious terrorism is not necessarily the same thing as ethnic or ethno-religious terrorism. While religion can reinforce ethnic identities, the extent to which the two intersect can vary widely by country. It is possible that not all members of an ethnic group share the same religion and vice versa. In Iraq, for example, religion and ethnicity constitute separate identities with little overlap between the two.

Extrapolating from this discussion, we can ascertain two traits of religious terrorism that distinguish it from secular terrorism. First of all, religious terrorism occurs along communitarian lines defined by the participants' religion. Many times, the lines are drawn between members of different faith traditions like Hindus versus Buddhists in Sri Lanka or Muslims versus Christians in Nigeria and the former Yugoslavia.[36] At other times, the fighting takes place between opposed camps within the same religion. These clashes may be between different intra-faith denominations (e.g., Sunnis versus Shiites in Iraq or Protestants versus Catholics in Ireland) or between rival movements within the religion (e.g., Hezbollah versus ISIS).

---

[35] Mark Juergensmeyer, *The New Cold War? Religious Nationalism Confronts the Secular State* (Berkeley: CA: University of California Press, 1993); Gabriel A. Almond, R. Scott Appleby and Emmanuel Sivan, eds., *Strong Religion: The Rise of Fundamentalisms around the World* (Chicago, IL: University of Chicago, 2003); Andrew H. Kydd and Barbara F. Walter, "The Strategies of Terrorism," *International Security* 31, no. 1 (2006): 49–80.

[36] Jonathan Fox, *Religion, Civilization and Civil War: 1945 through the New Millennium* (Lanham, MD: Lexington Books, 2004); Indra de Soysa and Ragnhild Nordas, "Islam's Bloody Innards: Religion and Political Terror, 1980–2000," *International Studies Quarterly* 51, no. 4 (2007): 927–943.

Religious terrorists make use of religious rhetoric and symbols in establishing this group identity. According to political scientist Assaf Moghadam, "[t]he out-group is identified with a certain behavior that, according to the narrative offered by the ideology, undermines the wellbeing of the in-group."[37] The establishment of group solidarity through the identification of characteristics common to those who share the same interpretation of their faith can serve as a powerful tool when a group finds itself in a disadvantaged position or crisis vis-à-vis an enemy out-group. For this reason, religious terrorist groups often prefer explicitly religious names so as to distinguish the righteousness of their organization versus that of their enemies. Similarly, they will also use religious terms – crusader, infidel, Satan – to describe their enemies.

The second trait unique to religious terrorism is the presence of a discernable religious ideology – a meta-narrative that helps religious adherents understand all aspects of the world that surrounds them and that justifies violent actions – usually built upon a selective reading and interpretation of sacred texts. For the religious terrorist, violence is a holy act undertaken with the sanction of a higher power.[38] It is violence for which religion supplies "the motivation, the justification, the organization, and the worldview."[39] As such, religious terrorism is a distinct form of political violence, profoundly different from other types of violence.[40] This ideology imbues a particular cause held by a terrorist group with sacred meaning and justifies the actions taken. It serves to create a set of beliefs about the nature of reality (including political reality) that members of the group internalize, leading combatants to perceive their acts of political violence against enemy out-groups as a divine duty.

Thus, terrorist agendas are based on interpretations of religious traditions and derived from religious symbols rather than from ethnicity, nationality or class. Religious ideologies may serve to define ultimate political goals as is the case with fundamentalist terrorist groups, or they may simply function as collective action frames through which the perceptions of the group's members are created and its tactics are legitimated.[41] This does not preclude the possibility of groups and individuals being motivated by additional concerns like nationalism, but it does mean that they perceive themselves to be, first and foremost, religious actors intent on advancing their interpretation of proper religion.[42] Political scientist Peter S. Henne explains that "[e]ven if they are motivated by political grievances, religious

[37] Moghadam, *Globalization of Martyrdom*, 46.
[38] Ayla Schbley, "Defining Religious Terrorism: A Causal and Anthological Profile," *Studies in Conflict & Terrorism* 26, no. 2 (2003): 105–134.
[39] Juergensmeyer, *Terror in the Mind of God*, 7.
[40] Hoffman, "'Holy Terror'"; Ranstorp, "Terrorism in the Name of Religion"; Juergensmeyer, *Terror in the Mind of God*.
[41] Peter S. Henne, "The Ancient Fire: Religion and Suicide Terrorism," *Terrorism and Political Violence* 24, no. 1 (2012): 38–60.
[42] Jonathan Fox, *Ethnoreligious Conflict in the Late 20th Century: A General Theory* (Lanham, MD: Rowman & Littlefield Publishers, 2002).

terrorist groups base their calculus for success and concerns about public responses on religious standards."[43] Consider Osama bin Laden's famous 1998 fatwa declaring, "[t]he killing of Americans and their civilian and military allies is a *religious* duty for each and every Muslim to be carried out in whichever country they are [found]."[44] In short, religious terrorists are different than secular terrorists in that they perceive themselves as religious actors *and* make plain the religious ends of their violence.

This is not to suggest, of course, that all religious terrorist organizations necessarily share the same underlying ideology or motivation. Indeed, at times, these groups may have significant differences with each other as in the cases of Hamas and al Qaeda.[45] Faith beliefs can also motivate militants to pursue a range of religiously defined goals. For terrorism rooted in religious fundamentalism, the goal is to return religion, state and society to a proper "golden age" that existed at some point in the past. For terrorism rooted in apocalyptism, by contrast, the goal is not to return to the past, but rather to hasten the "end of days" through the initiation of "cosmic war."[46] At other times, the goals are oriented around concrete and more limited issues: ending abortion, achieving self-determination for a faith community, removing a political leader from office or implementing religious law throughout all of society. So, then, tremendous variety exists among the world's religious terrorist movements. Yet, despite the range of beliefs and pursuits, what ties them together is a belief that they have divine sanction to carry out acts of violence, their bloodshed rooted in their particular faith tradition's texts, traditions and history.

THE UNIQUENESS OF RELIGIOUS TERRORISM

The foregoing discussion suggests that there are good reasons to disaggregate religious and secular terrorism but leaves unanswered the question of why to focus specifically on terrorism motivated by religion. Because religious terrorists look to their faith as a source of inspiration, legitimation and worldview, a totally different incentive structure emerges than exists for their secular counterparts.[47] If the sacred bases for acts of religious violence are real, then the consequences of such actions are bound to be striking.[48] In terms of behavior, religious terrorists are distinguishable

---

43 Henne, "The Ancient Fire," 43.
44 "The Allies Case against Bin Laden," *The Guardian*, last modified October 5, 2001, www.theguardian .com/uk/2001/oct/05/afghanistan.september11.
45 Mahmood Mamdani, *Good Muslim, Bad Muslim: America, the Cold War and the Roots of Terror* (New York, NY: Random House, 2004); Heather Selma Gregg, "Three Theories of Religious Activism and Violence: Social Movements, Fundamentalists, and Apocalyptic Warriors," *Terrorism and Political Violence* 28, no. 2 (2016): 338–360.
46 Juergensmeyer, *Terror in the Mind of God*.
47 Juergensmeyer, *Terror in the Mind of God*, 125–126.
48 Jonathan Fox, "Ethnoreligious Conflict in the Third World: The Role of Religion as a Cause of Conflict," *Nationalism and Ethnic Politics* 9, no. 1 (2003): 101–125; Isak Svensson, "Fighting with Faith," *Journal of Conflict Resolution* 51, no. 6 (2007): 930–949; Monica Duffy Toft, "Getting

from nonreligious terrorists with respect to two unique traits: their ruthlessness and resilience.

Ruthlessness

First, terrorism in the name of God results in greater levels of bloodshed and overall devastation than other forms of terrorism. Religious terrorists operate from an entirely different incentive structure than do secular terrorists, and this, in turn, shapes their goals and tactics in radically different ways. In the words of terrorism expert Bruce Hoffman, "terrorism motivated either in whole or in part by a religious imperative, where violence is regarded by its practitioners as a divine duty or sacramental act, embraces markedly different means of legitimization and justification than that committed by secular terrorists, and these distinguishing features lead, in turn, to yet greater bloodshed and destruction."[49] Sociologist Mark Juergensmeyer argues that "[w]hat makes religious violence particularly savage and relentless is that its perpetrators have placed such religious images of divine struggle – cosmic war – in the service of worldly political battles."[50] Economist Eli Berman provides a different logic for the relative lethality of religious terrorism.[51] He argues that radical religious groups have developed ways to screen terrorists, control defection and weed out potential free riders by requiring from recruits sacrifices as signals of commitment to the group.

One factor that makes religious terrorists especially deadly is that they seek not just independent states or a voice in government but religious control over governmental decision-making and the suppression of groups with differing ideologies once in power. Religious militants seeking to impose their version of a religiously pure, theo-political system on everyone in society makes conflicts rooted in divergent value systems extraordinarily difficult to resolve. Unlike most secular movements, some religious terrorist groups like al Qaeda and ISIS declare war on entire societies, cultures and ways of life, not just individual governments, though battles against domestic regimes certainly constitute one facet of their overarching spiritual struggle against those believed to be infidels. All members of these infidel societies, including the most vulnerable, are considered to be legitimate targets of terrorist violence, which is undertaken as an outward expression of determination and devotion to God. This logic helps explain why tactics such as suicide bombings, soft target attacks and assaults

    Religion? The Puzzling Case of Islam and Civil War," *International Security* 37, no. 4 (2007): 97–131; Isak Svensson and Emily Harding, "How Holy Wars End: Exploring the Termination Patterns of Conflicts with Religious Dimensions in Asia," *Terrorism and Political Violence* 23, no. 2 (2011): 133–149.
[49] Hoffman, *Inside Terrorism*, 83.   [50] Juergensmeyer, *Terror in the Mind of God*, 146.
[51] Eli Berman, *Radical, Religious, and Violent: The New Economics of Terrorism* (Cambridge, MA: Massachusetts Institute of Technology, 2009).

against members of the same religious or national community are much more prevalent with religious rather than secular terrorist groups.[52]

Evidence confirms the hypothesis that religiously motivated terrorism is more lethal than other forms. In a study that compared religious and secular terrorist organizations, political scientists Victor Asal and Karl Rethemeyer found that organizations acting on religious or ethno-religious ideologies caused more devastation than other types of terrorist groups.[53] Terrorism scholar James A. Piazza revealed that in terms of those wounded or killed by terrorist strikes, assaults by religious actors resulted in more than four times as many casualties as attacks by nationalist-separatist terrorists, more than four times as many casualties as attacks by leftist (anarchist, anti-globalization, communist, socialist and environmentalist) groups, and almost sixteen times as many casualties as attacks by rightist (racist, right-wing conservative and right-wing reactionary) groups.[54] Data on terrorist strikes from the US State Department also indicate that attacks motivated by a religious imperative are four times as lethal as attacks by secular groups.[55]

My own analysis of the Global Terrorism Database confirms these findings. Of the fifty deadliest terrorist attacks from 1970 to 2014 in which the perpetrator could be identified, thirty-eight (76 percent) were carried out by religious actors. This statistic is quite remarkable considering that religious terrorism did not really become a widespread phenomenon until the 1990s and that religious terrorist organizations comprise only a percentage of all terrorist groups. Of the 12,371 individuals killed in these attacks, 8,779 (71 percent) were slain by religiously motivated terrorists.

One of the most important factors that helps explain the relative lethality of religious terrorist groups involves the rise of extremist Islamist organizations since the 1980s. These organizations have proven to be exceptionally dangerous because they often hold to political theologies and practices derived from foundational Islamic texts that are believed to sanction bloodshed.[56] The Islamic conception of jihad represents one such doctrine. Though often equated with an internal struggle for personal betterment to decipher between right and wrong and do the will of God,

[52] Bruce Hoffman and H. Gordon McCormick, "Terrorism, Signaling, and Suicide Attack," *Studies in Conflict & Terrorism* 27, no. 4 (2004): 243–281.

[53] Victor Asal and R. Karl Rethemeyer, "The Nature of the Beast: Organizational Structures and the Lethality of Terrorist Attacks," *Journal of Politics* 70, no. 2 (2008): 437–449.

[54] James A. Piazza, "Is Islamist Terrorism More Lethal? An Empirical Study of Group Ideology, Organization and Goal Structure," *Terrorism and Political Violence* 21, no. 1 (2009): 62–88.

[55] Berman, *Radical, Religious and Violent*, 8.

[56] Amir Taheri, *Holy Terror: The Inside Story of Islamic Terrorism* (London: Hutchinson, 1987); Mark Juergensmeyer, "Terror Mandated by God," *Terrorism and Political Violence* 9, no. 2 (1997): 16–23; David C. Rapoport, "Fear and Trembling: Terrorism in Three Religious Traditions," *American Political Science Review* 78, no. 3 (1984): 658–677.

the radical Islamist interpretation of jihad features an external construal – a literal
holy war against infidels who do not succumb to the reign of Islam.[57]

The practice of martyrdom (*istish'had*) – self-sacrifice in service to the faith – is
another Islamic precept that sheds light on the prevalence of suicide bombings by
Islamic groups, especially those espousing a radical form of Sunni Islam known as
Salafi-Jihadism.[58] Al Qaeda agents, for example, hold a steadfast conviction that
Allah will reward those who sacrifice themselves in a noble mission of death with
entry into paradise and an audience with God. Accordingly, suicide attacks based in
religion have been on the rise in recent years. One study found there was an average
of 4.7 suicide attacks per year throughout the 1980s, 16 per year in the 1990s and 180
per year from 2000 to 2005. It also observed that from 2000 to 2003, 70 percent of
suicide missions had an overtly religious motivation.[59] Religiously motivated suicide
terrorism is also comparatively lethal. Assaf Moghadam finds that suicide attacks by
Salafist groups resulted in an average of fifty-six victims per attack (both killed and
wounded), whereas attacks by groups espousing a secular ideology killed or
wounded between eleven and twenty victims on average.[60] With respect to the
argument of this book, those preaching ideas of jihad and *istish'had* are much
more likely to gain a sympathetic following under conditions of pervasive repression
than where religious freedom exists in abundance.

Militant secular movements, in contrast, tend to be less lethal because they have
more easily identifiable, pragmatic, circumspect and limited ambitions such as
attaining political power, redressing class-based grievances or seeking autonomy
from a central government.[61] Unlike their religious counterparts, secular groups
do care about generating public support and will generally avoid risky, high-casualty
tactics that may provoke backlash from the public and consequently undercut their
demands and estrange valuable constituencies. Steven Simon and Daniel Benjamin
explain that "[b]y avoiding egregious bloodshed, [secular] group leaders preserve
their eligibility for a place at the bargaining table and, ultimately, a role in successor
governments."[62] In these cases, because conflicts are seen through non-transcendent
lenses, compromise and negotiation are possible, in contrast to religious terrorists
who consider such actions a betrayal of their divinely ordained mission. Secular
conflicts, in other words, tend not to be viewed as all-or-nothing battles in which all

57 Bernard Lewis, *The Crisis of Islam: Holy War and Unholy Terror* (New York, NY: Modern Library, 2003); Fawaz A. Gerges, *The Far Enemy: Why Jihad Went Global* (Cambridge: Cambridge University Press, 2005).
58 James Dingley and Michael Kirk-Smith, "Symbolism and Sacrifice in Terrorism," *Small Wars and Insurgencies* 13, no. 1 (2002): 102–128; Farhad Khosrokhavar and David Macey, *Suicide Bombers: Allah's New Martyrs* (London: Pluto, 2005).
59 Scott Atran, "Mishandling Suicide Terrorism," *Washington Quarterly* 27, no. 3 (2004): 65–90.
60 Assaf Moghadam, "Suicide Terrorism, Occupation, and the Globalization of Martyrdom: A Critique of *Dying to Win*," *Studies in Conflict & Terrorism* 29, no. 8 (2006): 707–729.
61 Toft, "Getting Religion?"; Svensson, "Fighting with Faith"; Svensson and Harding, "How Holy Wars End."
62 Steven Simon and Daniel Benjamin, "The Terror," *Survival* 43, no. 4 (2001): 5–18.

enemies must be destroyed. Rather, once the goals of the organization have been achieved or an equitable solution has been mutually agreed upon, secular terrorists usually cease violent activity. In such cases, we are less likely to witness capricious destruction or a wanton disregard for human life associated with religiously based terrorism.[63]

Of course, this does not mean that nonreligious terrorists are incapable of inflicting enormous damage and loss of life. The Revolutionary Armed Forces of Colombia (FARC) in Colombia, the Tamil Tigers in Sri Lanka, the Shining Path in Peru and the Kurdistan Worker's Party in Turkey – all self-identified as secular organizations – have been more lethal and less restrained in their efforts than many terrorist groups typically classified as "religious."[64] Secular groups like the Japanese Red Army and the Irish Republican Army have also carried out mass casualty attacks. Counterexamples also exist of supposedly religious terrorist groups whose behaviors resemble more the logic of secular terrorism. These groups may indeed identify themselves on the basis of religious identity, but their political or nationalist goals lead them to shun the use of mass causality tactics. This is the case with the American Christian Identity movement, for example. Such groups may target civilians at times, but they also attack military and government sites. Keeping these exceptions in mind, it is clear that religious terrorism generally embodies a markedly different form of violence than more traditional forms of terrorism, and this results in greater devastation most of the time.

Resilience

The second key behavioral difference between religious and nonreligious terrorists involves their high resilience. Studies have shown that religious terrorists fight harder and last longer than their secular counterparts.[65] The reason why is straightforward: religious terrorists consider the physical self to be fleeting and mortal but the spiritual self to be immortal and eternal, leading them to discount physical survival more so than secular terrorists who fight for purely terrestrial goals.[66] Accordingly, this key difference also means that religious terrorists commonly respond to the effects of repression – particularly religious repression – differently than secular terrorists.

An important study by Seth G. Jones and Martin C. Libicki of the RAND Corporation reveals that religious terrorist groups differ from those otherwise classified in their levels of resilience. "The most salient fact about religious terrorist

---

[63] Jonathan Fine, "Contrasting Secular and Religious Terrorism," *Middle East Quarterly* 15, no. 1 (2008): 59–71.

[64] Gunning and Jackson, "What's So 'Religious' about 'Religious Terrorism'?" 378.

[65] Seth G. Jones and Martin C. Libicki, *How Terrorist Groups End: Lessons for Countering Al Qa'ida* (Santa Monica, CA: RAND Corporation, 2008); Asal and Rethemeyer, "The Nature of the Beast"; Piazza, "Is Islamist Terrorism More Lethal?"

[66] Toft, "Getting Religion?" 100.

groups," they write, "is how hard they are to eliminate."[67] Specifically, they note that while 62 percent of all terrorist groups have ended, this is true of only 32 percent of religious terrorist groups. They also observe that this finding cannot be attributed to the fact that religious terrorism is a recent phenomenon because the survivability of religious groups is substantially higher within cohorts examined by decade. Of the forty-five religious terrorist groups that ended, twenty-six splintered and only sixteen succumbed to state pressure, including policing and military operations. Military actions have been successful at terminating only three religious terrorist groups.

The same conclusion is reached by analyzing terrorist attacks by group ideology and a country's level of liberty since the end of the Cold War. Non-democracies are far more likely to birth religious terrorists, while liberal democracies are more likely to experience attacks by groups motivated by nonreligious concerns. Seventy-four percent of religious attacks transpired in countries that were "not free" according to standards developed by democracy watchdog group Freedom House. Twenty-three percent of attacks occurred in "partly free" countries. Only three percent of attacks took place in liberal democracies. By contrast, only 10 percent of nonreligious attacks took place in authoritarian, unfree countries. Two-thirds of these attacks occurred in partly free countries. Yet nearly a quarter of attacks transpired in liberal democracies. Simply put, religious terrorists appear not to be deterred by the same structural conditions that apparently deter their secular counterparts, which tend not to stage attacks in authoritarian countries.[68]

Those claiming that repression works against terrorism might point to the successes of authoritarian governments in crushing terrorist threats in countries like Argentina, Sri Lanka, Uruguay and Peru. Notice, however, that the successes of illiberal regimes against terrorism in these countries occurred against self-professed *secular* terrorist organizations – the Montoneros (in Argentina), the Tamil Tigers (in Sri Lanka), the Tupamaros (in Uruguay) and the Shining Path (in Peru). Regimes that attempt to quash or prevent *religious* terrorism through such brutality tend not to be as successful over the long term. Examples include Takfir wal-Hijra in Egypt, Jundallah in Iran and the Eastern Turkistan Movement in China, all of which survived despite attempts at brutal suppression on the part of the state. At other times, "defeated" religious terrorist groups reconstitute themselves under different names like Algeria's Armed Islamic Group (AIG), which later became the Salafist Group for Preaching and Fighting.

If religious and secular terrorists really are different in fundamental ways, then it stands to reason that the ways in which these groups end might be different as well. It is conceivable that terrorism motivated by a religious impulse might be less amenable to negotiations and more resilient in the face of police and military operations – strategies that have been successful in ending many secular terrorist campaigns. This

[67] Jones and Libicki, *How Terrorist Groups End*, 36–37.
[68] Nilay Saiya, "Religion, Democracy and Terrorism," *Perspectives on Terrorism* 9, no. 6 (2015): 51–59.

book contends, on the other hand, that extremist religious groups and ideologies lose support in environments of liberty, which serve to deprive terrorists of the much-needed logistical sustenance they require to carry out attacks.

WHAT IS RELIGIOUS LIBERTY?

History shows that most human beings, regardless of age, socioeconomic status, race or gender, share a desire to know and have a relationship with the transcendent. Mircea Eliade famously described humans as "homo religiosus," born with a natural and powerful yearning to pursue answers to the ultimate questions of existence in this life and in the hereafter.[69] Religious liberty empowers people to embark on this spiritual quest, both individually and corporately.

Freedom of religion embraces the full array of thought, belief and behavior motivated by faith. Rooted in human dignity, it encompasses the right of people to think freely about the purpose of their existence, to live in accordance with their understanding of ultimate truth, to bear witness to faith-based commitments, to worship together with those of like mind, to carry out rituals and practices central to their faith, to renounce or change their faith (or to have no faith at all) and to bring their religiously informed views into the public square. Religiously free individuals have the right to the uninhibited peaceful practice, selection and profession of their faith and are protected from acting against the dictates of their conscience.

Religion also carries a natural public dimension. Religious actors are generally motivated by their understanding of spiritual imperatives to conduct themselves in the world in a manner consistent with their faith beliefs. Therefore, freedom of religion not only guarantees the right of people of faith to seek transcendent reality privately, it also empowers them to engage in public religious activity and to bring their faith-based convictions into the public square by influencing societal norms and public policy within broad limits.

The international community – including countries comprised of different majority faith traditions – has long recognized religious liberty as a fundamental human right, enshrining it in international covenants and national constitutions. Perhaps the most important document discussing the inherent right individuals have to religious liberty is the 1948 United Nations Declaration on Human Rights (UNDHR). Article 2 of the document asserts that rights cannot be derogated on the basis of religion, while Article 18 stipulates:

> Everyone has the right to freedom of thought, conscience and religion; this right includes freedom to change his religion or belief, and freedom, either alone or in community with others and in public or private, to manifest his religion or belief in teaching, practice, worship and observance.

---

[69]   Mircea Eliade, *The Sacred and the Profane: The Nature of Religion* (New York, NY: Harcourt, 1959).

Though nonbinding, the UNDHR paved the way for religious freedom to become enshrined in future international laws like the 1966 International Covenant on Civil and Political Rights and the 1981 Declaration on the Elimination of All Forms of Intolerance and of Discrimination Based on Religion or Belief. The national constitutions of several countries also adopted the language of the UNDHR in guaranteeing basic religious rights to citizens. Only a handful of countries today fail to provide guarantees of religious freedom. That said, even in countries where religious liberty is constitutionally guaranteed, a gap often remains between assurances of religious freedom in word and their realization in practice.

Finally, it is worth mentioning what freedom of religion does not mean. While religious freedom empowers minority and majority religious groups to carry out practices central to their faith and compete with each other in the public arena on the basis of their beliefs, it does not grant them free rein to take *any* action on the grounds that their faith requires it. It does not permit, for instance, the right to engage in violence or coercion that negatively impinges upon the fundamental rights of others, to use civil authority to privilege membership in their organizations or to create a world in which only their religion is permitted to exist. As is the case with any other freedom, the right to religion is not absolute and presupposes justifiable limits on the expression of faith. Just as people should be free to pursue the religious quest, they must also be free from coercion by civil or religious authorities in their search to understand and have relationship with the divine or to reject this quest altogether. There can be religious contention, but only within the bounds of civility and the presumption of legal equality – what the late Richard John Neuhaus referred to as the "civil public square."[70]

Unfortunately, religious freedom has not been given the attention it is due by academics, policymakers or even large parts of the human rights community. Described by political scientist Allen Hertzke as the "orphan of human rights," religious liberty has been relegated to second-class status in favor of "more important" human rights concerns.[71] Indeed, although religious persecution remains one of the most common ways in which human rights are repressed, it is also one of the most overlooked and least understood facets of human rights practice. As argued in this book, it also stands at the center of many of the world's most urgent security challenges.

THE UNIQUENESS OF RELIGIOUS FREEDOM

Some might reason that any argument about the causal importance of religious liberty is really one about human rights more generally, since religious freedom is

---

[70] Richard John Neuhaus, *The Naked Public Square: Religion and Democracy in America* (Grand Rapids, MI: William B. Eerdmans Publishing Company, 1986).

[71] Allen Hertzke, *Freeing God's Children: The Unlikely Alliance for Global Human Rights* (Lanham, MD: Rowman & Littlefield Publishers, 2004), 230.

simply a subset of a broader culture of rights. It is true that religious freedom often comes as part of a "bundled commodity" and is intertwined with other freedoms like expression, assembly and association. A good case can be made, however, that religious liberty is not just a derivative subset of broader political and civil rights, but is rather an *independent* and the most foundational of rights, which shelters, nurtures and forms the basis for the whole spectrum of rights in society. States that cede to religious communities the right to exist and operate independently of the state implicitly acknowledge that the ultimate issues of life lie outside of their domains, and that people are answerable to an authority higher than any temporal government. This recognition provides the basis for limited government and the cornerstone for all other human freedoms.

Throughout history, the reality of existence and the certainty of death have forced people to contend with questions of transcendence and supernatural reality. The right to religious liberty, therefore, lies in human nature itself, grounded in the inherent worth and dignity of all people. Indeed, the capability to think freely about the ultimate questions of one's existence and the quintessential pursuit of meaning and purpose – whether God exists, the purpose of life, the way to ultimate flourishing – is an essential part of human nature and constitutes the most basic form of liberty of conscience.[72] If people are not free to explore such timeless and fundamental questions – the ability to control their own thoughts – and to worship with others holding similar views without interference, they really cannot be considered "free" in any other area or to be living fully human lives.[73] Political philosopher Timothy Samuel Shah describes freedom of religion as "the thin end of liberty's wedge."[74] Others have referred to it as the proverbial "canary in the coalmine"; when religious freedom begins to be curtailed in a society, other civil and political restrictions are likely to follow.[75] In practice, this means that generally liberal countries can take steps to restrict religious liberty specifically. On the other hand, once religious groups have their faith-based rights secured, they can use their position of autonomy to press for other civil liberties for themselves or others, which strengthens a state's commitment to human rights generally.

Just as it would be a mistake to conflate religious freedom and the broader category of human rights, an even bigger error would be to assume that religious freedom and democracy are synonymous. While it is true that almost all genuinely religiously free countries are also democracies, the opposite is not always the case. Democracy does not guarantee the protection of religious liberty and respect for those with dissenting religious views; in fact, democracy can even facilitate abuses

---

[72] Justin L. Barrett, *Why Would Anyone Believe in God?* (Lanham, MD: AltaMira Press, 2004); Jesse Bering, *The Belief Instinct: The Psychology of Souls, Destiny, and the Meaning of Life* (New York, NY: W. W. Norton, 2011).

[73] David Novak, *In Defense of Religious Liberty* (Wilmington, DE: ISI Books, 2009).

[74] Timothy Samuel Shah, *Religious Freedom: Why Now? Defending an Embattled Human Right* (Princeton, NJ: Witherspoon Institute, 2012), 21.

[75] Grim and Finke, *Price of Freedom Denied*, 202–213.

against people of faith when a religious majority imposes its will on religious minorities or dissenters. Such countries may be democracies in an electoral sense – marked by public participation in selecting leaders, contested elections and the peaceful transfer of power – but illiberal to the extent that they impose restrictions on religion among other individual freedoms – what political analyst Fareed Zakaria has termed "illiberal democracy."[76]

In the Islamic world, we see such patterns today in Indonesia, Turkey, Malaysia, Iraq and Pakistan – electoral democracies that hold regular free and fair elections but also simultaneously pursue policies restricting religious liberty for minorities, often at the behest of illiberal Islamist parties that seek the implementation of restrictive laws based in sharia. In Indonesia, a country largely believed to be politically free, certain illiberal, religiously based civil society groups have been instrumental in pressuring the state to enact a series of laws that sharply curtail the rights of religious minorities, even banning the Ahmadiyya sect outright. In 2017, an Indonesian court found the Christian governor of the country's capital, Jakarta, guilty of blasphemy against Islam, sentencing him to a two-year prison term. In Turkey, persecution of dissident Muslim and Christian groups remains despite the presence of a free and fair electoral process and many in the West hailing the country as a model for democracy in the Muslim world. Similarly, Malaysia has long been considered a robust democracy, but one that curtails the religious rights of minorities. After decades of dictatorship, Iraq today is a democracy, but one in which religious repression of the most serious kind is present, owing, in large part, to Shia persecution of Sunnis and militant Sunni backlash. Since partition from India, Pakistan has enjoyed a mostly democratic history, periods of emergency rule notwithstanding, yet it also severely curtails the practice of faith through its blasphemy code and social persecution of religion.

Outside of the world of Islam, restrictions on religion have also been rising in fully consolidated democracies. In European countries like Austria, Belgium, France and Germany, governmental and societal regulation of religion have sharply increased in recent years. In Austria and Belgium, Jewish and Muslim leaders have reported alarmingly high levels of anti-Semitism and Islamophobia, including vandalism of holy sites, hate speech and physical violence against individuals. In France, a law remains in place prohibiting the covering of one's face in certain public spaces and government buildings and the wearing of religious symbols at public schools. Germany bans male circumcision. In North America too, such restrictions have been on the rise in both Canada and the United States. In the Canadian province of Quebec, the former Parti Québécois' proposed a "Charter of Quebec Values," a document intended to reaffirm Quebec's secular character by, among other things, prohibiting public sector employees from wearing or displaying "conspicuous"

[76]   Fareed Zakaria, *The Future of Freedom: Illiberal Democracy at Home and Abroad* (New York, NY: W. W. Norton, 2007).

religious symbols, but that was interpreted by many people of faith as an attack on religion. In the United States, hate crimes against Muslims have increased exponentially in the twenty-first century. These are all cases of democracy and religious liberty having parted company.

Electoral democracies may also enact distinctive restrictions on the political activities of religious groups as the cases of Ethiopia, Portugal and Uganda show. On the other hand, there are also examples of autocracies that impose relatively few restrictions on religion as seen in the cases of Cameroon, Gambia, the Republic of Congo and Swaziland. All of these cases suggest that a country's level of democracy is a far from perfect indicator of its level of religious liberty insofar as the latter captures something crucial about tolerance and minority rights that the former lacks. In short, that religious freedom can be conceived of separately from the general categories of human rights and democracy coupled with its natural relationship to religion justifies the more limited focus of this book.

OUTLINE OF BOOK

This book proceeds in five chapters. The opening chapter presents a quantitative analysis examining how the compromising of religious liberty can create conditions ripe for the emergence of religious terrorism. When states restrict religious belief and practice through oppressive laws and policies, prevent certain religious groups from participating in politics, promote sectarian polarization in society, fail to confront intolerance based in religion or engage in brutal counterterrorism campaigns, they foster alienation and sow the seeds for radicalization. This chapter examines two ways through which states commonly repress religion: minority religious discrimination and majority religious cooptation. Both forms of restriction carry the potential to generate terrorism in unique ways.

Yet quantitative analysis alone cannot demonstrate the linkages connecting the restriction of religion to terrorism or show how religious liberty can serve as a buffer against terrorism in individual countries. The next three chapters examine eleven different country case studies investigating the relationship between regulation of religion and terrorism, on one hand, and religious liberty and peace, on the other. The cases chosen provide for a wide range of geographic, religious, political and economic variation so as to isolate the explanatory power of religious liberty. The cases support the argument that religious liberty is a key factor preventing faith-based terrorism in the presence of high degrees of religiosity and pluralism.

Building off data presented in the opening chapter, Chapter 2 takes a global look at the connections between minority religious discrimination and faith-based terrorism, examining current or recent religious terrorism within six of the world's great faith traditions. It accomplishes this through case studies of Islamist terrorism in Pakistan, Christian terrorism in Central Africa, Hindu and Sikh terrorism in India, Buddhist terrorism in Burma and Jewish terrorism in Israel. All of these cases represent countries hardest hit by terrorism rooted in a specific religious tradition outside those currently in the midst of a civil war. Contrary to conventional wisdom and media portrayals, problems of religious freedom and violent religious extremism are not limited to the Middle East or Muslim-majority countries, but exist in every religion and region of the world. Many of these situations have deteriorated as a result of a failure on the part of states to adequately confront intolerance, uphold the rule of law and protect religious liberty.

While the second chapter examines several cases of how religious repression in the form of minority religious discrimination can beget terrorism, Chapter 3 sheds light on how *secular* repression in the form of majority religious cooptation contributed to violent religious extremism both before and especially after the so-called Arab Spring. Arab states have long used the specter of Islamist radicalism and terrorism to vindicate authoritarian practices, thus spawning cycles of repression and violent resistance in the countries of the Middle East and North Africa. An examination of the three secular repressive countries that have to date experienced regime change as a result of the processes generated by the Arab Spring (Egypt, Libya and Tunisia) reveals that attempting to fight religious extremism with repression invariably makes the situation worse. Interestingly enough, all of these countries actually became *more* democratic after their revolutions (though Egypt eventually reverted to a military dictatorship). At the same time, they uniformly became less religiously tolerant. In this chapter, I provide a brief background of religious repression in each of these countries, and argue that this legacy of repression masked widespread discontent and extremism that was brewing behind the veneer of stability. The process of state breakdown allowed these violent forces to emerge in horrible ways. This chapter also discusses the rise of ISIS in this context and tackles the controversial question of whether the religion of Islam is inherently prone to terrorism.

Just as religion can be a contributor to division, exclusivism and violence, so too can it be a crucial enabler of peace. Religious communities, drawing on their scriptures, beliefs and practices, have historically made incredibly positive contributions to society, which have led to more peaceful and stable settings. In many parts of the world, religious communities have been instrumental in increasing literacy, reducing poverty, promoting development, providing access to potable water and administering health care. "Militants for peace," as historian R. Scott Appleby refers to them, have also played constructive roles in conflict prevention, peace building and reconciliation in the wake of mass atrocities like civil war, genocide and terrorism, often with the same intensity as the destructive forces of religion.[77]

The fourth chapter examines some of the ways in which the presence of religious liberty can help generate peace and stability in highly religious and religiously plural

---

[77] R. Scott Appleby, *The Ambivalence of the Sacred: Religion, Violence and Reconciliation* (Lanham, MD: Rowman & Littlefield Publishers, 2000), 121.

settings. Past studies have found that sometimes terrorism emerges from communities and ideological movements that live together in isolation from the rest of
society, whose members are exposed only to those who share their ideological
perspective and not a diversity of opinions. Such environments of seclusion facilitate
indoctrination and control over group members. They can also generate extremist
ways of thinking and lionize those who carry out violence against the "other." On the
other hand, freedom of religion has the opposite effect, bringing diverse communities together and creating cultures of tolerance. This chapter discusses the cases of
Senegal, South Africa and the United States – countries where high levels of
religiosity and religious heterogeneity might have combined to foment violence as
they have elsewhere, but that have instead witnessed relative harmony between faith
groups, made possible, in part, by their commitment to freedom of religion.
Importantly, the case of South Africa demonstrates the profound impact of religious
liberty, not only in combating the rise of violent religious extremism but also in
empowering Christian and traditional African conceptions of restorative justice and
reconciliation in the aftermath of the atrocities associated with apartheid, which
helped prevent a relapse into conflict. The South African case thus illustrates how
the positive benefits of religious liberty extend to the whole of society.

The question of the relationship between religious repression and religious
terrorism carries significant policy ramifications. The fifth chapter situates the
arguments of the book in the context of American foreign policy. Because religious
freedom is not only a universally recognized fundamental human right but also a
crucial marker of secure and flourishing societies, protecting it at home and advancing it abroad should be a key ingredient in American national security, conflict
prevention and counterterrorism strategies. I argue that the United States needs to
move beyond mere rhetorical salutes to religious freedom and condemnation for its
violation to embracing it as a central component of its foreign policy, taking the lead
in promoting religious freedom abroad and working to rebuild the consensus in
favor of religious freedom with its allies. Doing so would advance not only America's
ideals, but its national security interests as well. The chapter offers ten practical
suggestions for how the United States can responsibly and successfully accomplish
this goal.

1

A Global View of Religious Repression and Terrorism

In 2013, the world's most brutal terrorist organization, known variously as the Islamic State in Iraq and Syria (ISIS), the Islamic State in Iraq and the Levant (ISIL), the Islamic State in Iraq and ash-Sham, the pejorative Arabic acronym *Daesh* or simply the Islamic State (IS), burst its way into public consciousness. ISIS commenced a campaign of unfathomable cruelty, engaging in mass murders, forced conversions, expulsions of religious and ethnic minorities, rape, human trafficking, sexual slavery, kidnappings, forced marriages and destruction of hundreds of houses of worship in its self-styled quest to create an Islamic caliphate according to its extremist interpretation of Islam. So barbarous were the actions of ISIS that al Qaeda leader Ayman al-Zawahiri condemned and formally disavowed it in 2014.

While ISIS is certainly the most prominent violent religious group today, it is hardly the only one. Indeed, individual zealots, violent sects, apocalyptic cults and faith-based terrorist groups have all become common in recent times. Why has the world witnessed an increase in violent religious extremism as represented by ISIS over the past three decades?

EXPLANATIONS FOR RELIGIOUS TERRORISM

Explanations for religious violence – and by extension religious terrorism – generally fall into two camps. The first emphasizes the rational character of terrorism. These accounts stress that terrorism has less to do with religious belief than with the underlying "real" rational motivations for violence. According to this school of thought, religion is used as a mobilizing force, an expedient justification, to gain leverage in sectarian conflicts, rather than being an underlying cause. Former American ambassador Michael Sheehan succinctly summarized this logic: "A number of terrorist groups have portrayed their causes in religious and cultural terms. This is often a transparent tactic designed to conceal political goals, generate popular support, and silence opposition."[1] For these individuals, "religious"

---

[1] Michael Sheehan, "Terrorism: The Current Threat," last modified February 10, 2000, www.brookings.edu/events/2000/0210terrorism.aspx.

violence has less to do with sacred texts and core teachings and can be attributed instead to factors like poverty, foreign interventions, political grievances and profit seeking.

Two prominent rationalist explanations for terrorism include poverty and foreign military occupation. The poverty–terrorism link is particularly popular among policymakers. After the 9/11 attacks, Presidents George W. Bush and Bill Clinton were quick to link terrorism to economic conditions in the Middle East. British Prime Minister Tony Blair made similar comments after the 2005 suicide attacks in London. The argument linking poverty to terrorism is as follows: because economic prosperity relieves competition over scarce resources, higher levels of wealth result in greater satisfaction among the general populace, and thus reduce the likelihood of individuals turning to violence in order to redress their impoverished situations. On the other hand, it is believed that poverty creates large pools of potential terrorist recruits.

However, much of the research has failed to show conclusively that poverty leads to increased levels of terrorism. Some work determines that economic development and equality serve as a bulwark against terrorism.[2] Other work finds the opposite: wealthier countries are more prone to terrorism.[3] Research has also shown that many members of religious terrorist groups enjoy a higher standard of living and better education than the general populace.[4] A surprisingly high proportion of terrorists has professional occupations.[5] In short, a causal argument linking economic deprivation to terrorism has not found conclusive support in the empirical record.[6]

Foreign military occupation is another popular rationalist explanation for terrorism. The most vocal supporter of the occupation thesis is University of Chicago professor Robert A. Pape, who has argued that religion plays only a marginal role in explaining the phenomenon of suicide terrorism.[7] He contends instead that suicide terrorists attack countries perceived as occupiers in the hopes of yielding territorial

---

[2] Quan Li and Drew Schaub, "Economic Globalization and Transnational Terrorism," *Journal of Conflict Resolution* 48, no. 2 (2004): 230–258; Brian Burgoon, "On Welfare and Terror," *Journal of Conflict Resolution* 50, no. 2 (2006): 176–203; Brian Lai, "Draining the Swamp: An Empirical Examination of the Production of International Terrorism," *Conflict Management and Peace Science* 24, no. 4 (2007): 297–310.

[3] Alberto Abadie, "Poverty, Political Freedom and the Roots of Terrorism," *American Economic Review* 96, no. 2 (2006): 159–177.

[4] Alan B. Krueger and Jitka Maleckova, *Education, Poverty, Political Violence and Terrorism: Is There a Causal Connection?* (Cambridge, MA: National Bureau of Economic Research, 2002); Claude Berrebi, "Evidence about the Link between Education, Poverty and Terrorism among Palestinians," *Peace Economics, Peace Science and Public Policy* 13, no. 1 (2007): 1–36.

[5] Marc Sageman, *Understanding Terror Networks* (Philadelphia, PA: University of Pennsylvania Press, 2004).

[6] James A. Piazza, "Rooted in Poverty? Terrorism, Poor Economic Development, and Social Cleavages," *Terrorism and Political Violence* 18, no. 1 (2006): 159–177; Alan B. Krueger, *What Makes a Terrorist: Economics and the Roots of Terrorism* (Princeton, NJ: Princeton University Press, 2007).

[7] Robert A. Pape, *Dying to Win: The Strategic Logic of Suicide Terrorism* (New York, NY: Random House, 2005).

concessions and that democracies are more often the target of suicide campaigns than authoritarian governments because they are more likely to acquiesce to terrorist demands. Thus, for Pape, suicide terror is considered an effective method available to weak actors fighting against stronger central governments.

The claim that suicide terrorists are not religiously motivated but are instead infuriated nationalists fighting against foreign military occupation raises a number of empirical problems, however. First, why did suicide terrorism only become a terrorist tactic beginning in the early 1980s instead of in the 1960s when it could have been used by nationalists fighting for independence from colonial occupiers throughout Asia, Africa and Latin America? Second, why do many suicide bombers travel to and carry out attacks in countries they have no national allegiance to? Most of the suicide bombings that occurred in Iraq, for example, were carried out by individuals from other countries – those countries often under no foreign military occupation. Third, why do suicide bombers often target members of the same national community if the goal really is to expel foreign occupiers? Finally, why does suicide terrorism continue (and often increase) after an occupation ends? These empirical contradictions call the foreign occupation thesis into question.

On the opposite end of the spectrum are those who believe that religion itself lies at the heart of much of the conflict and terrorism in the modern world. Some studies in this vein point to differences in religious identity as a key source of religious conflict. The late Harvard scholar Samuel Huntington, for example, claimed that after the Cold War, cultural differences (based primarily in religion) would replace ideological struggles as the primary driving force of contention in global politics.[8] Writing in response to those who believed that liberal democracy and free-market capitalism would flourish with the end of the Cold War, he argued that "the principal conflicts of global politics will occur between nations and groups of different civilizations," these conflicts stemming from differences in cultural values.[9]

Renewed attention has been given to the "clash of civilizations" thesis in recent times. Huntington correctly predicted that religion would be an important feature in post–Cold War global politics and a contributor to various conflicts around the world. His thesis sparked new thinking on the relationship between religion and conflict and inspired social scientists to take religion more seriously. In this sense, his argument presents an important challenge to the reductionist viewpoint taken by academics enamored of secularization theory who did not believe that religion could exhibit any independent effect on conflicts. At the same time, the mere presence of different faith traditions is rarely enough to spark conflict on its own. The United States, for instance, is the most ethnically and religiously diverse country in the world but experiences relatively little religiously inspired conflict. Similarly,

---

[8]   Samuel P. Huntington, *The Clash of Civilizations and the Remaking of World Order* (New York, NY: Simon and Schuster, 1996).
[9]   Samuel P. Huntington, "The Clash of Civilizations?" *Foreign Affairs* 72 (1993): 22.

in Singapore, Muslims, Hindus, Catholics and Protestants all live in peace with one another despite occupying the same tiny island. Interreligious conflict has been similarly absent in countries like Japan, South Korea and Vietnam despite the many different forms of religious expression. Senegal is home to a wide variety of ethnic groups and a sizeable religious minority, yet it has not experienced the radicalization of religion in ways that the clash thesis would predict. Greater still is the tremendous diversity found in any *one* of Huntington's "seven or eight" civilizations. Indeed, today there are more conflicts *within* rather than *between* civilizations.

Other work points instead to the ideas particular to certain militant groups – their "political theologies" – that not only permit, but in some cases command, the use of violence. These studies emphasize a range of motivations for religious violence rooted in the nature of religious belief itself: metaphysical battles of good versus evil that manifest in "cosmic war," spiritual insecurity and the lure of eternal rewards.[10] They argue that religious militants are different from secular combatants insofar as the former believe they are waging a *spiritual* battle for transcendent truth sanctioned by a divine authority. The audience for religious extremists, therefore, is a supernatural one – God – whereas groups moved by secular ideologies like Marxism, secular nationalism or anarchism speak to an earthly audience and do not claim to have divine sanction. Then there are those who believe that it is not just radical religious ideologies but religion itself that promotes violence. The so-called new atheists like Richard Dawkins, Sam Harris and the late Christopher Hitchens hold that religion necessarily leads to absolutism, division, irrationality, extremism and violence. As Dawkins put it in an op-ed written for *The Guardian* four days after the attacks of September 11, 2001: "To fill a world with religion, or religions of the Abrahamic kind, is like littering the streets with loaded guns. Do not be surprised if they are used."[11]

While theology obviously matters, it is incorrect that terrorism is the *inevitable* upshot of sacred texts and religious teachings as the neoatheists claim. Though the pairing of the words "religious terrorism" is common, there does not necessarily exist a natural connection between them. Some of history's greatest supporters of human rights and civic activists – Martin Luther King Jr., Archbishop Desmond Tutu, the Dalai Lama, Mohandas Gandhi and many others – were strongly motivated by religion. By the same token, some of history's greatest mass murderers – Mao Zedong, Adolf Hitler, Joseph Stalin and Pol Pot – were staunch atheists. With respect to terrorism, research has shown that a high level of religious devotion is a poor predictor of support for or participation in terrorist organizations.[12] On the

---

[10]   Hoffman, "Holy Terror"; Ranstorp, "Terrorism in the Name of Religion"; Juergensmeyer, *Terror in the Mind of God*; Stern, *Terror in the Name of God*; Moghadam, *The Globalization of Martyrdom*.

[11]   Richard Dawkins, "Religion's Misguided Missiles," *The Guardian*, last modified September 15, 2001, www.theguardian.com/world/2001/sep/15/september11.politicsphilosophyandsociety1.

[12]   Peter Mandaville and Melissa Nozell, *Engaging Religion and Religious Actors in Countering Violent Extremism* (Washington, DC: US Institute of Peace, 2017).

contrary, some work even finds that depth of religious knowledge and high levels of religious observance reduce the likelihood of individuals accepting extremist narratives steeped in religion.[13] It is thus far too simplistic to claim, as one of the new atheists does, that religion "poisons everything."[14]

A MIDDLE GROUND

This book seeks a middle ground: I argue that religion alone is prone neither to violence nor to peace but is instead a latent variable that becomes activated in either direction depending on its interaction with its political environment. This range of dramatic and contradictory responses by religious actors to their surroundings has been termed the "ambivalence of the sacred."[15] All great faiths are multivocal and contain within them numerous doctrinal currents and interpretations – some peaceful, others violent.[16]

I argue that it is not religion per se that generates terrorism, but rather its restriction. Until recently, scholars of conflict tended to ignore the importance of religious repression as a determinant of violence. This has been an unfortunate and surprising oversight considering that religion remains one of the most important aspects of people's identity in the modern world and that faith believers comprise the vast majority of the global population.[17] Against the predictions of modernization theorists that social, political and economic progress would ultimately spell religion's demise, religion has defied the odds. Recent scholarship has shown that religion is gaining in strength worldwide. This is especially true with respect to religion's influence on politics, which has witnessed a tremendous global upsurge in recent decades and is one of the great forces shaping the world today.[18]

For the faithful, the freedom to believe, perform faith-based rituals, proselytize, observe holy days, worship with those of like mind, don religious garb and otherwise live by the guidelines of their faith is of paramount importance and constitutes a crucial component of their sense of place in the world. Yet, according to a series of quantitative reports by the Pew Research Center that measure the level of restrictions on religion around the globe for 190 countries, about 75 percent of people in the world today live under conditions of "high" or "very high" restrictions on

[13] Richard A. Nielsen, *Deadly Clerics: Blocked Ambition and the Paths to Jihad* (Cambridge: Cambridge University Press, 2017).
[14] Christopher Hitchens, *God Is Not Great: How Religion Poisons Everything* (New York, NY: Twelve, 2009).
[15] Appleby, *Ambivalence of the Sacred*.
[16] Stepan, "Religion, Democracy, and the 'Twin Tolerations.'"
[17] Pippa Norris and Ronald F. Inglehart, *Sacred and Secular: Religion and Politics Worldwide* (Cambridge: Cambridge University Press, 2004).
[18] Almond, Appleby and Sivan, *Strong Religion*; Daniel Philpott, "Has the Study of Global Politics Found Religion?" *Annual Review of Political Science* 12 (2009): 183–202.

religious belief and practice.[19] As argued in this chapter, where this right becomes compromised, the prospects for religious terrorism increase dramatically.

If religion really is such an intrinsic part of the human experience, profoundly integral to human fulfillment and pervasive throughout human history – an anthropological response to what is considered "ultimate" in one's perception of reality – it stands to reason that its restriction is bound to have especially unfortunate consequences and likely to generate violence in ways that purely secular forms of repression do not, permitting religious terrorists to overcome barriers to violent activity prevalent in many authoritarian countries. For example, some previous research has revealed that grievances generated over religious repression help dissidents overcome collective action problems, thus making religion-related rebellion more likely.[20] This is because restriction of religion inhibits or prevents altogether people from fulfilling their quintessentially human pursuit of meaning and purpose: to understand and achieve harmony with transcendent reality.

Indeed, the 1948 United Nations Declaration on Human Rights grounds religious freedom in the "inherent dignity" and "worth of the human person." As Timothy Samuel Shah explains, "Because religious beliefs and social practices have proven so ineradicable, so *natural* in their immense variety and mutability, to repress them is to repress human dignity itself. Religious repression is the denial of the very essence of what it means to be human" (emphasis his).[21] In other words, governments that impede the quest for the divine do not simply undercut the ability of their people to vote, form political parties or pursue economic equality – though such limitations certainly have the potential to breed aggression – they restrain the more fundamental and intrinsic rights of people to think freely about the purpose of their existence and to otherwise fulfill their sacred duties that spring from a power that is both prior to and higher than the state. People of faith are therefore likely to believe that restrictions on their religious liberty run counter to the will of God. It is one thing to restrict materialist conceptions of liberty; it is quite another to deny the timeless and inborn pursuit of purpose, meaning and destiny. For this reason, regimes that hinder the knowledge or pursuit of the supernatural play with fire when they interfere with an individual's innate aspiration for transcendent and eternal truth. In such settings, even moderates might be tempted to turn to the gun in defense of their faith.[22] Religious repression becomes all the more problematic in a world where religion is

[19] Pew Research Center, "Latest Trends in Religious Restrictions and Hostilities," last modified February 26, 2015, www.pewforum.org/2015/02/26/religious-hostilities/.
[20] Matthias Basedau, Georg Strüver, Johannes Vüllers and Tim Wegenast, "Do Religious Factors Impact Armed Conflict? Empirical Evidence from Sub-Saharan Africa," *Terrorism and Political Violence* 23, no. 5 (2011): 752–779; Matthias Basedau, Birte Pfeiffer and Johannes Vüllers, "Bad Religion? Religion, Collective Action, and the Onset of Armed Conflict in Developing Countries," *Journal of Conflict Resolution* 60, no. 2 (2016): 226–255.
[21] Shah, *Religious Freedom: Why Now?*, 15.
[22] Omar Ashour, *The De-Radicalization of Jihadists: Transforming Armed Islamist Movements* (New York, NY: Routledge, 2009); Shadi Hamid, *The Islamist Response to Repression: Are Mainstream Islamists Radicalizing?* (Washington, DC: Brookings Institution, 2010).

of increasing importance in people's personal lives and becoming more politically assertive.

Returning to the example of the Islamic State, much of the public discourse before its decline as a territorial entity concerned how the international community should respond to its barbarity. More important, though, is addressing the conditions that gave rise to it in the first place. The growth of ISIS can be directly linked to the brutal and arbitrary treatment of Iraq's religious minority communities. Systematic discrimination along religious lines served to create a sense of desperation and angst among Sunnis who believed they would have no place in the new Iraq after the US-led invasion in 2003. The government of Shia strongman Nouri al-Maliki pursued a punitive policy toward Iraq's Sunni community, including using the security forces to suppress opponents and bully rivals. For example, when peaceful Sunni protests broke out in the Anbar province in 2012, Maliki responded with an intense crackdown, leading to the shelling of villages and the arrests of hundreds of Sunnis. The following year he crushed a peaceful gathering of Sunnis in Ramadi – the same city that ISIS was able to overrun in 2015. These repressive acts allowed ISIS to portray itself as the protector of Sunnis and assemble tribal allies throughout much of the western parts of the country. Maliki's authoritarian turn directly fueled the insurgency by creating an environment of impunity, marginalizing the Sunni population and fostering a sense of fear among the country's minority religious populations. Threatened and insecure, Iraq's Sunni community turned to extremist groups for protection. Had Maliki chosen a different path – one of accommodation, tolerance and inclusion – ISIS likely would have never received support from some parts of Iraq's Sunni population.

As the case of ISIS shows, the global resurgence of religion necessarily means that the issue of religious freedom is both inevitable and strategically important. In this chapter, I examine two ways in which states restrict religion and how these restrictions often generate religious terrorism both domestically and against other countries.

HOW STATES RESTRICT RELIGION

Perhaps the most obvious violation of religious liberty stems from the laws, policies and actions of states. Official restrictions on religion may target certain or all faith traditions operating within the borders of particular countries. These limitations most commonly entail restrictions on the ability of religious communities to believe what they want and to practice their faith as they see fit.[23] At some times, states may have seemingly mundane statutes that limit certain activities like publishing litera-

---

[23]   Grim and Finke, *Price of Freedom Denied*, 33–40; Jonathan Fox, *Political Secularism, Religion, and the State: A Time Series Analysis of Worldwide Data* (Cambridge: Cambridge University Press, 2015), 39–63.

ture, fund-raising and building houses of worship.[24] In more extreme manifestations, states may restrict religious liberty through overt violence against particular religious constituencies.

States commonly restrict religion because they see it as a source of problems that needs to be controlled. Political leaders may consider it in their best interest to curb the free flow of religious ideas (other than officially sanctioned ones) and restrict faith-based institutions because they fear that their own political power might be threatened if they allow religion (which focuses authority away from the state) to exist uninhibited. They might also enact restrictions only on specific religious communities in order to appease their own. These fears are understandable given religion's proven ability to function as a great source of unity among and mobilizer of people – powerful enough to bring down regimes and compel sociopolitical change. Research has shown that political elites take the potential threat posed by religion so seriously that they are more likely to suppress religiously motivated dissidents than other regime opponents.[25] Even during periods of peace and stability, elites often remain suspicious of religion. On the other hand, government leaders also understand the tremendous power of religious identity in building nationalism, owing to religion's deep and intimately intertwined relationship with a nation's culture and history. In some cases, by controlling religion, leaders hope to mobilize it to their advantage.

However, when states act in a discriminatory manner and block channels for political and cultural engagement, they also create conditions ripe for the development of insular, bellicose political theologies if people of faith perceive their religious beliefs are being attacked and are in need of defense. When states restrict religious economies, they inevitably make religion a source of conflict, insofar as these restrictions are targeted at a primary source of peoples' identities and are often interpreted as an affront to their very being.[26] For this reason, religious suppression works to radicalize religious actors, weaken moderates and increase the support of extremists by creating grievances among those religious groups prevented from practicing their beliefs or bringing their religiously informed views into the public square.[27] Though some might argue that such repression serves to quash terrorism, this tends to be only a short-term gain (if initially successful) and, more often than not, ends up hardening opposition to the state. Young people in these kinds of societies are especially prone to extremist narratives when alternative ones are unavailable. In short, religious terrorists are much more likely to find a receptive

---

[24] Paul A. Marshall, *Religious Freedom in the World* (Lanham, MD: Rowman & Littlefield Publishers, 2008).

[25] Cullen S. Hendrix and Idean Salehyan, "A House Divided: Threat Perception, Military Factionalism, and Repression in Africa," *Journal of Conflict Resolution* 61, no. 8 (2007): 1653–1681.

[26] Jonathan Fox, "The Effects of Religious Discrimination on Ethno-Religious Protest and Rebellion," *The Journal of Conflict Studies* 20, no. 2 (2000), https://journals.lib.unb.ca/index.php/jcs/article/view/4310/4922.

[27] Anderson, "Fulfilling Prophecies."

audience to their message that their faith is under siege under conditions of pervasive governmental repression.

Generally, states restrict religious liberty in one of two ways, both of which carry the potential to breed religious terrorism. The first category involves restrictions on religious *minorities* – limits on religious practices and institutions that are not placed on majority groups.[28] When states limit the practice of religion by minority groups, they implicitly favor adherents of other religious traditions, either purposely or unintentionally, thereby creating an unbalanced religious playing field.[29] A second type of restriction takes the form of limitations on the practices and institutions of religious *majorities* or all religions. In these settings, the state seeks not to partner with a particular religion, but rather to vigorously monitor, manipulate or restrict the activities of religious groups and individuals. While the specific policies and actions that are part and parcel of minority and majority religious restriction may appear similar, the distinction in motivation is crucial, and the implications for resultant violence can be markedly different. This means that both forms of restrictions are qualitatively different from each other and encourage violence in different ways. Distinguishing between limitations placed on majority religions from those placed only on minority faith traditions provides a clearer understanding of the different ways in which distinctive forms of restrictions can help produce terrorist violence. The following discusses these dynamics.

Minority Religious Discrimination

The contemporary realities of global migration and the consequent increasing of religious diversity require states to design policies for dealing with their religious minorities, but the ways that countries handle this task can differ markedly. In some cases, governments have been successful at integrating and protecting minorities and heterodox believers in the majority faith who depart from conventional religious belief and practice. At other times, individuals belonging to minority religious communities suffer from an institutional bias against new or historically repressed religions in the form of legal discrimination – laws or official policies that inhibit or prevent members of certain or all minority religious communities from carrying out practices central to their faith-based commitments but that do not apply to the majority religion. Examples of these violations include, but are not limited to, onerous restrictions on building and maintaining houses of worship, arbitrary confiscation of property, prohibitions on the wearing of religious garb, mandatory religious identification on legal documents, restrictions on proselytizing, discriminatory school curricula and laws prohibiting blasphemy or apostasy. Official laws and policies such as these serve to create an unbalanced playing field in the state's

---

[28]   Yasemin Akbaba and Jonathan Fox, "The Religion and State-Minorities Dataset," *Journal of Peace Research* 48, no. 6 (2011): 807–816.

[29]   Grim and Finke, *Price of Freedom Denied*, 22–24, 206–210.

religious economy, resulting in minorities facing discrimination in ways that majority groups in society do not.[30] Minority religious restriction says less about a country's
general attitude toward religion and more about how it treats specific religious
communities. The ideology of Islamism, which advocates the use of state power to
promote a conservative form of Islam throughout all of society, law and politics,
represents the most important way by which states restrict the belief and practice of
religious minorities in the modern world.

The plight of religious minorities is commonly worsened by the fact that religiously
restrictive states usually also have policies in place that favor religious majorities,
including special legal privileges or the ability to regulate religious or political life at
the expense of others.[31] The state itself need not be religious in its makeup in order to
ally with religious groups in society. In some cases, the regime may take on the
religious character of the group it has partnered with as in Iran, Nigeria or prewar
Afghanistan under the Taliban; in others, the secular state has found it politically
expedient to extend patronage to certain religious factions but not to others. This is the
case in countries like Pakistan and India. Governments may justify their partnership
with majority religions on the grounds that it is necessary for fostering a common
identity, social stability and national security, which they believe are under threat from
religious outsiders.[32] These policies are often supported by the religious majority,
which, in turn, legitimates the authority of the government.

Two of the most important but underappreciated legal instruments of minority
religious discrimination are blasphemy and apostasy laws. Blasphemy laws are legal
prohibitions against speech or actions considered to be contemptuous of one's faith.
Passed for the ostensibly noble purpose of protecting religion from defamation by
curbing "hate speech," such laws actually serve to coerce religious conformity and
silence opposing religious views. For this reason, human rights watchdog groups
have criticized blasphemy laws for their violations of fundamental civil liberties,
including freedoms of speech and expression. Similarly, laws prohibiting apostasy
prevent people from leaving their faith or converting to another religion. In some
places, apostasy laws have existed for thousands of years. Far from being artifacts of
history, however, in dozens of countries around the world, both blasphemy and
apostasy laws remain on the books and are often enforced, with penalties ranging
from fines to capital punishment.[33] In countries with blasphemy and apostasy codes,

---

[30] Nazih N. M. Ayubi, *Political Islam: Religion and Politics in the Arab World* (London: Routledge,
      1991); Oliver Roy, *The Failure of Political Islam* (Paris: Esprit/Seuil, 1994); W. Cole Durham Jr.,
      "Perspectives on Religious Liberty: A Comparative Framework," in *Religious Human Rights in Global
      Perspective: Legal Perspectives*, ed. Johan D. van der Vyver and John Witte Jr. (The Hague: Kluwer
      Law International, 1996); Grim and Finke, *Price of Freedom Denied*, 160–201.
[31] Finke and Harris, "Wars and Rumors of Wars."
[32] Ani Sarkissian, *The Varieties of Repression: Why Governments Restrict Religion* (New York, NY:
      Oxford University Press, 2015).
[33] Angelina E. Theodorou, "Which Countries Still Outlaw Apostasy and Blasphemy?" last
      modified July 29, 2016, www.pewresearch.org/fact-tank/2016/07/29/which-countries-still-outlaw-
      apostasy-and-blasphemy/.

the authority of the dominant religion and the authority of the state are profoundly intertwined, often to the detriment of religious minorities. Such laws are also a convenient way for political leaders to strengthen their domestic standing by claiming that they are defending religious values.

Generally, as a state's level of minority religious discrimination increases, so too does its level of religious terrorism. In states practicing this form of discrimination, terrorism may erupt via three different pathways. In the first pathway, *minority backlash*, terrorism occurs against governments or their supporters deemed to be acting unfairly toward a particular minority religious group or groups by favoring dominant religions. The idea that discrimination can foster grievances resulting in violence has a long pedigree in the contentious politics literature, including the study of terrorism.[34] According to the "relative deprivation" theory first laid out by Ted R. Gurr, groups in society feel "deprived" when they experience some form of political, economic or cultural exclusion compared to similarly situated groups.[35] This discontent leads to frustration, anger, a sense of injustice, the hardening of in-group solidarity and an atmosphere of distrust and intolerance; if severe enough, eventually deprivation results in armed opposition against the state by those attempting to redress their grievances.

There is no reason to believe that this logic would not also apply to religious minorities who experience discriminatory policies on the part of the state.[36] In such settings, religious discrimination leads to the generation of resentment on the part of minorities and heightens the likelihood that such groups will take up the gun against governments deemed to be acting unfairly toward them.[37] As political scientists Yasemin Akbaba and Zeynep Taydas explain:

> Members of the religious minority perceive discriminatory policies as fundamental threats to their moral framework and develop antagonistic feelings towards the perpetrators of such policies. Acts of discrimination are perceived by the victims as evidence of the government's intolerance and lack of respect for other belief systems. Rebels who feel subordinate stop perceiving the state as a neutral entity but rather identify the state as an agent responsible for promoting the identity of the dominant group.[38]

In short, while religious minority discrimination might lessen the likelihood of grievance formation among favored groups, inequalities between religious groups

[34] Dogo Ergil, "The Kurdish Question in Turkey," *Journal of Democracy* 11, no. 3 (2000): 122–135; James A. Piazza, "Types of Minority Discrimination and Terrorism," *Conflict Management and Peace Science* 29, no. 5 (2012): 521–546.
[35] Ted R. Gurr, *Why Men Rebel* (Princeton, NJ: Princeton University Press, 1970).
[36] Fox, "Effects of Religious Discrimination on Ethno-Religious Protest and Rebellion"; Fox, *Ethnoreligious Conflict in the Late 20th Century*; Fox, *Religion, Civilization and Civil War*.
[37] David C. Rapoport, "Some General Observations on Religion and Violence," *Terrorism and Political Violence* 3, no. 3 (2007): 127–134; Jonathan Fox, "The Influence of Religious Legitimacy on Grievance Formation by Ethnoreligious Minorities," *Journal of Peace Research* 36, no. 3 (1999): 289–307.
[38] Yasemin J. Akbaba and Zeynep Taydas, "Does Religious Discrimination Promote Dissent? A Quantitative Analysis," *Ethnopolitics* 10, no. 3/4 (2011): 271–295.

also generate grievances on the part of disadvantaged groups toward the more privileged religions, which can create a fertile ground for radicalization. Thus, minority religious discrimination is dangerous because it has the potential to engender grievances, facilitate collective action and provoke backlash on the part of beleaguered groups.[39]

Take Sudan, for example. The third largest African country has been ravaged by two devastating civil wars, the second of which (1983–2005) was explicitly religious in nature and fought over which religion should be partnered with the state. The conflict can be traced back to the late 1950s when the Sudanese government, under General Ibrahim Abboud, allied with northern Islamist forces against Christians, animists and other minority faiths in the non-Muslim south in its attempt to forcibly impose a draconian version of Islam throughout all of Sudan, leading to several years of bloody religious conflict and the eventual breakup of the country in 2011.[40] Under the autocratic rule of Islamist president Omar al-Bashir, political opponents and religious minorities turned to the gun. These religious dynamics have underpinned the formation of oppositional terrorist groups in Sudan, the most important of which was the Sudan People's Liberation Army – a militant organization opposed to the Islamist regime in Khartoum.

Similar dynamics can be seen in India, where partnership between Hinduism and the state provoked violent reaction on the part of embattled groups. In the northern region of Punjab, the militant wing of the Sikh resistance movement arose in response to centuries of brutal repression by successive national governments dating back to the time of the Mughal Empire. The most vivid example of anti-Sikh discrimination and the roots of modern Sikh terrorism occurred on June 4, 1984 when a government-orchestrated massacre took place in the Sikhs' central place of worship, the Golden Temple (Harmandir Sahib) complex in Amritsar, Punjab, as well as forty-one other houses of worship (*gurdwaras*). Operation Blue Star, as it was called, commenced a spiral of Sikh terrorism and violent state reaction that would define India's relationship with its Sikh minority in the coming years. Following the attack on the Golden Temple, Prime Minister Indira Gandhi was killed by two of her Sikh bodyguards in Delhi on October 31, 1984. The assassination, in turn, led to a hardening of religious identities and sparked a widespread pogrom against Sikhs and their property in northern Indian cities with significant Sikh populations.[41]

In Yemen, where the constitution recognizes Islam as the official religion of the state and declares sharia to be the source of all legislation, the law criminalizes blasphemy, and apostasy can theoretically be met with the death penalty. Interfaith marriages between Muslims and non-Muslims are prohibited. Non-Muslims are

---

[39] Martha Crenshaw, "The Causes of Terrorism," *Comparative Politics* 13, no. 4 (1981): 383.
[40] Francis M. Deng, "Sudan – Civil War and Genocide: Disappearing Christians of the Middle East," *Middle East Quarterly* 8, no. 1 (2001): 13–21.
[41] Scott W. Hibbard, *Religious Politics and Secular States: Egypt, India, and the United States* (Baltimore, MD: Johns Hopkins University Press, 2010), 144–148.

forbidden from running for parliament. The regime of Ali Abdullah Saleh imposed sharp religious restrictions on the minority Zaidi sect in the north, particularly in the province of Saada – limiting the hours of operation for mosques, removing allegedly extremist imams, restricting materials espousing Zaidi doctrine, banning public commemorations of Shia holy days and repressing the opposition Islah Party. The government also prohibited conversion from Islam and non-Muslim groups and individuals from proselytizing to Muslims. In addition to Zaidis, Christians and Jews faced severe restrictions on the practice of their faith. Social regulation of religion involved abuses and discrimination on the basis of religious belief or practice. For example, leading Salafi clerics often used accusations of blasphemy or apostasy to harass atheists and religious minorities.[42]

Consistent with other states practicing discrimination against religious minorities, Yemen's empowering of a religious majority at the expense of minorities resulted in terrorist attacks carried out by both. Since the uprising that led to the formal resignation of Saleh, sectarian clashes between minority Houthi rebels, state-backed Sunni Islamists (also supported by Saudi Arabia) and the Yemeni military have become commonplace in northern Yemen. Al Qaeda in the Arabian Peninsula (AQAP), the most dangerous of the al Qaeda affiliates, regularly carries out attacks against government targets or individuals it accuses of immoral behavior. Extremist Zaidi and Sunni leaders invoke *takfir* (declaring a Muslim an apostate) as a justification for attacking members of the opposition. Meanwhile, in the south, militant Islamist groups and a separatist movement have competed for control.

A second pathway connecting minority religious discrimination to terrorism takes the form of religious *outbidding*. While terrorism is often thought of as a "weapon of the weak," paradoxically, minority religious discrimination can also result in terrorism carried out by members of the very religious community with which the state has entered into alliance. Outbidding occurs in states that obtain their authority from their perceived commitment to a particular religious dogma, even as they repress groups not subscribing to this orthodoxy. Such regimes are considered legitimate, however, only to the extent that they retain their faith-based purity. If the state strays too far from the acceptable path, it may find itself at odds with ultra-conservative factions who claim that it has compromised its purity and therefore lost its legitimacy. Religious radicals then try to "outbid" the regime in its claim to be the true guardian of the authentic faith, and may attempt to overthrow the political leadership through violence in order to establish a more sacrosanct order. This tactic often forces the state to become more repressive and align itself even more closely with illiberal religious factions in order to retain its hold on power, thus making violence more likely.[43]

---

[42] US Department of State Bureau of Democracy, Human Rights and Labor, "Yemen," 2013 *International Religious Freedom Report*, last modified 2013, www.state.gov/j/drl/rls/irf/religiousfree dom/index.htm#wrapper.
[43] Toft, "Getting Religion?"

During the 1956 general election in Sri Lanka (then known as Ceylon), the Sri Lankan Freedom Party (SLFP), a party comprised mainly of Sinhalese Buddhists, promised the Buddhist majority a privileged status at the expense of Hindu Tamils upon winning the election. When Prime Minister S. W. R. D. Bandaranaika failed to sufficiently fulfill his "Sinhala only" campaign pledge, he was assassinated by a disaffected Buddhist monk in 1959.[44] Similar dynamics can be seen in Israel, a state founded as a "Jewish democracy." Israel's claim to being a Jewish state has left it vulnerable to the charge leveled by extremist Jewish organizations that it has compromised its Jewish character. The dynamic of outbidding has underpinned acts of violence by terrorist groups like the Jewish Underground, Keshet, Yad La'achim and Kach. Such groups have been implicated in the assassination of Prime Minister Yitzhak Rabin in 1995, the murder of twenty-nine Muslims in a 1994 mosque attack and the killing of four Arab-Israelis and the wounding of an additional nine on a commuter bus in 2005.[45] These groups strive to establish a more religiously pure state in accordance with their interpretation of the Bible, and thus oppose any efforts in support of a two-state solution in the Holy Land. Ironically, in the cases of Sri Lanka and Israel, implicit or explicit discrimination against religious minorities ended up producing a violent backlash by those associated with the religious majority against the state itself.

Finally, minority religious discrimination can encourage *vigilante terrorism* by dominant groups against minority communities. When states limit the religious activities of certain faith traditions, they sometimes contribute to the belief in society that violence against these groups is supported by official laws and policies.[46] An important example of this dynamic involves laws against religious defamation, which, though passed by the state (often to coopt a majority religious group into supporting the government), are often enforced by society at large more than official state institutions. Religious defamation laws preclude the development of a multiplicity of views at the society level. Instead, the prevention of peaceful dialogue on the role of religion and the lack of intellectual diversity stifles the healthy exchange of ideas and insulates radical theologies by smothering open debate and discourse regarding the proper construal of religion instead of allowing for the exposing of logical inconsistencies and incorrect interpretation by extremists.

Not only do defamation codes promote intolerance and increase the political salience of religion, in restricting the limits of acceptable discourse, they also encourage a culture of vigilante justice in society. In countries enforcing these laws, terrorists, claiming to be the defenders of a particular faith tradition, routinely attack those they believe are guilty of heresy. Vigilante terrorists have often attacked

44 Gregg, "Three Theories of Religious Activism and Violence."
45 Nachman Ben-Yehuda, *Theocratic Democracy: The Social Construction of Religious and Secular Extremism* (New York, NY: Oxford University Press, 2010), 99.
46 Nilay Saiya, "Blasphemy and Terrorism in the Muslim World," *Terrorism and Political Violence* 29, no. 6 (2017): 1087–1105.

with impunity individuals, homes, places of worship and businesses of those believed to be blasphemers or apostates, using the very laws passed by the state to justify their violence. In reply, the state commonly turns a blind eye to violence carried out by adherents of the dominant faith tradition on whose behalf it proscribes religious defamation in order to retain its good standing with that religious group. Terrorists thus feel empowered to commit acts of violence with little or no fear of governmental reprisal because defamation laws, in effect, lend the authority of the state to religious figures and reinforce extreme views. For this reason, rather than controlling the forces of extremism, such laws appease and encourage them.

In Pakistan, for example, jihadis have killed dozens of people whom they accuse of blasphemy, including politicians like Salmaan Taseer and Shabbaz Bhatti, who dared to criticize the country's blasphemy culture. In 2013, an accusation of blasphemy against a Pakistani Christian sparked a wave of attacks on the predominantly Christian neighborhood of Lahore known as Joseph Colony, resulting in the destruction of at least 150 Christian homes, businesses and churches. Hundreds of Christians were forced to flee for their lives. At the time of this writing, none of the suspected terrorists has been convicted for the attack. Similar incidents have occurred in Saudi Arabia, Iran, Egypt, Afghanistan and in various other Islamic countries with blasphemy laws.[47] In the Western world, charges of blasphemy by Islamists have resulted in the deaths of filmmakers, satirists and authors.

Blasphemy laws demonstrate one way in which minority religious restrictions can encourage vigilante terrorism. A second way involves apostasy (anti-conversion) laws. The Indian state of Odisha (formerly Orissa), one of six Indian states to have formal anti-conversion laws in place, has witnessed a high level of Hindu–Christian hostility. The root of the enmity can be traced to right-wing Hindu organizations such as the Vishwa Hindu Parishad and the Bajrang Dal, both of which promote anti-Christian propaganda in an effort to coerce the state's Christians to convert to Hinduism. They also accuse Christians of forcing lower-caste Hindus (Dalits) to convert to Christianity and leave the caste system. Such groups were behind the "Orissa Freedom of Religion Act" of 1967, which, despite its auspicious title, was an anti-conversion law that effectively prevented people from converting to Christianity. In 2008, this hostility turned violent when Christians attacked Hindu homes and businesses and Hindus burned down or otherwise destroyed hundreds of Christian churches and thousands of Christian homes. Vulnerable groups caught in the middle were forcibly displaced into relief camps. The violence in Odisha occurred while the state turned a blind eye; local police only registered 827 cases of more than 3,500 reports of violence they received.[48] A more recent example of

---

47 Paul Marshall and Nina Shea, *Silenced: How Apostasy and Blasphemy Codes Are Choking Freedom Worldwide* (Oxford: Oxford University Press, 2011).

48 Stoyan Zaimov, "Christians in India Demand Justice for 2008 Orissa Massacre," *Christian Post*, last modified January 3, 2012, www.christianpost.com/news/christians-in-india-demand-justice-for-2008-orissa-massacre-66264/.

vigilante terrorism in India involves the rise of Hindu "cow protection" groups who have attacked alleged smugglers, merchants and consumers of beef products, primarily Muslims and Hindu Dalits. These cow vigilante groups, acting on the belief that cow slaughter and beef consumption constitute an affront to Hindu deities, have been emboldened by official laws found in twenty-four of India's twenty-nine states imposing partial-to-full restrictions and penalties on the slaughter of bovines.[49]

Majority Religious Cooptation

Minority religious discrimination represents one way in which repression of religion can encourage terrorism; a second involves restrictions on religious majorities or all religions. It is important to examine majority restrictions on religion separately from minority restrictions as the two are qualitatively different from each other. In the case of minority restrictions, the state singles out particular religious groups for unfair treatment. Thus, it is a form of religious repression. Majority religious restriction, by contrast, says less about how a country treats specific religious communities (though the state may still single out a particular faith tradition for especially harsh treatment) and more about its general attitude or approach toward religion. Countries regulating religion in this manner seek to put religion under state control due to leaders' fear or suspicion of religion, even if this entails some degree of outward support for religion in certain cases. Nevertheless, the objective here is not to advance some idealized vision of a proper religious society, but instead to perpetuate the state's authority by subjugating or coopting religion, with the goal being the primacy of *nonreligious* principles in the political realm to the largest extent possible. Such states are grounded in political theologies of secularism imported from the West.

Why do states restrict religious majorities? Sometimes such restrictions owe to guiding ideologies that are anti-religion in nature and take the form of outright hostility toward religion with the goal of eradicating independent religious expression in society. Communist states like the former Soviet Union, North Korea and China under Chairman Mao fall into this category. After the end of the Cold War and the waning of communism, this form of religious regulation is becoming increasingly rare, with very few countries in the world practicing outright hostility to all religions across the board.

A far more common form of majority restrictions involves *religious cooptation*. In contrast to states that are hostile to any form of religious expression, other states that restrict religious majorities may allow certain forms of religiosity to exist so long as they are subservient to the state. Political elites in these countries may not necessarily be hostile toward religion and may even support the private practice of

[49] US Department of State Bureau of Democracy, Human Rights and Labor, "India," *2016 International Religious Freedom Report*, last modified 2016, www.state.gov/j/drl/rls/irf/religiousfreedom/index.htm #wrapper.

religion. In fact, religion can even serve a legitimating function in these states if it can be properly controlled in the service of boosting nationalism, helping to pacify citizens or preventing disorder. Instead, the restrictions on religion that are part and parcel of cooptation seek to prevent religion from acquiring an independent power base from which it can challenge or otherwise constrain the regime.

Paradoxically, many state leaders believe that the best way to keep religion's public power in check is to support a moderate strain of the predominant faith tradition within their countries, making it dependent on or beholden to the government. Jonathan Fox explains that political elites do this "because supporting religion is among the most effective strategies to make religious institutions dependent on the government, and thereby more subject to its control."[50] He finds that "no state regulates, controls, or restricts religion without also supporting it in at least some small way."[51] In other words, the support given to these religious institutions and actors comes with strings attached; the sustenance ends if religion begins to encroach on the territory of those in power. According to Fox, religious regulation is simultaneously intertwined with government support for religion.[52]

For example, Middle Eastern states in which secular nationalism took root, unlike communist countries, sought not to eliminate religion but to manage it in such a way so as to help entrench the power of secular dictators, usually by coopting a particular strain of Islam believed to be conducive to their political objectives – development, Westernization, unity – while banning those that did not faithfully adhere to their ideology and policies. One might point to Jordan – a country where all mosques are controlled by the state and Muslim clergy draw their salaries from the government – or Turkey – a secular republic that has generally been repressive of religious freedoms throughout its history in order to uphold the secularist legacy of its founder, Mustafa Kemal Atatürk, and where the Directorate of Religious Affairs manages mosques and religious schools and oversees all Islamic leaders. These are classic ways in which secular regimes have attempted to control religion within their borders. In short, if states restrictive of religious minorities impede religious liberty through the politicization of religion, states restrictive of majorities hinder it through the principle of secularism, seeking to manage religion, even if this means adopting a veneer of support for certain religious groups.

Majority religious cooptation can certainly encourage terrorism from embattled religious minority communities as in states featuring minority religious discrimination, but a more common form of violent resistance involves *majority backlash*. This is logical given that secular regimes, by their very definition, restrict the religious rights not only of minority religious groups but also of the predominant faith traditions. In the Middle East, for example, majority religious cooptation has given rise to an assertive, confrontational and sometimes violent religion.

[50] Fox, *Political Secularism, Religion, and the State*, 2.
[51] Fox, *Political Secularism, Religion, and the State*, 105.
[52] Fox, *Political Secularism, Religion, and the State*, 105–106.

In Turkey, the extremist Sunni group Turkish Hezbollah, though initially supported clandestinely by the Turkish state to counter the activities of the Kurdistan Workers' Party, eventually turned against the government itself in response to a worsening context of religious marginalization in the 1990s. The overarching goal of the terrorist group is to establish an Islamic state by the force of arms. In the Arab world, conservative religious movements were frequently forced underground, and religious institutions became the only social venue available for like-minded individuals to vent their frustration against the state and thus served as a space for group coalescence and the dissemination of radical ideologies. Restricted from public life and driven underground, these banned movements gave rise to the most feared transnational terrorist networks in history. In some places, disillusionment with the state exploded into full-blown religious civil wars as in Algeria and Syria.

Majority religious regulation is also practiced in other parts of the world (albeit in different forms) with often similar results. In China, the restriction of religion has helped foment violent resistance among Muslim Uyghurs in the western Xinjiang region.[53] In the former Soviet republic of Tajikistan, the government has pursued policies like disallowing women and minors from attending mosques, arresting imams who teach Islam to minors, closing hundreds of mosques, forbidding women from wearing the *hijab*, banning the Islamic Renaissance Party of Tajikistan, forcing Muslim men to shave their beards and criminalizing all unregistered religious activity, all in an attempt to curb extremism.[54] Yet Tajikistan's own recent history shows that such treatment of religion generates rather than squelches violence. After the fall of the Soviet Union, the repression of a neo-communist regime in Dushanbe provoked a violent civil war between Islamists and the state, claiming the lives of nearly 100,000 people. Terrorism has swollen as well, as demonstrated in the 2010 terrorist attack by the Islamic Movement of Uzbekistan, which resulted in the deaths of twenty-five Tajik soldiers. The attack was a direct response to Tajikistan's oppressive religion laws.[55] In 2015, the head of Tajikistan's security forces, Gulmuod Halimov, left the country for Syria in order to join ISIS, in part because the Tajik state no longer permitted Muslims "to pray and wear Islamic *hijabs*."[56]

This chapter has thus far argued that religious restrictions work to generate terrorism in two specific ways: minority religious discrimination and majority religious cooptation. The correlation graphs that follow show that countries repressive of religion do, in fact, experience significantly higher rates of terrorism than

---

[53] Remi Castets, "The Uyghurs in Xinjiang – The Malaise Grows," *China Perspectives* 49 (2003): 34–84.
[54] US Commission on International Religious Freedom, *2017 Annual Report* (Washington, DC: US Commission on International Religious Freedom, 2017), 96–102.
[55] Knox Thames, "Defending Religion from Itself," *Foreign Policy*, last modified July 30, 2015, http://foreignpolicy.com/2015/07/30/defending-religion-from-itself/.
[56] Radio Free Europe/Radio Liberty, "Missing Tajik Police Commander Appears on Internet, Says Has Joined IS," *RFE/RL's Tajik Service*, last modified May 28, 2015, www.rferl.org/a/tajikistan-police-commander-video-says-joined-islamic-state/27041183.html.

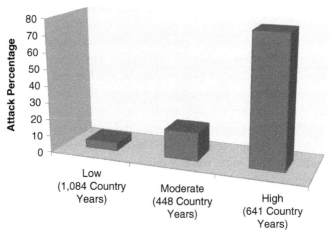

FIGURE 1.1 Government regulation of religion and religious terrorist attacks, 2001–2013
Sources: Data on attacks derived and coded from National Consortium for the Study of
Terrorism and Responses to Terrorism (START). *Global Terrorism Database*. 2016,
accessed January 28, 2017, www.start.umd.edu/gtd. See appendix for complete coding
procedures of terrorist attacks. Data for religious freedom scores derived from Association
of Religion Data Archives, International Religious Freedom Data, 2001, 2005,
accessed July 3, 2015, www.thearda.com/Archive/Files/Descriptions/IRF2001.asp;
Association of Religion Data Archives, International Religious Freedom Data, 2003,
2005, accessed July 3, 2015, www.thearda.com/Archive/Files/Descriptions/IRF2003.asp;
Association of Religion Data Archives, International Religious Freedom Data, 2005,
2005, accessed July 3, 2015, www.thearda.com/Archive/Files/Descriptions/IRF2005.asp;
Pew Research Center, *Global Restrictions on Religion*, December 17, 2009, www
.pewforum.org/2009/12/17/global-restrictions-on-religion/; Pew Research Center, *Rising
Restrictions on Religion – One Third of the World's Population Experiences an Increase*,
August 9, 2011, www.pewforum.org/2011/08/09/rising-restrictions-on-religion2/; Pew
Research Center, *Rising Tide of Restrictions on Religion*, September 20, 2012, www
.pewforum.org/2012/09/20/rising-tide-of-restrictions-on-religion-findings/

their religiously free counterparts. Figure 1.1 examines countries by their levels of
general government regulation of religion and the number of identifiable religious
terrorist attacks they suffered over the period 2001–2013. It reveals that countries in
which the government restricts religion generally are far more likely to witness
higher levels of religious terrorism than countries with low levels of religious
restrictions. Looking at countries further by their yearly terrorist attack averages
shows that states with low levels of governmental regulation suffered only 0.30
terrorist attacks per year; countries with moderate levels of restrictions saw 5.37
attacks on average; countries in the high category experienced 7.35 attacks, or nearly
twenty-five times as many attacks as countries with low restrictions. Countries with

a generally high level of governmental religious restrictions are thus associated with higher levels of attacks on average.[57]

Figures 1.2 and 1.3 examine the relationship between the two specific forms of government restrictions on religion – minority religious discrimination and majority religious cooptation – and their relationship to religious terrorism.[58] Figure 1.2 looks at restrictions placed by the state on the practice of religion by some or all minority religious groups that are not placed on the majority group. This category of restrictions attempts to gauge if and to what extent governments single out some or all minorities for unequal treatment vis-à-vis the majority group. These policies include restrictions on minority practices, minority institutions, conversions and missionary activity and other forms of minority religious restrictions. The figure reveals that countries in which the government restricts minority religious communities are far more likely to witness higher levels of religious terrorism than countries that do not engage in minority discrimination. Roughly 70 percent of religious terrorist attacks occurred in states marked by high levels of minority discrimination. These states also experienced about nine times the number of attacks as countries with low levels of persecution against minority communities.

Figure 1.3, which looks at restrictions placed by the state on the majority religion or all religions instead of discrimination against minorities, continues the same story of religious repression's deleterious effects on terrorism. Religious majority regulation includes restrictions on religion's political role, restrictions on religious institutions and clergy, restrictions on religious practices and other forms of regulation, control and restrictions. The figure reveals that countries in which the government restricts religion across the board experience substantially more religious terrorism than countries that do not attempt to regulate religion in this manner. About 80 percent of all religious terrorist attacks occurred in countries with high levels of majority religious restriction. These countries suffered almost ten times as many attacks as countries free of majority persecution.

The complete statistical models found in the appendix of this book reveal that governmental restriction of religion remains a statistically significant and substantively important variable in predicting religious terrorist attacks, even when controlling for other standard variables that might explain terrorism like the size of

[57] Government Regulation index of Religion (GRI) attempts to gauge the extent to which governments try to control religious groups or individuals through official policies and legislation. Government regulation is defined as "the restrictions placed on the practice, profession, or selection of religion by the official laws, policies, or administrative actions of the state." GRI data were coded by Brian Grim and Roger Finke from the 2001, 2003, 2005 and 2008 State Department International Freedom Report. Subsequent scores were derived from successive Pew Research Center reports from 2009 to 2013. The score for this index ranges from 0 to 10, with 10 representing the most egregious offenders of religious freedom. These scores were then consolidated into three categories with the first third of scores coded as "low," the second third as "medium" and the final third as "high," producing religious freedom scores for 196 countries and territories.

[58] Due to skewing caused by a few extreme outliers, countries were grouped into "low," "moderate" and "high" categories by creating equal country tertiles.

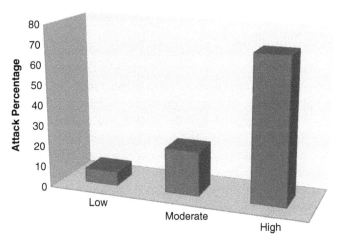

FIGURE 1.2 Minority religious restrictions and religious terrorist attacks, 1991–2009
Sources: Data for minority religious restrictions taken from Jonathan Fox, Religion and State Dataset, 2016, www.religionandstate.org. For terrorism data, see earlier in this chapter.

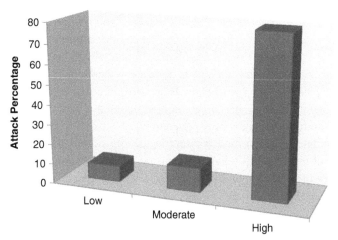

FIGURE 1.3 Majority religious restrictions and religious terrorist attacks, 1991–2009
Sources: See Figure 1.2.

a country's population, level of wealth, geographic size, level of democracy, religious fractionalization, the presence of other forms of violent conflict and whether a foreign military occupation was present. This suggests that religious repression is an important part of the story behind religious terrorism. Moreover, it appears that it is religious restrictions specifically and not a lack of democracy more generally that lead to these negative outcomes. Indeed, the statistical models confirm that electorally democratic countries are *more* likely to experience religious terrorist attacks. As discussed previously, the reason for this seemingly paradoxical finding is that many of the world's democracies are of the illiberal variety, which impede the free practice of faith. Clearly, then, religious terrorism is more closely associated with a country's level of religious liberty rather than its level of democracy.

In sum, the way religion is sanctioned by a state's government explains a good deal about when, where and why religious actors take up the gun. The more a government mediates and regulates religion, the higher the likelihood of religious terrorism occurring. Minority religious discrimination increases the ability of dominant religious traditions to wield undue political power, exacerbating the grievances held by minority religious communities or empowering religious terrorists from the favored religious community to carry out attacks against these minorities. Majority religious cooptation stifles the practice of religion for majority or all religious groups, contributing to widespread feelings of resentment by religious communities against the state. Both arrangements contribute to the lack of fully realized religious liberty in society and can become problematic with respect to religious terrorism.

RELIGIOUS RESTRICTION AND TRANSNATIONAL TERRORISM

"All politics is local" – a refrain popularized by former Speaker of the US House of Representatives Tip O'Neill – encompasses the idea that what happens in politics is directly linked to domestic circumstances. The same is true of terrorism. More than 90 percent of all terrorist attacks are domestic in nature; the perpetrator and victim are of the same nationality.[59] Yet in a globalized world where ideas rarely remain confined to individual countries, religious ideologies (including violent ones) can easily spread across borders and be taken up by like-minded individuals and groups in other countries.

Although most terrorists have local grievances and objectives, domestic conditions of religious repression can also give rise to groups and individuals who attack targets in other countries, a phenomenon that political scientists Monica Toft, Daniel Philpott and Timothy Samuel Shah refer to as the "glocalization" of terrorism.[60] While repressive governments may sometimes succeed at thwarting terrorism within their borders, they have at times simultaneously served to export it to other countries. Likewise, repressive domestic conditions can also invite terrorism from abroad. This connection between domestic politics and international terrorism has been exacerbated by the revolution in global communications, ease of travel and increased cross-cultural contact.

[59] Ignacio Sanchez-Cuenca and Luis de la Calle, "Domestic Terrorism: The Hidden Side of Political Violence," *Annual Review of Political Science* 12: 31–49.

[60] Toft, Philpott and Shah, *God's Century*, 123.

Just as state repression of religion works to generate domestic terrorism, it can inspire transnational terrorism as well in three general, sometimes overlapping, ways: (1) an outside-in strategy called *solicitation*, (2) an inside-out dynamic called *incubation* and (3) direct *state support* of terrorism.

In the outside-in strategy known as solicitation, religious actors, operating in a context of suppression by a state practicing either minority religious discrimination or majority religious cooptation, may attempt to solicit the support of coreligionists – in terms of money, weapons or recruits – from outside the state's borders to help undermine or overthrow the home regime through violence. Following the American invasion and occupation of Iraq, for example, Sunni militants from around the Middle East traveled to the country with the expectation that terrorist violence would both convince the United States to leave the region and overthrow the regime of Iraqi Prime Minister Nouri al Maliki, whose time in office witnessed the creation of an environment of impunity, the marginalization of the Sunni population and the fostering of a sense of fear among the country's minority religious populations. In Eurasia, Russia's brutality toward Chechnya led to thousands of Muslim warriors traveling to the Caucasus to battle Moscow. The US National Counterterrorism Center estimates that foreign fighters from more than ninety countries have joined the fight against Syrian leader Bashar Assad since Syria's civil war began in 2011.[61] Finally, in Burma, a new militant organization calling itself the Arakan Rohingya Salvation Army (ARSA) fights against an oppressive Burmese state on behalf of embattled Muslims. ARSA is led by a committee of Rohingya emigres in Saudi Arabia, and the Rohingya cause has been used propagandistically by international jihadi groups for several years.[62]

In the dynamic of incubation, in contrast to solicitation, religiously repressive environments give rise to religious extremism, but the states in which this militancy is birthed may not be where terrorists actually carry out attacks. These regimes incubate extremist groups who then operate in other countries – a classic case of "the friend of my enemy is my enemy."[63] As Kai Hafez explains, "[in] hard authoritarian states such as Iraq (under Saddam Hussein), Syria, Libya or Tunisia, it was ... impossible for an opposition to take shape in the first place, unless it move[d] abroad."[64] In the 1980s, nationals from repressive countries in the Arab world made their way to the battlefields of Afghanistan to support the *mujahidin* resistance to the Soviet invasion. Known as the "Arab Afghans," these foreign fighters had over

[61] Jamie Crawford and Laura Koran, "U.S. Officials: Foreigners Flock to Fight for ISIS," *CNN*, last modified February 11, 2015, www.cnn.com/2015/02/10/politics/isis-foreign-fighters-combat.

[62] International Crisis Group, *Myanmar: A New Muslim Insurgency in Rakhine State* (Brussels: International Crisis Group, 2016).

[63] Eric Neumayer and Thomas Plumper, "Foreign Terror on Americans," *Journal of Peace Research* 48, no. 1 (2011): 3–17.

[64] Kai Hafez, *Radicalism and Political Reform in the Islamic and Western Worlds* (Cambridge: Cambridge University Press, 2010), 107.

time become radicalized due to their treatment by their own governments and found an outlet for their rage in a holy war against the atheistic Soviet Union. After successfully repelling the Soviet military, these Arab volunteers returned to their home countries with a renewed sense of purpose about achieving political change through militancy at home just as they had done in Afghanistan. The same dynamic of incubation occurred during the conflict in the Balkans in the 1990s (which involved many Afghan veterans) and can be seen today in Iraq and Syria.

Today, Central Asia, one of the most religiously repressive regions of the world, illustrates well the connection between domestic religious repression and the incubation and exportation of terrorism to other countries. After the end of the Cold War and the fall of the Soviet Union, the newly independent republics of Tajikistan, Turkmenistan, Kazakhstan, Kyrgyzstan, Uzbekistan and Azerbaijan, often ruled by former communist officials, fell prey to a renewed round of secular authoritarianism deeply hostile to religion. This new wave of secular repression has encouraged religious radicalization. Several of the states of Central Asia have suffered less than other countries in terms of domestic religious terrorism, but they have also inadvertently incubated and exported radicalism abroad through their restrictive policies. In Uzbekistan – a country so repressive of religion that the US Commission on International Religious Freedom has listed it as a Tier 1 "country of particular concern" every year since 2006 – several thousands of people have been imprisoned and tortured for their Islamic beliefs. This state of affairs has forced indigenous Islamist movements such as the Islamic Movement of Uzbekistan to flee repression and leave the country. Many of these individuals, radicalized at home, went on to join extremist organizations like the Taliban and al Qaeda in the 1990s and the Islamic State and al-Nusra more recently. A disproportionate number of foreign fighters involved in the Iraq and Syria conflicts hails from Uzbekistan. In 2017 alone, Uzbek nationals carried out several high-profile attacks around the world: the New Year's shooting in Istanbul, the bombing of a St. Petersburg metro and a truck attack in Stockholm in April, and another truck attack in Manhattan in November. Formed in 1998, the Islamic Movement of Uzbekistan sought the overthrow of that country's authoritarian leader, Islom Karimov, but has since evolved into a transnational terrorist threat, officially aligning itself with ISIS in 2015.

In some cases, the dynamics of solicitation and incubation coexist and reinforce each other. After the attacks of September 11, 2001, the Yemeni government used the threat of terrorism as a justification to begin a campaign of systematic repression against its citizens, especially members of Islamic groups and students at religious schools. Supported by tens of millions of dollars in US aid annually, the state subjected thousands of citizens to arbitrary arrest – many of whom were imprisoned incommunicado, tortured or deported without access to legal counsel – and ruthlessly suppressed opposition movements. The post–September 11 crackdown precipitated the arrival of foreign radicals (most notably John Walker Lindh, the American Taliban member), the emergence of armed religious groups affiliated with al Qaeda in Yemen and the outbreak of violence. At the same time, Yemen also continued its exporting of terrorism abroad as terrorist organizations like AQAP and Ansar al-Sharia used the safe haven found in Yemen to train jihadis and plot attacks against external targets. AQAP claimed responsibility for the 2015 Paris attack against the headquarters of the satirical magazine *Charlie Hebdo*, which resulted in the deaths of twelve individuals. The two shooters in the attack, brothers Saïd and Chérif Kouachi, spent several months in the country and formed close ties to AQAP. The elder brother, Said, had attended al-Imam University, an extremist Sunni religious school.[65] AQAP was also the group behind the failed plot to blow up a US airliner over Detroit on Christmas Day 2009.

Local grievances and conflicts can sometimes also morph into international terrorism against third-party states believed to be supporting repressive regimes at home, even if those third parties are themselves not religiously restrictive. When states (including religiously free ones) offer unqualified support to repressive leaders, they themselves end up becoming accomplices in the denial of religious liberty and the perpetuation of persecution. In such cases, even though terrorists ultimately seek domestic regime change, they target the foreign sponsors of their home regimes in an attempt to drum up support for their cause and improve their recruitment and mobilization prospects. Terrorists hope to make foreign cooperation with repressive regimes costly in human terms.

In Algeria, after the Islamist opposition known as the Islamic Salvation Front (FIS) won the first round of the country's first multiparty parliamentary elections in 1992, the military-controlled government, with support from France, officially canceled the results, prevented a second round of voting, formally dissolved the FIS and declared martial law. Some members of the disbanded FIS, infuriated by their experience with politics, went on to form the Armed Islamic Group (GIA) the following year, launching a bloody terrorist campaign throughout the country. The GIA, however, did not confine its violence to Algeria but also staged several attacks in France and against French nationals living in Algeria. In 1994, four members of the GIA hijacked an Air France Airbus en route from Algeria to France. In 1995, the GIA carried out an unrelenting campaign of violence in France, which resulted in the deaths of scores of French citizens. The GIA engaged in this anti-French terrorist campaign in an attempt to force Paris to end its support for the incumbent Algerian government.

The United States has also been a victim of international religious terrorism arising from similar dynamics. Islamist terrorists from Egypt, Yemen, Pakistan, Uzbekistan and Saudi Arabia – countries with regimes sharply repressive of religious liberty but with which the United States has cultivated close alliances – have singled out the United States for its support of these oppressive governments.

---

[65]   Alan Yuhas, "How Yemen Spawned the Charlie Hebdo Attacks – the Guardian Briefing," *The Guardian*, last modified January 14, 2015, www.theguardian.com/world/2015/jan/14/yemen-aqap-civil-war-extremism?CMP=share_btn_tw.

The malcontent behind the most devastating terrorist attacks in history, the strikes against New York City and Washington, DC, in 2001, can be directly linked to the American backing of unpopular governments in the Muslim world. In Saudi Arabia, discontented Islamist groups have violently confronted a repressive state that has allied itself with a strain of Islam believed to be amenable to the rule of the Saudi monarchy. But the jihadist movement in Saudi Arabia seeks not just the domestic transformation of political life but also international political change. One key reason why jihadis of Saudi origin target the United States today is for its financial and military backing of a regime that sharply suppresses the freedom of those groups not aligned with the state.

A third pathway linking restrictions on religion to interstate religious terrorism involves state support for terrorism abroad. State support for terrorism arises in conditions similar to the ones that give birth to "outbidding" (discussed earlier). Political regimes that derive their legitimacy from their faithfulness to a particular religious dogma may not only favor or repress certain faith communities at home but also support or sponsor violence abroad. They do this because they see violence carried out by terrorist organizations as a useful way to wage war by proxy against their enemies. This can become especially problematic if the antagonistic countries are comprised of religiously distinct majorities.

For example, state-supported terrorism has also been an enduring feature of Pakistan's conflict with neighboring India. The Pakistani military, in particular, has cultivated strong ties to extremist groups, seeing them as a strategic asset against India, as a bulwark against communism during the Cold War and as a key proxy against Bangladeshi secessionist forces in East Pakistan in the 1960s. During the 1980s, the state's Inter-Services Intelligence (ISI) and military supported the Afghan *mujahidin* through military training and financial assistance in a proxy war against the Soviet-controlled Democratic Republic of Afghanistan. Yet even after that particular conflict came to an end, some elements within the establishment continued to support several extremist spin-off groups – reconstituted in the forms of Lashkar-e-Taiba, Harkat-ul-Mujahideen, Tehrik-i-Taliban and others – in ongoing insurgency operations in Afghanistan and India. Of course, Pakistan is not alone in its support of religious radicalism abroad. Theocratic governments also support religious terrorism against other countries. Owing to its alliance with Islamist factions, in 1991 Sudan invited Osama bin Laden to operate his transnational al Qaeda network from within that country until he was eventually expelled five years later under international pressure. To this day, the American government still considers Sudan a state sponsor of international terrorism. Iran and Saudi Arabia have acted in a like manner in this respect. Terrorist groups, supported by states such as these, provide a religious justification for attacking their enemies – a justification that would have far less credence in societies that uphold religious liberty.

Sometimes the connection between local forms of religious restriction and international acts of terrorism is more subtle than the three pathways outlined earlier.

Consider again the case of the 2015 massacre at the headquarters of *Charlie Hebdo*, a satirical newspaper based in Paris. Just before noon on January 7 of that year, two French brothers of Algerian descent, Saïd and Chérif Kouachi, opened fire at a staff meeting and proceeded to kill twelve newspaper employees, including the editor in chief, and injure another eleven. The gunmen believed that *Charlie Hebdo* had blasphemed the religion of Islam by publishing cartoons of the Prophet Mohammed – a sin they deemed deserving of death. As they went on their shooting spree, the brothers shouted that they had "avenged the Prophet."[66] The Kouachi brothers believed, mistakenly, that Islam prescribes death as a proper punishment for blasphemy (words or actions considered contemptuous or critical of Islam, Allah, Mohammed or Muslims) against their faith. However, Islam's holy book, the Quran, never mentions blasphemy, nor does it mandate any punishment for depictions of Mohammed, regardless of how irreverent or offensive they may be. The brothers' erroneous interpretation of their own faith likely originated from blasphemy codes prominent in large swaths of the Islamic world. Political leaders have long exploited such laws as a crafty way to use religion for political purposes, including inflaming religious sensibilities, silencing criticism of the regime, generating patriotism, fostering national cohesion, coopting Islamic supporters and undercutting detractors.[67] Yet, as demonstrated by the *Charlie Hebdo* attack, the criminalization of religious defamation can have violent ramifications even for countries far away, as blasphemy-related terrorist incidents have been increasing around the world.

An analysis of international terrorism data derived and coded from the RAND Database of Worldwide Terrorism Incidents shows that religiously restrictive states were the targets of 294 international religious terrorist attacks (80 percent) in the post–Cold War era (1991–2013). By contrast, moderately restrictive states endured 45 attacks (12 percent), while religiously free countries saw only 29 attacks (8 percent). Moreover, the vast majority of international religious terrorist groups also *originated* from religiously repressive settings: 91 percent emanated from highly restrictive countries; 8 percent from moderately restrictive countries; and slightly more than 2 percent from religiously free settings. In short, as Figure 1.4 reveals, religiously repressive countries have both experienced and given rise to far more international religious terrorist strikes than religiously free countries. As with domestic religious terrorism, this phenomenon does not appear to be related to a state's level of institutional democracy.

In sum, religiously repressive countries are more likely to both give rise to international religious terrorism and be targeted by religious terrorists who operate across national boundaries. To the extent that religiously free countries suffer from faith-based terrorism, the incidents can usually be linked in some way to another

[66] Dan Bilefsky and Maia de la Baume, "Terrorists Strike Charlie Hebdo Newspaper in Paris, Leaving 12 Dead," *New York Times*, last modified January 7, 2015, www.nytimes.com/2015/01/08/world/europe/charlie-hebdo-paris-shooting.html?_r=1.

[67] Ron E. Hassner, "Blasphemy and Violence," *International Studies Quarterly* 55, no. 1 (2011): 26.

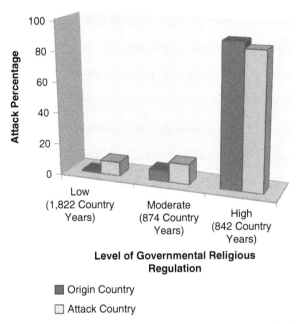

FIGURE 1.4 Governmental religious restrictions and international religious terrorist attacks, 1991–2013

Sources: Data on attacks derived and coded from RAND Database of Worldwide Terrorism Incidents (RDWTI), 2016, http://smapp.rand.org/rwtid/search_form.php; data for religious freedom were taken from David L. Cingranelli, David L. Richards and Chad Clay, "The CIRI Human Rights Dataset," 2014, www.humanrightsdata.org.

country under repressive governance. Furthermore, regardless of where international religious groups operate, the *ideas* underpinning such groups can usually be traced back to ideologues like Sayed Qutb, Abul A'la Maududi, Ayman al Zawahiri and Omar Abdel Rahman – intellectuals who developed their violent theologies while themselves living under conditions of pervasive repression, further demonstrating the connection between repression and transnational terrorism.

SUMMARIZING THE ARGUMENT

The flowchart presented in what follows summarizes the argument of this book, illustrating visually how restrictions on religion are related to religious terrorism. At the governmental level, religious restrictions arise in states that feel threatened by assertive religion or desire to promote stability through religiously based identity building. These governmental restrictions on religion generally take the forms of minority religious discrimination or majority religious cooptation. Minority discrimination is a strategy religious states – theocratic or religiously nationalist – pursue

Pathways to Terrorism

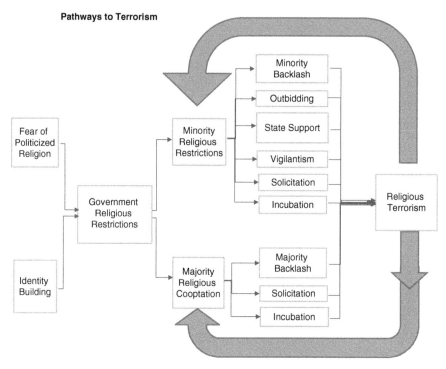

FIGURE 1.5 Pathways to terrorism

in an effort to appease dominant religious communities, thereby garnering faith-based legitimacy. These restrictions can generate domestic terrorism in three ways: minority backlash, outbidding and vigilantism. Because they stake their legitimacy on their fidelity to a particular religious dogma, such states may also incubate terrorists who operate in other countries, invite it from abroad or engage in direct state support of terrorist groups abroad. Majority cooptation, by contrast, is practiced by leaders of secular states who see religion as a potential threat to their regimes. They seek not to take on a religious character but instead to leverage religion in the pursuit of essentially secular goals. For this reason, leaders in these states often attempt to coopt a nonthreatening, mainstream version of the dominant religion in their countries, while at the same time ensuring that no religion becomes too powerful. Like minority religious discrimination, restrictions on religious majorities can also give rise to terrorism carried out by embattled groups, usually of the religious majority who seek to overthrow the regime. They can also spawn terrorism against other states or provoke terrorism from abroad via the pathways of incubation and solicitation. Governments commonly use the realization of terrorism as a pretext to enact further restrictions on religion, and the cycle begins again.

THE PEACEFUL BENEFITS OF RELIGIOUS FREEDOM

Thus far, this chapter has argued that religiously free countries are far less likely to both suffer from and export religious terrorism. If religious restrictions contribute to both domestic and international terrorism, how does religious freedom promote peace? It does so in at least five ways.

First, in religiously free settings, radicals will have their views challenged and critiqued in the marketplace of ideas and have to defend them. Extremist ideas tend not to flourish in open religious systems marked by healthy "religious economies" where religious actors and ideas enjoy protection and access to political and social life, where states and societies do not attempt to impose a religious monopoly and where governments do not selectively subsidize religious groups in a partial manner.[68] Because proponents of policies that encourage despotism and violate human rights often use religious arguments to support their stances, space must also be made available for people of faith to challenge these ideas and promote respect for individual and communal rights from within a religious discourse. Countries that refuse to systematically discriminate against religious groups in society allow for a wide range of religious practices and doctrinal interpretations to flourish.[69] Whereas religiously restrictive environments facilitate radical theologies by stifling open debate and the channels of discourse about the proper interpretation of religion, religiously free settings allow for the exposing of logical inconsistencies and incorrect construal of religious dogma by radicals, thus permitting diverse perspectives to emerge and the possibility of good theology overcoming misguided doctrine. Scholar of Islam Quintan Wiktorowicz has found, for example, that individuals less knowledgeable about Islam were more prone to the appeal of terrorist recruiters insofar as they lacked the spiritual knowledge necessary to counter extremist narratives.[70] On the other hand, when the interpretation of scriptures, beliefs and traditions is up for debate, no single voice can corner the market on truth, and the appeal of extremism diminishes.

An embrace of religious pluralism can therefore serve to undermine the claims of religious militants that their faith is under attack by the state and that violence is the best way to achieve whatever religiously informed goals they might have, thus allowing liberal political theologies to emerge. Religious extremists holding violent political theologies in religiously free settings may well exist, but the environment of religious freedom can serve to deprive terrorists of the much-needed logistical support they require to carry out attacks. For this reason, terrorism in religiously free countries tends to be limited in scope. In short, freedom granted to religious communities allows for the proliferation of doctrines, interpretations and practices

[68]   Rodney Stark, *The Victory of Reason: How Christianity Led to Freedom, Capitalism and Western Success* (New York, NY: Random House, 2006).
[69]   Gill, *Political Origins of Religious Liberty*.
[70]   Quintan Wiktorowicz, *Radical Islam Rising: Muslim Extremism in the West* (Lanham, MD: Rowman & Littlefield, 2005).

and generally has the effect of diminishing support for extremist groups. On the other hand, the silencing of the voices of moderation through legal and social structures serves to create an environment of ignorance, superstition, prejudice and distrust; unsurprisingly, in such climates the forces of extremism usually end up winning.

This religious pluralism argument is not new. Political philosophers and religious dissenters have been making this very case for hundreds of years. John Locke, for instance, believed that religious conflict was not the result of religious difference per se, but rather a defensive reaction to threats against conscience and belief. In his *Letter Concerning Toleration*, Locke wrote:

> [H]ow much greater will be the security of government, where all good subjects, of whatsoever church they be, without any distinction upon account of religion, enjoying the same favor of the prince and the same benefit of the laws, shall become the common support and guard of it.[71]

Essentially, Locke believed that people of faith would have no reason to rebel in a society that did not discriminate on the basis of religion. While religious liberty on its own cannot eradicate terrorists, it can isolate their ideas, insofar as all mainstream versions of the world's major religions contain voices of moderation, tolerance, harmony and nonviolence. These voices and the religious knowledge they bring to the table, however, can only emerge in contexts that provide for freedom of belief. Therefore, one of the key ways to combat the extremist and violence-inducing ideologies associated with individuals like Muhammad ibn Adbd al-Wahab (the founder of Wahhabism), Sayed Qutb, Joseph Kony or Ashin Wirathu – those who distort religious teachings for their own purposes – is to promote a culture of tolerance and coexistence in which counter narratives to radical ideas can arise naturally. In this sense, religious freedom is not just a victim of religious extremism but a vehicle that can play an important role in defeating it by isolating and marginalizing radical ideas.

Second, the political advantages that accompany genuine and widespread religious freedom afford would-be religious militants the ability to work through alternative and legitimate channels – electoral participation, grassroots activism and civic engagement – by which they can seek to shape religion, politics and society. In free countries, religious actors, by and large, do not react against political institutions but instead use them to their advantage, making it less likely that they will feel the need to turn to violence. A curious thing occurs when religious communities (including illiberal ones) are allowed to participate in political processes: they are forced to compete with each other for votes and thus must appeal to the political center in order to capture the widest proportion of the electorate.[72] This "democratic

---

[71] John Locke, *A Letter Concerning Toleration* (Indianapolis, IN: Bobbs-Merrill, 1955[1689]), 55.
[72] Jillian Schwedler, *Faith in Moderation: Islamist Parties in Jordan and Yemen* (New York, NY: Cambridge University Press, 2007).

bargain," as Samuel Huntington referred to it, encourages moderation of demands, modification of tactics and the development of cross-cutting cleavages and diverse platforms among groups that "play by the rules."[73] The presence of even limited forms of freedom can help spur changes in political theology and moderate previously extremist groups by making them stakeholders in the political game. We see evidence for such a hypothesis in countries where religious parties have been allowed to compete electorally like Indonesia and Turkey. On the other hand, when religious actors do not have an outlet for their religiously informed ideas in the public square, they are much more likely to see violence as the only way to change the status quo as they did in places like Egypt, Algeria and Tajikistan when religious parties were prevented from participating in the political game. In short, religious liberty in the political arena can marginalize or even prevent the rise of extremist religious groups by making it difficult for certain faith traditions to preserve political monopolies and by providing incentives for previously excluded groups to participate in the political system and renounce violent tactics.[74]

Third, not only does religious liberty protect the rights of people of faith to worship freely, perform rituals and engage in politics, it also frees them to provide social services and engage in peace-building activities that reduce the personal grievances that people have, thus making faith-based terrorism less likely. Around the world, religious actors have been at the forefront of leading efforts at conflict transformation and peace building. In Mozambique, a Catholic lay organization, the Community of Sant'Egidio, was instrumental in helping bring that country's devastating civil war to an end. Similarly, in South Africa, Guatemala, Peru, East Timor and Sierra Leone, religious communities contributed logistical support to their countries' truth commissions, assisting in organizing and carrying out hearings, finding and encouraging victims and witnesses to testify, and providing counseling once hearings were over.[75] Elsewhere, religious leaders have led interfaith dialogue initiatives as a way to deescalate tensions and promote understanding and respect between religious groups.

Because people in religiously tolerant countries do not have to focus their time, energy and resources on avoiding persecution and maintaining their identities and practices, they are freed to make positive contributions to society. Freedom of religion thus unlocks the "spiritual capital" of faith-based actors.[76] In many parts of the world, religious communities have been instrumental in increasing literacy,

---

[73] Samuel P. Huntington, *The Third Wave: Democratization in the Late Twentieth Century* (Norman, OK: University of Oklahoma Press, 1991), 165–170.

[74] Charles Kurzman and Ijlal Naqvi, "Do Muslims Vote Islamic?" *Journal of Democracy* 21, no. 2 (2010): 50–63; Marc Lynch," Islamists in a Changing Middle East," *Foreign Policy*, July 8, 2012, http://lynch .foreignpolicy.com/posts/2012/07/08/islamists_in_a_changing_middle_east.

[75] Daniel Philpott, *Just and Unjust Peace: An Ethic of Political Reconciliation* (Oxford: Oxford University Press, 2012).

[76] Corwin Smidt, ed., *Religion as Social Capital: Producing the Common Good* (Waco, TX: Baylor University Press, 2003).

reducing poverty, promoting development, providing access to potable water, administering health care, running counseling centers and leading peace and reconciliation processes.[77] In fact, it is estimated that between 30 and 50 percent of global health care providers are faith-based institutions.[78] Religious freedom is strongly related to a host of other goods that are hallmarks of stable societies, including "better health outcomes, higher levels of earned income, and better educational opportunities for women."[79] In short, religious communities, acting on the most fundamental teachings of their faith, have made incredibly positive contributions to societies that might have otherwise been suppressed through religious restrictions. This religious influence has led to more peaceful and stable countries.

Fourth, the free exercise of religion works against forces of authoritarianism and tyranny – political characteristics that tend to fuel terrorism in the first place. States that grant religious freedom to their people necessarily limit their own authority by conceding the existence of a power greater than the government. Several of the American Founding Fathers – George Washington and James Madison perhaps most famously – believed that religion could not only serve as a check on people's unrestrained passions but also maintain a free society by instilling key values like tolerance, trust, respect and altruism. Subsequent generations believed that religion, especially its public manifestation, was necessary for the overall health of democracy. French philosopher Alexis de Tocqueville even went so far as to suggest that successful political democracy requires moral instruction grounded in religious faith, stating that "despotism may govern without religion, but liberty cannot."[80] Furthermore, when people of faith have their rights secured, they are far more likely to remain loyal to the state and not try to take it over and establish a religious monopoly over those of different religions. In short, because religion focuses attention away from the state and stresses the primacy of transcendent realities, it is likely to emphasize the limited power of government, resist efforts toward authoritarian rule and cultivate socially beneficial values.

Fifth, religious freedom contributes to counterterrorism efforts. History teaches, and many studies confirm, that religiously restrictive counterterrorism policies that discriminate against entire religious groups work at cross purposes with the desired goal of effectively combating terrorism by driving ordinary people toward terrorist organizations. In such contexts, religious terrorists are much more likely to find

---

77 Robert D. Woodberry, "The Missionary Roots of Liberal Democracy," *American Political Science Review* 106, no. 2 (2012): 244–274. On peace and reconciliation, see Philpott, *Just and Unjust Peace.*

78 W. Cole Durham Jr. and Elizabeth A. Clark, "The Place of Religious Freedom in the Structure of Peacebuilding," in *The Oxford Handbook of Religion, Conflict and Peacebuilding*, ed. Atalia Omer, R. Scott Appleby and David Little (Oxford: Oxford University Press, 2015), 297.

79 Brian Grim, "Religious Freedom: Good for What Ails Us?" *The Review of Faith & International Affairs* 6, no. 2 (2010): 3–7.

80 As quoted in Jochim Wach, "The Role of Religion in the Social Philosophy of Alex De Tocqueville," *Journal of the History of Ideas*, 7 (1946): 90.

a receptive audience to their message that their faith is under siege and that violence is justified. This is true for three reasons. First, when states, in the name of combating terrorism, act indiscriminately and treat all people in a particular religious community as terrorists, they waste valuable time, energy and resources monitoring entire religious communities when they instead should be focused very narrowly on those who actually are terrorists. Only a very small percentage of individuals in any faith tradition believes that terrorism is justifiable; many fewer still actually take up the gun. Second, such actions inevitably serve to generate sympathy *for* terrorism, lead people to turn to terrorist groups for protection and end up creating more terrorists. Third, religiously repressive counterterrorism policies make it far less likely that individuals from targeted communities will cooperate with law enforcement officials on counterterrorism efforts. These logics explain why terrorist groups hope to provoke overreactions by states against the communities they claim to be defending. For counterterrorism efforts to succeed, they must marginalize terrorists from the wider populations they claim to represent. Terrorist organizations die when states refuse to play into their hands by overreacting, when they are no longer able to appeal to new recruits and when sympathizers in the wider population turn against them.

Japan provides an illustrative example. In 1995, the terrorist cult Aum Shinryko released sarin nerve gas in the Tokyo subway system, killing twelve passengers and injuring several thousand others. In response to the attack, the Japanese government acted decisively, aggressively going after those responsible for the attack and their supporters. Japan did so, however, in a manner respectful of religious freedom. The state did not ban Aum Shinryko, nor did it take anti-religious measures by targeting all religious groups. Aum ended up imploding, eventually splitting in 2007. It carried out no further terrorist attacks, and thousands renounced membership in the organization. Such a happy outcome would have been less likely had Tokyo chosen a counterterrorism strategy repressive of religion. While religious freedom in counterterrorism may not be completely without problems, ultimately, as highlighted by the case of Japan, counterterrorism efforts that are respectful of religious freedom empower moderate ideas and voices to denounce extremist hatred and violence.

Combined, these five logics suggest that the presence of religious tolerance mitigates against terrorism. This is not to suggest, of course, that religiously free countries are *always* peaceful, as there is no panacea for religious extremism. However, as a "force multiplier," religious freedom has contributed to peaceable and stable societies in numerous and profound ways by helping ease political and religious conflict.[81] Thus, societies that embrace the free exchange of religious ideas and encourage diversity of belief tend to be safer and more secure than their restrictive counterparts. Conversely, where the right to religion becomes embattled, the turn to the gun becomes more likely.

---

[81] Toft, Philpott and Shah, *God's Century*, 216.

CONCLUSION

This chapter has shown how state regulation of religion can create a fertile breeding ground for terrorism. States encourage religious terrorism when they discriminate against religious minorities or when they attempt to repress religion across the board through cooptation of a nonthreatening religion. These dynamics can even fuel international religious terrorism in various ways.

Conversely, freedom of religion has the opposite effect, mitigating the turn to the gun in five ways. First, in religiously free countries, individuals belonging to different religious communities tend to see each other as legitimate, even if they disagree on matters of faith and practice. This results in a marketplace of ideas in which religious extremists must contend with competing ideas (secular or religious) about freedom, justice, equality, morality and violence. Second, religious liberty extends to religious actors the opportunity to work toward their religiously informed goals through legitimate political institutions. The presence of the ballot renders the bullet less necessary as a means to exact political change. Third, religious freedom empowers people of faith to do good in the world in accordance with their religiously based convictions. The positive contributions religious actors have made to their societies have resulted in them being more peaceful and stable places. Fourth, countries that honor assurances of religious liberty acknowledge the right of their people to seek ultimate truth outside of the state. This concession, though perhaps threatening in the minds of authoritarians, is essential in maintaining the overall health of countries. Finally, religious liberty contributes to successful counterterrorism efforts by driving a wedge between terrorists and their constituencies. Repressive counterterrorism measures, by contrast, play into the narrative propounded by terrorists of a spiritual war between the state and believers.

The following chapters present several brief case studies demonstrating the link between religious restrictions and faith-based terrorism, on one hand, and religious freedom and peace, on the other. The next chapter takes a closer look at how minority religious discrimination has encouraged terrorism in different countries, each dominated by a different religious tradition. It shows that, despite the differences in religion, geographic location and development, the dynamics underpinning religious terrorism often flow from similar sources of repression.

2

Minority Religious Discrimination and Terrorism across Faith Traditions

In the previous chapter, I argued that states repress religion in two fundamental ways – minority religious discrimination and majority religious cooptation – and that both forms of restriction are positively correlated with both domestic and international terrorism. The cases in the present chapter demonstrate the former pathway at work. When states practice minority religious discrimination by partnering with a dominant faith tradition, they often end up generating terrorism in two broad ways. First, and most obviously, religious minorities in these countries might rebel against their marginalized and suppressed status. In this sense, terrorism functions as a classic "weapon of the weak." These kinds of religion–state arrangements, however, can also transform terrorism into a "weapon of the strong" by empowering religious terrorists to attack religious minorities. The cases in this chapter show how discrimination against religious minorities can result in both forms of terrorism while also giving rise to terrorism against third-party states.

The previous chapter presented a "bird's-eye" view of global religious terrorism. This chapter and the next attempt to move from the global to the local, examining the connections between the denial of religious liberty and religious terrorism in different contexts. In each case, I survey a country or region that has been most afflicted by a particular form of religious terrorism: Islamic terrorism in Pakistan, Christian terrorism in Central Africa, Buddhist terrorism in Burma, Sikh and Hindu terrorism in India and Jewish terrorism in Israel. These cases were selected for four reasons. First, these locations represent the countries (or region in the case of Central Africa) most afflicted by religious terrorism arising from one of the world's major religious traditions (not including Middle Eastern war zones, which are covered in the next chapter) since the turn of the century. Thus, these cases allow for higher-order insight and balance and represent "crucial cases" demonstrating the link between religious repression and religious terrorism. Second, all of these countries have high levels of religiosity, and each is a religiously plural setting. Third, the countries vary in their levels of political freedom, showing that it is how states treat religion rather than their levels of political freedom per se that matters more in generating religious terrorism. The specific manifestations of religious liberty denials, however, vary from country to country. Fourth, the cases come from four different regions of the world – the Middle East, South Asia, Southeast Asia and Central Africa – allowing for cross-cultural and cross-regional comparisons. Importantly, they also demonstrate that all religions contain the potential for violence, depending on political contexts and specific theologies. To be sure, the cases in this chapter differ in both form and intensity of religious restriction and level of terrorism, but they all demonstrate, in varying ways, how states practicing minority religious discrimination beget terrorism. I begin by discussing the case of Pakistan – a country where various repressive forces have intersected to produce a cauldron of faith-based domestic and international terrorism.

ISLAMIST TERRORISM IN PAKISTAN

While many countries (both Muslim-majority and non-Islamic) have suffered from an increase in Islamist terrorism in recent years, Pakistan may be the most important of these states due to the high number of attacks it has suffered, its exporting of jihadism abroad and its possession of nuclear weapons. The country represents a case where various forms of religious regulation have combined to create a terrorism nightmare for the people of Pakistan, its immediate neighbors and even distant countries. According to my analysis of the Global Terrorism Database, Pakistan ranked fourth globally in total number of terrorist attacks from 1991 to 2014 (2,384) and sixth in identifiable terrorist attacks motivated by a religious imperative (313) in that same period.[1] In 2016 alone, Pakistan witnessed at least 736 terrorist incidents, with virtually all of the identifiable attacks being orchestrated by Islamist militants. The South Asia Terrorism Portal documents that nearly thirty-eight terrorist organizations were active within Pakistan in 2018.[2] The government's long-standing failure to preempt or prosecute the agents of Islamist terrorism has served to create a climate of impunity that has only emboldened further extremism.

In terms of religious freedom and the type of relationship that has historically existed between religious and state institutions, Pakistan shares many of the characteristics of other countries in the region. A 2015 report by the Pew Research Center finds that Pakistan has "high" levels of governmental religious restrictions and "very high" social hostilities involving religion.[3] This dearth of religious liberty can be directly tied to Pakistan's terrorism problem. Compounding these issues have been the many social and economic challenges Pakistan faces like gender inequality, illiteracy and poverty, which further contribute to the country's terrorism problems.

---

[1] These rankings almost certainly underestimate the levels of religious terrorism in Pakistan since many of the perpetrators of the attacks could not be clearly identified but were likely motivated by religion.

[2] South Asia Terrorism Portal, "Pakistan – Terrorist, Insurgent and Extremist Groups," last modified December 2017, available from www.satp.org/featurelist.aspx?countryid=2&featurename=Terrorist%20Groups.

[3] Pew Research Center, *Latest Trends in Religious Restrictions and Hostilities.*

Although Pakistan was originally founded as a secular state after partition from India, successive Pakistani governments attempted to regulate religious life in order to gain the support of certain Islamic groups – ones that have pushed Pakistan further in the direction of partnership between mosque and state. The 1956 constitution declared Pakistan to be an "Islamic republic" – making it the world's first officially Islamic country – and prohibited the passage of any law contrary to the Quran. The constitution requires the president and the prime minister to be Muslims; all members of parliament must swear an oath to uphold Islamic principles. This alliance between religion and the state has resulted in a situation where Islam retains a privileged position in public life and is afforded the right to dictate key aspects of law and politics at the expense of minority groups like Christians, Hindus, Sikhs and Ahmadi Muslims, who are often refused jobs and housing and are frequently the target of physical assaults.[4] Government manipulation of religion (of which the intelligence services and military have also taken part) has served to empower radical elements and engender religiously based social hostilities as political leaders appeal to fundamentalists in order to make electoral gains, thus lending an aura of legitimacy to their views. A strong case can be made that had Pakistan shunned the temptation to cater to fringe elements in the Islamist movement soon after independence, it might not be experiencing the kind of terrorism problem it faces today.

Though Pakistan's founder, Muhammad Jinnah, desired his country to be a secular state, subsequent leaders appealed to Islam in order to garner support from religious leaders. Pakistan took an extreme turn toward Islamization under the military rule of General Muhammad Zia ul-Haq, a devoutly religious man who sought to revive a fundamentalist brand of Islam and pushed the country toward an intolerant rendering of religion after he seized power in a coup against Zulfikar Ali Bhutto in 1978. "Pakistan," he claimed, "was created in the name of Islam [and] will continue to survive only if it sticks to Islam ... [the] Islamic system [is] an essential prerequisite for the country."[5] Zia toed the Islamist line by implementing such measures as "the compulsory collection of *zakat*, the strengthening of existing antiblasphemy laws, and a law instituting *hudood* [fixed penalties for breaking Islamic law] punishments" – moves that empowered sectarianism and fostered a climate of impunity.[6] Furthermore, Zia's laws banned the sale of alcohol, fornication, lying and the intermingling of sexes in public – crimes punishable by "flogging, amputation, or stoning to death."[7] The Pakistani leader also bolstered Islam's judicial and

---

4   Lawrence Ziring, *Pakistan in the Twentieth Century: A Political History* (Karachi: Oxford University Press, 1997).

5   As quoted in William L. Richter, "The Political Dynamics of Islamic Resurgence in Pakistan," *Asian Survey* 19, no. 6 (1979): 555.

6   Peter S.Henne, Sarabrynn Hudgins and Timothy Samuel Shah, *Religious Freedom and Violent Religious Extremism: A Sourcebook of Modern Cases and Analysis* (Washington, DC: Berkley Center for Religion, Peace and World Affairs, 2012).

7   Shahid Javed Burki, Craig Baxter, Robert LaPorte and Azfar Kamal, *Pakistan under the Military: Eleven Years of Zia ul-Haq* (Boulder, CO: Westview, 1991), 36–37.

educational influence and granted the Islamist political party Jamaat-e-Islami some official powers, especially in Karachi and South Punjab.[8] Public schools and madrassas in Pakistan began using textbooks that taught from a strongly Islamist point of view, often depicting religious minorities in a negative or uninformed light. Zia further granted a great deal of political power to religious bodies such as the Majlis-e-Shoora, an advisory council comprised of Islamic jurists and scholars empowered to vet official laws for their compatibility with Islam and Islamic law. Zia's empowering of Islam had the effect of sowing seeds of religious intolerance against non-Muslims, especially Ahmadis, Hindus, Sikhs and Christians.[9]

The rule of Zia would have far-reaching consequences for terrorism, both domestic and international. Domestically, Zia's moves encouraged violence on the part of both privileged majority and marginalized minority religious groups. The vagueness of the greatly strengthened blasphemy laws, for example, allowed radicals to interpret the code in very loose ways and open-endedly persecute those believed to be guilty of defiling, in any way, "the sacred name of the Holy Prophet Muhammad." Zia's actions similarly led to conflict between majority Sunni and minority Shia communities, which manifested in attacks by Sunni militant groups like Ahle Sunnat Wal Jamaat (formerly Sipah-e-Sahaba) and reprisals by extremist Shia groups such as Sipah-e-Muhammad. During this time, several other religious terrorist organizations came into existence, including Jamiat al-Mujahedin, Hizbul Mujahedin, Abu Nidal and others. Some of these groups carried out attacks against religious minorities; others focused their efforts against what they perceived to be a corrupt and insufficiently pious government.

After the temporary transition to civil government, subsequent leaders continued many of Zia's policies by allying with an illiberal rendering of Islam. Such actions included increased restrictions on women and the attempted passage of a new sharia bill.[10] The upshot of these moves was the intensification of social hostilities between different religious communities as well as the deepening of the conflict between religious militants and the state. After the return to military rule under Pervez Musharraf, communitarian violence continued, especially attacks against Shia and Ahmadi Muslims throughout the country. The Musharraf era witnessed a number of assassinations and assassination attempts against several high-level Pakistani officials, including at least five attempts on the president himself.

At the time of this writing, levels of sectarian violence have reached an all-time high as Islamist militants have killed hundreds of religious minorities, women and liberals in terrorist attacks in recent years. One of the most gruesome attacks occurred on December 16, 2014, when militants loyal to the Pakistani Taliban attacked a school in Peshawar, killing 148 people. Most of the victims were

[8] Husain Haqqani, *Pakistan: Between Mosque and Military* (Washington, DC: Carnegie Endowment for International Peace, 2005).
[9] Burki, Baxter, LaPorte and Kamal, *Pakistan under the Military*.
[10] Ziad Haider, *The Ideological Struggle for Pakistan* (Stanford, CA: Hoover Institute Press, 2010).

schoolchildren who were gunned down as they hid under their desks. A report by Human Rights Watch attributes blame for the recent spate of bloodshed to the actions of the Pakistani government, which it accuses of not doing enough to stop the violence and protect vulnerable religious minority communities.[11]

Minority Muslim groups, including Sufis, Shias and Ahmadis, have been the victims of increasing suicide attacks and targeted killings by Sunni extremists, resulting in the deaths of hundreds. One particularly grisly assault took place in 2012 when four buses carrying Sufi worshippers were stopped and the passengers executed by al Qaeda–affiliated extremists. Another attack the following year, this time carried out by the Sunni group Lashkar-e-jhangvi, killed at least eighty-four people and wounded another 180 when a bomb exploded in a market in the city of Quetta. A 2015 attack in Shikarpur carried out by Jundallah resulted in the deaths of sixty-one Shias who had gathered for Friday prayers. At least eighty-eight people were killed and more than 350 others were injured in a February 2017 attack when a suicide bomber blew himself up in the Shrine of Lal Shahbaz Qalandar, a Sufi shrine dedicated to the thirteenth-century Islamic mystic in Sehwan. The following month a blast outside of a Shia commemoration hall in Parachinar resulted in 115 casualties. Attacks against Pakistan's Ahmadi community, a population that has long suffered from institutional discrimination and legal restriction, have also been on the rise. In June 2016 alone, three different Ahmadi doctors were assassinated in the city of Karachi. In December of that same year, several Ahmadi worshippers were wounded in an attack on a community mosque in Chakwal.[12]

Christians too have been targets of numerous attacks. On Easter Sunday 2016, a suicide attack in the city of Lahore by Jamaatul Ahrar, a splinter group of the Pakistani Taliban, killed seventy-eight people and injured hundreds of others, the majority of whom were Christian women and children who had gathered at Gulshan-e-Iqbal Park to celebrate the religious holiday. On December 17, 2017, two suicide bombers affiliated with ISIS killed nine Christians and injured another fifty-seven when they attacked a Methodist church in Quetta. All of these attacks, against Shias, Ahmadis and Christians, were carried out by Sunni extremists.

One of the major sources of terrorism against religious minorities is Pakistan's culture of blasphemy. The continued enforcement of blasphemy laws, with punishment for violators ranging from life in prison to capital punishment, has empowered vigilante terrorists to carry out attacks on religious minorities like Christians, Ahmadi Muslims and Hindus, which together, though comprising only 3 percent of the country's population, have accounted for roughly half of those accused of blasphemy-related offenses over the past two decades. The majority of these cases have occurred in Punjab Province, where most of Pakistan's minority religious communities reside. Found in Sections 295 and 298 of the Pakistan Penal Code,

[11] Human Rights Watch, "World Report 2015: Pakistan," last modified 2015, www.hrw.org/world-report /2015/country-chapters/pakistan.
[12] US Commission on International Religious Freedom, *2017 Annual Report*, 63.

blasphemy covers a number of offenses, including defiling houses of worship, marring the Quran or speaking negatively about Islam or Mohammed. In no other country have more people been prosecuted for committing blasphemy or killed extra-judicially for blasphemy-related offenses. Those accusing others of blasphemy are not required to present any evidence that the crime of blasphemy even occurred, often leading to abuse and false allegations. In 2016, at least forty-five individuals were imprisoned on blasphemy charges, with at least seventeen sentenced to death.[13]

The connection between blasphemy laws and terrorism can be seen vividly in three high-profile murders of those who criticized the blasphemy codes or were themselves inculpated as blasphemers. In each case, the attackers invoked blasphemy laws to justify their vigilantism. In 2011, Salman Taseer, a Pakistani businessman and governor of the Punjab province, was assassinated in a cosmopolitan area of Islamabad by his own bodyguard, Mumtaz Qadri. A renowned supporter of religious minority rights and a sharp critic of blasphemy laws, Taseer earned the ire of extremists within the country. Taseer's greatest sin involved his opposition to the death sentence of Aasia Bibi, a Christian farm laborer convicted of blasphemy. In court, Qadri admitted that he had shot Taseer twenty-seven times because of his support for Bibi.[14] The same year that Taseer was murdered, another prominent politician, Shahbaz Bhatti, met with the same fate. Bhatti, a devout Roman Catholic and the minister for minority affairs, received international acclaim for his defense of religious minorities, but, like Taseer, was deeply unpopular with supporters of blasphemy laws. He was also an ardent supporter of Aasia Bibi and others accused or convicted of blasphemy, which ultimately cost him his life. On March 2, 2011, Bhatti was shot multiple times after leaving his mother's home. Eerily, just months before his murder, Bhatti predicted his death at the hands of Islamist extremists saying, "I am living for my community ... and I will die to defend their rights."[15] Tehrik-i-Taliban, the same group responsible for the 2014 Peshawar school massacre, quickly claimed responsibility for the attack, leaving flyers at the scene of the crime. The group's spokesman referred to Bhatti as a blasphemer and warned that "we will continue to target all those who speak against the law which punishes those who insult the prophet. Their fate will be the same."[16] Bhatti was explicitly murdered for his opposition to anti-blasphemy laws as evidenced by the spokesman's comments. The assassination was meant to silence those who oppose the existence of blasphemy laws or defend those accused of blasphemy. A third assassination

[13] US Department of State Bureau of Democracy, Human Rights and Labor, "Pakistan," *2016 International Religious Freedom Report*, last modified 2016, www.state.gov/j/drl/rls/irf/religiousfreedom/index.htm#wrapper.

[14] Tom Wright, "Leading Pakistani Politician Killed," *Wall Street Journal*, last modified January 3, 2011, www.wsj.com/articles/SB10001424052748704723104576061371508098218.

[15] Aryn Islamabad, "In Pakistan, Justifying Murder for Those Who Blaspheme," *Time*, March 21, 2011, http://content.time.com/time/printout/0,8816,2058155,00.html.

[16] Orla Guerin, "Pakistan Minorities Minister Shahbaz Bhatti Shot Dead," BBC News, last modified March 2, 2011, www.bbc.com/news/world-south-asia-12617562.

occurred in 2014 when Rashid Rehman, a prominent attorney, human rights activist and blasphemy law critic, was killed for his defense of Junaid Hafeez, a university lecturer charged with blasphemy. After his murder, pamphlets were distributed throughout Multan, stating Rehman was justly murdered for attempting to "save someone who disrespected the Prophet Mohammed. We warn all lawyers to be afraid of God and think twice before engaging in such acts."[17] In sum, the assassinations of Taseer, Rehman and Bhatti graphically illustrate the permissive culture of impunity created by blasphemy laws in Pakistan, which emboldens extremists to commit acts of violence by providing them with a ready-made pretext for attacking their adversaries.

Restrictive conditions in Pakistan have resulted in international terrorism as well. Since the rule of General Zia, a close relationship between Pakistani governments and extremist religious networks has been an enduring feature of Pakistan's domestic *and* foreign policies. Former presidents Asif Ali Zardari and Pervez Musharraf admitted that Pakistan had, in the past, "deliberately created and nurtured [terrorists] as a policy to achieve some short-term tactical objectives."[18]

During the 1980s, Pakistan's Inter-Services Intelligence (ISI) and military supported the Afghan *mujahidin* through military training and financial assistance in a proxy war against the Soviet-controlled Democratic Republic of Afghanistan. Zia favored the more radical factions of the *mujahidin* – groups like Hizb-I-Islami that would later form close ties to the Taliban and Osama bin Laden (whom, it should be noted, found refuge and was eventually killed in Abbottabad, the Pakistani equivalent of West Point) – and vowed to support them not only until the Soviets were defeated but until an Islamic government had been established in Kabul.[19] After the Soviets withdrew their forces, the state continued to support many of these same extremist groups – reconstituted in the forms of Lashkar-e-Taiba, Harkat-ul-Mujahideen and others – in continuous insurgency operations in Afghanistan and India. The ISI has also been linked to the Haqqani network – the deadliest and most effective arm of the Afghan resistance that fights against the United States and the Afghan government. During the Afghan insurgency following the American invasion, the Haqqani network provided space for al Qaeda and other extremist groups to stage attacks against Western targets from the wild Af-Pak border region known as Waziristan – an area over which the government has complete control. In short, religious repression has served to create a cauldron of violent extremist forces in

[17] Matthew Blake, "Fearless Pakistani Lawyer Murdered for Continuing to Defend Man Accused of Blasphemy Despite Receiving Death Threats from the Prosecution," *Daily Mail*, last modified May 9, 2014, www.dailymail.co.uk/news/article-2624073/Fearless-Pakistani-lawyer-murdered-defending-man-accused-blasphemy-despite-death-threats-PROSECUTION.html.

[18] Dean Nelson, "Pakistani President Asif Zardari Admits Creating Terrorist Groups," *The Telegraph*, last modified July 8, 2009, www.telegraph.co.uk/news/worldnews/asia/pakistan/5779916/Pakistani-president-Asif-Zardari-admits-creating-terrorist-groups.html.

[19] Omar Noman, "Pakistan and General Zia: Era and Legacy," *Third World Quarterly* 11, no. 1 (1989): 43.

Pakistan, some of which support the state and its foreign policy objectives while others work to overthrow it.

Beyond Afghanistan, state-supported terrorism has also been an enduring feature of Pakistan's conflict with India, as elements of the Pakistani government have attempted to forge alliances with militant Sunni Islamic groups in an attempt to destabilize its neighbor and enemy to the east. For example, Pakistan has used Islamic militants, including both Afghan war veterans and home-grown terrorists, to wage a proxy war in Indian-held Kashmir. The ISI even used al Qaeda camps in Afghanistan as a place to train covert operatives for its war in Kashmir.[20] A disputed piece of territory between India and Pakistan and the only Muslim-majority state in India, Kashmir has witnessed a fluctuating insurgency since 1989 in which tens of thousands of people have lost their lives. After the Soviet invasion of Afghanistan, *mujahidin* fighters slowly began to infiltrate Kashmir, assisted by the Pakistani state, with the objective of spreading an Islamist ideology. When the indigenous Kashmiri insurgency began to diminish in the 1990s, Pakistan attempted to revive its indirect war in Kashmir through a policy of externally sponsored subversion and clandestine war, sending in Pakistani and Afghan commandos to carry out suicide missions against the Indian state.[21] In short, terrorism in Kashmir illustrates vividly how domestic religious conditions in one country can spur religious militancy in another. Through state sponsorship of terrorism, Pakistan has sought to use its alliances with radical Sunni groups as a way to advance its foreign policy vis-à-vis India.

This strategy, however, has proven to be a double-edged sword. In cultivating a desired form of terrorism that it can use against India and Afghanistan through groups like the Afghan Taliban, the Haqqani network, Jaish-e-Mohammed and Lashkar-e-Taiba, Pakistan has also inadvertently left itself vulnerable to another form of terrorism – a less enviable kind – that wages holy war against the Pakistani state itself, seeking to replace the government with one based upon sharia. Yet these "bad terrorists" were birthed in the very same repressive context that gave rise to the "good terrorists" whom Pakistan sees as furthering its strategic interests.[22] Some parts of the Pakistani establishment appear to have reached this same conclusion. One former ISI chief lieutenant-general declared that "we must not be afraid of admitting that the Jaish was involved in the deaths of thousands of innocent Kashmiris, bombing the Indian Parliament, Daniel Pearl's murder and even attempts on President Musharraf's life."[23] International security expert Brahma Chellaney explains that "the scourge of transnational terrorism ... cannot be effectively

[20] Brahma Chellaney, "Fighting Terrorism in Southern Asia: The Lessons of History," *International Security* 26, no. 3 (2002): 98; Praveen Swami, "The Well-Tempered Jihad: The Politics and Practice of Post-2002 Islamist Terrorism in India," *Contemporary South Asia* 16, no. 3 (2008): 303–322.
[21] Chellaney, "Fighting Terrorism in Southern Asia," 104.
[22] C. Christine Fair, *Fighting to the End: The Pakistan Army's Way of War* (Oxford: Oxford University Press, 2014).
[23] As quoted in Swami, "Well-Tempered Jihad," 305.

stemmed if attempts are made to draw distinctions between good and bad terrorists, and between those who threaten *their* security and those who threaten *ours*. The viper reared against one target state is a viper against another or against oneself" (emphasis his).[24] This metaphor describes how anti-Indian extremists trained and enabled by Islamabad have come to threaten Pakistan's own security. The actions of the state, therefore, have contributed to what terrorism scholar Jessica Stern terms a "jihad culture" that has morphed into a transnational threat across the Indian subcontinent and beyond.[25] At the same time, that these terrorist organizations target Pakistani civilians and governmental offices seriously reduces the will of the state to address the egregious religious freedom conditions that give rise to such violence in the first place.

As difficult as it might be to believe given the reality today, Pakistan has its roots in religious freedom. Pakistan founder Muhammad Jinnah established the country as a homeland for Muslims, but also believed that it should provide religious freedom for those of minority faiths. In his 1947 speech to the Constituent Assembly, Jinnah gave an eloquent defense of religious freedom, which he hoped would provide a necessary basis for tolerance and inclusivity given his new country's diversity:

> You are free; you are free to go to your temples, you are free to go to your mosques or to any other place of worship in this State of Pakistan. You may belong to any religion or caste or creed – that has nothing to do with the business of the State . . . We are starting in the days where there is no discrimination, no distinction between one community and another, no discrimination between one caste or creed and another. We are starting with this fundamental principle: that we are all citizens, and equal citizens of one State.[26]

Pakistan has strayed a long way from these founding ideals. Indeed, subsequent leaders did not seek to promote tolerance or inclusivity as Jinnah had hoped, but rather defined citizens and their rights on the basis of their faith and empowered sectarian forces. This has resulted in a dire terrorism problem, both at home and abroad.

CHRISTIAN TERRORISM IN CENTRAL AFRICA

While terrorism rooted in Islam has captured the lion's share of media attention since the 9/11 terrorist attacks, Christianity has its own long and troubling history with violence. The Crusades from the eighth to the thirteenth centuries were a series of military religious campaigns aimed at recapturing the Holy Land for Christ and laid the groundwork for medieval Christian society. In early modern Europe,

---

[24] Chellaney, "Fighting Terrorism in Southern Asia," 109.
[25] Jessica Stern, "Pakistan's Jihad Culture," *Foreign Affairs* 79, no. 6 (2002): 115–126.
[26] Quoted in Knox Thames, "Pakistan's Dangerous Game with Religious Extremism," *Review of Faith & International Affairs* 12, no. 4 (2014): 41.

warring Catholic and Protestant states fought against each other for centuries. Christian beliefs were also instrumental in motivating the Spanish Inquisition and the Salem Witch Trials in the fifteenth and seventeenth centuries, respectively.

But Christian violence is not an artifact of the past. Christianity's dark side can be seen in various extremist movements around the world ranging from the apocalyptic Eastern Lightning Church of the Almighty God group in China to the secessionist National Liberation Front of Tripura in India to the various loosely affiliated groups that are part of the Christian Identity movement in the United States. Apart from these established extremist organizations, lone-wolf terrorists moved by Christian belief continue to carry out terrorism around the world.

The Lord's Resistance Army

The region of Central Africa, including the countries of Sudan, Uganda and Central African Republic, has been especially plagued by an increase in Christian terrorism in recent times. In Uganda, although it is a country today generally tolerant of religious diversity and different beliefs, political manipulation of ethnic and religious differences and religious repression of minority Christian Acholis in the past by the political leadership greatly affected the country's development and sparked cycles of violence and retribution. This repression laid the groundwork for the emergence of violent Christian extremism.

After independence in 1962, Uganda was ravaged by internal conflict, particularly between the northern and southern parts of the country, ultimately leading to General Idi Amin overthrowing the sitting president, Milton Obote. Both Obote and Amin were infamous for their human rights abuses and tyrannical ways. Upon assuming power, the Amin regime engaged in severe ethno-religious discrimination against the primarily Christian Acholi people of the north due to their support of Obote. Under Amin, a convert to Islam, approximately 400,000 Christians were killed or fled the country between 1971 and 1976. Amin himself purportedly shot and killed Anglican Archbishop Janani Luwum in 1977.

The Tanzanian invasion of Uganda in 1979 had the effect of unifying and strengthening various anti-Amin forces who came together to form the Acholi-dominated Uganda National Liberation Army, leading to the overthrow of Amin and a succession of three presidents within the course of less than two years, the last of which was Obote himself, who returned to power in 1980 until he was deposed again in 1985. Obote's successor, an Acholi named Tito Okello, was overthrown the following year when Uganda's current president, Yoweri Museveni, came to power in the aftermath of the Ugandan Bush War (1981–1986). Museveni's National Resistance Army engaged in a campaign of revenge against the Acholi. The government held more than two million people in concentration camps in the north, and Museveni's army engaged in rape, torture, village razing and genocide against the Acholi. Millions of people were internally displaced. The repression in northern Uganda was accompanied by relative economic disadvantage and lack of development, which further contributed to a narrative of grievance against the central government.

It was this context of instability and repression that gave rise to Uganda's most brutal religious terrorist groups. The Acholi, who combine elements of mysticism, indigenous spirituality and Catholicism, have looked to their faith as a source of resistance against Kampala. When Museveni first came to power, many Acholi turned to the guidance of a Catholic spiritualist named Alice Auma. In 1985, Auma changed her name to "Lakwena" after claiming to have been overtaken by the spirit of a dead army officer by the same name. Auma and the Acholi believed that Lakwena's spirit was a manifestation of the Christian Holy Spirit, who had endowed her with supernatural powers.[27] Auma subsequently established a group known as the "Holy Spirit Movement" (HSM), which she believed had been given the divinely ordained mission of both retaking the capital from Museveni's National Resistance Army and ridding Uganda, particularly the Acholi people, of impure spirits. As stated by Isaac Ojok, a former minister and convert to the HSM, "the guidance from the Holy Spirit is enabling us to fight this war of liberation and I'm sure that with more prayers from those who care for Uganda we will win."[28] Led by Auma, the military wing of the HSM, the Holy Spirit Mobile Forces (HSMF), achieved a series of spectacular victories as it moved southward from Acholiland to Kampala. In the end, however, the government forces proved too powerful for the HSMF and ultimately defeated Auma's sect, forcing her to flee to Kenya, where she lived until her death in 2007.[29]

Auma's forces ultimately fragmented but formed successor movements. The year after the HSMF defeat, Joseph Kony, the son of a lay catechist of the Catholic Church, quickly filled the spiritual leadership void among the Acholi left by Auma and began his own movement, claiming to have inherited Lakwena's spirit from Auma. Kony declared that he had been sent by God to free the people of northern Uganda from the yoke of oppression imposed by Museveni. Originally known as the Lord's Salvation Army and then the United Salvation Christian Army, Kony's faction eventually took the name "Lord's Resistance Army" (LRA) in 1994, owing to its conviction that it had been charged with the divine mandate to serve as soldiers of the Lord commissioned to bring the world back to a proper theocracy. Kony perceived himself as a modern-day lawgiver, akin to the role played by Moses in the Hebrew scriptures.

---

[27] Heiki Behrend, "Is Alice Lakwena a Witch? The Holy Spirit Movement and Its Fight against Evil in the North," in *Changing Uganda: The Dilemmas of Structural Adjustment and Revolutionary Change*, ed. Michael Twaddle and Holger Bernt Hansen (London: James Currey Publishers, 1991), 162–177.

[28] Jonathan Wright, "Uganda Army Marches on Voodoo Priestess," *Glasgow Herald*, October 6, 1987.

[29] Heike Behrend, *Alice Lakwena & Holy Spirits: War in Northern Uganda 1986–97* (Athens, OH: Ohio University Press, 2000).

Like the HSMF, the LRA grounds its theology and actions in mystical Christian syncretistic beliefs, including divine revelation and spirit possession. Kony claims to draw inspiration from the Holy Spirit regarding how to conduct his military operations, going so far as to name the three divisions of the LRA "Father," "Son" and "Holy Ghost."[30] The objectives of the LRA, as articulated by Kony, are explicitly religious: "fighting for Uganda to be a free state governed by the Ten Commandments, a democratic state, and a state with a freely elected president."[31] Kony's tactics and theology have been condemned by the vast majority of Uganda's Christian population and all mainstream denominations.

Due, in part, to documentaries produced by the organization Invisible Children, the LRA has become a well-known terrorist organization infamous for its brutal tactics and use of child soldiers to serve as frontline troops or sex slaves. Since its inception, the LRA has kidnapped more than 60,000 children. Kony has been indicted by the International Criminal Court (ICC) for war crimes and crimes against humanity. In October 2005, the ICC issued arrest warrants for five LRA commanders, including a bounty of $5 million for Kony himself.

Although peace talks took place between the LRA and Kampala in 1993 and 2006, they ultimately failed and the conflict continued. Eventually, Kony's movement morphed into a transnational terrorist threat. The LRA draws strong support from the religiously repressive Sudanese government, which has used Kony's army to wage a war by proxy against Museveni who, in turn, provides support to the Sudan People's Liberation Army to wage war against Khartoum. What was once a relatively local conflict at times morphed into a sporadic de facto war by proxy between Uganda and Sudan. Beginning in 2008, Ugandan, South Sudanese and Congolese militaries launched offensives against LRA bases, and in July 2011, the United States deployed special forces personnel to help Uganda combat LRA rebels. Though terrorist attacks carried out by the LRA have waxed and waned since the early 1990s, its violent activities remained fairly constant from 2014 to 2017, with the organization averaging twenty-six attacks per year during that time period. Today the LRA remains a transnational terrorist threat, operating in the tri-border region of South Sudan, the Democratic Republic of Congo and Uganda.

The Antibalaka Militias

Though it is the most infamous of Central Africa's Christian terrorist organizations, the LRA is not the only militant Christian group operating in the region. In neighboring Central African Republic (CAR) – an impoverished landlocked country at the geographic center of the continent – brutal Christian militias

---

[30] James C. McKinley, "Christian Rebels Wage War of Terror in Uganda," *New York Times*, March 5, 1997.
[31] Eric Patterson, *Politics in a Religious World: Building a Religiously Informed U.S. Foreign Policy* (New York, NY: Continuum, 2011), 77.

known collectively as "antibalaka" ("anti-machete" in the local Mandja and Sango languages) have waged a religious war against the country's minority Muslim population (Muslims account for about 15 percent of the total population) in a relentless wave of coordinated attacks, forcing the exile of entire Muslim communities to the neighboring states of Chad, Cameroon, Nigeria, Niger and Sudan. The victims of the violence appear to have been targeted solely on the basis of their religious identity. In 2014, the human rights watchdog group Amnesty International referred to the situation in CAR as a clear-cut case of "ethnic cleansing."[32]

Though the violence began recently, its seeds had been sown many years before. For much of the history of CAR, different religious groups lived in relative harmony with each other. This situation changed in 2003 after the deposing of President Ange Felex Patasse and the coming to power of General Francois Bozizé. A devout Christian, Bozizé deliberately cultivated an anti-Muslim political narrative and used religion as a weapon against the country's minority Muslim population, who suffered from social shame, discrimination, political marginalization and religion-based socioeconomic inequalities, all of which contributed to their status as second-class citizens. Anti-Muslim discrimination also existed at the society level. In many churches, pastors preached sermons contemptuous of Islam, with services attended by "cadres of the Bozizé administration."[33] This state of affairs naturally bred resentment among CAR's Muslim population.

The current conflict in CAR began in 2013 when extremist Muslim rebels known as the "Seleka" (or "union" in Sango) came to power in a quick but bloody coup that toppled President Bozizé and proceeded to wage a campaign of systematic reprisals against the country's majority Christian population, which included the destruction of entire Christian villages, homes, churches and crops; indiscriminate killings; rapes; lootings; abductions and executions. Shocking levels of violence at the society level resulted in the displacement of nearly one-quarter of the country's Christian population. Under pressure from the international community, Seleka president Michel Djotodia resigned in 2014.

A self-defense group originally established to combat bandits and cattle thieves, the antibalaka (comprised primarily of Christians, some of whom had served in the Bozizé administration) reconstituted itself as a vigilante movement to avenge the abuses committed by the Selekan rebels, taking advantage of the power vacuum and climate of general instability to wage its own campaign of terror against Muslims. Eric Zalo, an antibalaka leader, described the group as "exclusively Christian" with its aim to "liberate the Christian population from the yoke of the Muslims."[34]

[32] Amnesty International, "Central African Republic: Ethnic Cleansing and Sectarian Killings," last modified February 12, 2014, www.amnesty.org/en/articles/news/2014/02/central-african-republic-ethnic-cleansing-sectarian-violence/.

[33] Henry KAM Kah, "Anti-Balaka/Seleka, 'Religionisation' and Separatism in the History of the Central African Republic," *Conflict Studies Quarterly* 9, no. 4 (2014): 30–48.

[34] Mouhamadou Kane, "Interreligious Violence in the Central African Republic," *African Security Review* 23, no. 3 (2014): 313.

Antibalaka attacks have themselves been characterized by horrific brutality – lynch-ings, mutilations, immolations, lootings and razings – including attacks against women, children and innocents trapped by fighting or trying to flee. The violence proved particularly ghastly among rural Muslim populations in the northern part of the country. A series of attacks in the capital city of Bangui in 2014 resulted in the deaths of more than 1,000 civilians and the displacement of more than 100,000 people, many of whom sought refuge in Mpoko Airport.

In the course of only two years, Christian violence decimated the country's Muslim population. Peter Bouckaert, the emergencies director at Human Rights Watch, decried the evaporation of long-standing Muslim communities, stating that the continuation of anti-Muslim violence would ultimately result in "no Muslims left in much of the Central African Republic."[35] By 2015, more than one-quarter of the total population had fled the country; about 60 percent were in need of humanitarian assistance, the majority of whom desperately required emergency food aid.[36] Ninety-six percent of the country's mosques have been destroyed in interreligious fighting, and 80 percent of the country's Muslim population have been driven out of CAR to the neighboring countries of Cameroon and Chad.[37] In Bangui alone, the Muslim population fell by 99 percent. Of the Muslims who remained in the country, 20,000 took refuge in various enclaves in the central and western parts of the country, with antibalaka violence preventing people from leaving or aid from entering.[38] Of the Muslims who remain in CAR, many report facing constant faith-based discrimination, including lack of access to basic neces-sities, the banning of public Muslim worship, the forbidding of traditional Muslim garb and forced conversions at gunpoint. Thousands of UN peacekeeping person-nel, joined by French and African Union forces, were deployed to the country for the purpose of protecting vulnerable communities and fostering stability.

The conflict between Christians and Muslims in CAR has also given rise to the dynamic of "solicitation" discussed in the opening chapter. After the ouster of Bozizé and the rise of the antibalaka, Islamist terrorists from Chad and Sudan began seeking the liberation of the country's embattled Muslim population, the creation of an independent Islamic state and the implementation of sharia. These

[35] Human Rights Watch, "Central African Republic: Muslims Forced to Flee: Christian Militias Unleash Waves of Targeted Violence," last modified February 12, 2014, www.hrw.org/news/2014/02/12/central-african-republic-muslims-forced-flee.
[36] US Commission on International Religious Freedom, *2017 Annual Report*, 29; USAID, "Central African Republic – Complex Emergency: Fact Sheet #10, Fiscal Year (FY) 2015," last modified March 2, 2015, www.usaid.gov/sites/default/files/documents/1866/car_ce_fs10_03–02-2015 .pdf.
[37] US Department of State Bureau of Democracy, Human Rights and Labor, "Central African Republic," *2015 International Religious Freedom Report*, last modified 2015, www.state.gov/docu ments/organization/256217.pdf.
[38] Human Rights Watch, "Central African Republic: Muslims Trapped in Enclaves," last modified December 22, 2014, www.hrw.org/news/2014/12/22/central-african-republic-muslims-trapped-enclaves.

aspirations were endorsed by Bozizé's successor, Michel Djotodia, in a written letter to the Organization of the Islamic Conference calling for a "new Islamic Republic" in CAR.[39]

In December 2015, Pope Francis called for peace between religious communities when he embarked on an apostolic journey to one of the last remaining mosques in the war-torn capital, the Central Mosque of Koudoukou. The pope urged reconciliation, calling on Christian and Muslim "brothers and sisters" to "say no to hatred, to revenge and to violence, particularly that violence which is perpetrated in the name of a religion or of God himself."[40] Over the following year, it appeared as if Muslim and Christian militants had taken the pope's words to heart. Fighting eased after the country elected a new prime minister in 2016, math teacher Faustin Archange Touadéra, and the establishment of a more inclusive government and national mediation efforts. The election of Touadéra marked the CAR's second peaceful transfer of power since its independence. A new constitution taking effect in March 2016 provided for freedom of religion and equal protection under the law for all religious groups. Nevertheless, the state's inability to exercise control or influence throughout much of the country, ensure the rule of law or administer justice allowed abuses by Christian militias and terrorists to continue, leading to retaliatory attacks and spirals of violence. Sectarian violence grew in the months following the election, displacing more than 100,000 individuals. At the time of this writing, religious violence continues to ravage the CAR, with partition remaining a very real possibility. Ironically, the CAR has historically experienced very little interreligious violence since its independence (although instability in other forms has been present). Going as far back as the nineteenth century, the CAR was governed as a secular state in which Christians, Muslims and animists coexisted peacefully.[41] Official religious discrimination and persecution of minority religious groups have been recent occurrences, which have combined to spark waves of terrorism and retaliation.

HINDU AND SIKH TERRORISM IN INDIA

India is a puzzling case with respect to religious freedom. On the one hand, it is the world's largest democracy, one of the world's most religiously plural countries and the birthplace of several of the world's major faith traditions. It has historically been a highly stable, federal democracy in an area of the world marked by authoritarianism and little respect for human rights. Its constitution forbids discrimination on the

39 KAM Kah, "Anti-Balaka/Seleka, 'Religionisation' and Separatism in the History of the Central African Republic," 41.
40 Pope Francis, "Address of His Holiness Pope Francis," November 30, 2015, https://w2.vatican.va/content/francesco/en/speeches/2015/november/documents/papa-francesco_20151130_repubblica-centrafricana-musulmani.html.
41 Kane, "Interreligious Violence in the Central African Republic," 313.

basis of caste, race, sex, birthplace or religion. Instead, it recognizes the importance of religious equality and tolerance in a highly pluralistic and religiously devout country. The preamble to India's constitution, which reflects the thinking of India's early leaders that the majority Hindu population should not receive preferential treatment, declares India to be a secular country, with freedom of religion explicitly guaranteed in Article 15. In this way, official policies in India comport to Mohandas Gandhi's Hindu-inspired vision of a pluralist and tolerant democracy based in religious freedom and equality for all of India's religious communities.

On the other hand, despite these secular underpinnings, India has failed to live up to its liberal founding ideals in many ways after the death of its first prime minister, Jawaharlal Nehru. Subsequent leaders, including Nehru's daughter Indira and grandson Rajiv, worked to appeal to and coopt Hinduism in order to gain religious credibility, thus moving the country from the ideals of Nehruvian secularism toward a partnered relationship between religion and state and discrimination against minority religious communities – a development that paved the way for the growing communalization of Indian society and politics and for an illiberal political theology associated with Hindu nationalism. This theology calls not for equality among India's religious groups as declared in the constitution, but rather for an integration between religious and state institutions in which majority Hindus enjoy a special status. For their part, the national government and many state governments have actively supported Hindu nationalists and cultivated strong ties to Hindu leaders and bodies to the detriment of minority religious groups like Sikhs, Muslims and Christians. India's majoritarian emphasis has resulted in what India scholar Upendra Baxi terms a "Hindu-secular state" in which religious freedom is a right reserved only for Hindus.[42] This reality has had the effect of contradicting the spirit of the Indian constitution, which calls for a secular state in which no single religious tradition can impose its will on the rest. At the society level, interreligious tension has been a constant reality in India, its post-independence history checkered by coerced religious conversions, religious and cultural intolerance, riots and physical assaults on minorities.

Restrictions on religious liberty in India have contributed to the growth of violent religious extremism. Since its independence in 1947, India has been the site of numerous and severe terrorist campaigns, from Kashmir and the "Seven Sisters" states in the north to Gujarat in the west and Odisha in the east. In what follows, I examine religious terrorism in two of India's states hit hardest by religious militancy: Gujarat and Punjab. I argue that restrictions on religious freedom are strongly correlated with higher levels of religious violence in both of these states. The finding is robust in that the logic linking restrictions to terrorism operates in each state, albeit in different ways, regardless of the faith tradition involved.

---

[42]   Upendra Baxi, "The Constitutional Discourse on Secularism," in *Reconstructing the Republic*, ed. Upendra Baxi, Alice Jacob and Tarlok Singh (New Delhi: Har-Anand Publications, 1999), 231.

Hindu Terrorism in Gujarat

Perhaps nowhere else in India have religious tensions been more evident than in the religiously diverse northwestern state of Gujarat. Although Hindus constitute a majority at roughly 89 percent of the population, significant religious minorities include Muslims and Jains. In 2002, Gujarat fell victim to communal rioting and terrorism between Hindus and Muslims after the infamous Godhra train bombing, resulting in the deaths of thousands of people. The violence was propelled by the Hindu nationalist government of Gujarat, which, had it intervened to curb Hindu militancy, could have spared the lives of thousands of Muslims who died in the Gujarat pogroms.

The Gujarat violence had its roots in a series of incidents that took place ten years beforehand more than 800 miles to the northeast in the state of Uttar Pradesh. In that state lies an ancient holy city named Ayodhya, which, according to local legend, was the birthplace of the Hindu god Ram (the believed reincarnation of the god Vishnu). The actual birthplace, previously a Hindu temple, however, had been occupied for 430 years by a large Muslim place of worship in the center of the city called Babar's Mosque (Babri Masjid), named after the Mughal king who destroyed the temple.[43] For years, Hindu nationalists through organizations like the Vishva Hindu Parishad (World Hindu Council) (VHP) and its political ally, the Bharatiya Janata Party (BJP), attempted to liberate Ram's birthplace from Muslim control. A major turning point occurred in 1986 when a district judge ruled that the mosque should be opened to the Hindu public, essentially giving the Hindu majority control over it. This action could not have occurred absent the complicity of the central government. From then on, Hindu nationalists, under the auspices of the Ram Janmabhoomi Action Committee, worked to have the mosque removed, staging a number of demonstrative processions throughout the country. In 1991, building on the interreligious tensions associated with Babar's Mosque, the BJP became the major opposition party in the Indian parliament and took political control in a number of states. Religion and state were slowly becoming integrated at both the national and state levels.

Emboldened by their positions of power, Hindu fundamentalists became more brazen in their demands that the Babar Mosque be destroyed and replaced with a Hindu temple. Ultimately, Hindus prevailed at destroying the mosque during a rally in 1992 when a mob of 300,000, incited by the BJP and coordinated by other Sangh Parivar organizations, demolished the Muslim place of worship and proceeded to build a shrine dedicated to Ram, doing so as the local authorities stood by idly. The episode struck a major blow to India's pluralist identity as Hindu nationalists sought to redefine the country in explicitly Hindu terms. While the central government, still under the control of the Congress Party, took several steps the

---

[43] Sarvepalli Gopal, *Anatomy of a Confrontation: The Babri Masjid-Ramjanmabhumi Issue* (New Delhi: Viking, 1991).

following day to punish those involved in the incident – jailing leaders, prohibiting radical movements like the Rashtriya Swayamsevak Sangh RSS, VHP and Bajrang Dal and dismissing state governments and state legislative assemblies in Madhya Pradesh, Rajasthan and Himachal Pradesh – India rapidly became engulfed in a religious war between Hindus and Muslims in which upward of 2,000 people died in religiously motivated violence and terrorism across the country. Importantly, state complicity in the Ayodhya incident, both before and after the destruction of the mosque, revealed the extent to which Hinduism and the state had become interwoven to the detriment of religious minorities. Far from random or spontaneous events, evidence indicates that the BJP had been planning attacks against Muslims months beforehand. For example, the terrorist incidents that occurred in the city of Mumbai during this time were carried out with the aid of voter registration lists and other official documents to more effectively target Muslim communities.[44] No longer could Muslims count on a neutral state to protect their rights as religious minorities.

What happened at Ayodhya sowed the seeds for the violence that would take place in Gujarat ten years later. On February 27, 2002, Muslim militants purportedly attacked the Sabarmati express train in Gujarat carrying Hindu worshippers returning from a pilgrimage to Ayodhya at the Godhra train station. The pilgrims had gone to Ayodhya with the goal of building Ram's temple at the place where Babar's Mosque once existed. The attack resulted in the deaths of fifty-eight people, virtually all Hindus, and included women and children. Almost immediately, Muslims were singled out for their role in the attack, and the local police, operating under this assumption, began to question and arrest Muslims en masse. The Godhra incident sparked waves of retaliatory violence by Hindus against Muslims throughout Gujarat and beyond. It also laid the foundation for state-level collusion between Hindus and the state as well as high social hostilities between Hindus and Muslims, both of which worked together to create the tragic situation that would follow. Terrorism, both state-sponsored (on the part of Hindus) and directed against the state (on the part of Muslims) would characterize Gujarati violence post Godhra.

The precipitating train bombing allowed for the solidifying of a hardline political theology of *Hindutva* (the predominant form of Hindu nationalism) as ideologues worked to define India as a country for Hindus. Even before the Sabarmati bombing, right-wing Hindu groups had been involved in an anti-Muslim propaganda campaign in Gujarat, leading to the stockpiling of weapons and the distribution of lists of Muslim dwellings and businesses.[45] In the weeks following the Godhra attack, nearly 2,000 Muslims were killed by Hindu rioters, and Muslim businesses were burnt indiscriminately. Little attempt was made to distinguish between those believed to be responsible for Godhra and the general Muslim population. Many

---

[44] Hibbard, *Religious Politics and Secular States*, 165–168.
[45] Martha Nussbaum, *The Clash Within: Democracy, Religious Violence, and India's Future* (Cambridge, MA: Belknap Press, 2009), 20.

of the victims included women who had been raped and tortured before being killed. A report by the Indian tribunal investigating committee revealed that Hindu nationalist groups had deliberately targeted Muslim homes and shops. Philosopher Martha Nussbaum describes the context graphically: "Children were killed with their parents; fetuses were ripped from the bellies of pregnant women to be tossed into the fire."[46] Other forms of violence included torture, mutilation and the destruction of Muslim holy places.

The Gujarat pogrom, as it has come to be called, differed from earlier spates of interreligious violence in that the state (both national and local) actively aided and abetted rather than simply tolerated anti-Muslim violence, thus contributing to a more extreme form of aggression. This was not a case of mob violence run amuck, but rather a "coordinated attack on a minority community designed to polarize Indian society and strengthen the Hindu nationalists' hold on power" that was planned well in advance.[47] Meanwhile, as documented in a report by Human Rights Watch, the press presented the Godhra events in such a way (and in some cases deliberately fabricated stories about Muslim violence) so as to incite terrorism against Muslims throughout the state. The report goes on to note that BJP officials themselves directed and the police participated in the attacks with the full support of the government.[48] As in Ayodhya, the security forces failed to respond sufficiently to the unfolding crisis; the Gujarat police, acting in accordance with the orders given by politicians, refused to intervene and in some cases abetted the violence. Though the central government eventually sent troops to the state, it did so only well after the pogroms were already under way.[49] Gujarat's chief minister – the man who would eventually become the country's prime minister, Narendra Modi, whom many believed to be complicit in the violence – justified the Hindu retaliation: "What is happening is a chain of action and reaction ... The people in that part of Godhra have criminal tendencies."[50] Modi's complicity in the 2002 riots prompted the US government to ban him from the United States, but it also turned him into something of a national hero among Hindu extremists. His chief of police later testified that political leaders had pressured the security forces not to register rioters or simply let them go with a slap on the wrist. The result was that virtually none of the pogrom's leaders faced criminal charges for their involvement in the violence.

The national government also took an approach of indifference to what was going on in northwest India at the time. Like Modi, national officials suggested that the attacks on Muslims were inevitable and even warranted. In a 2002 speech, Prime Minister Atal Vajpayee had the following to say about Islam: "Wherever Muslims

[46]   Nussbaum, *Clash Within*, 2.   [47]   Hibbard, *Religious Politics and Secular States*, 151.
[48]   Human Rights Watch, *We Have No Orders to Save You: State Participation and Complicity in Communal Violence in Gujarat*, last modified April 30, 2002, www.hrw.org/report/2002/04/30/we-have-no-orders-save-you/state-participation-and-complicity-communal-violence.
[49]   Sharif Shuja, "Indian Secularism: Image and Reality," *Contemporary Review* 287 (2005): 38–42.
[50]   "Blame it on Newton's Law: Modi," *Times of India*, March 3, 2002.

live, they don't like to live in co-existence with others, they don't like to mingle with others; and instead of propagating their ideas in a peaceful manner, they want to spread their faith by resorting to terror and threats. The world has become alert to this danger."[51] Through such statements, the central government conveyed the message that it did not believe that all of India's citizens should be treated equitably; Muslims were not deserving of the full protection of the law.

The most vivid manifestation of *Hindutva* ideology crystallizing among the general populace occurred during the Gujarat elections eight months after the state-sponsored pogrom against Muslims in which the Hindu majority was mobilized electorally against the Muslim minority. The BJP ran on a blatant platform of Hindu–state partnership, with its electoral manifesto calling for "proposals to launch an antiterrorist movement by training youth and forming village-based cells in coordination with the defense ministry. It also promised an anti-conversion law in Gujarat and regulation of education in the state's madrasas."[52] It strived to paint Gujarati Muslims as agents of India's enemy, Pakistan, intent on destroying India's foundational Hindu character.[53] This tactic of identifying Muslims as an internal enemy that had to be dealt with by force proved an effective strategy among Hindus living in Gujarat, especially in the aftermath of September 11. In these elections, the electorate overwhelmingly supported the expressed goal of the Modi-led BJP of driving Muslims out of Gujarat and establishing a Hindu *rashtra* (polity) in the state. Modi was reelected as chief minister in a landslide. According to a poll conducted by the Centre for the Study of Developing Societies, the BJP took a two-thirds majority in the legislative assembly, and in more than half of the districts in which violence had broken out, the BJP captured 91 percent of the ballots cast.[54] The same survey revealed that 55 percent of Hindu respondents – including a significant number of voters aligned with the Congress Party – agreed with the statement that the violence occurring after the Godhra attacks was "necessary to teach a lesson to anti-national elements."[55] Ashok Singhal, the international working president of the VHP, explicitly endorsed the anti-Muslim violence, declaring, "we were successful in our experiment of raising Hindu consciousness, which will be repeated all over the country now." He was referring specifically to the fact that entire villages had been "emptied of Islam," and that the Muslims living there had been forced into refugee camps. India scholar Arvind Rajagopal concludes

---

[51]   Siddharth Varadarajan, "A Stench That Is All Too Familiar," *The Hindu*, March 24, 2009.
[52]   Arvind Rajagopal, "The Gujarat Experiment and Hindu National Realism: Lessons for Secularism," in *The Crisis of Secularism in India*, ed. Anuradha Dingwaney Needham and Rajan Rajeswari Sunder (Durham, NC: Duke University Press, 2007), 220–221.
[53]   Katharine Adeney and Andrew Wyatt, *Contemporary India* (New York, NY: Palgrave Macmillan, 2010), 192.
[54]   Aseem Prakash, "Re-Imagination of the State and Gujarat's Electoral Verdict," *Economic and Political Weekly* 38 (2003): 1601–1610.
[55]   Yogendra Yadav, "The Patterns and Lessons," *Frontline* 19, no. 26 (2003): 10–16.

that "Singhal not only refused to condemn the violence following Godhra but endorsed it."[56]

This sent a powerful message to Gujarat's Muslim community that Muslims were not considered equal citizens and did not deserve the same rights as the Hindu majority, undoubtedly contributing to the feelings of vulnerability held by many Muslims. The US Commission on International Religious Freedom documented an "atmosphere of impunity" that existed in Gujarat at the time and that corresponded with the national rise of the BJP.[57] The Gujarat tragedy also resulted in the strengthening of militant Islamist groups like the Students' Islamic Movement of India, Harakat al-Jihad and Lashkar-e-Taiba, which vowed revenge for the actions of the state-supported Hindu majority. The Students' Islamic Movement "incrementally radicalized in response to rising levels of communal violence" as a means of "influencing a system that appears unresponsive to their grievances" – a pattern of marginalization and violence not uncommon in societies that discriminate against religious minorities.[58] The climate of hatred made it easier for these groups to draw recruits while simultaneously providing an aura of legitimacy to their goals. It is clear from the evidence that politicians aligned with the Hindu right intentionally fanned the flames of communitarian strife in Gujarat, seeking to reap political rewards by doing so.

The case of Gujarat shows how repression of a religious minority served to create a spiral of violence between the majority Hindu and minority Muslim communities. The partnership between Hinduism and the state and the consequent unequal application of police and judicial powers sparked violence in two ways. First, the implicit governmental backing of the Hindu claim that Babar's Mosque in Ayodhya had been constructed on a sacred Hindu site and its subsequent demolition resulted in a Muslim backlash that boiled over ten years later at Godhra. Second, partnership also empowered Hindu fundamentalists to carry out violence against Gujarat's minority Muslim community, which, in turn, served as a catalyst for hundreds of young Muslims to join Islamist terror organizations. The Gujarat pogrom, in the end, contributed to the widespread feeling of Muslims that they could not trust the state to protect their freedoms, thus widening the gap between the Muslim minority and the majority Hindus who had captured the government and used their position of power to deepen the partnership between Hinduism and the state and to launch an assault against Muslims.

Sikh Terrorism in Punjab

India's terrorism problem involves not just Hindus and Muslims. In the north-western state of Punjab, the government found itself at odds with Sikh terrorists

---

[56] Rajagopal, "The Gujarat Experiment and Hindu National Realism," 222.
[57] Anna Bigelow, *Sharing the Sacred: Practicing Pluralism in Muslim North India* (Oxford: Oxford University Press, 2010).
[58] Henne, Hudgins and Shah, *Religious Freedom and Violent Religious Extremism*, 22.

who demanded a separate autonomous state called Khalistan (Land of the Pure) throughout much of the 1980s and 1990s, a conflict that resulted in the deaths of approximately 25,000 people. A brief examination of the recent history of the conflict reveals how partnership between religion and state led to discrimination and assaults against minority Sikh communities living in northern India. This inequity, in turn, gave rise to spirals of terrorism and further state repression.

Sikhs – known for their long beards and distinctive turbans – constitute the world's fifth largest religious group. Since Indian independence, the country's minority Sikh community has decried its marginalized status resulting from a perceived alliance between Hinduism and the state. This sense of discrimination arises partly from Article 25 of the constitution, which, though providing for religious freedom, implicitly denies Sikhs their own religious identity and instead identifies them as constituting part of India's Hindu community: "the reference to Hindus shall be construed as including a reference to persons professing the Sikh, Jaina, or Buddhist religion." This constitutional provision effectively subjects members of these religious traditions to Hindu Personal Status Laws and denies them access to social services available to other minority religious communities, despite their unique founders, histories, beliefs and practices. The Sikh community has long demanded that the constitution be amended to remove any references that might misconstrue Sikhs as Hindus, thus denying them their distinct identity.

Sikh discontent has also been the result of explicit actions on the part of the state. In 1946, India's first prime minister, Jawaharlal Nehru, essentially nullified a federal arrangement that granted Punjabi Sikhs numerous concessions in exchange for their support of an independent Indian state and an Indian constitution. From then on, Sikhs held a litany of economic, political and social grievances against the state, which they believed was actively engaging in discrimination and undermining their identity. Eventually these grievances came to be defined in explicitly religious terms.[59] In 1973, the Sikh leadership presented basic Sikh grievances to the government in the Anandpur Sahib Resolution, a document that raised a number of issues that contributed to the widespread perception among Sikhs that their faith and identity were under attack. The document would become the basis for Sikh political demands.[60] Of the seven objectives delineated in the Resolution, three dealt specifically with the issue of religious liberty: (1) the passage of the all-India Gurdwara Act; (2) protection of Sikh minorities living outside Punjab, but within India; and (3) the end to the policy introduced by Indira Gandhi of restricting the number of

---

[59]   Hibbard, *Religious Politics and Secular States*, 151.
[60]   Harjot Oberoi, "Sikh Fundamentalism: Translating History into Theory," in *Fundamentalisms and the State: Remaking Polities, Economies, and Militance*, ed. Martin E. Marty and R. Scott Appleby (Chicago, IL: University of Chicago, 1993), 256–285.

Sikhs who could serve in the armed forces.[61] Importantly, it did not yet demand an autonomous Khalistani state since Sikhs still considered themselves part of India.

Up to this point, the Khalistani movement had not turned violent. This changed as the central government under the leadership of Indira Gandhi began to manipulate the politics of Punjab and confront Sikh opponents, setting the stage for a violent showdown between Sikhs and the Indian state. The beginnings of religious violence in Punjab can be traced to one of the rare instances of *interreligious* partnership – that is, when a political apparatus dominated by members of one religion seeks out an alliance of repression with members of a different faith tradition. In the case of Punjab, the Gandhi-led Congress, in a move to delegitimize the moderate Akali Dal party (Army of the Devotees of Akal) – its chief political rival in the Punjab – attempted to create an alternative religious party under the leadership of a firebrand Sikh radical named Jarnail Singh Bhindranwale. Congress leaders like Sanjay Gandhi and Zail Singh hoped that in supporting the rise of Bhindranwale it could divide the Sikh community and attenuate the base of support enjoyed by the Akali Dal.[62]

Bhindranwale, an Orthodox Sikh leader who in 1977 had become the head of the revivalist Sikh organization known as the Damdami Taksal, called on Sikhs to return to their "pure roots." He fervently preached against drug use, alcohol consumption, pornography and the cutting of one's hair, in accordance with a strict interpretation of Sikh belief.[63] Along with his calls for a return to proper religious practices, Bhindranwale also articulated an overt political agenda. In the 1970s and early 1980s, he collaborated with the Congress Party in order to undercut support for the centrist Akali Dal in Punjab, which he accused of abandoning proper Sikh belief. In many ways, the alliance between the radical Sikh leader and the Congress Party indeed worked to raise his stature among ordinary Sikhs. His willingness to resort to violence against non-Orthodox Sikhs further cemented his reputation among the hardline faithful.

As is the case in many other parts of the world, however, attempts at partnering with an illiberal rendering of religion would have devastating consequences. Eventually, Bhindranwale's movement became so powerful that it no longer needed the support of the central government in order to survive; it took on a life of its own, and the Congress Party was no longer able to control it for its own purposes. Under Bhindranwale's leadership, the Khalistani movement turned toward extremism and sought to violently confront the Indian state. Although the Congress Party managed

---

[61] Joyce J. M.Pettigrew, *The Sikhs of the Punjab: Unheard Voices of State and Guerrilla Violence* (London: Zed Books, 1995), 6; Harnik Deol, *Religion and Nationalism in India: The Case of the Punjab* (London: Routledge, 2000), 102–106.
[62] Kuldip Nayar and Khushwant Singh, *Tragedy of Punjab: Operation Bluestar & After* (New Delhi: Vision Books, 1984).
[63] Pritam Singh, "Two Facets of Revivalism," *Punjab Today* (1987): 170–171.

to capture the state government in Punjab and marginalize the Akali Dal – the very goals Mrs. Gandhi desired – the support Bhindranwale received allowed him, in turn, to become increasingly violent toward what he deemed heretical Sikh groups as well as Hindus. Bhindranwale's supporters and other militant Sikh groups attacked a variety of targets, including the police, government officials, a heterodox Sikh sect known as the Narankaris, politicians, banks, railway stations and government property.[64] A particularly grisly attack took place in October 1983 when several Hindu travelers were pulled off a bus and shot. In the early 1980s, the Sikh revolutionary was involved in a series of assassinations, but remained protected by the Congress Party.

Meanwhile, the Akali Dal took more forceful steps to reestablish itself as the legitimate representative of Sikh interests in Punjab by confronting the Congress Party, which refused to budge on issues of key importance for the Khalistani movement. A race to the bottom ensued between Bhindranwale and the more moderate Sikh elements. Both had to compete for the hearts and minds of ordinary Sikhs as to who better represented Sikh interests in the face of minority religious discrimination – a competition that Bhindranwale was winning. As the Akali Dal moved closer to the ideology espoused by Bhindranwale, the central government was able to portray the party to the Hindu majority as extremist. The reason for this, as explained by political scientist Scott Hibbard, was that "[r]eligion and politics became so intertwined in this context – and Bhindranwale's religious militarism so popular – that secular Sikhs could stand aloof only at the risk of being called traitors to the Sikh cause."[65]

Eventually the initial moderation of the Akali Dal yielded to the radical narrative. The Akali Dal launched a *morcha* (agitation) in the 1980s to protest the discriminatory policies of the central government.[66] Toward this end, it founded the Group for the Battle for Righteousness (Dharam Yudh Morcha) in 1982 with the goal of seeing the Sahib Resolution become reality. Indira Gandhi, worried by the increasing strength of the organization, portrayed the Sikh movement as one bent on separatism and concluded that the best way to subdue it was through repression. As the violence continued, Mrs. Gandhi imposed president's rule in Punjab, which gave the security forces expanded powers. Instead of quelling the violence, however, the decision actually served to add fuel to the fire as radical Hindu groups, mobilized by the central government and various state governments, orchestrated anti-Sikh violence in Punjab and surrounding areas. Groups like the Hindu Suraksha Samiti (Hindu Protection Organization) incited mob attacks against Sikhs and their holy

[64] Pritam Singh, *Federalism, Nationalism and Development: India and the Punjab Economy* (London: Routledge, 2008), 40.
[65] Hibbard, *Religious Politics and Secular States*, 146.
[66] Virginia van Dyke, "The Khalistan Movement in Punjab, India, and the Post-Militancy Era: Structural Change and New Political Compulsions," *Asian Survey* 49, no. 6 (2009): 985.

places, resulting in the deaths of dozens of people in separate attacks.[67] In just two and a half months, the security forces arrested approximately 30,000 Sikhs.[68]

The most vivid example of anti-Sikh repression and a major catalyst for Sikh terrorism occurred on June 4, 1984 when a massacre took place in the Sikhs' central place of worship, the Golden Temple (Harmandir Sahib) complex in Amritsar, Punjab, as well as forty-one other houses of worship (*gurdwaras*). The military operation, ordered by Mrs. Gandhi, intended on removing Sikh separatists led by Bhindranwale who had sought refuge in the Golden Temple. Gandhi sent in 10,000 troops, armored vehicles and tanks as part of the three-day operation. While the assault at the temple proved successful in removing the separatists, the army, in the process, killed thousands of Sikhs (the majority of whom were pilgrims worshipping at the temple for a Sikh religious festival), caused great damage to Sikh religious sites (including the holiest Sikh shrine) and burned ancient manuscripts held in the shrine's library. Mrs. Gandhi, pandering to the Hindu right, justified the draconian measure by claiming that "the Hindu Dharma was under attack ... from the Sikhs, the Muslims and others."[69] Instead of following in her father's footsteps by attempting to assuage communal conflict, Mrs. Gandhi was now actively stoking its flames. All this served to generate outrage among Sikhs and a nationwide controversy over the timing of and tactics used in the attack. Some believed that the army deliberately targeted the civilian worshippers.

The handling of the operation led to widespread resentment among Sikhs directed against the central government. The temple attack and subsequent assassination of Bhindranwale coupled with the fact that the perpetrators of the massacre had not been brought to justice led many otherwise restrained Sikhs to conclude that Bhindranwale was correct in his assessment that the state was at war with the Sikh people and that it needed to be confronted militaristically if they wanted to survive.[70] Virginia van Dyke writes that "the action created martyrs and completely disaffected the Sikh population, including the Diaspora."[71] The Golden Temple attack was carried out "to suppress the culture of a people, to attack their heart, to strike a blow at their spirit and self-confidence."[72]

Operation Blue Star, as it was called, kindled an intense reaction by the Sikh community and commenced a spiral of Sikh terrorism and violent state reaction that would define India's relationship with its Sikh minority in the coming years.

---

[67] Jagtar S. Grewal, *The Sikhs of the Punjab*, Vol. 2. (Cambridge: Cambridge University Press, 1998), 229.

[68] Deol, *Religion and Nationalism in India*, 104.

[69] As quoted in Sumantra Bose, "Hindu Nationalism and the Crisis of the Indian State: A Theoretical Perspective," in *Nationalism, Democracy and Development*, ed. Sugata Bose and Ayesha Jalal (New Delhi: Oxford, 1998), 123.

[70] Paul R. Brass, "The Punjab Crisis and the Unity of India," in *India's Democracy: An Analysis of Changing State–Society Relations*, ed. Atul Kohli (Princeton, NJ: Princeton University Press, 1988), 169–213.

[71] Van Dyke, "Khalistan Movement in Punjab," 986. [72] Pettigrew, *Sikhs of the Punjab*, 8.

Following the attack on the Golden Temple, Indira Gandhi was killed by two of her Sikh bodyguards in Delhi on October 31, 1984. The assassination, in turn, led to a hardening of religious identities and sparked a widespread pogrom against Sikhs and their property in northern Indian cities with significant Sikh populations. Mobs in Delhi and several other cities killed approximately 2,000 Sikhs in retaliation for the assassination. The pogroms, though led by the political leaders of Gandhi's Congress Party, were condoned and at times assisted by state agencies like the police and military. Dutch anthropologist Peter van der Veer describes the hostilities at the time: "Trains and busses were stopped and Sikhs taken out and killed, and in the Punjab the reverse happened with the militants killing Hindu passengers." The actions by the state were undertaken with the intent to "teach the arrogant Sikhs a lesson they would not forget."[73] According to another account of the pogroms, senior politicians unleashed thugs upon Sikh communities who proceeded to burn Sikhs alive, rape women and destroy religious shrines.[74] Attacks also occurred against Sikh *gurdwaras* and businesses. Nevertheless, following the pogrom against the Sikhs, Indira's son, Rajiv, led the Congress Party to a major election victory; the Party gained the largest majority ever seen in an Indian parliament, winning 411 out of 542 seats.

As in the case of Gujarat, the violence that occurred in Punjab was not impulsive aggression against Sikhs for the assassination of Mrs. Gandhi, but rather a planned effort on the part of Congress Party politicians who used the murder as a pretext to wage a war in the Punjab.[75] As a result, state complicity exacerbated communalism in Indian society and pitted majority Hindus against minority Sikhs. These events served to further consolidate a partnership between Hinduism and the state to the exclusion of the Sikh minority. Many of those who had never sought their own Sikh state now backed the idea of secession.

Throughout the 1980s and 1990s, violence continued in the Punjab until the government finally defeated the Sikh rebellion. During this time, tens of thousands of people were killed. For their part, Sikh militants were responsible for assaults against Hindu communities: bomb attacks, political assassinations and the massacre of civilians in Punjab and the surrounding areas.[76] Sikh terrorism also contained an international component. In 1985, members of the Sikh separatist group called the Babbar Khalsa blew up Air India Flight 182 in mid-air off the coast of Ireland,

---

[73] Peter van der Veer, "Religious Nationalism in India and Global Fundamentalism," in *Globalization and Social Movements: Culture, Power* and *the Transnational Public Sphere*, ed. John Guidry, Michael D. Kennedy and Mayer Zald (Ann Arbor, MI: University of Michigan Press, 2000), 319.

[74] Jasakaran Kaur, *Twenty Years of Impunity: The November 1984 Pogroms of Sikhs in India* (Portland, OR: Ensaaf, 2006).

[75] People's Union for Democratic Rights and People's Union for Civil Liberties, *PUCL–PUDR Report: Who Are the Guilty? Report of a Joint Inquiry into the Causes and Impact of the Riots in Delhi from 31 October to 10 November 1984*, last modified April 1, 2003, www.pucl.org/Topics/Religion-communalism/2003/who-areguilty.htm.

[76] Ramachandra Guha, *India after Gandhi: The History of the World's Largest Democracy* (New York, NY: Ecco, 2007), 555–565.

resulting in the deaths of 329 individuals. The Air India bombing was also the deadliest terrorist attack involving the hijacking of a passenger airliner until the attacks of September 11, 2001. The attack is believed to have been retaliation against the Indian state for Operation Blue Star.

The security forces responded brutally in their counterinsurgency campaign between 1984 and 1995 and, according to Human Rights Watch, often engaged in the violation of fundamental physical integrity rights, including "arbitrary detention, extrajudicial execution, and enforced disappearance of thousands of Sikhs," usually without any fear of prosecution or punishment by the state. Meanwhile, the judicial system failed victims and their families seeking justice in the form of "prolonged trials, biased prosecutors, an unresponsive judiciary, police intimidation, and harassment of witnesses … and the failure to charge senior police officers despite evidence of their role in the abuses."[77] Government officials bearing significant responsibility were not brought to justice as the government routinely denied any wrongdoing. Mass arrests and prolonged detention of Sikh men and youth further contributed to the perception among Sikhs that their faith and community were under attack.

Today, the militant Khalistani movement has lost its popular support both in India and within the diaspora Sikh community abroad. Nevertheless, terrorist attacks by militant Sikh groups have continued sporadically even after the Punjab insurgency came to an end. Organizations like the Khalistan Zindabad Force (KZF) and Babbar Khalsa remain active and militant Sikh cells operate internationally as well.

In sum, events in the Punjab demonstrate how discrimination against Sikhs embittered moderates, fueled Khalistani militancy and contributed to ongoing societal tensions between Sikhs and Hindus. The prolonged nature of the conflict was due to the refusal of the government to acknowledge the systematic nature of the problem (including widespread human rights abuses) and to act in a manner that would address its roots causes. Moreover, the Indian government utilized the Punjab operations as a kind of counterinsurgency model that has been replicated in other parts of India dealing with their own problems with domestic order.

Today, India stands at a crossroads. Though the world's largest democracy, it has failed to live up to its human rights obligations in the area of religious freedom. Specifically, India's religion–state arrangements have not produced the kind of tolerant polity necessary for the successful functioning of a liberal, multi-religion state. Religious freedom conditions in India continue to deteriorate at the time of this writing, and the situation of India's religious minorities remains especially perilous (particularly with respect to religious conversion and interreligious marriages). Political parties retain their relationship with fundamentalist religious

---

[77] Human Rights Watch, *Protecting the Killers: A Policy of Impunity in Punjab, India*, last modified October 17, 2007, www.hrw.org/report/2007/10/17/protecting-killers/policy-impunity-punjab-india.

groups, and Hindu nationalism still commands the support of a sizable proportion of the Hindu population. After the election of Prime Minister Narendra Modi in 2014 – a politician long associated with India's Hindu nationalist movement, whom the United States denied a visa in 2005 for his role in the Gujarat pogroms and who remains a lightning rod due to his checkered past – minorities reported feeling increasing fear and concern for their future. While the national government may not necessarily have led efforts at persecution, critics of the leadership accused the Modi administration of sweeping religious freedom issues under the carpet and failing to rein in extremist elements in favor of focusing on issues like development and trade. Since Modi's Bharatiya Janata Party retook parliament, India witnessed a renewed assault on religious liberty, including vandalism, burglary and arson against minority houses of worship; "reconversion" programs; and bouts of communal violence, particularly against minorities like Sikhs, Christians and Muslims. By the end of 2017, faith-based terrorism in India had reached an all-time high, with attacks carried out by individuals associated with all of India's major faith communities.

While the impeding of religious freedom does not account for every instance of religious terrorism, it does shed light on an important structural cause behind terrorism in Gujarat, Punjab and elsewhere. A return to the ideals of religious liberty and equality set forth in the constitution would be the most appropriate way to confront religious terrorism in India. While this does not mean the end of religious violence, the final throes of communalism or even a return to secularist Nehruvian principles, a state that is neutral with respect to religious disputes yet simultaneously works to protect religious freedoms for all would likely be seen as an entity that can be trusted and have legitimacy with a large portion of India's religious communities. As India continues to experience widespread religious hostilities, the country's leaders would do well to remember Gandhi's timeless words: "If the Hindus believe that India should be peopled only by Hindus, they are living in dreamland. The Hindus, the Mahomedans, the Parsis and the Christians who have made India their country are fellow countrymen, and they will have to live in unity, if only for their own interest."[78] Only by accepting tolerance and religious freedom for all will India be able to overcome its sectarian divides and communal hostilities, which have all too often manifested in violence.

BUDDHIST TERRORISM IN BURMA

"Buddhist terrorism," a combination of words that might seem oxymoronic to many, belies Buddhism's stereotype of being an "other-worldly" pacifist religion and spiritual system known for practices like meditation, asceticism, tolerance, empathy

---

[78] Mahatma Gandhi, *The Collected Works of Mahatma Gandhi: Volume 10* (New Delhi: Government of India, Ministry of Information and Broadcasting, 1963), 29.

and nonviolent protest in accordance with the concept of *ahimsa* (nonviolence) – ideas central to the teaching of the Buddha, Siddhartha Gautama, 2,500 years ago. Yet like every other religious tradition, Buddhism's relationship to violence is ambivalent. Although the principle of nonviolence is arguably more central to Buddhism than any other faith tradition, militant Buddhists have been responsible for inciting religious animosity throughout much of the religion's history, including engaging in war and other forms of violent conflict.[79] In the fifth century, millenarian Buddhist monks led a series of revolts and insurrections in China. Monks in Korea and China fought wars against the Mongols and Japanese. In Thailand, Buddhist holy men staged bloody revolts against the government beginning in the 1700s. In the twentieth century, Buddhist violence was a prevalent theme in the Burmese anticolonial movement and the Sri Lankan civil war against the country's Hindu/Tamil minority. Examples of Buddhist warfare can be seen in each of the religion's main traditions – Theravada, Mahayana and Vajrayana – challenging romanticized notions of Buddhism as a faith absolutely committed to peace and nonviolence.

Underlying recent Buddhist violence in Burma has been the relationship between temple and state. Buddhism has played an important role in the country's history, politics and culture. About 90 percent of Burma's population identifies with the Theravada tradition of Buddhism. Buddhism retains a privileged status among state leaders, remains part and parcel of Burmese culture and identity, provides religious legitimacy to the ruling apparatus and gives nationalist ideologies an aura of transcendence. Buddhism was integral to Burmese nationalism and the anticolonial struggle against Britain, and every regime since the country's independence in 1948 has either endorsed Buddhism as the state religion or adopted "Buddhist values" to build political legitimacy. In turn, the monkhood (*sangha*) lends the state a certain spiritual authority to shape the country's policy.

These mutually reinforcing relationships between temple and state serve to promote Buddhist values, maintain social order and perpetuate the purity and legitimacy of the Buddhist state, while marginalizing religious minorities who are seen as hindrances to a homogenous Buddhist nation.[80] The government thus imposes serious restrictions on the practice of minority religious groups, especially Muslims and Christians. In 1961, Prime Minister U Nu, a devout Buddhist, enacted a bill enshrining Buddhism as the official religion of the country, a development that led to clashes between Buddhist monks and Muslims.[81] Than Shwe, who served as prime minister from 1992 to 2011, actively promoted a Burma consisting of "one race,

[79] See Michael K. Jerryson and Mark Juergensmeyer, eds., *Buddhist Warfare* (Oxford: Oxford University Press, 2010).

[80] Mark Juergensmeyer, "The Global Rise of Religious Nationalism," *Australian Journal of International Affairs* 64, no. 3 (2010): 268.

[81] Juliane Schober, *Buddhist Conjunctures in Myanmar: Cultural Narratives, Colonial Legacies, and Civil Society* (Honolulu, HI: University of Hawaii Press, 2011).

one language, one religion," despite the country's varied religious traditions.[82] While the 2008 constitution includes provisions providing for religious freedom and equality and Article 364 warns that "the abuse of religion for political purposes is forbidden," such assurances have not in practice protected religious minorities from discrimination, bloodshed or other religiously motivated crimes.

The 1982 Citizenship Act, for instance, recognized 135 minority groups living in Burma, but denied citizenship to the Rohingya – a Muslim community living in Burma for generations and one of the world's most persecuted religious groups – effectively making them a people without a state, encouraging a de facto segregation of society, perpetuating disenfranchisement and denying them access to basic social services. The government disallows the Rohingya citizenship on the basis that they are recent Bengali immigrants imported by the British during colonial rule but not one of the original ethnic groups present in Burma before the British conquest in 1824. Absent citizenship, the Rohingya have no property rights; forego equal treatment under the law; experience limited freedom of movement; have no access to employment, education, health care and property; cannot maintain religious buildings; and require government permission to marry or have children.[83]

Evidence of nationalistic xenophobia and discrimination against the Rohingya can be found at the highest levels of government. The Ministry of Religious Affairs openly works "for the purification, perpetuation, promotion and propagation of the Theravada Buddhist [religion]."[84] Former president U Thein Sein averred that the Rohingya were not Burmese citizens and even suggested that they ought to be deported to other countries – a proposition that finds much support among the Buddhist elite, as demonstrated in October 2012 when thousands of Buddhist monks across the country marched together in a demonstration of support for the president's position denying the Rohingya citizenship and deporting them from Burma. Some government officials have called for bans on Rohingya women having more than two children, and the president supported the drafting of a national law prohibiting interfaith marriage known as "Safeguarding the National Identity" – a measure promoted by nationalist monks to prevent Buddhist women from marrying Muslim men as a means to "preserve race and religion."[85] In 2012, the central government backed out of an agreement that would have allowed the Organization of Islamic Cooperation to open an office in Burma to help the Rohingya.

[82] Mikael Gravers, "Spiritual Politics, Political Religion, and Religious Freedom in Burma," *Review of Faith & International Affairs* 11, no. 2 (2013): 48.
[83] Mary Kate Long, "Dynamics of State, Sangha and Society in Myanmar: A Closer Look at the Rohingya Issue," *Asian Journal of Public Affairs* 6, no. 1 (2013): 79–94.
[84] US Commission on International Religious Freedom, *Burma: Religious Freedom and Related Human Rights Violations Are Hindering Broader Reforms: Findings from a Visit of the U.S. Commission on International Religious Freedom* (Washington, DC: US Commission of International Religious Freedom, 2014), 4.
[85] Human Rights Watch, "Burma: Scrap Proposed Discriminatory Marriage Law," last modified March 24, 2014, www.hrw.org/news/2014/03/24/burma-scrap-proposed-discriminatory-marriage-law.

The targeting of the Rohingya is not just rhetorical in nature. During the Naga Min (Dragon King) operation of 1978 under the direction of General Ne Win, the Burmese government attempted to rid the Arakan state of the Rohingya under the auspices of combating illegal immigration. The operation resulted in "widespread reports of forced labor, torture, rapes, and mass killing," leading 250,000 Rohingya refugees to flee to Bangladesh.[86] A second operation called Pyi Thaya (Clean and Beautiful Nation) commenced in 1991 for the same purpose, resulting in another 200,000 people leaving the country. After Pyi Thaya, the military ramped up its presence in the predominantly Rohingya western state of Rakhine. This period saw more persecution of the Rohingya, including confiscation of property, destruction of mosques (sometimes replaced with Buddhist temples), forced labor and more coerced migration.[87] Today, the government through various policies continues to subject Rohingya Muslims to "physical abuse, arbitrary arrest and detention, restrictions on religious practice and travel ... and various forms of discrimination."[88]

State policy has encouraged Buddhist extremism at the society level as well, which has been an ongoing reality in Burma since independence, particularly in Rakhine state. Several Buddhist nationalist groups have circulated anti-Muslim literature in print and online, and the Buddhist Committee for Protection of Race and Religion (Ma Ba Tha) endorsed the passage of Burma's 2015 "race and religion protection laws" – comprised of the Buddhist Women Special Marriage Law, the Religious Conversion Law, the Population Control Law and the Monogamy Law – which essentially codify religious discrimination in Burmese society. In some parts of the country, Buddhists have prevented Muslims from living in certain areas or refused to sell or rent them land. Inspired by the militant monk Ashin Wirathu – the charismatic and commanding spiritual leader of the extremist 969 nationalist movement (numbers believed to capture the key virtues of Buddhism), who takes the moniker "Burmese bin Laden" – Buddhist mobs have systematically targeted members of minority faiths, particularly the Rohingya.[89] Wirathu, the abbot of the Mesoeyein Monastery in Mandalay, who served a jail sentence from 2003 to 2010 for inciting mob violence against Muslims in 2001, has, since his release, preached a message of blatant hatred toward and fear of the Rohingya, believing that they represent an existential threat to the Buddhist character of Burma and whose presence compromises the country's religious purity: "They would like to occupy our country, but

---

[86] Karin Solveig Bjornson and Kurt Jonassohn, *Genocide and Gross Human Rights Violations in Comparative Perspective* (New Brunswick, NJ: Transaction Publishers, 1998), 263.
[87] Greg Constantine, "Exiled to Nowhere: Burma's Rohingya," last modified 2018, www .exiledtonowhere.com/.
[88] US Department of State Bureau of Democracy, Human Rights and Labor, "Burma," 2015 *International Religious Freedom Report*, last modified 2015, www.state.gov/documents/organization/ 256305.pdf.
[89] The numbers 969 refer to virtues of the Buddha, the practices of the faith and the Buddhist community.

I won't let them. We must keep Myanmar Buddhist ... Taking care of our own religion and race is more important than democracy."[90]

Wirathu's sentiments capture a deep-seated fear among the Buddhist population that high Muslim population growth endangers Burma's Buddhist heritage and identity. For example, Shwe Maung, the Rakhine government spokesperson, once lamented the Rohingya conspiracy to "Islamise us through their terrible birthrate."[91] The 969 movement seeks to build in-group cohesion among Buddhists and marginalize Muslims by, among other things, boycotting Muslim businesses while patronizing only Buddhist ones as part of its "Buy Buddhist" campaign. The movement is also violent – its leading spokespersons openly call for attacks against all Muslims living in Burma, not just the Rohingya. In 2017, for example, Wirathu praised the assassination of a prominent Muslim attorney and thanked the alleged killers.[92] Wirathu has been able to effectively spread his message of hate, intensify hostilities and incite violence through his adroit use of social media. His activities were praised by President Thein Sein and influential monks.[93] Even the country's highest Buddhist authority, the State Sangha Maha Nayaka Committee, until recently, failed to exercise its moral authority to condemn Buddhist violence.

Discriminatory laws and societal repression of religion have directly led to religious violence carried out by both Buddhists and minority religious groups, including many terrorist attacks. Since 2010, the country has witnessed a renewed spate of religious conflict, a development that has, interestingly enough, coincided with Burma's transition to parliamentary democracy. In 2012, Burma entered a particularly violent phase of religious conflict between Buddhists and Muslims in Rakhine state. The conflict, which began as an allegation of rape of a Buddhist Rakhine woman by three Muslim men, eventually led to 200 Rohingya casualties, the forced displacement of 100,000 civilians, the destruction of 3,000 homes and fourteen religious buildings and a state of emergency being declared in Rakhine state.[94] Victims of the violence included women and children. According to Human Rights Watch, coordinated terrorist attacks on Muslim neighborhoods were orchestrated by Burmese officials, community leaders and monks backed by the state's security forces.[95] The violence was not contained to Rakhine state but spread across

[90] Hannah Beech, "The Face of Buddhist Terror," *Time*, July 1, 2013, http://content.time.com/time/magazine/article/0,9171,2146000,00.html.

[91] Banyan, "Unforgiving History: Why Buddhists and Muslims in Rakhine State Are at Each Other's Throats," *The Economist*, last modified November 3, 2012, www.economist.com/news/asia/21565638-why-buddhists-and-muslims-rakhine-state-myanmar-are-each-others%E2%80%99-throats-unforgiving.

[92] US Commission on International Religious Freedom, *2017 Annual Report*, 24.

[93] Mikael Gravers, "Anti-Muslim Buddhist Nationalism in Burma and Sri Lanka, Religious Violence and Globalized Imaginaries of Endangered Identities," *Contemporary Buddhism* 16, no. 1 (2015): 1–27.

[94] Neghinpao Kipgen, "Conflict in Rakhine State in Myanmar: Rohingya Muslims' Conundrum," *Journal of Muslim Minority Affairs* 33, no. 2 (2013): 398–410.

[95] Human Rights Watch, *All You Can Do Is Pray: Crimes against Humanity and Ethnic Cleansing of Rohingya Muslims in Burma's Arakan State* (New York, NY: Human Rights Watch, 2013).

the entire country to include non-Rohingya Muslims. In Mandalay, mob violence against Muslims resulted in several casualties and vandalized property, including religious sites. In the town of Meiktili, several mosques and houses were destroyed; 8,000 civilians were displaced.[96] While the government has taken some efforts to contain the violence, the authorities have, by and large, failed to protect vulnerable communities, and many of the perpetrators of the violence have yet to be brought to justice.

Predictably, minority religious discrimination and increasing despair among the Rohingya have driven more of the country's Muslim population to consider violence against the state, despite the fact that the Rohingya have historically not been prone to extremism. In 2017, a new terrorist group calling itself the Arakan Rohingya Salvation Army (ARSA) emerged. Led by a committee of Rohingya emigres in Saudi Arabia, the organization claims to "defend, salvage and protect" the Rohingya from atrocities carried out by the Burmese government and its supporters. Operating primarily in Rakhine state, where the greatest persecution against the Rohingya has taken place, the ARSA (and its predecessor, Harakah al-Yaqin) claimed responsibility for several attacks against police officers and members of the security forces. In October 2016, Harakah al-Yaqin attacked border posts in Rakhine state, killing nine police officers. On August 25, 2017, the ARSA killed twelve individuals in an attack against thirty police posts in Rakhine state. These strikes prompted a renewed and, by all accounts, wildly disproportionate crackdown described by the Burmese military itself as "clearance operations," marked by "extrajudicial killings; death by shooting, stabbing, burning, and beating; killing of children; enforced disappearances; rape and other sexual violence; arbitrary detention and arrests; looting and destruction of property, including by arson; and enhanced restrictions on religious freedom."[97] The operations cut off humanitarian aid and caused more than 600,000 Rohingya to flee their homes and cross the border into Bangladesh, all of which prompted further backlash. By the end of 2017, violence committed by Rohingya extremists reached an historic high.

Religious conflict has also spread to the neighboring countries of Thailand, Indonesia and Malaysia – all states with sizable Rohingya minorities. Some worry that radical Islamic groups throughout Southeast Asia will have an easier time recruiting terrorists if they can effectively exploit the treatment of the Rohingya in Burma to their advantage. In Malaysia, several Buddhist migrants were killed in 2013 in retribution for Buddhist attacks against Muslims in Burma. In Indonesia, two men were arrested for a plot to bomb the Burmese embassy in Jakarta. The attack was planned to protest how Burma treats its Muslim minority. In 2013, Islamist terrorists

---

[96]   Gravers, "Spiritual Politics, Political Religion, and Religious Freedom in Burma," 50.
[97]   BBC News, "Myanmar: Who Are the Arakan Rohingya Salvation Army?" *BBC News*, last modified September 6, 2016, www.bbc.com/news/world-asia-41160679; Katie Hunt, "Rohingya Crisis: How We Got Here," *CNN*, last modified November 12, 2017, www.cnn.com/2017/11/12/asia/rohingya-crisis-timeline/index.html.

staged an attack on the Ekayana Buddhist Center in Indonesia. In 2016, extremist Islamist groups in Malaysia and Indonesia called on coreligionists to kill Buddhists. These developments might ultimately have the effect of reinforcing dominant Buddhist narratives of fear, dampening the plight of the Rohingya further and generating a refugee crisis in bordering countries.[98]

Beyond the Rohingya, governmental preference for Buddhism has led to maltreatment of Christian groups as well. Christian minorities, particularly the predominantly Christian Karen ethnic group, have accused the regime of forcing them to become Buddhists. In the western Chin state, for example, the army has pursued a policy of destroying Christian crosses on hillsides and forcing Chin Christians to build Buddhist pagodas in their place. The military has attempted to drive the Karen people across the border into neighboring Thailand, raping and murdering women in the process and forcing thousands into labor camps. Reports have also surfaced of the army forcing Chin Christian children to convert to Buddhism in military-run Buddhist monastic schools.[99] In the Kachin state, more than 100,000 Christians have been internally displaced since 2011 as a result of civil conflict. Since 1996, the military has destroyed more than 3,000 Christian villages, leaving more than one million people displaced, according to the nongovernmental organization Christian Solidarity Worldwide.

Like the Rohingya, minority Christian groups have also taken up the gun. Resistance movements like the Karen Independence Army have waged war against the central government since independence with the goal of achieving self-determination. The Karen situation has also attracted a number of foreign combatants who fight on behalf of their Christian brethren, an example of the "solicitation" pathway discussed in the opening chapter.[100] Though different ceasefire agreements have been signed at various points throughout the conflict, persecution of Christians by the Burmese authorities continues to this day, as does the violent resistance.

Today, Burma is in the midst of a transition to democracy after more than fifty years of military rule – a process with immensely significant ramifications for religious freedom and faith-based violence. Civil society is active and growing; the media have greater freedom; political actors can now organize in a way that was previously impossible. Optimists remain hopeful that Burma's transition to democracy will result in the realization of full human rights for all of Burma's religious communities. Thus far, however, Burma's democratic experiment has only served to further alienate the Rohingya – who are not allowed to participate either as candidates or as voters – and to embolden the voices of extremism who have abused the

[98] Elaine Coates, "Interreligious Violence in Myanmar: A Security Threat to Southeast Asia," *RSIS Commentaries* 117 (2013): 1–3.
[99] Christian Solidarity Worldwide, "Burma," last modified January 11, 2018, www.csw.org.uk/our_work_profile_burma.htm.
[100] Thomas Bleming, *War in Karen Country: Armed Struggle for a Free and Independent State in Southeast Asia* (New York, NY: IUniverse, 2007).

greater freedoms of expression to fan the flames of sectarian chauvinism, allowing individuals like Wirathu and his followers to spread their ideas of hate. Complicating matters has been the fact that Burma's first state counsellor (a position akin to prime minister) and winner of the Nobel Peace Prize, Aung San Suu Kyi, and her National League for Democracy (NLD) have not taken a strong stand on minority religious rights or made the plight of the Rohingya a governmental priority upon assuming office.

In summary, mutual support between the monkhood and the Burmese state has given rise to a nationalist discourse that aims to protect Buddhist national identity by segregating Buddhists from religious minorities. This dynamic has also fueled religious terrorism against minority Christian and Muslim groups by lending official support to attacks carried out by militant monks. In certain cases, it has also provoked a violent backlash from beleaguered groups. It is important to note, however, that the vast majority of Buddhists living in Burma do not identify with the goals of the 969 movement. They recognize that the political manipulation of Buddhism to justify discrimination and violence belies traditional Buddhist beliefs. In fact, at least 20,000 Buddhist monks, in the face of governmental threats, arrests, harassment and violence, led the antigovernment protests of 2007 collectively known as the Saffron Revolution, which was instrumental in ultimately paving the way for a new constitution and democratic elections. More recently, the official monk-led association known as the State Sangha Maha Nayaka Committee distanced itself from the extremism of Ma Ba Tha, asserting itself as the true representative of Burma's Buddhist community. These voices stand in stark contrast to the armies of hate sweeping across much of the country. Whether the forces of moderation prevail going forward will greatly depend on whether Burma chooses to reverse its integration of religion and state and the systematic persecution of its religious minorities. Until that time, Burma stands as yet another case demonstrating that religious liberty and democracy are not always coterminous.

JEWISH TERRORISM IN ISRAEL

Israel is a unique case. Though officially a liberal democracy that respects religious freedom for all religious communities, the Basic Law also identifies Israel as a Jewish state, represented by the Star of David adorning its flag. Immigration laws allow any Jew to migrate to Israel and receive citizenship. Although the founder of the Zionist movement, Theodore Herzl, envisioned a country in which "the state will be the supreme authority and ... the rabbis will be confined to their synagogues," religion and state have been inextricably linked from Israel's founding to the present day.[101] The dual characterization – Jewish and democratic – has led to the formation of

---

[101] Jonathan Cook, *Blood and Religion: The Unmasking of the Jewish and Democratic State* (London: Pluto, 2006).

a partnership between synagogue and state, leading some scholars to describe the country as a "theocratic democracy" or "semi-secular democratic state" that has at times curtailed the rights of minority religious communities.[102] Political scientists Jonathan Fox and Jonathan Rynhold note that Israel has the highest overall level of government involvement in religion of any democratic state.[103] Because Israel exists as a Jewish state, in practice "religion and state are deeply intertwined such that Orthodox Judaism effectively serves as the established religion."[104] According to the most recently available report on global religious restrictions by the Pew Research Center, in 2016, Israel exhibited "high" governmental restrictions on religion, joining the ranks of countries like Algeria, India and Iraq.[105]

Since its founding, Israel has privileged the Orthodox denominations of Judaism over other Jewish traditions such as Conservative or Reform Judaism. This situation has had political implications. Select government policies are determined by Orthodox interpretations of *Halacha* (religious law). The state recognizes Jewish marriages within Israel only if they are performed by the Orthodox Chief Rabbinate. The Rabbinate also determines who can be buried in Jewish state cemeteries based on whether the individual was considered Jewish by Orthodox standards.[106] Furthermore, Orthodox Judaism possesses "a virtual monopoly on funding for religious institutions [while] liberal movements like Conservative and Reform Judaism have traditionally been shut out."[107] Haredi (ultra-Orthodox) Jews are exempted from the compulsory military service required of Israel's Jewish citizens. In addition, the government subsidizes 55–100 percent of the costs for Haredi religious education.[108]

With respect to non-Jewish religions, the Israeli government generally protects religious freedoms. Arab citizens, for example, enjoy individual rights, including freedoms of speech, assembly and worship, and are allowed to maintain Arabic-language schools and their own religious courts. Yet this does not preclude instances of discrimination and the curtailment of certain liberties for non-Jews. Such discrimination can be seen in the "political, economic, educational, land allocation, and housing arenas."[109] While a 1977 law allows for proselytizing, the Israeli

[102]   Almond, Appleby and Sivan, *Strong Religion*, 131; Ben-Yehuda, *Theocratic Democracy*.
[103]   Jonathan Fox and Jonathan Rynhold, "A Jewish and Democratic State? Comparing Government Involvement in Religion in Israel with Other Democracies," *Totalitarian Movements and Political Religions* 9, no. 4 (2008): 524.
[104]   Fox and Rynhold, "A Jewish and Democratic State?" 509.
[105]   Pew Research Center, *Trends in Global Restrictions on Religion*.
[106]   US Department of State Bureau of Democracy, Human Rights and Labor, "Israel," 2014 *International Religious Freedom Report*, last modified 2014, www.state.gov/j/drl/rls/irf/religiousfree dom/index.htm#wrapper.
[107]   Joshua Mitnick, "Israel Moves to Improve Religious Freedom – for Jews," *Christian Science Monitor*, last modified June 6, 2012, www.csmonitor.com/World/Middle-East/2012/0606/Israel-moves-to-improve-religious-freedom-for-Jews.
[108]   US Department of State, "Israel."
[109]   Jerome Slater, "Zionism, the Jewish State, and an Israeli–Palestinian Settlement: An Opinion Piece," *Political Science Quarterly* 127, no. 4 (2012): 611.

government actively discourages it and many (incorrectly) perceive it to be illegal. The Ministry of the Interior has cited proselytism as a reason for denying student, work and religious visa extensions, applications for permanent residency and building permits. In 1986, the Mormon Church received permission to build its Jerusalem Center only after promising the Knesset that it would not engage in proselytizing.[110]

Regarding (predominantly Muslim) Arabs living in Israel, a 2003 internal governmental report concluded that the "[g]overnment handling of the Arab sector has been primarily neglectful and discriminatory."[111] Jonathan Fox notes that a particular area of discrimination relates to the construction of holy sites: "While illegally built synagogues are often left alone, illegally built mosques are more often closed by the government."[112] The 2014 US State Department *Religious Freedom Report* further notes that Arab schools receive "proportionately less than the funding for religious education courses in Jewish schools."[113] Muslim citizens of Israel may also face restrictions in performing the pilgrimage to Mecca as required by Islam. Muslim groups in the Occupied Territories also find traveling for religious purposes especially cumbersome as a result of border closures or extremely long waits due to security concerns.[114] Minority religious discrimination can also be seen in the realm of security. According to terrorism scholar Daniel Byman, "Israel does not impose restrictions on Jewish religious institutions that turn out militants and violent propaganda. Some rabbis who justify violence even receive government salaries."[115]

All this has contributed to high levels of tension between Israel's various religious communities, including many faith-based terrorist attacks from both Jewish and non-Jewish sources. My analysis of the Global Terrorism Database reveals that Israel has suffered the eighth most identifiable religious terrorist attacks from 1991 to 2014 (247 incidents). This violence has been carried out by various religious communities, most often stemming from extremist Islamic, but also at times, Jewish groups. Somewhat paradoxically, both the privileged and the disenfranchised have felt compelled to take up the gun in the Israel.

Islamist terrorist groups – mostly originating from the Occupied Territories – have committed acts of terrorism against the state and its citizens. This violence has erupted, in part, due to certain discriminatory policies toward Muslims. Consider the justification for terrorism offered by Mahmoud Zahar, one of the cofounders of Hamas: "The Jews made their religion their nation and their state. They have declared war on Muslims and our faith system of Islam. They have closed our mosques and massacred defenseless worshippers at Al Aqsa and in Hebron. They

---

[110] US Department of State, "Israel."
[111] "The Official Summation of the Or Commission Report," *Ha'aretz*, September 2, 2003.
[112] Jonathan Fox, *A World Survey of Religion and the State* (Cambridge: Cambridge University Press, 2008), 243.
[113] US Department of State, "Israel." [114] US Department of State, "Israel."
[115] Daniel Byman, *A High Price: The Triumphs and Failures of Israeli Counterterrorism* (Oxford: Oxford University Press, 2011), 293.

are the Muslim-killers and under these circumstances we are obliged by our religion to defend ourselves."[116] During times when Israeli repression of Palestinians intensified and became more indiscriminate and widespread, support for terrorism increased among ordinary Palestinians, especially in the first few months of the *intifada*.[117] In 2015, the government imposed restrictions on the ability of Palestinian Muslims to access the Temple Mount/Haram al-Shariff, leading to a series of attacks by Palestinians against Jewish targets on the Israeli side of the Green Line and reprisal "price tag" attacks carried out by Jews against Muslims and their holy sites. In one price tag attack, Jewish militants attacked a Palestinian home in the village of Duma, killing an eighteen-month-old boy and his parents. The perpetrators spray painted in Hebrew the word "revenge" and a Star of David on the house.[118] In the following months, a wave of interreligious violence occurred in Jerusalem, the West Bank and Gaza.

Although Islamist terrorism has been the more prevalent form of religious violence in the Holy Land, not all terrorism in Israel is perpetrated by jihadist groups, as the example just given shows. Modern Jewish terrorism began even before the State of Israel was founded in 1948.[119] Groups like the Irgun (led by Menachem Begin, a future Israeli prime minister) and the Stern Gang adhered to the militant Revisionist Zionism of Vladimir Jabotinsky, which sought the restoration of *Eretz Yisrael* (the ancient land of Israel). Early terrorist groups like these justified the use of violence against Palestinians and the British in order to create the Jewish state. Of the scores of attacks carried out by Irgun, the most well known involved the bombing of the King David Hotel in Jerusalem – the hotel housing British administrative authorities – in which ninety-one people were killed. Irgun members also attacked Arab population centers, killing hundreds of civilians.

Subsequent Jewish terrorist groups like Brit HaKanaim (Covenant of the Zealots), Malchut Yisrael (Kingdom of Israel), Gush Emunim Underground, Keshet, Bat Ayin Underground and Lehava worked to achieve explicitly religious objectives: fighting the widespread trend of secularization, protecting the ultra-Orthodox Jewish way of life, imposing Jewish religious law, preventing the integration of Jews and non-Jews and establishing a *Halakhic* (religiously pure) state.[120] Newer Jewish extremist groups like Kach and the Jewish Underground have also grounded their actions explicitly in religion, their networks consisting of religious Zionists and ultra-

[116] As quoted in Beverley Milton-Edwards and Stephen Farrell, *Hamas* (Cambridge: Polity, 2010), 14.
[117] Bader Araj, "Harsh State Repression as a Cause of Suicide Bombing: The Case of the Palestinian–Israeli Conflict," *Studies in Conflict and Terrorism* 31, no. 4 (2008): 284–303.
[118] US Department of State Bureau of Democracy, Human Rights and Labor, "Israel," *2015 International Religious Freedom Report*, last modified 2015, www.state.gov/documents/organization/256481.pdf.
[119] Ehud Sprinzak, *Brother against Brother: Violence and Extremism in Israeli Politics from Altalena to the Rabin Assassination* (New York, NY: Free Press, 1999).
[120] Ian Lustick, *For the Land and the Lord: Jewish Fundamentalism in Israel* (New York, NY: Council on Foreign Relations, 1988); Ami Pedahzur and Arie Perliger, *Jewish Terrorism in Israel* (New York, NY: Columbia University Press, 2011), 31–37.

Orthodox Jews usually living in isolated and homogenous communities. In 1994, for example, Baruch Goldstein, an Israeli physician and supporter of Kach, killed twenty-nine Muslim worshippers in the Cave of the Patriarchs massacre in Hebron. Goldstein was a firm believer that Arabs should be expelled not only from Israel but also from the Palestinian Territories.

The integrating of religion and state in Israel has fueled the ideology held by some radical organizations that the country should exist as a land only for Jews. That Israel has established itself as a religious state – a "Jewish democracy" – has left it vulnerable to the claim lodged by some right-wing reactionaries that it is not sufficiently "Judaized." In some ways, these terrorist incidents represent a classic case of religious outbidding; Jewish terrorist groups attack Jewish Israelis and Jewish targets as well. Extremist groups like Kach, Kahane Chai and the Hilltop Youth believe that government favoritism of Judaism does not go far enough, and seek to establish a more sacrosanct regime, by violence if necessary, based on their interpretation of the Bible. They consider themselves the vanguards of authentic Jewish values, and believe that the very presence of Muslims in the land of Israel constitutes a serious obstacle to the redemption of the Jewish people as promised in the Hebrew Scriptures. For this reason, they have declared war not only against Palestinians but also against their own government.

Moreover, when Israeli leaders take conciliatory steps toward Palestinians, such groups fear the loss of their privileged station, sometimes lashing out violently. Two examples illustrate this logic. In 1995, Yitzhak Rabin became the only Israeli prime minister to be murdered while in office. He was assassinated by Yigal Amir, a young law student and Orthodox Jewish radical influenced by militant rabbis. Declaring that he was acting on what he believed were direct orders from God, Amir assassinated Rabin in an effort to derail the Israeli–Palestinian peace process after the prime minister's "traitorous" signing of the Oslo Accords in 1993, which would have prevented Israel from establishing sovereignty over the "Greater Land of Israel" – a paramount goal of many Jewish terrorists. In his view, any peace agreement that divided the land of Israel by ceding parts of the West Bank to the Palestinians ran counter to the will of God and had to be opposed by any means possible, including murder. Amir also believed that his actions were justified by decrees issued by extremist rabbis calling for Rabin's death, without which, Amir stated, "it would have been very difficult for me to murder."[121] The murder of Rabin achieved its desired objective: dealing a death blow to the peace process initiated by the prime minister. Ten years later, another prime minister, Ariel Sharon, announced his plan to have Israel unilaterally disengage from the Gaza Strip and hand over the territory to Palestinian governance. In response, Jewish terrorist groups and extremist settlers, claiming that the action compromised Jewish heritage and the rules of *Halakha*,

---

[121]   Leslie Derfler, *Yitzhak Rabin: A Political Biography* (New York, NY: Palgrave Macmillan, 2014), 176.

plotted several attacks against Israeli targets in the following months.[122] Israeli scholar Nachman Ben-Yehuda notes, "[t]he continued existence of [theocratic Jewish extremist movements] and the pressure they exert on Israeli democracy and its law enforcement powers points to the willingness of religiously pious Israelis to ignore democracy and resort to direct action, violence, and terror activities to achieve a non-democratic goal."[123]

Simply maintaining the status quo has not always been the prime motivation of Jewish violence, however. Ben-Yehuda argues that Jewish violence in general seems to be carried out with the intention of moving Israel toward a pure theocratic political system, hastening the arrival of the Messiah and initiating the subsequent redemption process.[124] The founder of Kach, Rabbi Meir Kahane, famously called for the expulsion of all Arabs from Israel and the complete "Judaization" of the state.[125] Kahane and his followers sought to bring Israel out of its secular state of sin. The rabbi viewed armed action as an appropriate means of purification: "Jewish violence in defense of Jewish interest is never bad," he explained.[126] Though the intensity and frequency of Jewish terrorism has waxed and waned since even before Israel's formal establishment, it stems from the central paradox in Israeli society: its claim to be both a liberal, democratic state and, at the same time, an exclusively Jewish one.

In sum, the case of Israel shows how government partnership with religion coupled with minority religious discrimination can lead to religious terrorism via different pathways. While some radical Orthodox groups, emboldened by their privileged position, continue to push for a more Jewish state, Islamist jihadists seek the destruction of Israel altogether. Both types of violence – Jewish and Muslim – stem, at least in part, from how the state has elected to mediate religion. This minority religious discrimination plays an important role in contributing to the seemingly endless cycle of violence, a cycle in which ideology and environment collude to foment terror. Even though the vast majorities of both Israelis and Palestinians long for peace, the violent actions of extremists on either side serve to strengthen the radicals on the other at the expense of moderates, thus undermining momentum for a comprehensive peace initiative. In the end, it is difficult to imagine that a country founded as a "Jewish homeland" can ever completely separate the political and religious spheres. However, unless efforts are made to address issues of bias and systemic privilege, Israel may not be able to create an atmosphere in which extremism, either Islamic or Jewish, has little room to grow, especially as the prospects for a two-state solution grow increasingly grim.

[122] Pedahzur and Perliger, *Jewish Terrorism in Israel*, 123–128.
[123] Ben-Yehuda, *Theocratic Democracy*, 99.   [124] Ben-Yehuda, *Theocratic Democracy*, 216.
[125] Ehud Sprinzak, "Jewish Fundamentalism in Israel," in *Fundamentalism and the State: Remaking Polities, Economies, and Militance.*, ed. Martin E. Marty and R. Scott Appleby (Chicago, IL: University of Chicago, 1993), 478.
[126] Sprinzak, "Jewish Fundamentalism in Israel," 480.

ALTERNATIVE EXPLANATIONS

A lack of religious liberty is obviously not the only factor that leads to religious terrorism, though it is an important and neglected one. This section applies three common alternative explanations for terrorism – poverty, foreign occupation and lack of democracy – to the countries surveyed in this chapter. The general inadequacy of these explanations in explaining terrorism suggests that, at the least, religious repression should be considered a primary cause of faith-based terrorism, even if in conjunction with other factors. This is confirmed by the statistical appendix at the back of the book.

The first alternative explanation is a lack of political freedom. The Polity democracy database codes the authority characteristics of states using a scale that ranges from −10 (strongly autocratic) to +10 (strongly democratic).[127] The Polity scores tell us much about a country's level of political freedom. In 2015, of the countries surveyed here, three – Israel, India and Pakistan – were fully consolidated democracies according to Polity. Central African Republic, Uganda and Burma were anocracies (somewhere between democracy and autocracy). Even Burma, which scores lowest on democracy of the country cases, has been transitioning toward democracy since 2011. Yet democracy or moves toward it have not inoculated these countries from religious terrorism. The one thing that these countries have in common is not their level of political freedom but rather that they restrict religious liberty in different ways. Let us consider the countries surveyed in this chapter in turn.

Pakistan is the world's second largest Muslim-majority democracy, behind only Indonesia. Pakistan's political system has fluctuated between civilian and military governments throughout its history. Beginning in 2007, Islamabad started moving away from the authoritarianism that had defined its political system over the preceding decade. Today, Pakistan is as institutionally democratic as at any point in its post-independence history. This increased political freedom has not been accompanied by religious freedom, however. At the same time that Pakistan has been becoming more democratic, it has remained religiously restrictive. Consequently, in support of the argument of this book, this restriction has fueled both majority and minority religious terrorism. Its level of terrorism in 2017 was as high as it has ever been. Uganda and Central African Republic are anocracies – neither authoritarian nor democratic. Both countries have high levels of social religious regulation, however, and Uganda's governmental religious regulation has been increasing in recent years, while their levels of democracy have remained fairly constant. Christian terrorism in these countries tracks more closely with their levels of religious freedom rather than political freedom. The world's largest democracy,

[127] Monty G. Marshall, Ted Robert Gurr and Keith Jaggers, *Polity IV Project: Political Regime Characteristics and Transitions, 1800–2016*, Center for Systemic Peace, last modified July 25, 2017, www.systemicpeace.org.

India, has been classified by Polity as a consolidated democracy every year since its independence. In terms of religious liberty, however, India has seen moderate-to-high levels of governmental regulation and consistently very high levels of social regulation of religion. These forms of religious restriction have dovetailed to make India one of the world's most terror-prone countries, one that has experienced attacks by both majority Hindu and minority Sikh, Muslim and Christian groups. Unlike the previous three countries, Burma has only recently begun its democratic transition, having been under military rule from 1962 to 2011. To be sure, Burma is not a consolidated democracy, yet it is important to note that its democratic transition has coincided with a spike in terrorism. In 2017, Burma witnessed more terrorist attacks than at any point in the previous twenty years. As argued in this chapter, a good part of the explanation has to do with Burma's high levels of minority religious restriction, which have actually increased after the country's partial transition to civilian rule. Finally, Israel has functioned as a full-fledged democracy since its founding in 1948. Yet it is also a country that continually exhibits minority religious restriction, which has fueled Jewish terrorism against both the Jewish state and Palestinians as well as terrorism from Palestinian sources.

The second alternative explanation points to poverty as the main driver of terrorism. The countries examined here represent a broad spectrum of wealth. According to the World Bank, in 2015, Israel's GDP/capita stood at approximately $36,000. The other countries are poorer. India's GDP/capita was $1,582, Pakistan's $1,429, Burma's $1,203, Uganda's $676 and Central African Republic's $307. Israel ranks in the top 15 percent of countries in terms of GDP per capita. Yet despite its relatively high level of wealth, Israel has experienced more than 2,000 terrorist attacks since 1970, more than 1,000 of which have occurred since 2001. Countries in the same range of wealth as Israel like New Zealand, Japan, the United Arab Emirates and Brunei have witnessed only four religious terrorist attacks between them during the same timeframe. India, Pakistan and Burma rank 139, 140 and 150, respectively, in a global list of countries ordered according to their wealth. The first two countries are also among the most terror-prone states in the world. The states ranked just above and below India and Pakistan in 2017 by the World Bank – Laos, Djibouti, Ivory Coast and Ghana – saw a total of only 101 terrorist attacks from 1970 to 2015, and only two attacks were carried out by religious terrorist organizations. By contrast, India and Pakistan have witnessed more than 20,000 attacks during that same timeframe, with a sizable proportion of attacks carried out by religious militants. Likewise, Burma witnessed 430 terrorist attacks from 1970 to 2016, with a significant uptick in religious attacks since 2011. Yet Cambodia, a fellow Buddhist country ranked just one spot lower, has seen virtually no religion-related terrorism. Uganda and Central African Republic rank among the poorest countries in the world. Together they suffered 568 terrorist attacks from 1970 to 2016. Yet similarly impoverished countries like Malawi, Madagascar, Gambia and the Republic of Congo have seen virtually none of the terrorism that has afflicted those countries.[128] In short, though the poverty hypothesis remains a popular explanation for terrorism, especially among policymakers, there is little empirical evidence to suggest that such a link exists. This finding is confirmed by the statistical analysis found in the appendix.

A third popular explanation for terrorism involves foreign military occupation. University of Chicago political scientist Robert Pape has argued that (suicide) terrorism has little to do with religion per se, and is better understood as a tactic to compel democracies to withdraw their military forces from a territory the terrorists consider their homeland. This argument says little about the cases examined in this chapter. Pakistan has been a sovereign, independent state since 1947, which has not experienced foreign military occupation. In fact, in Pakistan the problem has more to do with endemic *state weakness*, especially in the volatile Federally Administrated Tribal Areas (FATA) along the Afghan border, which have become a training ground for violent jihadi groups. In Central Africa, both the Central African Republic and Uganda have experienced a good deal of internal strife. Yet neither country has been occupied by a foreign power. Religious terrorism in these states thus targets governmental institutions or religious groups, rather than outside actors. India too has not been occupied by a foreign power throughout its postcolonial existence. India itself does hold part of a disputed piece of territory between India and Pakistan – Kashmir – but this conflict has nothing to do with Hindu terrorism in India. Burma, unlike other Buddhist-majority countries in Southeast Asia, has not experienced a major foreign intervention or occupation since its independence. Finally, Israel's occupation of the West Bank and Gaza is certainly an important factor behind Palestinian terrorism and has led to Israeli settler terrorism against Palestinians, but the occupation thesis has little to say about Jewish terrorism as Jews constitute a religious majority in Israel and Israelis are themselves not under occupation.

CONCLUSION

In the West, it is difficult to consider the topic of religiously motivated terrorism without attention turning immediately to the religion of Islam. This is largely because the attacks of September 11, 2001, carried out by a group of Islamic radicals, forced many to consider religious motivations for political violence for the first time and that the most prominent terrorist groups active today – the Islamic State, al Qaeda, Boko Haram – claim a basis in Islam. The reality is, nonetheless, that all faith traditions have given rise to religious terrorism depending on the time and context, and contemporary religious terrorism stems from a variety of religious sources. As noted by political scientists Ami Pedahzur and Arie Perliger, "[r]eligious

[128] Data for this paragraph taken from World Bank, *World Development Indicators* 2017 (Washington, DC: World Bank, 2017); National Consortium for the Study of Terrorism and Responses to Terrorism (START), "Global Terrorism Database," last modified 2018, www.start.umd.edu/gtd/.

terrorism is not a one-faith phenomenon. In fact, identical patterns of radicalization and the use of terrorism can be traced to any counterculture that adheres to a totalistic ideology, be it religious or secular."[129]

This chapter has surveyed religious terrorism in six different faith traditions across several countries. It reveals that under certain conditions, Christianity, Sikhism, Hinduism, Buddhism and Judaism have all had their own issues with violent religious extremism. Interestingly, the terrorism that is associated with these very different faith traditions tends to arise in countries where religion and politics are intrinsically tied up and mutually dependent, leading to discrimination toward, exclusion of or repression against particular faith communities. While the impeding of religious freedom does not account for every instance of religious violence, it does help elucidate an important structural consideration in the perpetration of terrorism in the countries surveyed here.

At the same time, while religious terrorism can be found in every faith tradition, it must be acknowledged that today it is most prominent in the world of Islam. Six of the ten countries hit hardest by religious terrorism since the end of the Cold War are Muslim-majority states. The majority of religious terrorists today claim an Islamic mantle; in 2016 the top eight groups that perpetrated terrorist attacks were Muslim. This reality necessitates taking a closer look at what is going on in the Muslim world, especially the countries of the Arab world. The following chapter examines terrorism in the aftermath of the Arab Spring. It reveals that the problems of violent religious extremism in the Middle East and North Africa have less to do with Islam per se and can instead be linked to decades of secular repression followed by sudden state collapse. It was this context that gave birth to the world's most feared terrorist group, ISIS.

---

[129] Pedahzur and Perliger, *Jewish Terrorism in Israel*, xiv.

3

Majority Religious Cooptation, Terrorism and the Arab Spring

Political scientists have long noted that the so-called third wave of democracy seemed to have bypassed the Arab world. In Asia, Europe, South America and Africa, significant progress had been made with respect to democratization since the 1970s. The glaring exception was the countries of the Middle East and North Africa (MENA). For a short time in 2011, it appeared that this wave of democratization might have finally found an inlet into one of the region's unlikeliest places: the smallest of the North African Maghreb states, Tunisia.

From 2010 to 2012, a series of major anti-regime uprisings across the MENA collectively known as the "Arab Spring" – the Arab version of the democratic awakening that occurred in Czechoslovakia forty years earlier called the "Prague Spring" – took the world by storm, shocking even regional specialists and generating unprecedented political and social tumult across the Arab world.[1] In Tunisia, Egypt, Yemen, Libya and several other countries, millions of Arab citizens took to the streets in protest of the hated dictators who ruled them, for the first time demanding fundamental rights and freedoms. The revolutionary wave of demonstrations, protests, strikes, rallies, marches and other forms of civil resistance made possible by the adept utilization of social media for the purpose of effective organization resulted in the overthrow of dictators in four countries, a sectarian civil war in Syria and a renewed round of conflict in Iraq. Other leaders who were not forcibly removed from office like Sudan's Omar al-Bashir and Iraq's Nouri al-Maliki announced that they would voluntarily step down at the end of their terms. While the proximate causes of the Arab Spring were myriad and included factors like youth unemployment, sharp increases in income inequality, rampant elite corruption, uneven distribution of benefits and skyrocketing food prices, at its core, the Arab Spring represented a profound dissatisfaction with inadequate political representation, repressive state policies and the quest of ordinary Arabs to shape their own destiny. In the words of renowned economist Dani Rodrick, "Protesters in Tunis and Cairo were not demonstrating about lack of economic opportunity or poor social services.

---

[1] F. Gregory Gause III, "Why Middle East Studies Missed the Arab Spring: The Myth of Authoritarian Stability," *Foreign Affairs* 4 (2011): 81–90.

They were rallying against a political regime that they felt was insular, arbitrary, and corrupt, and that did not allow them adequate voice."[2]

For decades, the Arab world has been caught in a struggle between secular repressive dictatorships, on one hand, and intensely illiberal religious opposition movements whom these secular dictators see as the primary challengers to their rule, on the other. Governments in MENA countries have historically used the potential for social conflict as a convenient justification for restricting religious rights, often in brutal fashions. The conventional wisdom among regional leaders has been that restrictions on a wide range of freedoms – including religious liberty – may be a necessary evil in order to realize the greater goals of order and stability. To this end, states attempted to regulate religious spaces and activities – a strategy that often backfired by inadvertently strengthening extremist voices. The result, consequently, was often the exact opposite of that which was intended: more sectarian strife and violence. The more brutal the dictator, the more violent the resistance became. In Algeria, for example, a military coup that denied Muslims access to the political system, coupled with indiscriminate repression of Islam, directly contributed to the rise of violent extremism and a civil war in which 200,000 people died.[3] Political scientist M. Steven Fisch finds that between 1994 and 2008, Islamists operating in authoritarian or illiberal democratic settings (including many Arab states) committed 61 percent of high-casualty terrorist bombings, resulting in 70 percent of all deaths.[4] For a moment, it appeared that this dynamic of repression and violent resistance might finally be changing.

Optimists hoped that the largely peaceful, mass pro-democracy protests that were part and parcel of the Arab Spring signaled an end to this cycle of repression and violence. Historian of the Middle East Rashid Khalidi expressed delight that Arabs were finally "shaking off decades of cowed passivity under dictatorships that ruled with no deference to popular wishes."[5] World leaders conveyed optimism for a better future for the people of the Arab world. The day after Egyptian president Hosni Mubarak stepped down from power, American president Barack Obama proclaimed, "[t]he people of Egypt have spoken, their voices have been heard, and Egypt will never be the same."[6] The uprisings also cast a pall on the extremist ideologies underpinning groups

[2] Dani Rodrick, "The Poverty of Dictatorship," *Project Syndicate*, last modified February 9, 2011, www .project-syndicate.org/commentary/the-poverty-of-dictatorship.

[3] Mohamed Hafez, *Why Muslims Rebel: Repression and Resistance in the Islamic World* (Boulder, CO: Lynne Rienner Publishers, 2003).

[4] M. Steven Fisch, *Are Muslims Distinctive? A Look at the Evidence* (Oxford: Oxford University Press, 2011), 151–155.

[5] Rashid Khalidi, "The Arab Spring," *The Nation*, last modified March 21, 2011, www.thenation.com /article/arab-spring/.

[6] The White House, "Remarks by the President on Egypt," last modified February 11, 2011, www .whitehouse.gov/the-press-office/2011/02/11/remarks-president-egypt.

like al Qaeda and their principal claim that the only way to bring about change in the Muslim world and depose corrupt, secular and despotic regimes was through radical violence. The protestors who gathered in Arab public spaces did not raise pictures of bin Laden or chant his name as they demanded the resignation of the dictators who ruled them. Instead, they sought to bring about change through peaceful protest.

Moreover, the strategy proved successful. Within days, Tunisia's president, Zine El Abidine Ben Ali, was forced from power, as was Hosni Mubarak in Egypt. The following months witnessed the departure of Yemen's Ali Abdullah Saleh and Libyan dictator Muammar Qaddafi as well. The exit of these leaders made possible through democratic, secular and nonviolent revolutions effectively destroyed the notion that only violence and religious zealotry could topple oppressive Arab regimes, while simultaneously removing a key source of grievance that terrorists could exploit. Faith in people power seemingly replaced the seduction of violent religion to bring about change. The same secular political processes al Qaeda's leadership once denounced as sacrilegious became the vehicle of choice to usher in a new era of Arab politics. Many hoped that the new governments in these countries would implement guarantees of human rights, in particular religious freedom for long-repressed groups, and that democratic transitions would entice Islamists to turn to the ballot instead of the bullet.

Nevertheless, as the initial wave of protests subsided in 2012, the region witnessed a general *worsening* of religious freedom conditions, especially for religious minorities who could no longer count on the protection of leaders like Mubarak or Qaddafi. Successive annual studies by the Pew Research Center have consistently ranked the MENA region as worst in the world in terms of religious freedom. The chart presented in what follows contrasts religious freedom scores in the Middle East and North Africa with the global average from 2007 to 2014. They show the median level of government religious restrictions is at least twice as high as the global average each year, and in certain years the ratio is much more acute. Furthermore, there has been an upward trend in these scores since the Arab Spring first shook the region in 2011, even while global scores have remained fairly constant.

The removal of strongmen in four countries proved not to be a prelude to liberty but the opening salvo in a violent struggle to shape the post-authoritarian political order. Initial displays of interfaith unity such as the group of Egyptian Christian protesters who formed a human chain to protect vulnerable Muslims as they performed their Friday prayers in Tahrir Square gave way to renewed communal hostilities between religious groups. In the states that experienced regime change as a result of the Arab Spring, religious majorities often exhibited social attitudes toward those of minority communities that ranged from discrimination and intolerance to open warfare. In some cases, previously repressed groups took advantage of the changing religious and political landscape not only to carve out a social and political space for themselves but also to intensify the marginalization of other

108

Weapon of Peace

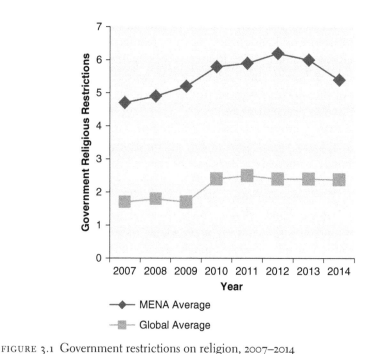

FIGURE 3.1 Government restrictions on religion, 2007–2014
Sources: Pew Research Center, *Global Restrictions on Religion*, last modified December 17, 2009, www.pewforum.org/2009/12/17/global-restrictions-on-religion/; Pew Research Center, *Rising Restrictions on Religion – One Third of the World's Population Experiences an Increase*, last modified August 9, 2011, www.pewforum.org/2011/08/09/ rising-restrictions-on-religion2/; Pew Research Center, *Rising Tide of Restrictions on Religion*, last modified September 20, 2012, www.pewforum.org/2012/09/20/rising-tide-of-restrictions-on-religion-findings/; Pew Research Center, *Arab Spring Adds to Global Restrictions on Religion*, last modified June 20, 2013, www.pewforum.org/2013/06/20/arab-spring-restrictions-on-religion-findings/; Pew Research Center, *Religious Hostilities Reach Six-Year High*, last modified January 14, 2014, www.pewforum.org/2014/01/14/ religious-hostilities-reach-six-year-high/; Pew Research Center, *Latest Trends in Religious Restrictions and Hostilities*, last modified February 26, 2015, www.pewforum .org/2015/02/26/religious-hostilities/; Pew Research Center, *Trends in Global Restrictions on Religion*, last modified June 23, 2016, www.pewforum.org/2016/06/23/trends-in-global-restrictions-on-religion/

religious groups, dispossess them of civic voice or repress religious minorities and heterodox believers in the majority faith. In these countries, despite headway at the ballot box, religious minorities continue to be persecuted; communal violence steeped in religion persists; and Islamic moderates remain silenced. In Egypt, members of the Muslim Brotherhood, their sympathizers and opposition leaders continue to be harassed, imprisoned and, in extreme cases, sentenced to death, while the conditions for Coptic Christians remain precarious. In Iraq, free, fair and frequent elections have become commonplace, yet the coming to power of hardline

Shia parties has left little room for Sunnis and religious minorities, who frequently are the targets of systematic discrimination, harassment and violent reprisals for injustices carried by out by Saddam Hussein. In the tribal societies of Yemen and Libya, the deposing of dictators has given rise to highly factionalized, post-authoritarian countries, leaving minorities vulnerable to high levels of social hostilities.

Terrorism, war and violence have increased as well. While the initial wave of revolutionary protests may have indeed represented a repudiation of jihadist ideas, this did not keep terrorists from exploiting the confusion and power vacuum that followed the toppling of long-standing dictatorships. Egypt and Tunisia, for example, disbanded their security forces and freed many jihadist political prisoners. Parts of Libya fell into utter chaos beyond the reach of the government, providing new openings for violent religious extremism to flourish. Instead of depriving jihadist groups of political space, the effects of the Arab Spring enabled terrorists who, initially left behind by the pro-democracy uprisings, took advantage of chronically weak central governments, fragility and instability. These developments led some to speculate that the Arab Spring had devolved into an "Islamist winter," characterized by widespread violence, abuses of human rights and instability.[7]

This chapter examines religious restrictions and faith-based terrorism in the Arab world, both before and after the Arab revolutions. Whereas the previous chapter surveyed countries employing a religion–state arrangement I call "minority religious discrimination," this chapter examines the second way in which government religious restrictions foment terrorism: majority religious cooptation. I focus on the Arab world inasmuch as many Arab leaders – most prominently Iraq's Saddam Hussein, Egypt's Gamal Nasser and Hosni Mubarak and Syria's Assads – have historically employed this *secular* version of religious repression. They have followed in the footsteps of Turkey's founder, Mustafa Kemal Atatürk, who desired to create a secular, Western Turkish state based in the principles of equality, modernity and nationalism. In contrast to states that discriminate against religious minorities at the behest of dominant faith traditions, regimes electing to regulate religion through its cooptation consider religion a potential or actual threat to their regimes and seek to keep its power in check, often through brutal force. At the same time, recognizing the deeply held religious convictions ubiquitous in their populations, Arab leaders have not sought the impossible goal of religious eradication, but rather its containment and exploitation made possible through cooptation. These leaders thus attempted to bolster loyalty to their regimes from among dominant religious communities through outward support for and even expressions of moderate faith, enforcing a temperate form of religion from above through the control and cooptation of religious institutions, religious political parties, school curricula, public

---

[7] Aaron David Miller, "For America, an Arab Winter," *Wilson Quarterly* 35, no. 3 (2011): 36–42; Howard J. Wiarda, "Arab Fall or Arab Winter?" *American Foreign Policy Interests* 34, no. 3 (2012): 134–137.

expression of religion and religious teachings. In countries governed by secular Arab nationalism, the state assumes responsibility for running mosques and schools, training and supervising clerics, monitoring sermons, conducting religious broadcasts, enforcing dress codes and publishing religious literature. At the same time that Arab regimes have attempted to coopt a nonthreatening, moderate version of Islam, they have simultaneously curtailed, often viciously, the practice of conservative or traditional Islamic interpretations, portraying their leaders as enemies of the state. The upshot is a form of government that, unlike communism, is not entirely irreligious, but at the same time, seeks to build modern nation-states through the subordination of Islam.[8]

This chapter proceeds in three parts. The first section takes a succinct look at the three Arab countries featuring the religion–state arrangement of majority religious cooptation that experienced regime change as a result of the Arab Spring at the time of this writing: Tunisia, Egypt and Libya.[9] I provide a brief background of religious repression in each of these countries, and argue that this legacy of repression masked widespread discontent and extremism that was brewing behind the veneer of stability. The process of state breakdown allowed these violent forces, already set in motion through secular repression, to emerge in horrible ways. These cases were selected for two reasons. First, because they are the Arab countries in which there was a regime change resulting from the Arab revolutions, they allow for an ideal test of whether a lack of political freedom generally or a lack of religious liberty specifically better explains the exponential increase in terrorism since the Arab Spring. Interestingly enough, all of these countries actually became *more* democratic after their revolutions (though Egypt eventually reverted to a military dictatorship). At the same time, they uniformly became less religiously tolerant. Second, in contrast to the previous chapter, which looked at the relationship between minority religious discrimination and terrorism, the cases in this chapter provide insight into the religion–state arrangement I term "majority religious cooptation" – a secular form of repression.[10] The second part examines the rise of the world's most infamous terrorist organization, ISIS, in the context of both secular and religious repression before and after the American invasion of Iraq in 2003. It makes the case that the American invasion and occupation of that country opened the door to an Iraqi government that systematically persecuted opposition groups, especially the minority Sunni community, which, in turn, fomented grievances, increased the appeal of terrorism and ultimately led to the rise of ISIS. These forces of terrorism, however, had been set into motion many years before the toppling of Saddam Hussein's regime. The final section takes on the contentious question of whether the problems

[8] Daniel Philpott, *Religious Freedom in Islam? Intervening in a Culture War* (Oxford: Oxford University Press, 2019).
[9] A fourth country, Yemen, also experienced regime change, but its form of religious repression was one of minority religious rather than secular repression.
[10] For this reason, I do not focus on theocratic-oriented countries like Iran or Saudi Arabia.

of repression and violent resistance in the Arab world are the product of Islam itself. It argues that the dearth of religious freedom in this part of the world has less to do with Islam per se and is tied more to the interests of those who wield power.

The Arab Spring began in one of the unlikeliest of places – the smallest of the Maghreb countries – with one of the least likely of people – an ordinary street merchant. On December 10, 2010, a 26-year-old fruit vendor named Mohamed Bouazizi began his day as normal, walking to the grocery store, where he purchased produce to fill his vegetable cart to sell at the market. Shortly thereafter, a policewoman confiscated his cart and spat in his face, a routine with which the merchant had become all too familiar. When he attempted to file a complaint with local authorities, he was refused an official hearing. Overwhelmed by these kinds of daily humiliations and frustrations, Bouazizi doused himself with paint thinner and lit himself on fire in front of the municipal government office.[11] What began with the immolation of an unremarkable fruit vendor quickly gave rise to countrywide protests against high unemployment and repressive state policies. The Tunisian "Jasmine Revolution" ultimately toppled the country's long-standing dictatorship and paved the way for massive revolutionary movements across the region and the demise of four authoritarian regimes.

Prior to the Jasmine Revolution, Tunisia had been ruled since independence by only two presidents: Habib Bourguiba (1957–1987) and Zine El Abidine Ben Ali (1987–2011), both of whom were ardent secularists and suppressed religious expression and democracy. These leaders positioned the Tunisian state in opposition to Islamic organizations, leading to official policies of religious marginalization. Though nominally a Sunni Muslim, Bourguiba governed as a committed secularist who emphasized a secular orientation over Islamic identity, modeling his regime on that of Kemal Atatürk's in Turkey.[12] Though making strides in the areas of education and women's rights, the Tunisian leader also prohibited the wearing of the *hijab* in public in 1957 through the Personal Status Law, eliminated sharia courts, confiscated religious buildings (including the historic Zaytuna Mosque, which eventually reverted to an Islamic university after the Jasmine Revolution), directed and supervised religious institutions through the Ministry of Religious Affairs (including training, paying and placing clerics), installed state-appointed imams and even appeared on state television during Ramadan drinking orange juice during

---

[11]   Yasemine Ryan, "The Tragic Life of a Street Vendor," *Al Jazeera*, last modified January 20, 2011, www .aljazeera.com/indepth/features/2011/01/201111684242518839.html.
[12]   Lewis B. Ware, "Ben Ali's Constitutional Coup in Tunisia," *Middle East Journal* 42, no. 4 (1988): 587–601.

daytime.[13] Bourguiba brutally suppressed the Islamic movements he believed posed a threat to his regime, arresting more than 3,000 Islamists and exiling many others, even as he controlled through cooptation nonthreatening forms of Islam.[14]

In a peaceful coup in 1987, General Zine El Abidine Ben Ali seized power from Bourguiba and clung to it via repressive laws, stifled political expression and a massive internal police force. After a brief thaw in relations between Islamists and the state, Ben Ali intensified state repression of Islam, and eventually worked to eliminate Islam from public life after certain groups became politically active.[15] Subsequently, all religiously based political parties were banned on the grounds that they promoted radicalism, social hostility and terrorism. As for social policy, Ben Ali restricted the rights of ordinary Muslims by, among other things, prohibiting women from wearing the *hijab* and other forms of "sectarian dress," banning the distribution of religious literature, censoring the content of mosque curricula and barring interfaith marriages between Muslims and non-Muslims.[16] Like his predecessor, Ben Ali detained, tortured, persecuted, jailed or exiled thousands of suspected Islamists, including members of the leading Islamic political party, Ennahda. Others had their passports or identity cards revoked. In sum, the Bourguiba and Ben Ali regimes sought to estrange Muslims from their religion, replace Islamic identity with an imported Western one and harshly suppress any political manifesta-tion of Islam. Thus, while Bouazizi's self-immolation may have been the proximate spark that ignited protests around the region, it was lit upon the tinder of several decades of political, social and religious repression and ended up causing a wildfire beyond anything the fruit vendor could have possibly imagined.

For many Islamists, the Tunisian state represented the enemy of Islam, and they did not recognize the legitimacy of either the Bourguiba or Ben Ali regimes. Yet Bourguiba and Ben Ali appeared successful at containing the forces of extremism and violence, due, in part, to Tunisia's tiny landmass, small population and lack of mountainous terrain that could sustain an anti-government insurgency. Still, violent forms of resistance were still present, as the state's harsh crackdown on Islam facilitated the development of radical Islamic theologies. On August 2, 1987, the day before Bourguiba's birthday, a group calling itself Islamic Jihad coordinated bombings on four hotels in the cities of Sousse and Monastir in which thirteen people were injured, most of whom were foreign tourists. Islamic Jihad and various other smaller groups carried out small-scale attacks throughout the 1980s and 1990s as part of a campaign by extremists to gain power.[17] For the most part, though, even if

[13]   Marion Boulby, "The Islamic Challenge: Tunisia since Independence," *Third World Quarterly* 10, no. 2 (1988): 590–614.
[14]   Susan Waltz, "Islamist Appeal in Tunisia," *Middle East Journal* 40, no. 4 (1986): 651–670.
[15]   Dalacoura, *Islamist Terrorism and Democracy in the Middle East*, 142.
[16]   Emad Eldin Shahin, *Political Ascent: Contemporary Islamic Movements in North Africa* (Boulder, CO: Westview Press, 1997), 100–101.
[17]   Michael Willis, *Politics and Power in the Maghreb: Algeria, Tunisia and Morocco from Independence to the Arab Spring* (Oxford: Oxford University Press, 2014), 175–177.

underlying discontent with the regime was widespread, the religious resistance to the secular state tended to occur through the nonviolent Movement of the Islamic Tendency (MTI) led by Rached Ghannouchi, which later became the Ennahda (Renaissance) Party. The government engaged in a policy of sustained repression of the MTI following its attempt to register as a political party in 1989, arresting more than 8,000 sympathizers.[18]

Bourguiba's and Ben Ali's anti-Islamist policies may have in some ways mitigated against the threat of terrorism at home, but this did not prevent the exporting of Islamist militancy to other countries via the dynamic of terrorist incubation discussed in the opening chapter. Tunisia, along with other Maghreb countries, provided thousands of radicalized foreign fighters known as the "Arab Afghans" to fight the Soviets after their invasion of Afghanistan in 1979. Many of these same war-hardened jihadis went on to fight against Bosnian Serbs in the 1990s. Circa 2000, an al Qaeda affiliate known as the Tunisian Combat Group emerged in Afghanistan, dedicating itself to the overthrow of the Ben Ali regime. One of the group's founders, Tarek Maaroufi, purportedly on orders from Osama bin Laden, assassinated the anti-Taliban commander General Ahmad Shah Massoud two days before the 9/11 attacks in the United States.[19] In 2001, Belgian authorities arrested Maaroufi on charges of recruiting men for training in the camps of al Qaeda.[20] A Tunisian, Serhane ben Abdelmajid Fakhet, masterminded the 2005 train bombings in Madrid, which killed 191 people and wounded another 1,841 – the most lethal terrorist attack in Europe since the 1988 Lockerbie bombing.[21] Finally, French-Tunisian Abubakr al-Hakim helped establish a network that sent jihadis from France to fight in Iraq. Among those who formed part of the network was one of the brothers responsible for the *Charlie Hebdo* attacks in Paris in 2015. The fact that many Tunisians elected to wage jihad in other parts of the world suggests that the secular repressive policies of the Bourguiba and Ben Ali regimes served to mask an underlying rage among the Tunisian polity at home while driving it elsewhere.

Unlike the other countries rocked by the Arab Spring, Tunisia has been hailed as its one success story. In short order, Tunis relaxed some of Ben Ali's oppressive policies, adopted a new progressive constitution, conducted successive free and fair elections and worked to include an Islamist opposition committed to democratic principles. In the country's first post-revolutionary elections of October 2011,

[18] Amnesty International, *Tunisia: A Widening Circle of Repression*, last modified June 8, 1997, www.amnesty.org/en/documents/mde30/025/1997/en/.
[19] Erin Cunningham, "Ahmad Shah Massoud, Assassinated by Al Qaeda but no Friend of the U.S.," *The National*, last modified September 6, 2011, www.thenational.ae/news/world/south-asia/ahmad-shah-massoud-assassinated-by-al-qaeda-but-no-friend-of-the-us.
[20] John Tagliabu, "A Nation Challenged: The Suspects; Arrests in Belgium Highlight Its Role as a Militant's Base," *New York Times*, last modified December 20, 2001, www.nytimes.com/2001/12/20/world/nation-challenged-suspects-arrests-belgium-highlight-its-role-militants-base.html.
[21] Elaine Sciolino, "Spain Struggles to Absorb Worst Terrorist Attack in Its History," *New York Times*, last modified March 11, 2004, www.nytimes.com/2004/03/11/international/europe/11CND-TRAI.html.

Ghannouchi's Ennahda Party won 37 percent of the vote. Forty-two women were elected to the newly formed Constituent Assembly. The new constitution was widely hailed as progressive, friendly to human rights and a positive step toward the consolidation of democracy, including decentralized and open government.[22] After coming to power, Ennahda openly professed its commitment to equality and civil freedoms as well as a more prominent role for Islam in public life. Further, Ennahda proved its commitment to tolerance by not seeking to implement religious law. Instead, the new constitution contained a number of provisions protecting freedoms of expression, belief and practice and the rights of women and religious minorities that were missing under the leadership of Bourguiba and Ben Ali. Although Islam remains the official state religion, it is not considered a source of legislation in the new constitution. State leaders have consistently urged protection for non-Muslim religious minorities, while denouncing acts of anti-Semitism and abuse of minority rights. Parliamentary and presidential elections in 2014 witnessed the decline in popularity of Ennahda, the rise of the secular Nidaa Tounes Party and the election of a secularist with ties to the Ben Ali regime, Beji Caid Essebsi. Ennahda surrendered its ruling party status peacefully and agreed to enter into a coalition government with Nidaa Tounes, thus completing Tunisia's transition to democracy.

Yet, despite the relative political progress made by Tunis, conditions of religious freedom became no better since the revolution, and the state's practice of majority religious cooptation continues. According to the Pew Research Center, Tunisia's government regulation of religion score stayed virtually the same from 2007 to 2014.[23] The years following the protests that brought down Ben Ali have witnessed a continuation of many of the same secular repressive policies, including strict oversight of the religious landscape and a new crackdown on Islamist organizations. The new constitution appoints the government as the "guardian of religion." The state continues to appoint, train and pay imams, preserves its privilege to appoint the country's Grand Mufti, maintains its power to remove imams it accuses of preaching "divisive theology" and has standardized mosque operations through-out the country. The state still has a penal code criminalizing insults directed at the government. In a manner consistent with majority religious cooptation, it also continues to imprison individuals for blasphemy against Islam. One such individual, an atheist named Jabeur Mejri, was sentenced to seven and a half years in prison for posting offensive cartoons of the Prophet Muhammad online.[24] The state has also been increasingly restrictive of religion in its counterterrorism policy. In response to

---

[22] Human Rights Watch, "Tunisia: Let Constitution Herald Human Rights Era," last modified February 1, 2014, www.hrw.org/news/2014/02/01/tunisia-let-constitution-herald-human-rights-era.

[23] Pew Research Center, *Trends in Global Restrictions on Religion*, 56.

[24] Amnesty International UK, "Jabeur Mejri, Imprisoned for Facebook Posts in Tunisia," last modified May 9, 2014, www.amnesty.org.uk/jabeur-mejri-imprisoned-facebook-posts-tunisia#.VcKFVqO89Kw.

separate terrorist attacks in 2013, the government closed eighty mosques and dismissed twenty imams, while the parliament passed a sweeping and repressive antiterrorism bill that allowed police to hold suspects for as long as two weeks without charge. The government also threatened to ban the nonviolent Hizb ut-Tahrir movement. The state of emergency declared after the 2015 Bardo Museum attack led to complaints by Islamists of discrimination, harassment and torture.[25]

Although the initial Jasmine Revolution protests revolved around secular concerns, the subsequent political reforms strengthened illiberal Islamic groups at the society level, as indicated by the Pew scores. Salafi hardliners exploited openings provided by the Arab Spring to impose sharia in their neighborhoods, threaten individuals they accuse of blasphemy, spread anti-Semitic propaganda, separate genders in public spaces, ban the sale of alcohol, enforce dress codes, shut down cultural events deemed un-Islamic, desecrate Sufi shrines and threaten secular activists.[26] Among the most important of these Salafist organizations was Ansar al-Sharia, a group devoted to establishing sharia as the law of the land. Clashes between secularists and Islamists seeking the application of conservative Islamic norms in society occurred regularly and sometimes turned violent. Some religious minorities complained that their communities have been subject to harassment, vandalism, intimidation and discrimination by Salafist groups on the basis of their religious affiliation, belief or practice.

Tunisia's transition from dictatorship to democracy has been complicated by the new space opened up for extremist groups to spread their ideologies of hate as a result of the democratization process. Less than three months after successful and peaceful legislative and presidential elections in 2015, the country suffered its worst terrorist attack in thirteen years – a shooting at the historic Bardo Museum in the heart of the capital, which killed twenty-one people and injured another forty. Another terrorist attack rocked the country just three months later when gunmen attacked a hotel in the coastal city of Sousse, killing thirty-seven people and wounding another thirty-six. Both attacks targeted tourists. In 2012, Salafi-inspired protestors attempted to ransack the American Embassy in Tunis after a YouTube video mocking the prophet Mohammed went viral. In 2013, a new group, the Uqba Ibn Nafaa Brigade, claimed responsibility for attacks on Tunisian security forces and political activists. My analysis of data derived from the Global Terrorism Database shows that from 1991 to 2011, Tunisia suffered an average of just 0.3 terrorist attacks per year; from 2011 to 2016, that number increased to twenty-three.

[25] US Department of State Bureau of Democracy, Human Rights and Labor, "Tunisia," 2016 *International Religious Freedom Report*, last modified 2016, available from www.state.gov/j/drl/rls/irf/religiousfreedom/index.htm#wrapper.
[26] US Department of State Bureau of Democracy, Human Rights and Labor, "Tunisia," 2013 *International Religious Freedom Report*, last modified 2013, available from www.state.gov/j/drl/rls/irf/religiousfreedom/index.htm#wrapper.

While domestic terrorism has increased since the Jasmine Revolution, the more important story regarding the connection between Tunisia and terrorism concerns its continued exporting of jihadism abroad, as measures increasingly repressive of Islam drive extremism elsewhere. In a reprise of the "Arab Afghan" phenomenon of the 1980s, Tunisia has become a fertile ground for recruiters from the Islamic State and Jabhat Fath al-Sham (formerly known as Jabhat al-Nusra), who have been able to exploit anti-state rage within Tunisia and channel it to the battlefields of Iraq, Syria and Libya, where many Tunisians have become suicide bombers. The country holds the dubious distinction of being the world's leading producer of international jihadism, far ahead of much larger countries like Russia and Saudi Arabia. As of 2015, more than 7,000 Tunisians were believed to have joined ISIS, and more than 3,000 Tunisians traveled to Syria to fight against the regime of embattled Syrian dictator Bashar al-Assad.[27] Others have flocked to radical groups like Ansar al Dine (Tunisians account for half of that jihadist rebel group) and al Qaeda in the Islamic Maghreb, both of which operate throughout northern Africa.[28] The fact that Tunisia has incubated and exported so many jihadists abroad – first to Afghanistan in the 1980s, then to the Balkans in the 1990s and more recently to Iraq and Syria – suggests that instead of eradicating militant Islam, secular repression has actually created a wellspring of underground rage and militarism.

In spite of these challenges, many hold up Tunisia as a successful model of an Arab country transitioning from dictatorship to democracy – indeed, the only country affected by the Arab Spring in which democracy can be said to have taken root.[29] Unlike in other countries, the birthplace of the Arab Spring has not ended up in state failure, civil war or authoritarian resurgence. Contrariwise, only ten months after Ben Ali's ouster, a new constituent assembly was elected and the legitimately elected government possessed the mandate and capacity to govern effectively. Tunisia's relatively successful experiment with democracy has been attributed to its ability to fall back on a strong and diverse civil society, including solid labor unions, robust civic organizations and viable secular opposition groups. Yet this is only half the story. Democracy alone has not been enough to curb the appeal of violent religious extremism. High unemployment rates, corruption, police brutality and worsening religious freedom conditions have all combined to increase the appeal of terrorism at home and abroad. How Tunisia deals with these issues, especially its stance on religious freedom, will determine much regarding the country's political stability and potential for violent religious conflict going forward.

[27]   Chris Stephen, "Fear of Tunisia's Democracy Led ISIS to Launch an Attack on Its Tourist Economy," *The Guardian*, last modified March 21, 2015, www.theguardian.com/world/2015/mar/22/tunisia-terror-attack-tourists.

[28]   John Zarocostas, "More than 7,000 Tunisians Said to Have Joined Islamic State," *Mclatchy DC*, last modified March 17, 2015, www.mcclatchydc.com/news/nation-world/world/middle-east/article24781867.html.

[29]   Alfred Stepan, "Tunisia's Transition and the Twin Tolerations," *Journal of Democracy* 2 (2012): 89–103.

EGYPT

The Tunisian "burning man" inspired revolutionary movements across the region, including in the Arab world's most populous and historically most important country, Egypt. A few short weeks after the Jasmine Revolution rocked Tunisia, Egyptian citizens, emboldened by their Tunisian counterparts, took to the streets of Cairo in protest of government corruption, endemic repression and failed economic policies. Hundreds of thousands of Egyptians joined together in the heart of the city, Tahrir Square, to demand freedom, justice, equality and an end to decades of autocratic rule. The world's largest Islamist organization, the Muslim Brotherhood (al-Ikhwan al-Muslimun), took part in the mass demonstrations, not to insist on sharia but to call for democratic elections. Despite the government shutting down the Internet to prevent the organization of further protests; using tear gas, live ammunition and water cannons to disperse the crowds; and a last-ditch effort by Egyptian leader Hosni Mubarak to placate protestors by offering limited political reforms, the demonstrations continued to grow.[30] The eighteen-day uprising eventually witnessed the resignation of Mubarak on February 11, 2011 – twenty-nine years after he first came to power in 1981 – and the transferring of power to the armed forces of Egypt.

Though freedom of belief and worship were discursively enshrined in both the old and new Egyptian constitutions, in practice, successive Egyptian leaders have suppressed it since independence through cooptation of Islam. At the same time that the constitutions provided for religious liberty, they also specified Islam to be the religion of the state and the principles of sharia to be the primary source of legislation. This deference to Islam, nonetheless, was an attempt to appease the Egyptian population, which always remained strongly Muslim in identity and highly religious in belief and practice. The political theology of the state remained resolutely secular in nature.

Following the Free Officer's Coup in 1952, Gamal Abdel Nasser sought to control, manipulate, subordinate and, most importantly, mobilize religion for his own purposes via a policy of majority religious cooptation, thereby preventing any challenges to his rule stemming from religious institutions, particularly the Muslim Brotherhood led by cleric Hasan al-Banna.[31] He placed public Islam under the direction of the state, specifically the Ministry of Religious Endowments, from which the government could gain greater jurisdiction over the country's mosques – more than 1,000 of which it constructed, funded and packed with state-endorsed clerics who sanctioned the goals and policies of the regime.[32] Nasser also confiscated religious property, closed Islamic courts and controlled

---

[30] Mohammed Abouelleil Rashed and Islam El Azzazi, "The Egyptian Revolution: A Participant's Account from Tahrir Square," *Anthropology Today* 27, no. 2 (2011): 22–27.

[31] Richard P. Mitchell, *The Society of the Muslim Brothers* (Oxford: Oxford University Press, 1993).

[32] Hibbard, *Religious Politics and Secular States*, 49–79.

religious television programming and education. At the same time, Nasser was also deliberate about publicly displaying his own fidelity to Islam, making the pilgrimage to Mecca shortly after coming to power. In these ways, Nasser's version of majority religious cooptation would become a pattern that future leaders in the region, both Egyptian and non-Egyptian, would emulate.

Yet in attempting to refashion Egypt as a secular society through the suppression of Islam, Nasser created the very conditions conducive for the growth of an anti-regime political theology of violence that rapidly gained support among the population, culminating in an assassination attempt on the Egyptian leader himself in 1954, which prompted a subsequent crackdown on the Brotherhood involving mass arrests of the Brothers, their removal from various branches of the government and the execution of the organization's top-tier leadership. In the 1950s and 1960s, the regime continued its mass arrests and detained tens of thousands of Brotherhood members in squalid prisons – an experience that greatly contributed to the radicalization of some Islamist segments and the development of the theology that would eventually be taken up by the likes of Osama bin Laden and other militant jihadis. This can be seen most vividly in the writings of the Muslim Brotherhood's leading ideologue, Sayed Qutb, who advocated a religious holy war (jihad) as a legitimate measure to overthrow what he believed was a thoroughly corrupt, secular, discredited and apostate (*takfir*) regime, which had led Egyptians into a renewed condition of religious ignorance (*neo-Jahliyya*).[33] Qutb's redefinition of jihad stemmed, in large part, from his own treatment at the hands of Nasser, who had Qutb imprisoned, tortured and eventually executed. Qutb's ideas would be taken up by radical groups like al-Jihad, al Takfir wa Hijra, Jund Allah, al-Gama'a al-Islamiyya and al Qaeda, all of which subscribed to the belief that violence was necessary in order to create a proper Islamic state in Egypt and beyond, thus globalizing Qutb's vision.[34]

Nasser's successor, Anwar al-Sadat, by contrast, tended (at least at first) to treat Islam quite differently than his predecessor. As part of his "Corrective Revolution," Sadat, known as the "believing president," attempted to partner with religion and use the institutions of the state to actively promote Islamic fundamentalism by expanding religious education, increasing Islamic television programming, cultivating a close relationship with the Brotherhood, backing Islamic student organizations on university campuses, giving Salafists prominent positions in the government and incorporating aspects of sharia into Egypt's statutory laws. These measures were undertaken in order to marginalize the left and holdover supporters of Nasser's Arab socialism, while buttressing Sadat's own legitimacy.[35]

---

[33] Sayyid Qutb, *Al-Adala al-Ijimaiyya fi-I Islam* (Beirut: Dar al-Kitab al-Arabi, 1979).
[34] Ahmad S. Moussalli, *Radical Islamic Fundamentalism: The Ideological and Political Discourse of Sayyid Qutb* (Beirut: American University of Beirut, 1992).
[35] Carrie Rosefsky Wickham, *Mobilizing Islam: Religion, Activism, and Political Change in Egypt* (New York, NY: Columbia University Press, 2002), 93–118.

Eventually, however, Nasser's successor came to the belated realization that in partnering with an illiberal rendering of religion, he had inadvertently empowered radical groups that jeopardized his rule. In September 1981, Sadat's security forces rounded up and jailed more than 1,500 individuals believed to be sympathizers of al-Gama'a al-Islamiyya. The following month Sadat was assassinated by one of the members of al-Jihad. Sadat's assassination occurred at the hands of Muslim radicals, despite his attempt at partnering with conservative Islam. It also resulted in the passage of an emergency law that has been in place ever since and used to justify sharp limits on basic human rights.

Hosni Mubarak initially followed in Sadat's footsteps. He tried to align with illiberal Islamic groups, but then repressed those same groups when they posed a threat to his regime. Increasing dominance of Islam on the part of the Egyptian government, especially its treatment of Brotherhood members, including arrests, imprisonments, indiscriminate sweeps and torture, resulted in an overall lack of legitimacy, which, in turn, added credence to the claims made by radical groups that violence was not only an appropriate response but a necessary one to defend Islam. Mubarak's actions directly contributed to the radicalized political theologies of embattled individuals like Ayman al-Zawahiri and Omar Abdel Rahman, thus sowing the seeds of al Qaeda. The state's blatant disregard for and assault upon the political and religious liberties of Islamists encouraged militant behavior, culminating in intermittent terrorist attacks on government and foreign targets in the 1980s and a prolonged insurgency during the 1990s led by al-Gama'a al-Islamiyya and al-Jihad. The insurgency targeted not only state officials and buildings but also tourists, civilians and journalists. Prominent attacks during this time included the assassination of former prime minister Atef Sedky, the killing of human rights activist Farag Foda, the attempted assassination of Noble Prize in Literature winner Naguib Mahfouz and several massacres of Copts and tourists. In 1995, an attempt was made on Mubarak's life in Addis Ababa. Although the state was ultimately able to put down the insurgency, it continued to harass both majority-Muslim and minority communities like Shia Muslims, Christians and Baha'is, contributing to the overall narrative of grievance against the regime. Prior to Egypt's revolution in 2011, regime legitimacy was extremely low.[36]

Although Tunisia's and Egypt's paths to democracy started down similar paths in 2011 – both overthrowing dictators and implementing democratic reforms at the same time – Egypt's brief experiment turned out quite differently. After Mubarak's overthrow, Islamist groups, taking advantage of the weak civil society they dominated, controlled the post-breakdown political landscape, gaining more than 70 percent of seats in the legislature.[37] Mohammed Morsi, the leader of the Islamist

[36] Mark Sedgwick, "Measuring Egyptian Regime Legitimacy," *Middle East Critique* 19, no. 3 (2010): 251–267.

[37] Jason Brownlee, Tarek Masoud and Andrew Reynolds, *The Arab Spring: Pathways of Repression and Reform* (Oxford: Oxford University Press, 2015), 115.

Freedom and Justice Party, became the country's first democratically elected leader. Before his election, Morsi purportedly made deeply troubling statements signaling what Egypt would be like under his presidency. As reported by the respectable Ria Novosti newswire, in a candid campaign speech to the students of Cairo University, Morsi declared, "The *Koran* is our constitution, the Prophet is our leader, *jihad* is our path, and death in the name of Allah is our goal." He went on to portend the "triumph of Islam" and the establishment of "*sharia* law" through his Freedom and Justice Party.[38]

In numerous ways, the Morsi government turned out to be an utter disaster. The Brotherhood ruled in an oppressive and sectarian manner, abused its authority, quashed its opposition by banning members of Mubarak's political party from holding office and excluded large portions of the population. The constitution drafted by the Brotherhood weakened protections for religious minorities, especially Baha'is, and banned blasphemy against Islam. Morsi's government was also inept, bringing the country into further economic and social malaise as unemployment and crime skyrocketed even as access to basic social services declined. To make matters worse, in November 2012, Morsi declared that his presidential decrees were above judicial review, in effect establishing a new form of dictatorship. In sharp contrast to Tunisia's Ennahda Party, the Muslim Brotherhood proved uninterested in sharing power or respecting minority rights. At the society level, Islamist watchdog groups, empowered by Islam's takeover of the state, began to police neighborhoods for inappropriate religious behavior, reportedly harassing unveiled women and those who purchased alcohol.[39] Christians, Shias and Baha'is faced widespread discrimination and persecution for "denigrating religion" or refusing to comply with Muslim cultural mores. Thus, as a result of both governmental and societal actions, non-Islamists were marginalized from Egypt's nascent democracy.

Violence increased under Morsi as well as the government failed to prevent, investigate or prosecute crimes against religious minorities.[40] Copts, in particular, witnessed large-scale attacks against their churches and reported physical abuse, intimidation and compelled expulsions by Islamist mobs and security forces from 2011 to 2013. On April 5, 2013, attacks by Islamist militants in al-Khusus resulted in the deaths of five Copts and one Muslim. As parishioners gathered at St. Mark's Cathedral in Cairo to mourn the victims two days later, the police joined together

---

[38] Ashley Lutz, "The New Egyptian President Reportedly Said 'Jihad Is Our Path and Death in the Name of Allah Is Our Goal,'" *Business Insider*, last modified June 25, 2012, www.businessinsider.com/morsi-says-jihad-is-our-path-and-death-in-the-name-of-allah-is-our-goal-2012-6#ixzz3gT13w97s.

[39] Robert C. Blitt, "Springtime for Freedom of Religion or Belief: Will Newly Democratic Arab States Guarantee International Human Rights Norms or Perpetuate Their Violation?" in *State Responses to Minority Religions*, ed. David M. Kirkham, (Farnham: Ashgate, 2013), 58.

[40] US Department of State Bureau of Democracy, Human Rights and Labor, "Egypt," 2013 *International Religious Freedom Report*, last modified 2013, www.state.gov/j/drl/rls/irf/religiousfreedom/index.htm#wrapper.

with a mob in laying siege to the mourners.[41] Morsi defended the Ministry of the Interior from criticism, saying that the police had tried to dispel the anti-Copt mob, despite evidence to the contrary.[42] In 2014, the Egyptian government released its fact-finding report regarding the unprecedented violence against Copts in the summer of 2013. It documented that fifty-two churches had been razed to the ground; twelve others had been damaged; numerous properties owned by Copts had been destroyed; and twenty-nine individuals had been killed. Most of the perpetrators of these attacks have not yet been prosecuted at the time of this writing, and the failure to protect Copts contributed to an environment of impunity.

In a short period of time, Morsi lost popularity and credibility, and the Brotherhood was poised to be defeated in the next round of parliamentary elections. But rather than letting the Brotherhood fail at the polls, on July 3, 2013, Morsi was officially ousted as president by Egypt's armed forces, which assumed power once again. The Morsi regime was succeeded by another round of military rule, this time in the person of General Abdel Fatah al-Sisi, chief of the Egyptian army. In May 2014, Sisi was formally elected president, reportedly receiving 96 percent of the vote. In 2015, a court issued a death sentence for Morsi (and sixteen other Brotherhood leaders) after being convicted on charges of breaking out of prison during the 2011 uprising against Mubarak that eventually brought him to power. Meanwhile, just months before, an Egyptian court dropped charges against Mubarak for his alleged role in killing protesters in 2011. The coup against Morsi and the coming to power of Sisi reflected a return to the days of Egypt's old authoritarian order. Not only did the military ouster of Morsi bring an end to Islamist rule, it also upended Egypt's first democratic experiment.

Upon assuming power, the regime of General Sisi increased its control over the country's religious institutions in a manner consistent with majority religious cooptation. Though touted by some in the West for his embrace of "moderate Islam," calls for religious pluralism and relative protection of minorities in contrast to his Islamist predecessor, Sisi's rule has witnessed a deepening persecution of Islam: the state has increased its control over all Muslim religious institutions and closed thousands of small mosques and hundreds of Islamic civil society and charitable organizations; the regime requires Muslim clerics to be vetted by the state and licensed through al-Azhar Mosque, which, according to the constitution, is "the main authority in theology and Islamic affairs," essentially making it an agent of the state; those who engage in preaching or religious teaching without a license from the Ministry of Religious Endowments or al-Azhar risk a prison term of one year and a fine of 50,000 Egyptian pounds; the Ministry of Education bans girls from wearing

---

[41] Wael Eskander, "In Search of a New Prayer: An Eye Witness Account of the Cathedral Attack," *Atlantic Council*, last modified April 8, 2013, www.atlanticcouncil.org/blogs/egyptsource/in-search-of-a-new-prayer-an-eye-witness-account-of-the-cathedral-attack.

[42] Human Rights Watch, "Egypt: Redress Recurring Sectarian Violence," last modified April 10, 2013, www.hrw.org/news/2013/04/10/egypt-address-recurring-sectarian-violence.

the *hijab* in primary schools and professors at Cairo University from wearing the *niqab*; Morsi's Freedom and Development Party has been outlawed; discriminatory laws and policies restricting freedom of thought, conscience and religion remain in place; courts have increased their prosecution, conviction and sentencing of citizens for blasphemy-related offenses in accordance with Article 98(f) of the Egyptian Penal Code; Baha'is and Jehovah's Witnesses remain banned by presidential decree; anti-Semitism persists in the state-controlled media; and the Brotherhood remains repressed, officially being designated a terrorist organization by the state in collusion with the once-independent judiciary.[43] In these ways, the Sisi regime has worked to eradicate Islamist groups as a social force in Egypt. The government maintains this oversight of Islam is necessary in order to effectively combat extremism and prevent radicalized clerics from inciting violence from within mosques.

These actions have also fueled religious repression at the society level between pro-Sisi sympathizers and the Muslim Brotherhood. For example, appearing on national television, a pro-regime preacher called for Muslim Brothers to be crucified or have their limbs cut off.[44] According to the Pew Research Center, Egypt's religious freedom scores for government regulation of religion and social hostilities involving religion jumped from 7.2 and 6.1, respectively, in 2007 to 8.2 and 7.7 by the end of 2015.[45]

The regime's heavy-handed approach to religion has also been marked by some of the bloodiest violence in modern Egyptian history. As Sisi broadly expanded the powers of the presidency, the military began a massive physical crackdown against political dissidents, journalists and civil society organizations, especially the Muslim Brotherhood, killing, jailing and torturing its members while driving the rest underground. In one particularly gruesome incident, the military systematically massacred 817 unarmed civilian protestors at Rabaa Square on August 4, 2013, as security forces ferociously disbanded two pro-Morsi sit-ins in Cairo. Human Rights Watch described the state's actions as likely constituting "crimes against humanity."[46] Yet not a single member of the security services was held to account for the massacre. By 2015, more than 40,000 Egyptians had been jailed, including both Islamic and secular critics of the government; hundreds of Muslim Brotherhood members had been sentenced to death in mass trials; hundreds more had "disappeared" as a result of extrajudicial abductions; more than 2,500 had been

---

[43] US Department of State Bureau of Democracy, Human Rights and Labor, "Egypt," 2016 *International Religious Freedom Report*, last modified 2016, www.state.gov/j/drl/rls/irf/religiousfree dom/index.htm#wrapper.

[44] Shadhi Hamid, "Rethinking the U.S.–Egypt Relationship: How Repression Is Undermining Egyptian Stability and What the United States Can Do," Prepared Testimony for the Tom Lantos Human Rights Commission, November 3, 2015.

[45] Pew Research Center, *Latest Trends in Religious Restrictions and Hostilities*, 61.

[46] Human Rights Watch, "Egypt: Rab'a Killings Likely Crimes against Humanity," last modified August 12, 2014, www.hrw.org/news/2014/08/12/egypt-raba-killings-likely-crimes-against-humanity.

killed and 17,000 wounded; and in 2014 security forces arrested Mohamed Ali Bishr, the sole remaining leader of the Brotherhood.[47] These developments led the US Commission on International Religious Freedom to recommend the State Department list Egypt as a "country of particular concern" every year since the Arab Spring first began.

Sisi's goals of achieving stability and security in the face of Islamist terrorism have been seriously undermined by his repressive policies; indeed, they have made the resort to violence on the part of beleaguered groups more likely. The coup, the massacres and the extreme crackdown gave the claims made by radical groups more credence than ever, fueling the very violent resistance the state claimed to be fighting. Egypt under Sisi experienced higher levels of violence and terrorism than at any point since the Islamist insurgency in the 1990s. My analysis of data derived from the Global Terrorism Database shows that from 1991 to 2011, Egypt suffered an average of slightly fewer than twenty terrorist attacks per year – and most of these occurred during the 1990s insurgency. After the 2013 coup until 2017, that number swelled to 276 – more than a tenfold escalation during Sisi's time as president. Under Sisi, sectarian violence has increased as well, particularly against Copts in Upper Egypt who have experienced "the most extensive [attacks] in Egypt's modern history."[48] Such developments also contributed to the formation of an Islamic State affiliate in Egypt calling itself the "Province of Sinai," which has seized on popular disillusionment with Sisi. This group coordinated attacks on July 1, 2015 that killed sixty-four soldiers in the deadliest terrorist attack in decades. That same year ISIS's Egyptian affiliate claimed responsibility for the bombing of a Russian charter jet over the desert north of Sharm el Sheikh, Egypt, which killed all 224 people aboard. Hundreds of soldiers and police officers have been killed in the Sinai; bombings in the capital, Cairo, have become commonplace.[49] In December 2016, twenty-nine people were killed in a suicide attack during Sunday services at Saint Peter and Paul Coptic Orthodox Church in Cairo, part of the Coptic Orthodox Cathedral in Cairo. In 2017, Islamist militants carried out the deadliest terrorist attack in modern Egyptian history inside a crowded Sufi mosque in the Sinai Peninsula, killing more than 300 people and injuring more than 100. ISIS-inspired attacks have also occurred in other parts of the country. On Palm Sunday 2017, ISIS coordinated bombings of Coptic churches in Tanta and Alexandria, killing at least forty-seven people and injuring more than 100.

47 Kristen McTighe, "Ex-Egyptian President Morsi's Death Sentence Upheld," *USA Today*, last modified June 16, 2015, www.usatoday.com/story/news/world/2015/06/16/former-egyptian-president-morsi-sentenced/28796565/.

48 Jocelyne Cesari, *The Awakening of Muslim Democracy: Religion, Modernity and the State* (Cambridge: Cambridge University Press, 2014), 179.

49 Editorial Board, "Stop U.S. Support for the Repressive Regime in Egypt," *Washington Post*, last modified October 28, 2014, www.washingtonpost.com/opinions/stop-us-support-for-the-repressive-regime-in-egypt/2014/10/28/0c871dca-5ebd-11e4-8b9e-2ccdac31a031_story.html.

Sisi used these attacks as a justification for expanding his powers as president in the fight against terror, further stifling moderates, alienating secular allies and aiding in the recruitment of jihadis. While the Sisi regime may have been successful at suppressing the Muslim Brotherhood and its supporters, this will likely prove a hollow victory insofar as it has fostered a climate unfavorable to the development of a moderate strain of political Islam. Especially problematic is what is happening behind the curtain in Egyptian prisons, where radical ideas and extremist movements steeped in religion have been incubated in the past. It is worth quoting at length Ahmed Maher, the leader of the nonviolent April 6 Youth Movement, who today finds himself imprisoned for violating Egypt's draconian protest law and advocating democracy:

> Prison has really become a breeding ground for extremists. It has become a school for crime and terrorism, since there are hundreds of young men piled on top of each other in narrow confines, *jihadists* next to Muslim Brotherhood members next to revolutionaries next to sympathizers. There are also a large number of young people who were also arrested by mistake and who don't belong to any school of thought.
> Everyone is suffering oppression and punishment inside the prisons.
> Everyone is accused of being either a terrorist or a member of the Muslim Brotherhood. This is turning the people arrested by mistake who don't belong to any movement into *jihadists*. Moreover, Muslim Brotherhood members are gradually becoming radicalized, since they suffer from inhumane treatment in the prisons. The authorities treat the prisoners like slaves, and this inspires a thirst for revenge, not to mention the undignified treatment that the families face when they visit. ISIS has exploited the situation. The Arab uprisings are not the cause, but rather the bloody authoritarian regimes that resisted change and resisted democracy, true justice, and concepts of tolerance, co-existence and freedom. This is what gave rise to ISIS and continues to drive it.
> Extremism found a foothold in Egypt because of Sisi's brutality and authoritarianism. The more the oppression and authoritarianism increased and the more freedom and democracy vanished, the more justifications ISIS and al-Qaeda have. ISIS is saying that your regimes are corrupt, unjust failures and we're the alternative. This is a disaster, because injustice generates extremism. For this reason, neither the coalition's strikes nor Sisi's raids will stop ISIS. Defeating ISIS requires freedom, democracy, justice and a culture of tolerance, co-existence and acceptance of the other.[50]

Going forward, Egypt faces major challenges with respect to guaranteeing religious liberty for all of the country's religious groups. The most important question confronting Egypt today concerns the lessons the Muslim Brotherhood will take away from its brief encounter with democracy now that it once again finds itself

[50] Moataz Shamseddin, "In Translation: April 6's Ahmed Maher on Egypt under Sisi," *Huffington Post Arabi*, July 29, 2015, https://arabist.net/blog/2015/8/17/in-translation-april-6s-ahmed-maher-on-egypt-under-sisi?utm_source=Sailthru&utm_medium=email&utm_campaign=New%20Campaign&utm_term=*Mideast%20Brief.

persecuted and excluded. For decades, extreme Islamist groups chastised the Brotherhood for its renouncing of violence and desire to institute change through politics. Will it now conclude that these underground groups were ultimately correct – that democracy is a dead end and that militancy represents the only way forward?

The Egyptian experience with religious terrorism is a familiar one throughout much of the Arab world. It is a story of repressive regimes, backed by the West, that became loathed by the population. These regimes became more repressive over time in order to survive, spurring the opposition to become more radical and violent. The lack of legitimate avenues for political expression and assaults on faith failed to disempower religion, however, but instead forced political activity into extremist mosques and madrassas, which served as important instruments of resistance under secular authoritarian regimes. From these centers of hatred and fanaticism arose both radicalized theologies and the recruits who declared war not only on their own governments but also on their key international backers.

LIBYA

Just two days after Ben Ali fled Tunisia, Libyan dictator Muammar Qaddafi appeared on state television publicly condemning the Jasmine Revolution.[51] On February 11, 2011, riots erupted in Benghazi, following the arrest of an outspoken critic of the regime. Protests quickly spread throughout the country and reached the capitol, Tripoli, on February 20. With these uprisings following the ousters of leaders of countries on both Libya's eastern and western borders, Qaddafi again appeared on television promising not to step down and urging loyalists to fight back.[52] Nevertheless, rebels quickly captured Libya's second and third largest cities, Benghazi and Misratah, respectively. After the fall of Misratah, attention turned once again to Benghazi, where pro-Qaddafi forces threatened to retake the city, despite the initial opposition success. As the situation deteriorated and momentum began turning against the rebels, on March 17, the UN authorized a no-fly zone over Libya and "all necessary measures" to protect civilians. Two days later, a NATO coalition led by the United States, France and the United Kingdom began airstrikes to cease the loyalist advance on Benghazi. By late August, rebel militias seized Tripoli, and in October, Qaddafi was captured and killed by rebels in his hometown of Sirte. Libya differs from the other Arab countries in which autocrats were forced from power in that, absent foreign intervention, Qaddafi likely would have remained in power.

---

[51] Matthew Weaver, "Muammar Gaddafi Condemns Tunisia Uprising," *The Guardian*, January 16, 2011.

[52] John Hemming and Dominic Evans, "Defiant Gaddafi Vows to Die as Martyr, Fight Revolt," *Reuters*, last modified February 22, 2011, www.reuters.com/article/us-libya-protests-idUSTRE71G0A620110222.

Muammar Qaddafi ruled Libya from 1969 to 2011 after coming to power via a military coup. The history of lacking consistent and centralized authority in Libya fostered the development of a system of power in which the state used tribal hierarchies to consolidate political power. Libya developed a patronage system in which economic benefits and political power were concentrated among the clans with strong connections to Qaddafi. As an oil-rich state, the Qaddafi regime was able to buy off the dissenters it did not repress. All political parties were banned, and civil society remained stunted.[53]

Although Qaddafi initially rewarded orthodox Muslims for their assistance in overthrowing the Sufi king, Idris asSanusi, by reinstating certain religiously based criminal codes, banning alcohol, appointing Muslims to important positions within the government, dismantling the Sanusi order and establishing Sufism as an enemy of the revolution, eventually he turned on the Muslim community in the wake of Sadat's assassination in Egypt, abandoning Islam as a source of governmental authority and establishing himself as the only leadership Libya needed.[54] In due course, Islamists, whom the Libyan leader now branded as "unjust heretics" and "allies of Satan," like every other group Qaddafi believed constituted a threat to the regime, came to be harshly suppressed in a "systematic, ruthless security crackdown."[55] The same was true for non-Muslim groups, including Baha'is, Hindus and Buddhists, all of whom were not permitted to practice their faith openly.

In a manner consistent with majority religious cooptation, the regime established a number of state-led religious institutions, closely monitored the activities of Islamic organizations, censored the content of sermons and publication of religious materials and passed several laws promoting Qaddafi's own understanding of Islam via the Ministry for Endowments and Islamic Affairs. Qaddafi proclaimed himself Libya's chief Muslim jurist and the only trustworthy interpreter of Islam and the Quran for the entire country, sharply repressing those who did not fall in line with his brand of Islam. After brutally suppressing and banning the Muslim Brotherhood in 1973, "most Islamic religious institutions [came] under direct government control."[56] Islamists, seen as a threat to the secular regime, were under constant pressure and surveillance, including the Sufi Sanusi order, which was banned due to its association with the pre-revolutionary monarchy. Qaddafi outlawed groups that refused to support official state doctrine or criticized the regime. The government backed and tightly controlled the Islamic Call Society (ICS), a moderate Islamic body, while banning all Islamic sects that did not fall in line with the organization.[57]

[53] Lisa Anderson, "Demystifying the Arab Spring: Parsing the Differences between Tunisia, Egypt, and Libya," *Foreign Affairs* 90 (2011): 2–7.
[54] Lisa Anderson, "Religion and State in Libya: The Politics of Identity," *Annals of the American Academy of Political and Social Science* 483, no. 1 (1986): 69–70.
[55] Yehudit Ronen, "Radical Islam versus the Nation-State," in *Religion, Politics, Society and the State*, ed. Jonathan Fox (Oxford: Oxford University Press, 2012), 139.
[56] Marshall, *Religious Freedom in the World*, 262.
[57] Fox, *World Survey of Religion and the State*, 235.

Individuals belonging to a competing brand of Islam were arrested; this was particularly true if they had attempted to mix religion and politics. Men were forced to shave their beards to avoid harassment, and, in extreme cases, death sentences were handed out to those suspected of being militant Islamists.[58] The manner in which Qaddafi manipulated and regulated Islam contributed to widespread grievances and support for the 2011 uprising.

Marginalized voices opposing the Qaddafi regime existed long before the Arab Spring swept over the Middle East and North Africa. In the 1980s and 1990s, the regime faced a serious threat from terrorist groups. The Libyan Islamic Fighting Group (LIFG), comprised of veterans who fought in the Afghanistan war on behalf of their Muslim brothers against Soviet forces, dedicated itself to overthrowing Qaddafi's government and implementing an Islamic state. In the 1990s, the LIFG confronted Libyan security forces in armed clashes on several occasions and attempted to assassinate Qaddafi in 1996 and again in 1998.[59] The LIFG officially joined with al Qaeda in 2007 and maintained ties to radical Islamic groups in various countries.

While the constitution discursively provides for religious freedom and some leaders have called for national reconciliation and peace, many of the laws that restricted religion under Qaddafi remain on the books, and the Ministry for Endowments and Islamic Affairs continues to administer mosques, supervise clerics and provide the content for Friday sermons, with no personal commentary allowed. In 2012, the National Transitional Council appointed a Salafist cleric to the position of Grand Mufti – the leading religious authority in the country – and in 2013, the General National Congress (GNC) voted that sharia would be the source of legislation in Libya and abandoned laws that contradict Islamic law. The interim constitution proclaims Islam to be the religion of the state.

Though the Arab Spring brought an end to the despised Libyan dictator and resulted in successful subsequent elections in 2012 and 2014, it did so at great cost, uncorking a violent Islamism brewing under the surface of Qaddafi's repression. The collapse of law and order that accompanied the regime's demise and the subsequent civil war allowed extremist elements – once effectively contained by Qaddafi – to gain traction and assert control throughout large parts of the country. Qaddafi's de-institutionalization of an already weak state left the country an "institutional wasteland" after his departure.[60] The political system remains fractionalized after fraudulent elections in 2014 and the creation of rival parliaments, each supported by different external powers, further contributing to the deterioration of

---

[58] Marshall, *Religious Freedom in the World*, 262.

[59] Gary Gambill, "The Libyan Islamic Fighting Group (LIFG)," *Terrorism Monitor* 3, no. 6 (2005), www .jamestown.org/single/?tx_ttnews[tt_news]=308#.VaBxe6OwXXs. Other groups like the Islamic Martyrs Movement had also attempted to assassinate Qaddafi on multiple occasions.

[60] Clement Henry, Jang Ji-Hyang and Robert P. Parks, "Introduction," in *The Arab Spring: Will It Lead to Democratic Transitions?*, ed. Clement Henry and Jang Ji-Hyang (New York, NY: Palgrave Macmillan, 2013), 20.

stability and national cohesion.[61] Libya remains plagued by tribal allegiances that jeopardize the prospects for achieving national unity and loyalty to Tripoli. The central government failed to exert authority evenly throughout the country or build the basic institutions of governance that would allow it to do so. As a result of its inability to maintain law and order, the government relied on a variety of outside militias and warlords to support the armed forces and police. For example, in the eastern part of the country, an armed group known as the "Libyan National Army" conducted a series of military campaigns against Islamist organizations, its commander publicly declaring his intention to rid the country of all Islamists, violent or peaceful.[62] In this power vacuum, militias and terrorist organizations that once fought against Qaddafi grew rapidly, became a source of social order and came to control different parts of the country. In cities like Darnah and Sirte, numerous reports surfaced of Islamist groups restricting religious practices, enforcing compliance with Islamic law and targeting those who violated their standards.

One such group, Ansar al-Sharia – an outfit that seeks the implementation of a strict form of sharia throughout the country and has connections to al Qaeda – has been linked to the September 11, 2012, attack on the US consulate and CIA annex in Benghazi that killed American ambassador Christopher Stevens, among others. In 2013, a group of policemen calling itself the Gunmen of the Revolutionary Operations Room of Libya kidnapped Prime Minister Ali Zeidan.[63] Another group, al Qaeda in the Islamic Maghreb (AQIM), has flourished after Qaddafi's departure and is currently one of the most lethal of al Qaeda's franchises. Also present in Libya is the Islamic State, which has taken advantage of the breakdown of order. Today, thousands of fighters associated with ISIS have found a favorable haven in Libya, carrying out targeted killings and suicide bombings, which have resulted in the deaths of hundreds of civilians. These groups have benefited from the flow of arms emanating from Sudan and Qatar.[64] In the five years following Qaddafi's ouster, Libya averaged an astonishing 276 terrorist attacks per year, according to my analysis of the Global Terrorism Database.

Religious minorities have suffered tremendously as violent Islamist groups have gained influence. Christians in particular have been the targets of escalating attacks. In 2013, the largest Coptic church in Benghazi was burned down. In 2015, Islamic State militants beheaded twenty Egyptian Christians and a Ghanaian construction worker living in Libya on a Mediterranean beach. ISIS threatened Libyan Christians

[61] Lin Noueihed and Alex Warrn, *The Battle for the Arab Spring: Revolution, Counter-Revolution and the Making of a New Era* (New Haven, CT: Yale University Press, 2012), 191–192.
[62] US Department of State Bureau of Democracy, Human Rights and Labor, "Libya," 2016 *International Religious Freedom Report*, last modified 2016, available from www.state.gov/j/drl/rls/irf/religiousfree dom/index.htm#wrapper.
[63] Carlotta Gall, "Show of Power by Libya Militia in Kidnapping," *New York Times*, last modified October 10, 2013, www.nytimes.com/2013/10/11/world/africa/libya.html?_r=0.
[64] Alan J. Kuperman, "Obama's Libya Debacle: How a Well-Meaning Intervention Ended in Failure," *Foreign Affairs* 94 (2015): 66–77.

with similar actions. Sufi communities have seen the graves of their saints desecrated (including the destruction of the 500-year-old Al-Andalusi Mausoleum in 2013) and their mosques and schools destroyed with impunity by militant Salafist groups who view the veneration of saints as a form of paganism.[65] These acts of terrorism have been committed by groups, once repressed under Qaddafi, which now have a place in the new Libya. For its part, the government has generally not brought those responsible for violence against Copts and Sufis to justice, contributing to a climate of impunity against religious minorities.

The chaotic situation in Libya contributed to violence in other countries as well. A 2007 report by the Combating Terrorism Center (CTC) at the US Military Academy concluded that Libya provided "far more" foreign fighters in Iraq's insurgency than any other country on a per capita basis.[66] This theme of incubation and exportation would continue after Qaddafi's fall. The instability in Libya has affected security not only within the country but also among its neighbors, as extremist elements pilfered large volumes of arms (including missiles and air defense systems) from Qaddafi's huge weapons stockpiles. These weapons made their way into the hands of other terrorist groups like Boko Haram in Nigeria and Hamas in the Gaza Strip. The massive deserts of the country have become smuggling routes for weapons bound for al Qaeda militants deep in the Sahara; some believe that the January 2013 terrorist attack on an Algerian natural gas complex may have been launched from across the border in Libya. AQIM took advantage of safe havens in Libya to establish an independent Islamic state in northern Mali, prompting a French intervention in 2013. Finally, terrorists responsible for the 2015 massacres at the Bardo Museum and Sousse beach resort in Tunisia received training, weapons and indoctrination at a jihadist camp in Libya.[67]

In sum, Libya illustrates the dangers that majority religious cooptation in the form of brutal, blanket repression can create in the long run. Under the veneer of stability provided by Qaddafi was a broken state with no civil society, rule of law or governing institutions. In Libya, widespread anti-government coalitions formed and banded together in defiance of the oppressive government and achieved unification through opposition to the regime. When Qaddafi was overthrown, those that fought for liberation were given support and held in esteem, even if they held extreme or little-supported political or religious ideologies. Because the regime was hostile toward and dominated religious institutions, it is not surprising that a great number of opposition factions were religiously motivated.

[65] US Department of State Bureau of Democracy, Human Rights and Labor, "Libya," 2013 *International Religious Freedom Report*, last modified 2013, www.state.gov/j/drl/rls/irf/religiousfreedom/index.htm #wrapper.

[66] Joseph Felter and Brian Fishman, *Al-Qa'ida's Foreign Fighters in Iraq: A First Look at the Sinjar Records* (New York, NY: Combating Terrorism Center at West Point, 2007).

[67] Howard LaFranchi, "Terrorists in Tunisia Attacks Trained at Islamic Camp in Libya," *Christian Science Monitor*, last modified July 2, 2015, www.csmonitor.com/USA/Foreign-Policy/2015/0702/Terrorists-in-Tunisia-attacks-trained-at-Islamic-State-camp-in-Libya.

THE RISE OF THE ISLAMIC STATE

From 2014 to 2017, ISIS captured the attention of security experts, academics and policymakers around the world. ISIS, an outgrowth of al Qaeda, arose in the aftermath of the upheavals that shook the Arab world. For this reason, it might be tempting to pin blame for the existence and growth of ISIS on the Arab Spring itself. While the vacuum in state authority in parts of the Middle East and North Africa no doubt provided a fertile breeding ground that ISIS exploited, the reality is that the conditions that contributed to the terrorist group's appeal were in place well before the democratic revolts touched the region. One could point to a number of factors: the bungled American occupation of Iraq, the collapse of the Iraqi security forces, the civil war in Syria and the backing of Sunni militants by certain Gulf States. Perhaps the greatest blame lies, however, with the brutal and arbitrary treatment of Iraq's and Syria's religious communities by the state.[68]

Prior to the US-led invasion in 2003, Iraq was governed by the Ba'athist regime of Saddam Hussein, who employed an extreme form of secular repression in order to promote a secular Arab identity as a source of national unity. Although the 1990 Iraqi constitution banned religious discrimination and guaranteed religious freedom, in actuality the state dominated the religious arena through brutal repression. Saddam was particularly wary of the threat posed by Shia militancy spreading from Iran in the wake of its Islamic revolution in 1979. Consequently, he quickly suppressed any signs of Shia political activity and expelled more than 15,000 Shia from Iraq during Iraq's eight-year war with Iran. The government, according to Jonathan Fox, "restricted religious freedom for all faiths [and] regulated and monitored all political and religious activity" via the Iraqi Ministry of Endowment and Religious Affairs, thereby controlling all houses of worship and religious publications.[69] Christians and Shia were especially discriminated against by Saddam, who, "for decades, conducted a brutal campaign of killing, summary execution, and protracted arbitrary arrest against religious leaders and followers of the Shia Muslim population and … sought to undermine the identity of minority Christian (Assyrian and Chaldean) and Yazidi groups."[70] With respect to Shia Muslims, the government banned communal Friday prayer, broadcasts on government radio or television and the processions and public meetings in honor of holy days. Furthermore, Shia mosques were often desecrated by Saddam's security agents, while the government continually interfered with Shia education and religious ceremonies.[71]

At the same time, true to the pattern of majority religious cooptation, Saddam simultaneously burnished his own religious credentials in an attempt to bolster

[68] Andrew Phillips, "The Islamic State's Challenge to International Order," *Australian Journal of International Affairs* 68, no. 5 (2014): 495–498.
[69] Fox, *World Survey of Religion and the State*, 238.
[70] US Department of State Bureau of Democracy, Human Rights and Labor, "Iraq," *International Religious Freedom Report*, 2003, http://m.state.gov/md24452.html.
[71] Fox, *World Survey of Religion and the State*, 238–239.

loyalty to the regime. In 1993, for example, he launched a "return to faith" campaign aimed at securing support from Sunni Muslims. The initiative saw the building of thousands of new mosques, a new statewide religious school curriculum and a series of new sharia-based laws. The overall orientation of the regime remained secular, nonetheless, even as the regime sought to promote a moderate and friendly form of Sunni Islam at the expense of Iraq's Shia population.

Saddam's brutal repression may have tempered the incidents of terrorism during his reign through the use of restrictive laws and violent suppression; however, underground resistance was still present in Iraq before the American-led invasion and exploded afterward. Here marginalization and repression of religion created a fertile breeding ground for radical political theologies to develop and flourish by mobilizing public opinion against the regime. Shia opposition groups like al-Da'wa al-Islamiya (Islamic Call) and al-Mujahidin (Muslim Warriors) took up the gun in response to Saddam's repressive actions.[72] Militant Sunni groups were active as well. Formed in 2001, the group Ansar al Islam, for example, called for the establishment of a Kurdish theocracy based on Islamic law and fought the Ba'athists before and after the US invasion. Other groups like Jund al-Islam and the Tawhid Islamic Front launched attacks against government targets throughout the Saddam era.

In 2003, the United States invaded and occupied Iraq for the stated purpose of eliminating Saddam's weapons of mass destruction program. The toppling of the Ba'athist regime, however, triggered a regional religious war in the Middle East that continues to this day. As a consequence of de-Ba'athification – the official policy of the George W. Bush administration implemented by the Coalition Provisional Authority (CPA), which involved disbanding the Iraqi army and purging Ba'athism from Iraqi society – hundreds of thousands of Sunni bureaucrats, school-teachers and soldiers nominally aligned with the Ba'ath Party found themselves jobless and barred from holding any government position in the future. De-Ba'athification also had the unintended effect of transforming Iraq's religion–state arrangement from one of majority religious cooptation to minority religious discrimination as an overt alliance between hardline Shia parties and the government of Prime Minister Nouri al-Maliki, actively supported by Iran, emerged in the years following the invasion. Known as the "Malaki State of Law," this alliance between Shiism and the state left little room for Sunnis, who quickly became the targets of systematic discrimination, harassment and violent reprisals for injustices carried by out by Saddam. In one fell swoop, the fortunes of Iraq's majority Shia and minority Sunni communities had practically reversed.

In a classic case of the "religious persecution paradox," formerly persecuted groups who endured the sharp curtailing of their religious freedoms under

---

[72] Hanna Batatu, "Shi'i Organizations in Iraq: Al-Da'wa al-Islamiyah and al-Mujahidin," in *Shi'ism and Social Protest*, ed. Juan Cole and Nikki Keddie (New Haven, CT: Yale University Press, 1986), 179–200.

Saddam ended up morphing into the role of persecutor themselves.[73] Long repressed under Saddam, uncompromising Shia groups used their newfound power to now repress Sunnis. For his part, Maliki, despite numerous promises, proved utterly uncompromising and extremely punitive toward the Sunni population – using an antiterrorism law as a pretense for targeting Sunni areas for security sweeps and arrests, detaining Sunnis without access to due process, mistreating Sunni prisoners, marginalizing Sunnis from security positions and refusing to enter into a power-sharing agreement with Sunnis. All of these actions had the effect of driving many angry, dispossessed and armed Sunnis (including many former agents of Saddam's regime) toward radicalism and violent opposition, while others simply refused to legitimize the government by not participating in the political process. In 2012, Maliki ousted his Sunni vice president, Tariq al-Hashimi (and later sentenced him to death in absentia), on flimsy terrorism charges, leading to mass protests and the escalation of sectarian violence over the next year. The prime minister resigned in August 2014 and was replaced by Haider al-Abadi. The change in leadership did not result in a different approach to governance, however, as human rights abuses by the state – torture, extrajudicial killings of Sunnis and arming of Shia militias – continued. At the society level, Muslim and non-Muslim minorities reported "threats, pressure, and harassment to force them to observe Islamic customs . . . such as wearing the *hijab* or fasting during Ramadan."[74]

The structural transformation of religion and state in Iraq ultimately led to the collapse of political order and the onset of widespread sectarian violence as the Iraqi military lacked the capacity to defend the country from extremist forces. After 2003, religiously motivated violence increased exponentially, especially against religious minorities. Some Sunni insurgent groups like Abu Musab al-Zarqawi's organization al Qaeda in Iraq (AQI), seeking to undermine the political process, carried out numerous attacks against Shia civilian communities and religious targets. Sunni extremist groups claimed responsibility for the 2006 bombing of the al-Askari Mosque, an important Shia holy site, which led to several months of heightened violence between Sunnis and Shia. In 2012 and 2014, Sunni militants staged major coordinated attacks during Shia religious holidays.

On the opposing side of the sectarian violence were militant Shia groups like the Badr Brigades, the Mahdi Army, Kata'ib Hizbullah and the Popular Mobilization Forces, all of which were empowered by the transformation of religion and state. Repression of the Shia for decades by Saddam had the effect of hardening Shia identity, solidarity, religiosity and political awareness vis-à-vis Sunnis. The strong sense of communal grievance experienced by the Shia population contributed to its desire to gain unilateral control over the new Iraq and resist compromise and

---

73 W. Cole Durham and Brett G. Scharffs, *Law and Religion: National, International, and Comparative Perspectives* (New York, NY: Aspen Publishers, 2010), 3.
74 US Department of State Bureau of Democracy, Human Rights and Labor, "Iraq," *2015 International Religious Freedom Report*, last modified 2015, www.state.gov/documents/organization/256479.pdf.

reconciliation. Some supported radical groups to counter the rising violence perpetrated by Sunni extremists. The Mahdi Army, a primary terrorist organization led by
radical Shia cleric Moqtada al-Sadr, engaged in acts of terrorism against Sunnis as
well as coalition and Iraqi government forces. Al-Sadr's group, believed to have
thousands of members, formed in opposition to Saddam and his Sunni-dominated
regime. In the chaos following Saddam's fall, the Mahdi Army was able to acquire
large supplies of munitions from unguarded Iraqi armories. This, in conjunction
with its sizable force, made it a significant terrorist and militia power. The group
enjoyed de facto control over many areas, especially Sadr City, and was responsible
for a large amount of the sectarian violence, often in retaliation for attacks carried
out by al Qaeda against Shia civilians. At times during the conflict, Mahdi "death
squads" controlled "no-go areas" in a fashion more typical of Sunni extremists who
lacked the government representation enjoyed by the Shia majority.[75]

The structural context involving religious persecution, lawlessness and the withdrawal of American troops in 2011 provided a fertile breeding ground for increased
sectarian conflict and the rise of the radical Sunni terrorist group ISIS in the
following years. Nearly three years after American troops left the country, ISIS
made rapid progress in gaining control over Iraqi territory, armored vehicles and
weapons stockpiles, which had been abandoned by the Iraqi armed forces.
The Islamic State's goals involved an Islamist takeover of Iraq and Syria and the
establishment of an Islamic caliphate in the broader Middle East. In early July 2014,
the group announced the official creation of a new religious state in Iraq and Syria,
and was even able to establish some institutions of governance in the areas under its
control.[76] After capturing Iraq's second largest city, Mosul, in 2014, the
following year it claimed the third largest city, Ramadi, and large swaths of territory
in northwestern Iraq and in Syria. Though most Iraqis despised ISIS, the punitive
actions of the Iraqi state, the abusive conduct of the security forces and high levels of
state fragility combined to pave the way for the terrorist group to take control. Many
Sunnis believed that the Islamic State was their only source of protection in the face
of government repression and threats from Shia militias.

ISIS's "state" also extended into Syria – a country that has been in the midst of
a sectarian civil war since 2011 – where ISIS captured a number of oil-rich provinces
and used the money from oil sales to arm itself and recruit fighters. Like Iraq, in Syria
a secular Ba'athist leader has, through the systematic targeting of a religious majority
(in this case Sunnis), created a climate conducive to the spread of ISIS. The Assad
regime, first of Hafez and then of his son, Bashar, has for decades practiced a harsh
form of majority religious cooptation, promoting a moderate form of Islam through
control of and support for religious institutions – schools, mosques and courts –
while sharply repressing conservative Islam. The regime, for example, banned the

[75] Peter Beaumont, "Iraq's 'Failing to Tackle Death Squads,'" *The Guardian*, last
modified September 29, 2006, www.theguardian.com/world/2006/sep/29/iraq.topstories3.
[76] Michael Crowley, "The End of Iraq," *Time*, June 19, 2014, http://time.com/2899488/the-end-of-iraq/.

Muslim Brotherhood, prohibited women from wearing the *niqab* in certain settings and detained and tortured suspected Islamists. The Assads banned membership in certain religious organizations, including any groups associated with Sunni fundamentalism. The penalty for breaking this law ranged from imprisonment to death. Today, the regime continues to monitor sermons, limit activities of religious groups and close mosques between Friday prayers. In 1982, President Hafez al-Assad brutally crushed a Sunni rebellion in the city of Hama, slaughtering tens of thousands of his own people in the process and utterly destroying the city. The "Hama Massacre" became an example to the people of Syria how the regime would handle any perceived threats to its rule. Hama also came to be indelibly seared on the collective consciousness of Sunnis throughout the Middle East and remains a pivotal moment in modern Syrian history.

Ever since demonstrations first broke out against Syrian dictator Bashar al-Assad in 2011, the regime declared an all-out war against all groups and individuals that opposed it, with tactics involving extrajudicial killings, rape, torture, the use of chemical weapons, barring humanitarian aid, indiscriminately attacking civilian areas (including holy sites) and other crimes against humanity.[77] Assad, who hails from the minority Alawite community, deliberately targeted towns for siege, shelling and aerial bombardment based on the religious affiliation of their residents. The state frequently targeted Arab Sunni places of worship, resulting in the destruction of numerous holy sites.

In a classic example of "solicitation," the barbarity of the regime's atrocities lured equally vicious Sunni extremist groups like al Qaeda, ISIS, Khorasan, Jabhat Fath al-Sham and thousands of nonaffiliated foreign jihadis, including many from the West, to fight against it. These groups and individuals considered it their religious obligation to fight on behalf of their fellow embattled Sunnis. Militant Shia groups from Iraq, Lebanon and Iran too have taken up the gun to protect Shia holy sites and defend the Alawite regime of Bashar Assad, including Hezbollah and Iraqi and Shia Afghan fighters recruited by the Iranian Revolutionary Guard. The war in Syria thus became a proxy war between the regional powers of Iran and Saudi Arabia, with the former supporting Assad and the latter those aspiring to overthrow him.

ISIS brought an unthinkable reign of terror and unprecedented persecution to the areas of Iraq and Syria under its control. The group oppressed Shia, Alawites, Christians and nonconformist Sunnis through indiscriminate attacks, kidnappings, public executions, enslavement and human trafficking. ISIS imposed a strict form of sharia in the areas under its control through its police force known as Hisbah, and destroyed numerous churches, Shia shrines and other religious heritage sites. The wars in both countries have had such a calamitous effect on civilians that in 2016 the US State Department declared ISIS's actions against religious minorities as

---

[77] US Commission on International Religious Freedom, *Annual Report 2015* (Washington, DC: US Commission on International Religious Freedom, 2015), 115–118.

"genocidal," marking the first time that an American administration proclaimed an ongoing campaign to constitute genocide since the atrocities in Darfur in 2004. Following suit, the US House of Representatives voted by a margin of 393 to 0 to designate Islamic State crimes as constituting "genocide."[78] More than half of the Syrian population fled to neighboring countries or became internally displaced within Syria. As the insurgency quickly took on a Sunni character, the Assad regime responded by using religious affiliation as a determinant in targeting towns and neighborhoods as part of its effort to defeat the armed opposition. Religious minorities, especially Yazidis and Christians, experienced torture, rape, mass killings, harassment, intimidation, robbery, destruction of personal property and religious sites, enslavement of women and children, kidnappings, crucifixions and beheadings for refusing to convert to Islam or pay a high tax (*jizya*) in order to continue living in ISIS-controlled territory. Members of ISIS kidnapped and sexually assaulted thousands of Yazidi and Christian girls and women, forcing them to become sexual slaves. Attacks on the institutions of these minorities became commonplace like the 2010 strike on the Sayidat al-Majat Syriac Catholic Church, which killed fifty-three people. In a 2014 attack against the predominantly Yazidi town of Sinjar in northern Iraq, ISIS massacred Yazidis, Assyrian Christians, Shia and others while destroying centuries-old holy sites.[79] Two-thirds of Iraq's Christian population fled the country, the number of Christians shrinking to fewer than 500,000 in 2015 from one and half million in 2003.[80] A climate of impunity was made possible by an Iraqi government that was either unwilling or unable to protect minorities from violence or bring perpetrators of violence to justice. The future of the Yazidi and Christian communities in parts of northern Iraq remains in jeopardy. In its self-declared capital of Raqqa, Syria, ISIS held thousands of enslaved Yazidi women and girls kidnapped in Iraq to be sold or distributed to ISIS fighters as "spoils of war." ISIS killed dozens of Syrian Christians – men, women and children – in the form of public executions, crucifixions and beheadings. The Islamic State also attempted to control the social religious landscape through its own police force, court system, school curriculum and training camps.

While non-Muslim religious minorities suffered unimaginable cruelty at the hands of ISIS, the vast majority of those killed by ISIS are of Iraq's majority Shia population, whom the militant Sunni group considers apostates deserving of death. ISIS also targeted Sunnis who departed from its extreme ideology. In 2014, for example, ISIS slaughtered 150 Sunni Muslims, dumping their bodies into a mass

[78] Adam Chandler, "The Long Thorny Path to Calling ISIS 'Genocidal.'" *The Atlantic*, last modified March 17, 2016, www.theatlantic.com/politics/archive/2016/03/isis-genocide-obama/474087/.
[79] US Commission on International Religious Freedom, *Annual Report 2015*, 95–99.
[80] Eliza Griswold, "Is This the End of Christianity in the Middle East?" *New York Times Magazine*, last modified July 22, 2015, www.nytimes.com/2015/07/26/magazine/is-this-the-end-of-christianity-in-the-middle-east.html?_r=0.

grave. The organization has also killed at least twelve Sunni clerics who rejected its extreme interpretation of Islam or attempted to protect religious minorities.

In its heyday in 2014, ISIS controlled vast swaths of territory in Iraq and Syria and governed a large percentage of populations in both countries. Beginning in 2016, ISIS experienced a serious reversal of fortunes as it began suffering a series of losses to the Syrian regime and its allies, relinquishing control of major strongholds in Homs City and Aleppo. By the end of 2016, the anti-ISIS coalition had recaptured more than half of the territory previously taken by ISIS in Iraq, including the cities of Ramadi and Fallujah. The following year, ISIS lost Mosul, Iraq's third largest city. In 2017, the fall of ISIS's capital city, Raqqa, essentially spelled the symbolic end of its rule in Syria. By the end of 2017, the Iraqi government proclaimed that the war against ISIS was over. Time will tell whether ISIS has truly been defeated or if it will reemerge in another form. Regardless of how much territory ISIS has lost, its ideology lives on, however. The fact that Sunni–Shia tensions and government regulation of religion remain high, that Syria's civil war continues and that a consensus has not been reached on establishing a genuinely representative government in Iraq – the very conditions that led to the formation of the Islamic State in the first place – suggest that victory celebrations sounding the death knell for ISIS may prove premature. Moreover, ISIS's regional branches continue to operate throughout parts of Asia and Africa, and it maintains its ability to inspire lone-wolf attacks in the West. ISIS has proven a resilient and protean force that is unlikely to disappear altogether. Many fighters will also likely return to their home countries and take up the war against their home regimes. For these reasons, the military defeat of ISIS notwithstanding, unless earnest attempts are made to battle ISIS's deep-seated ideological sources and to address the issues of systematic discrimination that led to its emergence, claims of victory could well prove hollow in time.

ALTERNATIVE EXPLANATIONS

How well do other explanations account for religious terrorism in the Arab world? A lack of democratic space in the Middle East and North Africa, which reduced citizens to the category of political observers, certainly played a role in the radicalization of Islam in the Arab world before the Arab Spring. The region's political desert gave fuel to radical movements as Islam became the language of opposition to corrupt, unresponsive, exclusionary and politically oppressive dictatorships, both secular and religious. This had the effect of reinforcing the political and ideological foundation for violent religious extremism.

To leave it at that, however, would miss an important contradiction brought on by the Arab Spring. Before the Arab uprisings began in 2011, Tunisia, Egypt, Libya and Syria were all deeply authoritarian states, and Iraq was in the midst of a violent transition period. The Arab Spring changed that reality in Tunisia, Libya and Iraq. In 2014, Tunisia passed the famous "two turnover" test, when it successfully completed a second peaceful transition of power. Following the initial protests, Tunisia steadily increased in its democracy, so that by 2015, Tunisia was considered a fully consolidated democracy by the Polity Project. Iraq today is officially a parliamentary democracy, introduced gradually following the American-led invasion in 2003. Like Tunisia, in 2014 it too passed the "two turnover" test, becoming for the first time a consolidated democracy, albeit a fragile and imperfect one. Libya has yet to become a democracy as of 2018, but it is today far more politically free than at any point in its history. The countries of Egypt and Syria are as politically repressive in 2018 as they have ever been, with the latter continuing in a state of civil war. Egypt became slightly more democratic in the year of its revolution, but then quickly reverted to previous levels of authoritarianism. If political freedom is the answer to terrorism, then we would have expected levels of terrorism to have fallen off in each of these countries as they allowed for greater political freedom. In fact, the exact opposite happened as terrorism levels reached all-time highs in these countries in the wake of the Arab Spring. What did not change, however, is that each of these countries, despite headway at the ballot box, retained or worsened in their levels of religious repression, and this reality, aided by state collapse, fueled cycles of religious violence.

A second major rival explanation for terrorism – poverty – also falls short in explaining religious terrorism in the region. Simple bivariate correlations between a country's level of wealth (measured by GDP/capita) and its level of religious terrorism indicate an inverse relationship between the two; poorer countries are not more susceptible to terrorism in the Arab world. As revealed in the appendix to this book, this inverse relationship holds even in statistical analyses incorporating other explanations for terrorism. In 2017, Egypt and Syria ranked in the bottom 40 and 25 percent of countries in terms of wealth, respectively. The other countries surveyed in this chapter – Iraq, Libya and Tunisia – ranked in the top 50 percent of countries ordered by wealth.[81] The range of wealth present in these countries suggests that poverty is not a key driver of religiously motivated terrorism. Evidence gathered at the individual level also indicates that economically marginalized individuals in the Arab world are not more likely to become terrorists than those with higher levels of education or who hail from middle- and upper-class backgrounds.[82] In the case of Egypt, for example, Saad Eddin Ibrahim revealed that those imprisoned on terrorism charges in the 1970s tended to come from middle-class families, and were "significantly above the average in their generation."[83] The poverty thesis thus fails to explain terrorism in the Arab world.

Finally, it is undeniable that foreign interventions in the Middle East and North Africa have had a deleterious impact on the emergence of violent religious

---

[81] Data derived from the World Bank, *World Development Indicators*, 2017.
[82] Sageman, *Understanding Terror Networks*.
[83] Saad Eddin Ibrahim, "Anatomy of Egypt's Militant Islamic Groups: Methodological Note and Preliminary Findings," *International Journal of Middle East Studies*, 12, no. 4 (1982): 440.

extremism in places like Iraq, Yemen and Libya. Upon first glance, Iraq, in particular, appears to represent a clear-cut case of foreign occupation opening the
floodgates to terrorism. A closer look, however, reveals a more complicated picture.
It is true that before the 2003 American-led invasion and occupation, Iraq experienced relatively little terrorism, and that terrorist attacks increased dramatically after
2003. But the case of Iraq itself raises serious contradictions. The occupation thesis
suggests that the carnage that took place in Iraq in the years following the foreign
intervention should have been largely carried out by Iraqi nationalists fighting
against the American occupation.[84] Yet the majority of terrorists who fought in the
Iraqi insurgency were themselves not Iraqi and therefore held no allegiance to the
Iraqi state, and the majority of their victims were not those of Western occupying
powers. The occupation thesis also cannot explain why terrorism continued well
after the withdrawal of American troops from the country in 2011. A more plausible
explanation concerns the dynamics of incubation, exportation and solicitation
discussed in the opening chapter. Militant Sunnis from around the region considered it a *religious* duty to fight on behalf of their embattled coreligionists in Iraq who
were suffering persecution at the hands of the Iraqi government and Shia groups in
society. Furthermore, as the cases of Egypt and Tunisia show – two countries that
have not undergone a major military occupation by a foreign power in decades –
religious terrorism can also emerge absent foreign intervention. Even in the cases of
Yemen and Libya, foreign intervention never led to full-scale military occupation,
and both countries retained their sovereignty. In short, the occupation hypothesis
remains an insufficient explanation for religious terrorism in the Arab world.

IS ISLAM THE PROBLEM?

Why has the Arab world been caught for so long between the forces of tyranny and
terrorism? Some implicate the religion of Islam as the primary culprit behind the
region's lack of religious freedom and consequent high levels of violent religious
extremism. Eighteenth-century French philosopher Montesquieu opined that
"moderate government is better suited to the Christian religion, and despotic
government to Mohammedanism." For this reason, "Mohammedan princes constantly kill or are killed."[85] More recently, the late Middle East scholar Elie Kedouri
argued that Islam was responsible for the lack of representational government,
religion–state separation and civil liberties in the Islamic world.[86] The famous
"clash of civilizations" thesis propounded most famously by Middle East historian

[84] Robert A. Pape, "It's the Occupation, Stupid," *Foreign Policy*, October 18, 2010, http://foreignpolicy
.com/2010/10/18/its-the-occupation-stupid/.
[85] Charles Baron De Montesquieu, *Montesquieu: The Spirit of the Laws*, ed. Anne M. Cohler, Basia
Carolyn Miler and Harold Samuel Stone (Cambridge: Cambridge University Press, 1989), 461.
[86] Elie Kedouri, *Democracy and Arab Culture* (Washington, DC: Washington Institute for Near East
Policy, 1992).

Bernard Lewis and the late political scientist Samuel Huntington maintains that most governments in the world of Islam care little for alien concepts of democracy, minority rights and religion–state separation.[87]

These individuals reach their conclusions about the compatibility of Islam and religious freedom based on their interpretation of Islam's foundational doctrines and sacred texts. The most commonly cited reason for Islam's dearth of freedom has to do with the refusal of Islamic countries to separate the religious and political spheres, leading to unchecked political power, little room for religious plurality and no development of cross-cutting societal cleavages on the basis of issues other than religion. "In Islam ... God is Caesar," Huntington explained.[88] In other words, because religious freedom stems from a separation of religion and state, it is a Western norm – not a universal one – that has little acceptance or understanding in the world of Islam. Individuals holding this view believe that efforts by the West to promote religious liberty in the Islamic world will ultimately prove at best insignificant and at worst counterproductive.

Upon first glance, it appears that the cynicism of the skeptics is justified. Indeed, the fusion of religion and politics in many Muslim societies *has* led to the open persecution of religious minorities and strong resistance to liberal formulations of human rights, including religious freedom. One might be tempted to point to the aftermath of the Arab Spring as evidence that a politically empowered Islam does not easily lend itself to religious freedom. Scholarship has found that religious restrictions are more common in the Islamic world than elsewhere.[89] Such restrictions are often very serious and involve bans on proselytizing, restrictions on basic religious practices, sharp limits on missionary activity and the dissemination of religious literature in the form of broadcasts or publications and outright discrimination and persecution of religious minorities. But, in support of the argument of this book, the ways in which religious liberty is inhibited in the Muslim world vary across states. Sometimes, hostility to religious freedom arises from Islamist forces, which work to restrict the rights of those belonging to minority faiths or believers in a heterodox version of the majority faith with respect to dress, public practice and legislation. Such patterns of minority religious discrimination can be discerned in countries like Pakistan, Iran and Saudi Arabia – countries that afford religious actors the capability to regulate political life to varying extents.

Importantly, though, restrictions of religious freedom in the Muslim world arise not only from politicized Islam but also from secular elites (like leaders in those countries examined in this chapter who were guided by official ideologies of secularism) who oppose independent religious expression and seek to suppress, manage or monitor Islam's political and social influence as well as that of other religions. Leaders in the Arab world often adopted traditional socialist ideas as a way

---

[87] Bernard Lewis, "The Roots of Muslim Rage," *Atlantic Monthly* 266 (1990): 47–60; Huntington, *Clash of Civilizations.*

[88] Huntington, *Clash of Civilizations*, 70.   [89] Grim and Finke, *Price of Freedom Denied*, 160–201.

to combat Western imperialism, and Arab socialism eventually became prevalent throughout the Middle East and North Africa.[90] States in which secular Arab nationalism took root sought to manage religion in such a way so as to help entrench the power of the secular dictators who ruled them. This was usually accomplished by coopting a particular strain of Islam believed to be conducive to their political objectives, while banning or persecuting those that did not faithfully adhere to the official ideology and policies endorsed by the state. Toward this end, government tactics typically included the state appointing Islamic clergy, paying their salaries, funding mosques, editing sermons and monitoring religious services. Political scientist Daniel Philpott implicates this type of "restrictive secularism" – or what I call "majority religious cooptation" – in 40 percent of cases where Muslim-majority states restrict religious practice. Although secular dictatorships of this sort worked to minimize the influence of religion, they actually served to increase the salience of Islam as the mosque became the center of political activity and opposition to the state. In Egypt, for example, the Muslim Brotherhood appealed to wide portions of the population because it had been suppressed for decades and was able to capitalize on this broad base of support and mobilize efficiently after the demise of Mubarak. Interestingly enough, when these secular states are taken out of the equation, there is virtually no difference between Muslim-majority countries and the rest of the world in terms of religious freedom. Thus, while the lack of religious freedom in the world of Islam needs to be recognized, Islam itself is not always why that shortage exists.

If there is evidence that religious restrictions in the Islamic world arise from both secularism and Islam, there is also evidence that religious liberty is not a Western norm that is incompatible with Islam. Muslim societies in the past were striking examples of religious diversity with many different sects, creeds and worldviews coexisting in environments of broad toleration. Today, virtually all Islamic countries have signed off on international concords that ensconce religious freedom as a universal and fundamental human value: the 1948 United Nations Declaration on Human Rights, the 1966 International Covenant on Civil and Political Rights and the 1981 Declaration on the Elimination of All Forms of Intolerance and of Discrimination Based on Religion or Belief. Importantly, these international standards were developed by a broad coalition representing many religions and countries around the world. More importantly, the push for religious liberty is arising from *within* an Islamic discourse itself with pro-freedom arguments being made by prominent Muslim intellectuals like Hamza Yusuf, Abdullah Saeed and Abdolkarim Soroush, all of whom strongly reject the assertion that freedom of religion is a Western imposition. In 2016, more than 250 Muslim religious leaders, scholars and government leaders from ten dozen countries convened in Morocco and affirmed the "Marrakesh Declaration" – a landmark statement drawing on the

[90] Adeed Dawisha, *Arab Nationalism in the Twentieth Century: From Triumph to Despair* (Princeton, NJ: Princeton University Press, 2005).

Charter of Medina, which champions the rights of religious minorities in Muslim countries and declares the oppression of religious minorities as contrary to Muslim values.[91] Two years later more than 400 religious leaders representing the three Abrahamic faith traditions assembled in Washington, DC, as part of an "Alliance of Virtue." The Alliance took its name from an initiative that took place in Mecca during the time of the Prophet Muhammed to ensure fair treatment of vulnerable communities, including non-Muslims. The renewed alliance issued a "Washington Declaration" to affirm its commitment to "joint action in the service of sustainable peace, justice, compassion and mutual respect," emphasizing the need to move beyond mere toleration to a future in which people of all religious convictions can flourish together.[92] These individuals and initiatives provide strong support for the notion that religious liberty is compatible with Islam.

Furthermore, sites of religious freedom exist in the Islamic world today. Of the forty-nine Muslim-majority countries or territories covered in the 2015 Pew Research Center report *Latest Trends in Religious Restrictions*, while 71 percent have "high" or "very high" levels of governmental restrictions on religion, 29 percent also have "moderate" to "low" levels of government-enforced restrictions. Forty-nine percent of countries have "high" or "very high" societal regulation of religion, while a majority of countries (51 percent) has "moderate" to "low" levels of social religious restriction. Outside of these countries, millions more Muslims in the Islamic diaspora fully embrace religious liberty in the non-Muslim world. Certainly the world of Islam has a way to go with respect to religious freedom, but these figures show that freedom of belief may not be as rare as some might believe.[93]

But what of the Arab world specifically? There is some evidence that limited forms of religious freedom have begun to sprout here as well. Of the twenty-two Arab countries/territories surveyed by the Pew report, seven have "moderate" or just slightly higher than moderate government restrictions on religion (Comoros, Lebanon, Libya, the Palestinian Territories, the United Arab Emirates [UAE], Somalia and Tunisia), while ten have "moderate" or "low" social hostilities involving religion (Bahrain, Comoros, Djibouti, Jordan, Mauritania, Morocco, Oman, Qatar, United Arab Emirates and Western Sahara). In contrast to highly restrictive states like Saudi Arabia, which bans the public expression of any religion other than Islam, non-Muslim places of worship and apostasy and blasphemy, other Gulf States are far less punitive toward religious minorities who often retain the right to worship freely and run their own institutions free from governmental interference. In the United Arab Emirates, for example, Christian churches are growing exponentially

---

91 Marrakesh Declaration, "Marrakesh Declaration," January 25–27, 2016, last modified 2016, www.marrakeshdeclaration.org/marrakesh-declaration.html.
92 Parliament of the World's Religions, "Alliance of Virtue for the Common Good – The Washington Declaration," February 5–7, 2018, https://parliamentofreligions.org/publications/alliance-virtue-common-good-washington-declaration.
93 Philpott, *Religious Freedom in Islam?*

and are protected under the law. Sheikh Nahayan Mabarak al-Nahayan, a senior member of the ruling family, summarizes the condition of religious freedom in the country: "In the UAE we enjoy a society that prizes tolerance and we value the benefits of living in a nation where people of many different faiths live, work, and pray in harmony and peace."[94] In the nearby tiny Gulf kingdom of Bahrain, seeds of religious diversity and tolerance can also be found. In 2017, Bahrain's king, Hamad bin Isa Al Khalifa-Manama, authored the "Bahrain Declaration on Religious Tolerance," calling for religious tolerance and peaceful coexistence not only in the Middle East but throughout the entire world. The declaration reads:

> For hundreds of years, different religious groups have lived harmoniously, side by side, in the Kingdom of Bahrain, fully practicing the tenets of their respective faiths in blessed, peaceful coexistence with each other. We humbly offer the centuries-old traditional Bahraini way of life as an example to inspire others around these principles.[95]

The UAE's and Bahrain's histories of relative religious harmony and diversity may offer signs of hope for other countries of the region. All these countries – including both the UAE and Bahrain – have a way to go with respect to particular areas central to religious freedom like governmental favoritism of religion, societal persecution and legal discrimination, but their examples allow for the possibility that religious freedom can exist in the Arab world.

Finally, even if the Arab world generally lags behind other regions in terms of religious freedom, this does not necessarily mean that countries with high levels of religious restrictions cannot become more hospitable to such freedoms over time. This was indeed the path taken by the Catholic Church.[96] Interestingly, what many claim to be impediments to religious freedom in Islam also hold true for Catholicism: its patriarchal structure, universal truth claims and historical distrust of democracy. But most Catholic countries did eventually become democratic and embrace religious freedom after the Church incorporated teachings about human rights and democracy into its framework at the Second Vatican Council beginning in 1962, an event that triggered what Samuel Huntington referred to as democratization's "third wave." In Europe, Catholics may have initially had designs of imposing their will on society through politics, but they ended up compromising on these objectives as they participated in the democratic game.[97] The Catholic Church never renounced its claims to spiritual universality, but it did relinquish its quest for political power and social domination of other religions. This did not lead to

[94] Jonathan Aitkin, "An Oasis of Tolerance," *American Spectator*, March 2013, 45–46.
[95] Hamad bin Isa Al Khalifa-Manama, "The Bahrain Declaration on Religious Tolerance," *Simon Wiesenthal Center*, last modified July 3, 2017, www.wiesenthal.com/site/apps/nlnet/content.aspx?c=lsKWLbPJLnF&b=8776547&ct=15004381.
[96] Daniel Philpott, "The Catholic Wave," *Journal of Democracy* 15, no. 2 (2004): 32–46.
[97] Stathis N. Kalyvas, *The Rise of Christian Democracy in Europe* (Ithaca, NY: Cornell University Press, 1996).

a complete separation of religion and state as even today the majority of predominantly Catholic countries sanction state support for religion in much the same way that many Islamic countries do. The major difference, however, is that state support for Catholicism does not ordinarily lead to discrimination against or persecution of religious minorities. Perhaps Catholicism's eventual embrace of religious liberty holds out some hope for those skeptical about the possibility of religious freedom in the Arab world.

In this light, it might make more sense to view the dynamics of repression and terrorism in the Arab world not as attributable to Islam per se but rather as a result of unique state–religion relations. Unlike communist totalitarian regimes, secular Arab dictatorships did not attempt to ban Islamic institutions, only religiously based political parties and activities that could pose a threat to their regimes. Knowing that they could never eliminate religious movements in their highly religious societies, these leaders attempted instead to place Islamic institutions under state control while promoting a moderate version of Islam from above. But religion itself never guided the thinking or goals of these secular state leaders, who considered nonofficial forms of Islam dangerous to their personal power and national aspirations. On the contrary, most states responded to the increasing assertiveness of Islam with heightened levels of repression, especially in the countries examined in this chapter. As a result, unofficial Islam gained an aura of authenticity and purity due to its distance from the state; Islamic institutions morphed into an "underground rallying point for political opposition";[98] Islam became the language of resistance to the repressive state; and radicals like Egypt's Sayed Qutb and Ayman al Zawahiri used religion to justify violence against their enemies, both foreign and domestic. Thus, repression increased the salience of Islam both as a form of collective identity and as a viable political alternative to secularism, often pushing it in a violent direction, while simultaneously undermining more moderate interpretations. Islamist terrorists certainly take their faith seriously and in it find a ready-made source of legitimacy, but it would be a mistake to blame Islam itself for either terrorism or the climate of authoritarianism that helped to produce it.

CONCLUSION

Since decolonization, the people of the Arab world have been caught in a dilemma of oppression: either support tyrants who promise security and stability or the violent extremists who seek to dethrone them and implement a tyranny of their own in the form of religious law. Though the Arab Spring momentarily represented an alternative to these two extremes, it proved short-lived and gave way to yet another cycle of repression and religious violence. Of the four Arab countries in which uprisings

[98] Cesari, *Awakening of Muslim Democracy*, 123.

brought down autocrats, three have failed to complete the democratic transition. In Yemen and Libya, a legacy of government repression, state fragility and social persecution of religion have combined to aid the proliferation of tribal and religious militias. The coup in Egypt led by General Sisi against that country's first genuinely elected president signaled a return to the secular authoritarianism the country has known for virtually all of its post-independence history. Only Tunisia can be said to have maintained its democratic transition, but here too the forces of jihadism have been at work.

Some might argue that these cases demonstrate precisely why straightforward repression of religion works. Though Ben Ali, Hosni Mubarak, Muammar Qaddafi and Saddam Hussein were undeniably brutal tyrants, at least their heavy-handedness was able to keep the forces of religious extremism at bay. Two points are worth mentioning. First, repression may provide the illusion of order, but it only fuels the underlying rage among the people against corrupt, repressive and unresponsive regimes. These contexts increase the likelihood that ordinary people will see radical ideologies and violence as justifiable, thus increasing support for terrorist groups. Eventually, the brewing discontent under the surface can no longer be contained. That the Arab Spring resulted in civil war, terrorism and other forms of religious violence is hardly surprising considering that the populations living under Arab dictatorships, though highly religious, were prevented from exercising their religious rights, sometimes through violent religious persecution on the part of the state. Repression of religion in these secular Arab dictatorships thus pushed Islamic groups in the direction of radicalism. Often they became militant opponents of the state. Second, the stability of authoritarian regimes such as these is far less certain than once believed. Just ten years before the Arab revolutions, it seemed unthinkable that the firmly entrenched Arab dictatorships in Tunisia, Egypt, Libya, Yemen, Iraq and potentially Syria could be overthrown. Yet when these regimes fell, the groups who filled the power vacuum were often highly illiberal ones that had been suppressed or banned for decades and were ill equipped to govern effectively, as demonstrated by the Muslim Brotherhood in Egypt. Newer religious extremist groups have also emerged from older ones, including the world's most brutal contemporary terrorist organization, the Islamic State in Iraq and Syria (ISIS).

Like their Arab counterparts, Western policymakers have been inculcated into believing that they too must choose between the forces of stability and extremism. They have often opted for the former, continuing their support for secular Arab dictators whom they see as a buffer against terrorism. After 9/11, Washington established ever-closer relations with authoritarians like Egypt's Hosni Mubarak, Yemen's Ali Saleh and Saudi Arabia's King Abdullah in its "war against terror." Yet far from being a bulwark against extremism, Arab leaders continue to directly support terrorist groups in Iraq and Syria, and their repressive policies at home garner hatred and play into the hands of extremists who exploit repression to mobilize support and justify their violence. Not only do these leaders repress extremist movements, they ruthlessly persecute the dissidents and supporters of human rights who present a viable alternative to both tyranny and terrorism. Moreover, the people of the Arab world will not soon forget that this despotism is enabled by Western governments.

After the Arab Spring, the choices have become even more extreme. Forces of secular repression have persisted in Tunisia, Egypt, Libya and Syria, where they continue the cycle of secular tyranny and violent religious resistance. In Egypt, General Sisi has murdered hundreds of opponents in the name of combating extremism. In Iraq and Syria, the Islamic State has slaughtered thousands of civilians in the most barbaric ways imaginable. It is the height of irony that the last name of Egypt's military leader – Sisi – is the name of the world's most brutal terrorist organization spelled backward – ISIS – a simple but powerful reminder that dictators and terrorists represent two sides of the same coin, both of which seek to rule by the sword and persecute their enemies. Both forces are intimately connected, and increasing the strength of one will inevitably lead to the growth of the other.

Fortunately, an alternative to tyranny and terrorism exists: religious liberty. Just as repression and radicalism feed off and strengthen each other, religious freedom promotes peace by undermining the forces of extremism. The following chapter examines how the presence of robust religious freedom protections in the vastly different countries of the United States, Senegal and South Africa has helped to keep religious violence at bay or prevent relapse into violent conflict. Religious liberty, it argues, is truly a weapon of peace.

4

A Weapon of Peace

The previous two chapters have examined some of the myriad ways in which restrictions on religion facilitate religious terrorism. The present chapter now turns attention to addressing how religious freedom can help hold religious violence at bay and even contribute to peace building and reconciliation in the aftermath of atrocity. I argue that in religiously free settings, religious extremists will have a difficult time attracting sympathizers to their cause. While religiously motivated attacks can certainly occur in religiously free states, they do so with far less frequency than in their repressive counterparts.

As discussed in the opening chapter, there are at least five logics that explain why this is the case. First, religious liberty creates a de facto marketplace of ideas in which religious extremists have their views openly challenged by peaceful groups – secular and religious – in society. Religious extremists holding violent political theologies may well exist, but the environment of religious freedom can serve to deprive terrorists of the much-needed ideological and logistical support they require to carry out attacks. For this reason, countries that strive for religious tolerance and encourage open dialogue are less likely to propagate extremism. Second, religious freedom also allows people of faith to advance their cause through legitimate political institutions, making it less likely that they will feel the need to turn to the gun. Third, religious liberty empowers religious individuals and communities to do good in the world in accordance with the imperatives of their faith. The positive contributions to society that might have otherwise been suppressed through religious restrictions – promoting social harmony, alleviating poverty and fostering development – have led to more peaceful and stable societies. Fourth, the free exercise of religion works against tendencies toward authoritarianism and tyranny – the very characteristics that facilitate religious radicalism in the first place. Finally, religious liberty can aid in counterterrorism efforts by driving a wedge between terrorists and their constituencies.

The opening chapter also argued that religion's relationship to violence or peace is best understood as ambivalent. Just as religious extremists use their faith to justify violence, religious peacemakers look to their faith in committing themselves to

146

ending violence and resolving conflict. Just as violent extremists can be found in every religious tradition, so too can religious peacemakers who channel their faith toward justice and peace. Conditions favorable to religious freedom can empower these forces for peace while undermining their violent counterparts.

This chapter takes a brief look at three countries where the presence of religious liberty has served to dampen the impetus toward religious violence: the United States, Senegal and South Africa. These contrasting cases to those covered in previous chapters were chosen for two reasons. First, as in the previous country cases, all three of these countries might seem like places where religious extremism should have been able to gain a foothold, due to their high degrees of religiosity and pluralism. Yet all three have been relatively immune to the forces of religious zealotry. Second, the cases cover very different parts of the world with entirely different histories and cultures. Yet in each case, the presence of religious liberty helped to keep religious violence (including terrorism) at bay.

The success of the American experience in preventing religious terrorism can largely be attributed to the flourishing of religious liberty enabled by its founding conditions and constitution. In the West African country of Senegal, the encouraging of religious pluralism and various Islamic traditions and practices has given rise to a moderate and tolerant Islam, and the country has seen virtually none of the religious terrorism that has engulfed similar nations. Finally, the South African case shows how, despite the presence of racial conflict, religion was never directly implicated in the violence of apartheid (though some churches did indeed support the policies of the National Party), and the culture of religious tolerance has held religious extremism at bay. Moreover, religious actors in South Africa were empowered to carry out valuable peace-building and reconciliation work in postapartheid South Africa, contributing to the country's healing, peace and stability.

THE UNITED STATES

The United States is unique among advanced industrial countries in that it is a highly religious society in terms of levels of belief and one of the world's most religiously plural societies.[1] Unsurprisingly, then, the potential for social conflict along religious lines has been present throughout American history from the beginning. The Puritans who helped found the country sought freedom of religion for themselves but not for those holding different religious convictions, sometimes exiling them from Puritan communities. In post-revolutionary Virginia, Anglicans, loyal to the Church of England, persecuted Presbyterians and Baptists. Friction between Catholics (particularly Irish immigrants) and Protestants was palpable throughout the nineteenth century and well into the twentieth. Fringe groups like

---

[1] Diana Eck, A New Religious America: How a "Christian Country" Has Become the World's Most Religiously Diverse Nation (New York, NY: Harper Collins, 2001).

the Ku Klux Klan and the Know-Nothings committed or approved of acts of violence against Catholics, seeing them as constituting a threat to American national identity. Mormons were violently chased out of several states until finally settling in Utah's Great Salt Lake Valley in 1847. Anti-Semitism was rampant throughout many northeastern cities during the Great Depression. After the attacks of September 11, 2001, hate crimes against Muslims increased dramatically.

One might think that the unusually high commitment to religion among the American people and the mixing of different religions would be a recipe for strife as it has been elsewhere in the world. What is remarkable, nonetheless, is how *little* religious conflict the United States has experienced, especially in recent times. Persecution of religious minorities eventually gave way to tolerance. Despite anti-Catholic sentiment, the violence against Catholics was limited in scope, and they always retained their religious freedoms. Today, Mormons, Jews and Muslims openly practice their faiths free from interference. While religious extremism has not been eradicated, its violent outgrowth has been largely contained.

Until very recently, the United States was one of the most religiously free countries in the world.[2] The high level of religious liberty stems from America's unique founding conditions. Settled largely by immigrants escaping religious persecution and discrimination in Europe, religious freedom has always been central to American society and politics, even if it was not always applied equally.[3] The Pilgrims were followed by millions more – Christians and non-Christians – who sought refuge in the religious liberty offered by the United States. Even today, those facing religious persecution in their native countries see the United States as a sanctuary of freedom in contrast to much of the rest of the world.

In such a setting, constitutionally mandated religious freedom serves as a guarantee that all may express their religious beliefs however they see fit without having to fear state repression or encroachments on their faith by other religious groups. Unlike most other countries in the world (including many liberal democratic ones), the American Constitution makes no attempt to either partner with religion or discriminate against it. The First Amendment of the Constitution states that "Congress shall make no law respecting an establishment of religion, or prohibiting the free exercise thereof." Article 6 of the document also forbids any "religious test . . . as a qualification to any office or public trust." These laws explicitly prevent the government from establishing any religion as the state religion; at the same time, they guarantee universal religious freedom, ensure equal status of all religious communities and protect religious communities from state interference or

[2] Fox, *World Survey of Religion and the State.*
[3] Martha Nussbaum, *Liberty of Conscience: In Defense of America's Traditions of Religious Equality* (New York, NY: Basic Books, 2008); John M. Barry, *Roger Williams and the Creation of the American Soul: Church, State and the Birth of Liberty* (New York, NY: Viking, 2012); Nicholas P. Miller, *The Religious Roots of the First Amendment: Dissenting Protestants and the Separation of Church and State* (New York, NY: Oxford University Press, 2012); Michael I. Myerson, *Endowed by Our Creator: The Birth of Religious Freedoms in America* (New Haven, CT:Yale University Press, 2012).

control. As former president Bill Clinton explained, "[r]eligious freedom is at the heart of what it means to be an American and at the heart of our journey to become truly one America."[4]

The paragon of separation found in the American Constitution and other statutes does not imply that religious actors cannot be involved in the public sphere or that the state cannot be friendly toward religion, only that it cannot be selective in doing so. Indeed, religious rhetoric and symbolism is pervasive throughout American political culture, from the national motto "In God We Trust," to the phrase "under God" in its pledge of allegiance, to the opening prayer of congressional and state assembly sessions to the use of religious language by every president since George Washington. The state also provides indirect financial support for religious institutions through tax exemptions, land grants and school vouchers.

State neutrality in religious matters, assurances of religious liberty and high rates of religious assimilation have resulted in low levels of religious violence in the United States. Writing of the United States, political scientists Monica Toft, Daniel Philpott and Timothy Samuel Shah explain that the "strong tradition of consensual independence between religion and state suggests that religious terrorists will always be a marginal force."[5] Furthermore, the United States' commitment to religious freedom provides all religious groups the ability to work through political channels in order to bring about societal change, and in this way undermines the narrative of extremists that their faith is under attack.

This is not to suggest that the United States has always been immune to religious terrorism. Certainly there have been and continue to be radical groups like the American Christian Identity movement motivated, at least in part, by a violent political theology. Today, many in the policy world take it as an article of faith that international Islamist terrorism poses the greatest threat to US national security. They also point to "homegrown terrorism" – terrorism committed by American residents and citizens – as a cause for alarm.[6] After 9/11, a culture of fear about terrorism quickly developed that has been internalized by many security experts, politicians and large segments of the population. Such sentiments continue to be echoed by a number of government officials. Yet how influential are violent religious groups and how systematic are attacks compelled by a religious imperative in the United States?

---

[4] William J. Clinton, "Remarks Announcing Guidelines on Religious Exercise and Religious Expression in the Federal Workplace," *The American Presidency Project*, last modified August 14, 1997, www.presidency.ucsb.edu/ws/index.php?pid=54535&st=&st1.

[5] Toft, Philpott and Shah, *God's Century*, 130.

[6] Sageman, *Understanding Terror Networks*; Daveed Gartenstein-Ross and Laura Grossman, *Homegrown Terrorists in the U.S. and the U.K.: An Empirical Study of the Radicalization Process* (Washington, DC: FDD Press, 2009); Brian Michael Jenkins, *Would-Be Warriors: Incidents of Jihadist Terrorist Radicalization in the United States since September 11, 2001* (Santa Monica, CA: RAND Corporation, 2010).

My analysis of the Global Terrorism Database shows that these fears, at least in historical perspective, are unwarranted. From 1990 to 2014, the United States suffered only twenty-four identifiably religious terrorist attacks, or an average of slightly more than one per year. This is quite remarkable given the country's large population and many diverse religious traditions. Since the 9/11 attacks, al Qaeda was not able to carry out even one successful attack on American soil, and, until the Boston Marathon attack in 2013, no terrorist had been able to detonate even a rudimentary bomb. In the fifteen years following 9/11, religious terrorism accounted for a maximum of forty-six deaths. Almost one-third of those victims (fourteen) were killed during the 2015 terrorist attacks in San Bernardino, California. The majority of post-9/11 terrorism plots involved "lone wolf" vigilantes who were not acting on behalf of an overarching organization. Put simply, the capabilities of actual terrorists and the propensity for radicalization among American Muslims have been "overblown."[7] Though the fear of terrorism following the 9/11 attacks was certainly justifiable – they were, after all, by far the most devastating terrorist strikes in history – these attacks now appear to have been more of an aberration rather than an omen of future attacks. To put it in perspective, John E. Mueller and Mark G. Stewart calculate the odds of an American being killed by terrorists to be about one in three and a half million.[8]

When religious terrorism occurs in the United States, it is often perpetrated by individuals from abroad who were incubated in conditions of religious repression. According to my analysis of violent jihadism in the United States, only fifty-four individuals were implicated in attacks or plots on American soil from 2001 to 2016. Of those individuals, thirty-four (63 percent) were American citizens. However, nineteen of these Americans (56 percent) were naturalized citizens who had been born abroad. Only sixteen individuals were American citizens by birth. The majority of those associated with jihadi attacks hailed from countries like Egypt, Yemen and Pakistan – places where religious liberty is sharply repressed. To be sure, radicalization has occurred among a few American citizens, but the far greater threat comes from individuals whose theologies of violence were incubated and nourished in conditions of repression abroad.

In the wake of the 2001 attacks, many worried about the possibility of domestic radicalization among the country's Muslim communities. However, scholarship and polls in the years after 9/11 reveal that American Muslim communities remained remarkably resistant to the ideas of religious radicals in contrast to Muslims in other

---

[7] John E. Mueller, *Overblown: How Politicians and the Terrorism Industry Inflate National Security Threats* (New York, NY: Free Trade Press, 2006); John E. Mueller and Mark G. Stewart, "The Terrorism Delusion: America's Overwrought Response to September 11," *International Security* 37, no. 1 (2012): 81–110.

[8] Mueller and Stewart, "Terrorism Delusion," 96, 103, 107.

parts of the world, while embracing core American values.[9] According to a survey by the Pew Research Center, the vast majority of American Muslims believes that violence cannot be justified in any context, especially when directed against fellow citizens. The survey also found that, compared to their religious counterparts in Europe who perceive themselves as perennial outsiders, American Muslims are better integrated into American culture, and despite being exposed to radical ideologies, have, by and large, rejected them.[10] Like Catholics before them, freedom of religion has allowed for the entry of Muslim groups into the broader society. For this reason, would-be militants have not typically been able to find complicit environments in the form of local sanctuaries within sympathetic communities from which to launch attacks. Furthermore, members of these communities (including family members and close friends) have been willing to alert authorities when those expressing extremist views engage in suspect behavior.[11] Several of the plots hatched since 9/11 were foiled as a result of tips from community informants, and it appears that strong Muslim communities in the United States function not as channels of radicalization (contrary to popular perceptions echoed by influential politicians) but rather as an important check against it. With respect to foreign terrorist recruiting, al Qaeda and ISIS have been relatively unsuccessful in attracting Americans to their cause. In short, the post-9/11 security environment has not become more permissive for religious zealots or threatening for American citizens.

Moreover, the context of religious liberty has empowered Muslim voices of peace who have used their positions of prominence to denounce Islamic extremism. According to one study of Muslim American terrorism, American Muslim organizations have "issued press releases, spoken out in mosques, and created community organizations to convey the message, in public and in private, that terrorism is religiously prohibited and strategically foolish."[12] A devout and prominent American Muslim, Dr. Zuhdi Jasser, for example, founded and currently heads the American Islamic Forum for Democracy, an organization dedicated to preserving American founding principles by directly countering extremist ideologies. Jasser has also served on the US Commission on International Religious Freedom. Sheik Hamza Yusuf, another Muslim-American intellectual whom *The Guardian* newspaper dubbed as "arguably the West's most influential Islamic scholar," has

9 Pew Research Center, "Muslim-Americans Middle Class and Mostly Mainstream," last modified May 22, 2007, www.pewresearch.org/files/old-assets/pdf/muslim-americans.pdf; Farooq Kathwari, Lynne Martin and Christopher B. Whitney, *Strengthening America: The Civic and Political Integration of Muslim Americans: Report of the Task Force on Muslim American Civic and Political Engagement* (Chicago, IL: Chicago Council on Global Affairs, 2007); Ihsan Bagby, "The American Mosque in Transition: Assimilation, Acculturation and Isolation," *Journal of Ethnic and Migration Studies* 35, no. 3 (2009): 476–490.
10 Pew Research Center, *Muslim Americans*.
11 Risa Brooks, "Muslim 'Homegrown' Terrorism in the United States: How Serious Is the Threat?" *International Security* 36, no. 2 (2012): 22–24.
12 Charles Kurzman, David Schanzer and Ebrahim Moosa, "Muslim American Terrorism since 9/11: Why So Rare?" *Muslim World* 101, no. 3 (2011): 473.

consistently and vigorously condemned violence committed in the name of Islam.[13] The voices of individuals like these, empowered by religious liberty, serve as an important counter to the influence of extremists, and they have courageously challenged radical interpretations of Islam from within an Islamic discourse itself.

The American context of religious liberty has also provided Muslim Americans with the ability to work through democratic institutions by which they can promote their rights and interests and channel their grievances. As in other democracies, Muslims have used the institutions of democracy to their advantage, thus dampening the impetus toward violence and integrating themselves into the democratic process. The political dimension of religious freedom has therefore marginalized and perhaps even prevented the rise of extremist Islamist groups in the United States.

It stands to reason that had the United States compromised religious freedoms, religious conflict would have been a much more prevalent theme throughout its history. Yet it is important to recognize that freedoms are fragile and often threatening to those in power. Recent evidence reveals a disturbing downward trend in religious freedom protections in the United States in terms of both governmental and social religious regulation, with some national politicians lodging blatant attacks on religious minorities. What was once the most religiously free country in the world now exhibits "moderate" levels of governmental religious restrictions and "high" social hostilities involving religion.[14] The future of religious conflict in America will be determined, in large part, by how well it respects religious liberty going forward. Even though freedom is enshrined in law and supported by the broader culture, the consensus behind religious freedom can erode if not vigorously defended, as recent history shows. This point is taken up at greater length in the concluding chapter.

SENEGAL

As noted in the previous chapter, many scholars and analysts have long noted the dearth of freedom in Muslim-majority countries. The democracy deficit is often attributed to Islamic theology, which, it is believed, does not allow for a separation between the religious and political realms. Senegal, a tiny West African country that lies along the Atlantic coast and one of the world's few Muslim-majority countries that is also a consolidated democracy, challenges the idea of a mechanistic relationship between Islam and authoritarianism.

Upon first glance, it might appear that Senegal should be susceptible to the same forces of violent religious extremism that have engulfed surrounding countries: it contains a dominant Muslim majority (94 percent of the population) coupled with a sizeable Christian minority (5 percent) and various ethnic groups; it has

---

[13] Jack O'Sullivan, "If You Hate the West, Emigrate to a Western Country," *The Guardian*, last modified October 8, 2001, www.theguardian.com/world/2001/oct/08/religion.uk.

[14] Pew Research Center, *Trends in Global Restrictions on Religion*, 52.

experienced a legacy of Western colonialism and a long-simmering secessionist conflict in the predominantly Christian southern part of the country; it has a highly religious populace (according to surveys conducted by the Pew Research Center's Forum on Religion and Public Life, 98 percent of Senegalese describe religion as "very important" in their lives);[15] and it has allowed Islam to play a significant role in political life in defiance of the prevailing view that Islam must be privatized if democracy is to flourish. Yet despite the presence of similar demographic and historical factors that have led to religious conflict between Muslims and Christians in other parts of Africa like Nigeria and Central African Republic, Senegal has remained highly stable and almost completely free from any form of religiously inspired violence. As noted by scholar of Senegal Leonardo Villalón, "socio-political cleavages based on religion, whether between Muslim and non-Muslim or between Sufi orders, are virtually nonexistent."[16] Indeed, in the post–Cold War era, Senegal has experienced virtually no instances of identifiable religiously motivated terrorism.

Many scholars have noted the "exceptional" character of Senegalese politics and society, including its high degree of democracy and religious tolerance.[17] Religious actors and theologies never became politicized in Senegal the way they have in other parts of the Muslim world where Islamists commonly seek to impose a fusion of religion and state. Rather, the variety of Islam practiced in Senegal is of a moderate and forbearing nature, leading to a general peaceful coexistence between Muslims and Christians.[18] For example, a devout Catholic, poet Léopold Sédar Senghor, served as the first president of the overwhelmingly Muslim country (1960–1980). Many families include both Christians and Muslims, and interreligious weddings are commonplace, even at the highest levels of government. The presidents who followed Senghor, Muslims Abdou Diouf and Abdoulaye Wade, had Christian wives. Religious tolerance between Muslims and Christians is thus high in Senegal. According to the Pew Research Center poll referenced earlier, only 2 percent of Senegalese Muslims believe Christianity is violent, in sharp contrast to countries like Djibouti, Kenya, Uganda and Cameroon, where between 25 percent and 40 percent of Muslims see Christians as violent.[19]

Some have attributed Senegal's high levels of social harmony and liberty to the presence and influence of competing yet tolerant and peaceful Sufi brotherhoods

[15] Pew Research Center, *Tolerance and Tension: Islam and Christianity in Sub-Saharan Africa*, last modified April 15, 2010, www.pewforum.org/2010/04/15/executive-summary-islam-and-christianity-in-sub-saharan-africa/.

[16] Leonardo A. Villalón, *Islamic Society and State Power in Senegal: Disciples and Citizens in Fatick* (Cambridge: Cambridge University Press, 1995), 2.

[17] For a review of works on the Senegalese exception, see Donal B. Cruise O'Brien, "The Senegalese Exception," *Africa* 3 (1996): 458–464.

[18] Sheldon Gellar, *Democracy in Senegal: Tocquevillian Analytics in Africa* (New York, NY: Palgrave Macmillan, 2005).

[19] Pew Research Center, *Tolerance and Tension*, 8. Figures for the percentage of Christians who see Muslims as violent are not available due to the low number of Christians surveyed in Senegal.

like the Tijaniyya (the largest order), the Qadiriryya (the oldest) and the Mouridiyya (the most influential) in Senegalese society.[20] Originating in South Asia in the early ninth century, Sufism is a non-dogmatic, mystical form of Islam that seeks to find divine love through a direct and personal encounter with God. In Senegal, different dynastic and hierarchical Sufi brotherhoods incorporate varied practices in accordance with how their particular beliefs have evolved. Due to its acceptance of democracy and pluralism, Senegalese Sufism is believed to constitute an important ideological bulwark against jihadism.

Numerous factors have no doubt contributed to peace, stability and religious harmony in Senegal, including the presence of Sufi theology. The content of Sufi theology, however, at best only partially explains the lack of religious conflict in Senegal. While Senegalese Sufism has been a *largely* peaceful, progressive and tolerant force throughout the country's modern history, Sufi brotherhoods also engaged in violent campaigns against the French and traditional African kings in the nineteenth century.[21] As noted by Villalón, "the jihads that swept West Africa in the late eighteenth and the nineteenth centur[ies] were in almost all cases led by leaders rooted squarely in the Sufi tradition, a tradition on which they based the inspiration for their movements of militant reformism."[22] So, put in historical context, even among Sufis, one can discern the Janus-faced and multivocal character of religion, even if modern Sufi theologies are peaceful.[23]

An especially noteworthy factor – and one that has made a viable peaceable Sufi presence in public life possible – is its low levels of governmental restriction of religion – a rare characteristic among Muslim-majority states but one that has fostered the development of a moderate and inclusive political theology. The French colonial state approached religion in Senegal in a very different way than in Algeria or even France itself. According to political scientist Alfred Stepan, instead of promoting a stringent secularism characteristic of *laïcité*, the French cultivated "vertical rituals of respect in regard to all of Senegal's major religious groups [and] all the religious groups, Muslim and Catholic ... reciprocated."[24] These "rituals of respect" between religious leaders and the secular state facilitated both peaceful coexistence among religious groups and policy cooperation between religious and political leaders that carried over into the post-independence era and continues to shape political and social life to this day.[25] Such a happy state of affairs

[20] Mamadou Diouf, ed., *Tolerance, Democracy, and Sufis in Senegal* (New York, NY: Columbia University Press, 2013).
[21] Alfred Stepan, "Rituals of Respect: Sufis and Secularists in Senegal in Comparative Perspective," *Comparative Politics* 44, no. 4 (2012): 383–384.
[22] Leonardo Villalón, "Negotiating Islam in the Era of Democracy: Senegal in Comparative Regional Perspective," in *Tolerance, Democracy, and Sufis in Senegal*, ed. Diouf, 241.
[23] Roman Loimeier, "The Secular State and Islam in Senegal," in *Questioning the Secular State: The Worldwide Resurgence of Religion in Politics*, ed. David Westerlund (New York, NY: St. Martin's Press, 1996), 183–197.
[24] Stepan, "Rituals of Respect," 380.   [25] Diouf, *Tolerance, Democracy, and Sufis in Senegal*, 14.

would not have been possible in Senegal's highly religious context absent mutual tolerance and respect between the state and religion, on one hand, and between different religious groups, on the other.

The Senegalese constitution defines the country as a secular state, provides for the free practice of religion and allows for the self-governance of faith-based groups without interference from the state. While religion and state are clearly separated in Senegal, the government does play a role in religious affairs, cultivating good relations with religious leaders and encouraging peaceful coexistence between faiths. The government's involvement in religion does not take a discriminatory character, however. In sharp contrast to the majority of Muslim countries, the state made no effort at coopting Islamic leaders or marginalizing religious minorities, thus precluding the formation of grievances on the part of either minority or majority religious groups. Conversely, religious groups made no attempt to take over the state or use it to further a religiously informed agenda against other religious communities.[26] Instead, both religious actors and the state have been content to respect each other's sphere of autonomy.[27]

For instance, the state provides direct financial and material assistance to all religious communities, primarily for the purposes of sponsoring special events and building or maintaining houses of worship.[28] The government also sponsors Muslim participation in the *Hajj* and Christian pilgrimages to the Vatican or the Holy Land, permits voluntary religious education in public schools and provides Arabic language training for Islamic schools.[29] Consequently, religiously based social tensions are also virtually nonexistent. According to the Pew Research Center, 93 percent of those surveyed said that people of different faiths are "very free" to practice their religion, and 90 percent of respondents agreed that this is a "good thing."[30] Constitutionally mandated freedom for all religious groups and individuals has thus helped prevent the rise of religious radicalism, even though the potential for religious violence has been an ever-present reality.

In the 1980s and 1990s, some feared that certain religious groups like the Association of Muslim Students of the University of Dakar (EIMUD) and the Moustarchidine would develop radical political agendas in challenging the state in the same way that analogous movements had done in places like Algeria. (Indeed, a militant form of Islam had begun to sprout in youth organizations throughout

---

[26] Leonardo A. Villalón, "Generational Changes, Political Stagnation, and the Evolving Dynamics of Religion and Politics in Senegal," *Africa Today* 46, no. 3 (1999): 130.

[27] Alfred Stepan, "The Multiple Secularisms of Modern Democratic and Non-Democratic Regimes," in *Rethinking Secularism*, ed. Craig Calhoun, Mark Juergensmeyer and Jonathan van Antwerpen (Oxford: Oxford University Press, 2011), 132–135.

[28] US Department of State, Bureau of Democracy, Human Rights and Labor, "Senegal," 2014 *International Religious Freedom Report*, last modified 2014,/www.state.gov/j/drl/rls/irf/religiousfree dom/index.htm#wrapper.

[29] Alfred Stepan and Juan J. Linz, "Democratization Theory and the Arab Spring," *Journal of Democracy* 24, no. 2 (2013): 19.

[30] Pew Research Center, *Tolerance and Tension*, 7.

Dakar in the early 1980s, fueled by economic crisis and a severe drought.) Yet, as noted by Alexander Thurston, the state's willingness to compromise and give space to these groups prevented their further radicalization and the acceptance of their ideas among the general populace. Thurston argues that "[b]y permitting Islamic activists to function openly, the regime prevented their radicalization along political lines. It also seems that permitting a vocal opposition to function with minimal interference and repression, at least in comparison with many other parts of the world, meant that Islam did not become the last bastion of political contestation."[31] A general move toward the taking up of arms would not have been unthinkable during this time as occurred in other parts of the Muslim world that experienced similar dynamics, but the Diouf regime's willingness to grant autonomy to and engage constructively with potential religious opposition movements appears to have had a moderating effect by facilitating an atmosphere in which religious leaders were free to make their case against extremism from within Islam. Further, like the various existing Sufi orders, Catholics too have crafted a political theology that respects the beliefs and practices of other faith traditions. While the secessionist conflict in the Christian-dominated southern region could have easily taken on a religious dimension as in other parts of the world, the presence of religious freedom created a marketplace of ideas and prevented radical voices from dominating the discourse.

In sum, Senegal stands out among Muslim-majority countries in its pursuit of policies that respect religious differences, rather than discriminating against religious minorities or regulating religious life in a manner consistent with majority religious cooptation. This has had the effect of strengthening moderate forces in the country, combating the growth of religious radicalism and consolidating democracy. While other social, economic and political factors have certainly contributed to this happy state of affairs, religious liberty has been an important part of the equation. For these reasons, Senegal presents an interesting challenge to the assumption that Islam must be relegated to the private sphere in order for democratic consolidation to occur and social harmony to flourish. At a time when religious tensions have gripped many parts of the Islamic world, respect between faiths in Senegal remains unshaken. Senegal's interreligious harmony stands as a model from which African countries in the midst of religious conflict can learn much.

SOUTH AFRICA

More than 4,000 miles southeast of Senegal lies the African continent's southernmost state, the Republic of South Africa – a country hobbled by a long and tumultuous history of conflict along ethnic and racial lines. From 1948 to 1994,

---

[31] Alexander Thurston, "Why Is Militant Islam a Weak Phenomenon in Senegal?" *Working Paper No. 09–005*, Institute for the Study of Islamic Thought in Africa (ISITA) (Bufett Center for International and Comparative Studies, Northwestern University, March 2009), p. 8.

South Africa was governed by a brutal and inhumane system of institutionalized racism and social oppression made possible by an elaborate set of laws known as apartheid ("apartness" in Afrikaans) until imprisoned civil rights leader Nelson Mandela rose to the presidency. During apartheid, the Afrikaner-dominated government engaged in state violence and human rights abuses (torture, imprisonment, forced resettlements and assassinations) in order to maintain its control. Blacks were excluded from government and were often forced to renounce their South African citizenship. Since the end of apartheid, Mandela's African National Congress party has dominated the political scene. The case of South Africa is a prime example of the Janus-faced character of religion; although certain churches propped up the apartheid regime, the climate of religious freedom after the end of apartheid empowered religious actors to engage in peace-building activities and helped prevent a relapse into conflict. Thus, South Africa demonstrates the profound value of religious freedom not only in combating terrorism and discouraging conflict but also in contributing to the overall health of society.

Religion mattered during the apartheid era. During this time, the state effectively coopted the Dutch Reformed Church (DRC), which it used to provide biblical sanction and theological justification for its discriminatory racial policies and structural violence, thus linking Afrikaner nationalism, apartheid and religion.[32] Some Christian churches (most notably the DRC but also certain Methodist, Catholic and Anglican fellowships) promoted apartheid in myriad ways, including, but not limited to, failing to use their moral standing to speak out against the injustices of apartheid; allowing segregation during worship services, thus reinforcing the racist backbone of apartheid; preaching a theology that the Bible forbids the intermingling of different races; or actively providing military chaplains to the armed forces.[33] This was not the only role played by religion, however. Christian theologians and religious leaders also led the struggle against the apartheid government beginning in the 1960s.[34] Through important statements like the 1960 Cottesloe Declaration and the 1986 *Kairos Document*, a group of progressive theologians boldly rejected the status quo, challenged the regime from a Christian perspective, demanded respect for all citizens of South Africa and helped pave the way for the country's religiously informed Truth and Reconciliation Commission in the mid-1990s.[35]

[32] Kairos Theologians, *The Kairos Document: Challenge to the Church: A Theological Comment on the Political Crisis in South Africa*, 2nd edn. (Grand Rapids, MI: William B. Eerdmans Publishing Company, 1986).

[33] Truth and Reconciliation Commission, *Volume Four: Truth and Reconciliation Commission of South Africa Report*, last modified October 29, 1998,/ www.justice.gov.za/trc/report/finalreport/Volume%204 .pdf/.

[34] Erik Doxtader, *With Faith in the Work of Words: The Beginnings of Reconciliation in South Africa, 1985–1995* (East Lansing, MI: Michigan State University Press, 2008).

[35] Tristan Anne Borer, *Challenging the State: Churches as Political Actors in South Africa, 1980–1994* (Notre Dame, IN: University of Notre Dame Press, 1998).

Despite the considerable racial and ethnic divisions and legacy of injustice, South Africa has not been plagued by the same religious turmoil found in other African states (even during apartheid religion was never a major source of conflict). The lack of religious tensions stems largely from the country's environment of religious freedom. South Africa is officially a secular state with a neutral stance toward religion. The constitution provides robust protections for freedom of religion, belief and opinion, and the government does not interfere in the free practice of religion. Robust antidiscrimination laws reinforce the culture of religious tolerance, while social regulation of religion remains very low (minor incidents of religious insensitivity notwithstanding).[36] As in Senegal, religious terrorism in South Africa has been virtually nonexistent.

In postapartheid South Africa, religion has not functioned as a source of conflict as much as a resource for social justice, peace building and reconciliation after the end of apartheid. Religious actors played a crucial role in breaking cycles of political violence and putting the country on a path to healing. As noted by W. Cole Durham and Elizabeth Clark, "religious freedom recognizes and values the contributions of religious actors and ideas, which can empower both religious leaders and members to become helpful resources to the peace process."[37] This has certainly been the case in South Africa, where the context of religious freedom has empowered religious actors to lead restorative processes that promoted national unity, rebuilt trust and restored relationships following decades of legalized discrimination against and suppression of the country's nonwhite population.

Largely the brainchild of Nobel peace prize winner and South Africa's most influential cleric, Archbishop Desmond Tutu, the newly elected government immediately following apartheid's end approved the establishment of a "Truth and Reconciliation Commission" (TRC) – a governmental body established to facilitate a peaceful transitional period from authoritarianism to democracy. South Africa's TRC was tasked with the twin goals of exposing and documenting the causes, nature and extent of violence and human rights abuses during apartheid and promoting reconciliation.[38] Unlike other truth commissions, the TRC took on an undeniably religious character, being chaired by Archbishop Tutu – always dressed in his purple clerical robes and wearing a conspicuous pectoral cross – and Alex Boraine, a former president of the Methodist Church of South Africa.[39] Seventeen of its commissioners came from faith communities; four were ordained ministers. With its emphasis on the biblically based concept of restorative rather than retributive

[36] Johan D. van der Vyver, "The Contours of Religious Liberty in South Africa," *Emory International Law Review* 21 (2007): 77–110.

[37] Durham and Clark, "The Place of Religious Freedom in the Structure of Peacebuilding," 296.

[38] Charles Villa-Vicencio and Wilhelm Verwoerd, eds., *Looking Back, Reaching Forward: Reflections on the Truth and Reconciliation Commission in South Africa* (Cape Town: UCT Press, 2000).

[39] Desmond Tutu, *No Future without Forgiveness* (New York, NY: Doubleday, 1999); Alex Boraine, *A Country Unmasked: Inside South Africa's Truth and Reconciliation Commission* (Cape Town: Oxford University Press, 2000).

justice, spiritual values like forgiveness, confession, repentance, reparation, redemption and reconciliation dominated the proceedings, while religious rituals like hymn singing, prayer and the reading of scripture were all commonplace.[40] The spiritual ethos that was part and parcel of the TRC was undeniable but also crucial to its ultimate success, largely due to the highly religious orientation of South Africa's population and the high level of trust, respect and influence commanded by the country's religious leaders.[41]

Religious communities also contributed logistical support to the truth commissions, assisting in organizing and carrying out hearings, finding victims and witnesses, encouraging them to share their stories and providing counseling once hearings were over.[42] As the focal point of the local community, the church was able to play a positive role in fostering peace because of the moral authority, community stature, knowledge of institutional resources, credibility, trust and empathetic neutrality it brought to the table. The religious communities that supported the work of the TRC most visibly were the same ones that most strongly and consistently opposed the policies of apartheid. Many have praised South Africa's unique approach to transitional justice as indispensable in avoiding a potential civil war and recovering from its bloody past. Though controversial for its supposed lack of accountability and denial of legal justice for victims of apartheid (perpetrators of atrocities publicly acknowledged their crimes in exchange for amnesty from prosecution), it is difficult to know how successful South Africa would have been in moving away from the injustices and tribulations of the past and toward reconciliation and healing in the absence of the religiously informed commission. Religious calls for repentance, forgiveness and reconciliation animated the populace to overcome anger and work toward a solution in the interest of the entire country.

Apart from the establishment and day-to-day operations of the TRC, the state has also invited religious actors to play a vital role in improving the overall quality of life within the country, recognizing that religious leaders are well positioned to build upon their successes with the reconciliation process begun with the TRC. For example, the government has welcomed the endeavors of groups like the Africa Cooperative Action Trust, a Christian organization that works to alleviate poverty, combat HIV/AIDS, strengthen civil society and sustain the environment; Caritas Southern Africa, a Catholic organization that, inter alia, has developed a peacebuilding curriculum for use in South African schools; the National Interfaith Council of South Africa, which brings together religious leaders to address various public policy issues; the Damietta Peace Initiative, a Pretoria-based Franciscan interfaith outreach program that promotes interfaith cooperation with the goal of

---

[40]   Janine Natalya Clark, "Religious Peace-Building in South Africa: From Potential to Practice," *Ethnopolitics* 10, no.3/4 (2011): 350.

[41]   James Cochrane, John de Gruchy and Stephen Martin, *Facing the Truth: South African Faith Communities and the Truth & Reconciliation Commission* (Athens, OH: Ohio University Press, 1999).

[42]   Philpott, *Just and Unjust Peace*, 100.

spreading peace throughout Africa; and Mercy Ministries, a Christian nonprofit group that works toward forgiveness, reconciliation and healing.[43] In these ways, the state has been able to harness the positive benefits of religion while discouraging its negative outgrowth, thus furthering the process of reconciliation.

In sum, far from being a roadblock to stability, prosperity and modernity, religion has been instrumental in helping South Africa overcome significant historical challenges, avert a relapse into conflict, build healthy cooperative relationships and pave the way for a brighter future. The government's encouraging of positive engagement by religious actors is exemplified by the successful reconciliation process, faith-based involvement in promoting social welfare and lack of religious terrorism. In particular, the South African approach to religion-led reconciliation made possible by the presence of religious freedom provides a model for how countries can grapple with a troubling past while moving toward sustainable democracy, averting a relapse into conflict and establishing a bulwark against religious violence. South Africa's religious approach to reconciliation has also had a global impact, shaping the thinking about justice in the aftermath of atrocity in other parts of the world. Of course, the reconciliation process is incomplete given the myriad injustices committed during apartheid, and, as Archbishop Tutu himself has admitted, "[t]he TRC process was an important turning point for South Africans – but it was only a starting point. We need to keep working at reconciliation."[44] Today, the country remains hobbled by serious economic problems – including a low economic growth rate, high unemployment and poverty rates and uneven wealth distribution – significant levels of criminal violence and rampant racism – all of which hamper genuine peace. Racism and self-imposed segregation remain important obstacles even within churches. While religion does not provide all of the answers to South Africa's problems, the process of addressing the deep emotional and psychological wounds of the past has begun, in large part made possible by the presence and creative work of religious actors who have proven capable of building bridges across cultural, ethnic and religious lines, thanks principally to the opportunities provided by religious liberty.

CONCLUSION

In his classic work *Political Liberalism*, political philosopher John Rawls argued that achieving an "overlapping consensus" in favor of liberty and democracy in plural societies necessarily means taking the "truths of religion off the political agenda."[45] However, in a deeply religious world where religion remains central to many conflicts, attempts to exclude religion will likely result in greater divisions and

---

[43]   Clark, "Religious Peace-Building in South Africa," 353–357.
[44]   As quoted in Charles Villa-Vicencio and Fanie Du Toit, *Truth and Reconciliation in South Africa: 10 Years On* (Cape Town: New Africa Books, 2006), v.
[45]   John Rawls, *Political Liberalism* (New York, NY: Columbia University Press, 1993), 151.

further conflict. On the other hand, empowering religion in these situations can play a constructive role in countering extremist narratives, averting violence and promoting peace. The cases of the United States, Senegal and South Africa suggest that giving voice to religious actors (even extremists) is a far better way to achieve the goals Rawls discusses, especially in countries where the population is comprised of a significant number of faith believers. In South Africa, for instance – the most important country in what is arguably the most religious region of the world – Christian themes played an indispensable role in reconciling hostile parties and mending broken communities. Peace and stability require that people of different backgrounds and religious views respect each other's rights. Religious freedom makes this possible for it empowers spiritual leaders who value the norms and habits of tolerance, trust and respect to advance theologically compelling arguments rooted in their particular faith traditions.

In all three cases examined here, religious liberty has helped hold religious militancy generally at bay in highly religious contexts. While religiously based tensions have been increasing in the United States, its long history of and robust protections for religious freedom have insulated it from religious terrorism for much of its past. Likewise, in the highly religious country of Senegal, widespread religious tolerance appears to have played a critical role in preventing religious radicalization and terrorism, despite the presence of several of the same precipitating factors that have led to violence elsewhere. The case of South Africa highlights another but commonly overlooked benefit of religious freedom: religiously based peace building in the aftermath of injustice, which can serve as a bulwark against civil conflict and terrorism. Without religious figures like Desmond Tutu and Alex Boraine, South Africa's TRC would have never come about. In this case, religious peacemakers performed rituals of reconciliation, imparted moral vision and promoted forgiveness and, in this way, helped offer spiritual healing to a country desperate to move beyond the injustices of the past. Of course, South Africa is not alone in this sense. Religious communities have been forces for peace in various countries – Mozambique, Guatemala, Uganda, Liberia, Ivory Coast, Burundi, Kosovo, Congo and many others – but only when they have enjoyed the necessary space created by religious freedom to carry out their crucially important work. Conversely, though, where religious freedom is inhibited, so too is the ability of religious actors to carve out a position of independence for themselves from which they can help create more stable and secure societies.

This book has thus far made the case that the presence of religious liberty works to combat violent religious extremism and that its violation has the opposite effect. The final chapter considers this argument in the context of policymaking, paying particular attention to the United States. It argues that the promotion of religious liberty ought to be an integral part of any broader effort designed to achieve security at home and abroad. The chapter offers ten practical suggestions for how the United States can responsibly and successfully accomplish this goal.

5

Religious Liberty and American Foreign Policy

American policymakers generally take religion more seriously today than they did after the end of the Cold War. The US Congress and State Department have taken practical steps toward integrating religious concerns into the conduct of American foreign policy, expanding its engagement with religious communities abroad via various special representatives and envoys. The State Department periodically offers a course on Religion and Foreign Policy at its Foreign Service Institute, and in 2013 it formally established the Office of Religion and Global Affairs. In late 2016, Congress passed an important update to the 1998 International Religious Freedom Act (IRFA). The new law allows the State Department to single out not just countries but also people and groups who threaten religious liberty. The law also elevates the role of the Ambassador at Large for International Religious Freedom, an appointee nominated by the president and confirmed by the Senate who heads the International Religious Freedom Office within the State Department. Moreover, it addresses a fundamental deficiency in the original Act by highlighting religious liberty as both a humanitarian and national security concern.

Yet, despite these positive developments, American foreign policy is not obtaining its objectives with respect to defeating religious terrorism or advancing religious freedom. Over the past decade, the global landscape for religious liberty has shifted markedly as levels of religious persecution and violent religious extremism are higher today than ever. The negative consequences that accompany religion's persecution threaten not only the well-being of the countries where those violations occur, but they also carry significant ramifications for regional and even global peace and security. The tragic recent events that have unfolded in countries as diverse as Egypt, Iraq, Nigeria, Syria, Burma, Belgium, the United States, Britain and France underscore the reality of violent religious extremism and the necessity of formulating effective policy responses.

In practice, the United States not only has failed to take advantage of the various tools offered by IRFA, in some cases it actively continues its support for many of the policies of religiously repressive states, implicitly accepting the argument that stability and US interests are best achieved by backing strongmen or illiberal policies. This wisdom is incorrect. Not only does it undermine the principles of popular consent and human dignity that the United States and the West more generally claim to champion, it also ensures the exact opposite outcome of that which is intended: diminished stability, extremism, terrorism and a tarnished reputation for those who support local repression. This understanding requires a fundamental rethinking of how the United States can best protect its interests, from blindly supporting autocrats to linking stability and security to the legitimacy of government.

American foreign policy has been particularly egregious in the Middle East and North Africa, where the same cycle of repression and violent resistance has been repeating itself for decades. Regimes repressive of religious liberty, backed by the West, generate discontent among the masses who view them as corrupt and illegitimate. In an effort to cling to power, these regimes become even more repressive over time and the opposition becomes more extreme as well. The polarized environment leaves little room for compromise, tolerance and liberty. Often the resistance turns violent. Although terrorists and those on whose behalf they claim to speak have mostly local grievances, Washington's support for the dictators of these countries puts the United States at risk as well. The reality of anti-American transnational terrorism, especially after the terrorist attacks of September 11, 2001, confronted the United States with an opportunity to contemplate the structural causes behind such a breathtakingly audacious act of violence.

Unfortunately, instead of critically examining how the United States' own policies may have contributed to the most devastating terrorist attack in history, American leaders doubled down on their default strategy of giving foreign assistance to leaders of the very states from where this anti-American belligerence emanates, thus ignoring the possibility that financial and military support given to unpopular, oppressive local regimes could contribute to further anti-American grievances among the masses in these countries. Osama bin Laden referred to this very injustice, among a litany of other charges, in his 2002 "Letter to America," writing:

> Under your supervision, consent and orders, the governments of our countries which act as *your agents*, attack us on a daily basis ... The freedom and democracy that you call to is for yourselves ... only; as for the rest of the world, you impose upon them your monstrous, destructive policies and governments, which you call the "American friends." ... When the Islamic party in Algeria wanted to practice democracy and they won the election, you unleashed your agents in the Algerian army onto them, and to attack them with tanks and guns, to imprison them and torture them ... These governments give us a taste of humiliation, and place us in a large prison of fear and subdual ... The removal of these governments is an obligation upon us.[1]

---

[1] Osama bin Laden, "Letter to America," *The Guardian*, last modified November 24, 2002, www.theguardian.com/world/2002/nov/24/theobserver. Emphasis added.

To understand the roots of Islamic rage toward the United States, it would be advantageous to carefully consider what the mastermind of al Qaeda himself had to say on the issue of American support for repressive regimes in the Islamic world.

In choosing a policy of stability over liberty, the United States ended up producing neither. American support enabled Arab security states to continue to ruthlessly suppress their people in an effort to shore up their rule. Repression also led to the development of extremist theologies and religious militancy, greatly aiding the recruitment efforts of groups like ISIS. It is no coincidence that most of the major terrorist threats to the United States today originate from the countries of the Arab world, a region that not only features some of the world's most repressive regimes but also one whose repressive leaders receive a substantial amount of aid from the United States. In Egypt, for instance, the United States has given large amounts of financial support to the military-backed government of President Sisi and remained conspicuously silent as he cracked down on religious, human rights and civil society groups. Ongoing religious persecution in Egypt, however, will likely advance the cause of extremism, threatening the security of not only that country but also that of its allies. Already, an active affiliate of ISIS has emerged in Egypt. US policy undermines the goal of stability and its own credibility by supporting a government that fails to respect human rights and the rule of law in a country where such actions have bred violent extremism in the past. In the Arab world, as elsewhere, religious repression is the problem, not the solution.

Despite its shortcomings on religious freedom policy, the United States is in the best position to champion the cause of international religious freedom. Not only is it the world's most powerful country, but religious liberty is also part and parcel of America's founding ideals. It therefore has a unique ability to explain to the world how liberty can promote stability and combat terrorism.

FAITH, FREEDOM AND FOREIGN POLICY

Several of the world's leading religious and political figures have drawn an explicit link between religious freedom and societal flourishing in recent years. The Archbishop of Canterbury, Justin Welby, made an unequivocal connection between the two: "societies which respect freedom guard their own freedom and flourishing in every area, with robust and respectful conversation, they become more like the societies in which we dream of living; vigorous, diverse, generous, hopeful, exciting."[2] In a 2013 conversation sponsored by Georgetown University, prominent American evangelical pastor Rick Warren declared that religious liberty is integral

---

[2] Justin Welby, "Archbishop of Canterbury on Religious Freedom," last modified July 16, 2015, www.archbishopofcanterbury.org/articles.php/5591/archbishop-of-canterbury-on-religious-freedom.

to solving the world's major problems.[3] Finally, no less than Pope Benedict XVI referred to religious liberty as "an authentic weapon of peace with an historical and prophetic mission."[4]

Political leaders have also in rhetoric recognized the connection between religious repression and violence. Many American policymakers from both sides of the political aisle, including those at the highest levels of government, have been vocal in their support for religious freedom as a key ingredient in American national security. Florida senator and 2016 Republican presidential candidate Marco Rubio declared that "attacks on religious freedom are both a moral and strategic national security concern for the United States."[5] Speaking in her capacity as secretary of state in a 2012 speech to the Carnegie Endowment for International Peace, Hillary Clinton declared religious freedom to be in the American national interest, explicitly proposing that international religious freedom could be an effective antidote to religious extremism and terrorism. Clinton touted religious freedom as a "cherished constitutional value, a strategic national interest, and a foreign policy priority." The secretary continued:

> Religious freedom is both an essential element of human dignity and of secure, thriving societies. It's been statistically linked with economic development and democratic stability ... And because the impact of religious freedom extends beyond the realm of religion and has ramifications for a country's security and its economic and political progress, more students and practitioners of foreign policy need to focus more time and attention on it.[6]

Clinton's speech was the first by such a high-level American governmental official to so forcefully and eloquently draw the connection between religious liberty and national security.

Clinton's successor, John Kerry, also drew an unambiguous connection between religious liberty and violent religious extremism:

> [T]rying to dictate an artificial conformity of religious expression is not a prescription for harmony. It is a prescription for frustration, anger, and rebellion. And we have learned time and again that if citizens are denied the rights to practice and express their beliefs peacefully, they are far more likely to explore other and more often than not dangerous alternatives ... No nation can fulfill its potential if its

---

3 Rick Warren, "Rick Warren on Religious Freedom – A Conversation," February 12, 2013, remarks to Georgetown University, Washington, DC.

4 Pope Benedict XVI, "Religious Freedom, the Path to Peace," last modified January 1, 2011, www.vatican.va/holy_father/benedict_xvi/messages/peace/documents/hf_ben-xvi_mes_20101208_xliv-world-day-peace_en.html.

5 Marco Rubio, "Rubio Comments on the Release of the International Religious Freedom Report," last modified October 14, 2015, www.rubio.senate.gov/public/index.cfm/press-releases?ID=6d9c39fb-1df2-4a8a-8915-fa52aeacdfd9.

6 Hillary Rodham Clinton, "Remarks at the Release of the 2011 International Religious Freedom Report," last modified July 30, 2012, www.state.gov/secretary/20092013clinton/rm/2012/07/195782.htm.

people are denied the right to practice, to hold, to modify, to openly profess their innermost beliefs.[7]

The last three presidential administrations too have voiced support for religious liberty. Addressing a summit on Christian persecution held in Washington, DC, Vice President Mike Pence promised that "[p]rotecting religious freedom is a foreign-policy priority of the Trump administration."[8] Trump's presidential predecessors, George W. Bush and Barack Obama, provided strong rhetorical support in high-profile speeches regarding the importance of religious freedom. In a 2003 speech delivered to the National Endowment for Democracy, Bush recognized the connection between (religious) liberty and national security saying, "[s]ixty years of Western nations excusing and accommodating the lack of freedom in the Middle East did nothing to make us safe, because in the long run stability cannot be purchased at the expense of liberty."[9] In 2008, Bush offered another strong defense of religious liberty. "Whenever and wherever I meet leaders, I'm going to constantly remind them that they ought to welcome religion in their society, not fear it. I'll remind them someone pledged to love a neighbor like they'd like to be loved themselves is someone who will add to their society in constructive and peaceful ways."[10]

President Obama too, at times, spoke favorably about the need for religious liberty. In his first and most important foreign policy speech, the president identified religious freedom as one of seven key areas of concern in US–Islamic relations, declaring that "freedom of religion is central to the ability of peoples to live together."[11] He made this statement while speaking in the heart of the Arab world: Cairo, Egypt. Again, in 2011, he spoke about the idea that freedoms, including religious liberty, constituted a "top priority that must be translated into concrete actions, and supported by all of the diplomatic, economic and strategic tools at our disposal."[12] He declared insightfully at the 2014 National Prayer Breakfast: "History shows that nations that uphold the rights of their people, including the freedom of religion, are ultimately more just and more peaceful and more successful. Nations that do not uphold these rights sow the

[7] John Kerry, "Remarks at the Rollout of the 2014 Report on International Religious Freedom," last modified October 14, 2015, www.state.gov/secretary/remarks/2015/10/248198.htm.
[8] Julie Zauzmer, "Pence: America Will Prioritize Protecting Christians Abroad," *Washington Post*, May 11, 2017, accessed June 20, 2017, www.washingtonpost.com/news/acts-of-faith/wp/2017/05/11/pence-america-will-prioritize-protecting-christians-abroad/?utm_term=.afof98b2e443.
[9] George W. Bush, "President Bush Discusses Freedom in Iraq and Middle East," November 6, 2003, http://georgewbush-whitehouse.archives.gov/news/releases/2003/11/20031106-2.html.
[10] George W. Bush, "Remarks on the 10th Anniversary of the International Religious Freedom Act," July 14, 2008, http://georgewbush-whitehouse.archives.gov/news/releases/2008/07/20080714-1.html.
[11] Barack Obama, "Remarks by the President at Cairo University," last modified June 4, 2009, www.whitehouse.gov/the-press-office/remarks-president-cairo-university-6-04-09.
[12] Barack Obama, "Remarks by the President on the Middle East and North Africa," last modified May 19, 2011, www.whitehouse.gov/the-press-office/2011/05/19/remarks-president-middle-east-and-north-africa.

bitter seeds of instability and violence and extremism. So freedom of religion matters to our national security." He further declared, "promoting religious freedom is a key objective of U.S. foreign policy. And I'm proud that no nation on Earth does more to stand up for the freedom of religion around the world than the United States of America."[13] Finally, in a speech at the Countering Violent Extremism summit in 2015, the president identified freedom of belief as integral to political stability, saying that "when people are free to practice their faith as they choose, it helps hold diverse societies together."[14]

These rhetorical salutes to religious freedom notwithstanding, the promotion of international religious freedom did not figure prominently into any of these presidents' approaches to foreign policy, nor did their administrations devote necessary resources for its promotion. To his credit, President Trump did nominate an individual to the post of Ambassador at Large for International Religious Freedom, Governor Sam Brownback, widely supported by religious freedom advocates. However, through a series of measures, the president simultaneously undercut America's commitment to religious freedom. In an executive order on refugees and immigration, Trump ordered the State Department to prioritize refugee claims for those of minority (non-Muslim) faith communities, while temporarily banning all citizens of several Muslim-majority countries in the Middle East and North Africa from entry to the United States. The president also barred all refugees from Syria – the country where religious persecution is arguably the greatest. These moves served to alienate strategic partners in the fight against terrorism, increase the distress of the victims of terrorism and create rifts among those in Trump's national security team.

Though Bush centered his foreign policy on the promotion of democracy in Afghanistan and Iraq and verbally acknowledged the freedom–security nexus, he generally ignored the highly complex and vitally important religious configurations of those countries and the role religious freedom could have played in fostering peace and stability after the American-led invasions. Unfortunately, rhetorical denunciations of religious subjugation alone were not enough to stem the tide of faith-based persecution worldwide.

Obama provided strong rhetorical support for religious freedom, but it is clear from the administration's actions that such concerns were in practice relegated to the back burner. In a speech before the United Nations in 2013, the president did not mention religious liberty (or any human right for that matter) as a key pillar of US grand strategy. The Obama administration's 2010 *National Security Strategy* – a document that broadly reflects the president's approach to major national security

---

[13] Barack Obama, "Remarks by the President at the National Prayer Breakfast," last modified February 14, 2014, www.whitehouse.gov/the-press-office/2014/02/06/remarks-president-national-prayer-breakfast.

[14] Barack Obama, "Remarks by the President at the Summit on Countering Violent Extremism," last modified February 19, 2015, www.whitehouse.gov/the-press-office/2015/02/19/remarks-president-summit-countering-violent-extremism-february-19-2015.

concerns – made no mention of religious freedom as a weapon that can fight extremism. Finally, during much of Obama's tenure as president, the position of Ambassador at Large for International Religious Freedom remained vacant, although it is a post required by law. Inattentiveness to religious freedom could also be detected with respect to specific foreign policy decisions. For example, although human rights organizations consistently documented massive rights abuses in Egypt, the president failed to roundly condemn these atrocities, instead describing the country as on the path to democracy. In practice, the Obama team defaulted to the conventional belief that support for authoritarian allies can lead to stability.

TEN PROPOSALS FOR AMERICAN FOREIGN POLICY

The reality of rising global religious terrorism necessitates the development of fresh approaches to counter it. In this battle, no single solution will suffice in addressing the myriad sources of religious radicalization. At the same time, it is clear that the undue regulation of religious belief and practice often lies at the root of extremism and that incorporating religious liberty into efforts to confront terrorism can play an indispensable role in the struggle against religious terrorism. In this section, I highlight ten practical ways in which American foreign policy can help break the cycle of religious repression and religious terrorism.

1. First, practical steps should be taken to make the promotion of religious freedom a higher priority within the foreign policy and national security establishment. As mentioned earlier, the United States has had a statutory requirement to promote religious freedom abroad since 1998 when Congress unanimously passed the International Religious Freedom Act (IRFA), a law mandating the United States to oppose persecution on the basis of faith wherever it exists. IRFA established the Office of International Religious Freedom within the State Department – a body tasked with writing the annual *International Religious Freedom Report*, which systematically evaluates each country in the world with respect to its record on religious freedom and designates certain egregious offenders as "countries of particular concern" (CPCs) – and the independent and bipartisan US Commission on International Religious Freedom (USCIRF), which monitors worldwide violations of religious freedom and makes policy recommendations. IRFA further created the position of Ambassador at Large for International Religious Freedom as a principal advisor to the president and secretary of state on matters of international religious freedom. Many hoped that the law's passage would send a clear signal that the right to religious freedom is a priority in American foreign policy. Generally, however, the provisions of the Act have been ignored by policymakers, and, despite its foresight and good intentions, religious freedom conditions continue to decline in most parts of the world. One key reason behind the disappointment with IRFA revolves around the fact that the Act, though correctly framing religious liberty as a humanitarian concern, did not attempt to connect it to American national security until the

passage of a major substantive update to IRFA, the 2016 Frank R. Wolf International Religious Freedom Act, which better equips the US government to address current religious freedom conditions.

The US State Department thus needs an integrated, flexible and comprehensive strategy aimed at promoting international religious freedom and curbing the rising tide of religious intolerance.[15] Several steps can be taken. The Office for Religious Freedom, instead of being buried in the State Department's Bureau of Democracy, Human Rights and Labor, should be integrated into broader discourses and programs designed to promote civil society and enhance American national security and agencies directly responsible for foreign policy, intelligence and national defense. The Ambassador at Large for Religious Freedom should also be equipped with the same resources and status as those in similar posts (such as the Ambassador at Large for Global Women's Issues) and should also be required to have regular briefings with the secretary of state and attend the highest-level meetings at the State Department and National Security Council. In line with the requirements of IRFA, diplomats – from ambassadors all the way down to the entry level – should receive education on the nature, causes and consequences of religious freedom as part of their training at the Foreign Service Institute in accordance with the provisions of the 2016 Wolf Bill. Furthermore, the *National Security Strategy* and other influential policy documents should contain clearly articulated statements about the importance of promoting international religious freedom as part of an overall strategy to counter terrorism and foster stability. Finally, Congress should increase funding and staffing for USCIRF, which can inform decisions on foreign policy and national security. In short, there is a dire need for a stronger infrastructure, better coordination, increased resources and concrete strategies for advancing religious freedom abroad. These changes would send a powerful message both to American officials and to foreign governments that the United States takes religious liberty seriously and considers it a priority in pursuing its normative and strategic goals.[16]

2. Second, foreign policymakers need to accept that a wide variety of secularisms and religion–state relations exists, which can broadly be classified as "religiously free." Even religiously free countries in the West exhibit vastly different religion–state arrangements, ranging from England's established state church to America's "wall of separation." Therefore, American diplomats must do everything in their power to overcome the perception that religious freedom is a Western norm that has little acceptance or understanding outside of the West. They should be clear to their counterparts around the world (particularly in the Arab countries) that religious freedom does not mean a Rawlsian, French-style, hostile separation of religion and

[15] R. Scott Appleby and Richard Cizik, *Engaging Religious Communities Abroad: A New Imperative for US Foreign Policy* (Chicago, IL: Chicago Council on Global Affairs, 2010), 56–61.
[16] Thomas F. Farr, "International Religious Freedom Policy and American National Security," Witherspoon Institute, last modified September 19, 2014, www.thepublicdiscourse.com/2014/09/13818/.

state – the relegation of religious expression to the private realm and its banning from policy debates – something that the highly religious publics around the world would (or should) never accept. Put differently, American foreign policy should make no attempt to divorce people's religious ideas and identities from their participation in politics. In the Middle East, for example, where the marginalization of religion has only led to social stagnation and extremism, establishing liberal orders can only be accomplished by including people of faith in what one scholar has termed "religiously-friendly" democracy.[17] This type of responsible promotion of religious freedom can serve to undercut the assertion that religious freedom is simply a form of Western cultural imperialism rooted in a particular American Protestant understanding of religion and state designed to remove Islam from public life. Properly understood, religious liberty means that the practice and expression of religion is free, not that public life is free of religion. In this sense, the United States can draw on its own experience as a country that welcomes the participation of religious groups in the social and political arenas.

3. Third, these same foreign policy officials should strive to explain to their counterparts why weaving religious liberty into the fabric of their societies is in *their* national interest. The promotion of religious liberty abroad is more likely to succeed when it can be tied directly to the material self-interest of other states. Research by sociologists and political scientists has found that religious freedom is strongly correlated with other social and political goods like stability and economic development. The implication is clear: if countries are serious about making headway in the areas of civil society, security and the economy, religious freedom needs to be part of the strategy. In this same vein, in addition to using existing targeting tools against officials, groups and states involved in severe violations of religious liberty – visa denials, asset freezes and adding names to the Treasury Department's list of "specially designated nationals" – the United States should also recognize and reward countries for making progress on religious freedom issues in the form of public commendation, development aid and other economic incentives. Specific inducements might include American support for accession to the World Trade Organization, new or enhanced bilateral trade agreements, sanctions relief or loan support from international economic organizations.

4. Fourth, the US government should do a better job highlighting the plight of religious heroes of conscience who are persecuted for their faith and prioritize the release of prisoners identified as being imprisoned for their religious beliefs and practices. These are the very individuals who challenge extremist narratives that give rise to violence and instability. Hundreds of religious dissidents remain persecuted or imprisoned in countries that are close allies of the United States like Egypt and

---

[17] Michael Driessen, *Religion and Democratization: Framing Political and Religious Identities in Muslim and Catholic Societies* (Oxford: Oxford University Press, 2014).

Saudi Arabia. These are countries where the United States has a great deal of clout and should use its military and economic leverage to urge those governments to grant their people fundamental religious rights. To this end, the US Commission on International Religious Freedom should swiftly work to compile and publish a current and comprehensive list of prisoners held abroad owing to their religious beliefs, practices or identities.

5. Fifth, policymakers should recognize that violations of religious liberty stem not only from the policies of regimes but also from religious and nonreligious actors in society. In many parts of the world, public opinion supports the establishment of democratic institutions and processes but is less favorable to the idea of liberty for all groups in society. In fact, as the experience of the Arab Spring demonstrated, democratically elected governments can actually worsen the plight of religious minorities in countries where society at large opposes free religious expression. Therefore, efforts to address religious liberty issues should focus not only on elite violations but also on threats at the society level. This can be accomplished through education programs that can both offer alternative narratives to extremism and intolerance, and counter rumor-based cultures and segregation of religious communities that plague societies marked by religious persecution. Through awareness-raising, such programs can teach the importance of ending cycles of persecution and securing rights for all. These "civil society initiatives" can help overcome societal prejudice and divisions by working directly with organizations and individuals at the grassroots level. Such nongovernmental organizations are not merely humanitarian watchdog agencies; they are also important instruments of peace. The Office of Faith-Based Community Initiatives would be an ideal vehicle to accomplish this goal. In the Muslim world, for example, the empowering of Sufi brotherhoods at the society level could be an important strategy in the battle against religious extremism as seen in the previous chapter. As explained by scholar of religion Philip Jenkins: "Where Islamists rise to power, Sufis are persecuted or driven underground; but where Sufis remain in the ascendant, it is the radical Islamist groups who must fight to survive."[18] An approach that recognizes Sufis as a natural ally can help counter the voices of hatred prevalent in too many mosques and schools throughout the Muslim world. In short, by directly engaging with and, where appropriate, assisting religious groups in society, the United States can generate goodwill among these crucially important religious communities, instead of engaging solely with regimes.

6. Sixth, and related to the aforementioned point, foreign policy officials should actively collaborate with local religious leaders abroad. While the United States can and should defend religious freedom from abroad in the defense of "universal human rights," the most effective response is likely to come from local religious leaders who make religiously based arguments in support of religious freedom and against religious extremism (and the various

---

[18] Philip Jenkins, "Mystical Power," *Boston Globe*, January 25, 2009.

forces that give rise to it). These spiritual leaders possess moral standing and pervasive influence based on a shared set of values, credibility with their constituencies and an intimate knowledge of cultural values and local issues that no outside actor can possibly have.[19] Because they have personal relationships with members of their communities, they possess a unique ability to credibly verbalize counter narratives, positively influence would-be militants and mobilize support for peace. They are the ones best positioned to carry out conflict resolution between warring communities, mediation, reconciliation, the re-humanizing of relationships and context-specific rituals of healing, which can all help in preventing relapses into conflict and the onset of violent religious extremism. Indeed, religious actors have time and again proven instrumental in mediating peace agreements in places like Mozambique, Algeria, Kosovo, Guatemala and Uganda. For these reasons, a successful policy will combine American diplomatic efforts with homegrown initiatives to support religious liberty.

7. Seventh, the United States should be skeptical of the idea that military intervention alone can help transform countries from repressive autocracies to religiously liberal democracies free of terrorism. Recent history has shown the limits of American power in achieving this objective. The use of force alone cannot eliminate faith-based terrorism. While the American armed forces have proven exceptionally adroit at removing repressive dictators from power in places like Libya and Iraq, American-led interventions have also paved the way for state collapse and militia rule in these countries, directly contributing to radicalization and increasing sympathy for terrorists. Since the terrorist strikes of September 11, 2001, the United States has spent breathtaking sums of money in the quest to combat terrorism – missions that have resulted in the deaths of thousands of servicemen and women and claimed the lives of hundreds of thousands of innocent civilians. For example, since 2011, the United States, in collaboration with the Yemeni government, has been conducting a shadow war via CIA operatives and drone strikes in an effort to assassinate key leaders associated with al Qaeda and its affiliates. The most prominent of these leaders was Anwar al-Awlaki, an American-born Islamist militant who was the first citizen of the United States to be targeted and killed in an American drone strike. While the strikes have been effective in assassinating a number of alleged terrorists, they have also killed an unknown number of civilians, which has likely increased radicalization and support for militant groups. As Osama bin Laden once pointed out in a videotaped speech aired on al Jazeera:

> All that we have to do is to send two *mujahidin* to the furthest point east to raise a piece of cloth on which is written al-Qaeda, in order to make the generals race there to cause America to suffer human, economic, and political losses without their

---

[19]   Douglas Johnston and Brian Cox, "Faith-Based Diplomacy and Preventive Engagement," in *Faith-Based Diplomacy: Trumping Realpolitik*, ed. Douglas Johnston (New York, NY: Oxford University Press, 2003), 11–30.

achieving for it anything of note other than some benefits for their private companies.[20]

Not only has the unabashed use of American military power failed to secure many foreign policy objectives, served to create a national security state domestically and contributed to record fiscal deficits, in the cases of both Iraq and Afghanistan, post-invasion planning failed to incorporate the religious freedom dimension, which could have helped prevent the onslaught of extremism and persecution that subsequently engulfed those countries.

Instead, the United States and its allies should seek to combine a "light-footprint" strategy (including intelligence gathering and sharing, law enforcement and the use of Special Operations forces) with a surge in religiously informed diplomacy as part of a broader national security strategy.[21] The struggle against global religious extremism is better understood as a war of ideas rather than a battle of bombs. To this end, a war must be fought – but one aimed against religious intolerance and extremist ideologies. Groups that pervert religion according to their twisted interpretations of sacred texts like ISIS and its ilk can only be defeated when people are free to choose better ideas, and these ideas emerge only in the free marketplace of beliefs that are part and parcel of religious freedom, which naturally weakens extremism at its root. The focus, therefore, should be not only on stopping the violence of radical groups but also on dissuading people from joining them in the first place and empowering those groups who offer a critique of and an alternative to the extremist agenda. The robust protection of religious freedom is central to that objective and more likely to succeed over the long term than military measures, not to mention being far less costly.

8. Eighth, and related to the point given earlier, the United States must aggressively tackle the profound problem of failed and failing states. Religious repression is especially dangerous in contexts where states that restrict religion are simultaneously too weak to provide security and basic services for all people living under their jurisdiction. In fragile and failing states, national and local authorities lack the capacity to prevent violence and engage in counterterrorism, which renders violence more feasible. Because governments lack the monopoly on the legitimate use of force within their territories, radical groups have an easier time gaining loyalty in states marked by instability, breakdown of governance, widespread lawlessness and challenges to authority. The government's difficulty in providing for the essential well-being of its people (including basic infrastructure, services and personal security) allows radical religious groups to make inroads among the local populace, delivering goods and services that the government cannot and setting up autonomous political and social institutions. As noted by terrorism expert James A. Piazza,

---

[20] "Full Transcript of bin Laden's Speech," *Al Jazeera*, last modified November 1, 2004, www.aljazeera.com/archive/2004/11/200849163336457223.html.

[21] Seth G. Jones, *Hunting in the Shadows: The Pursuit of al Qa'ida since 9/11* (New York, NY: W. W. Norton, 2013).

"Failed states, through their incompetence, create 'political goods vacuums' into which terrorist groups can step and parcel out personal security, economic assistance, or other services to win the support of the local population and widen their activities."[22] Large numbers of insecure, marginalized, and unhappy citizens provide important opportunities for terrorists by making it easier for them to gain the sympathy of ordinary people, recruit, train, fundraise and plot attacks.[23] The absence of authority in producing violence has a long academic pedigree and is central to contemporary policy discussions regarding religious terrorism.[24] Former American Secretary of Defense Robert Gates identified "fractured or failing states" as "the main security challenge our time."[25] Similar sentiments have been raised by a slew of academics, pundits and diplomats.[26] Some of the worst cases of religious terrorism occur in countries where state collapse immediately follows years of religious repression by the state.

Unfortunately, as shown in Chapter 4, American policies have at times been responsible for helping to *create* conditions of fragility in certain parts of the Middle East and North Africa. In some countries, governing institutions have completely collapsed, leading to civil war and internecine fighting. Such countries create the kinds of anarchic conditions that generate social hostilities and religious persecution, provide sanctuary for extremist networks and allow them to thrive and export their radicalism to other states. Often, the only sources of law and order in these countries come from extremist organizations who engage in severe violations of human rights.

While the ability of the United States to influence events on the ground in these countries is obviously limited, the goal of American policy should be to improve responsible and liberal state authority structures in countries with ungoverned spaces, particularly Yemen, Pakistan, Somalia and Libya, to the extent that such states are at least capable of maintaining order within their territories. In these areas, the United States must do what it can to protect vulnerable communities as it did in the humanitarian mission undertaken by the Obama administration in 2015 to save those trapped on Mount Sinjar in northern Iraq and facing certain death at the hands of ISIS. Another positive step would be congressional passage of the Iraq and Syria Genocide Emergency Relief and Accountability Act (H.R. 390). The law

---

[22] James A. Piazza, "Incubators of Terror: Do Failed and Failing States Promote Transnational Terrorism?" *International Studies Quarterly* 52, no. 3 (2008): 472.

[23] Ray Takeyh and Nikolas Gvosdev, "Do Terrorist Networks Need a Home?" *Washington Quarterly* 25, no. 3 (2002): 97–108.

[24] National Security Council, "Strategy for Winning the War on Terror," last modified 2006, www.whitehouse.gov/nsc/nsct/2006/sectionV.html.

[25] Robert M. Gates, "Helping Others Defend Themselves: The Future of U.S. Security Assistance," *Foreign Affairs* 98 (2010): 2.

[26] For example, see Joel S. Migdal, *Strong Societies and Weak States: State–Society Relations and State Capabilities in the Third World* (Princeton, NJ: Princeton University Press, 1998); Susan E. Rice, *The New National Security Strategy: Focus on Failed States* (Washington, DC: Brookings Institution, 2003).

ensures that humanitarian assistance reaches the victims of genocide whose very survival is at risk in an effort to preserve minority religious communities in their ancestral homelands in the Middle East. Similarly, the United States should do more to help refugees fleeing severe persecution at the hands of radical jihadi groups by continuing the US Refugee Admissions Program (USRAP), while at the same time addressing long-standing flaws in the treatment of asylum seekers. An embrace of refugees will also likely generate goodwill from among Muslim communities at home and abroad, thus making counterterrorism easier. Conversely, bans on immigrants from predominantly Muslim countries would likely constitute a propaganda victory for religious terrorists by reinforcing the claims of jihadists that the West is at war with Islam.

9. Ninth, Washington needs to understand that foreign policy takes place not just with diplomatic counterparts but also with the people whom those officials represent. As the United States implicitly or explicitly backs and legitimizes repressive regimes, it should recognize the effect this has on those who bear the brunt of religiously oppressive policies. Such unholy alliances not only turn public opinion against the domestic government, they also poison ordinary peoples' views of the United States. When individuals in these countries see their despised regimes being propped up by the United States, inevitably that rage turns against the "far enemy" as well.[27] Western support for autocrats may give policymakers a sense of security in an age of terrorism, but one must always question what is happening behind the curtain of repression, particularly in religious institutions, where terrorists feed off of popular discontent and make credible arguments that violence is the answer. It should be very worrying indeed that the standing of the United States in the Arab world today hovers around record lows in several countries. For this reason, the United States needs to fundamentally rethink its increasingly close relationship with repressive regimes like those in Yemen, Egypt and Saudi Arabia and make security and counterterrorism assistance contingent upon human rights outcomes in accordance with the provisions of the "Leahy Law," which prohibits the Departments of Defense and State from providing military assistance to foreign units implicated in serious rights abuses.

10. Tenth, it is imperative for the United States to lead in example by vigorously protecting religious freedom at home. Unfortunately, reports by the Pew Research Center show that religious freedom in the United States is decreasing, especially for religious minorities. Yet history shows that the robust defense of religious freedom for minority faith communities within its borders will have the effect of increasing the legitimacy of the United States in its dealings with foreign governments. For example, American president Dwight Eisenhower successfully appealed to Zahir Shah, the king of Afghanistan, to allow Afghan Christians to build churches. In making his appeal, Eisenhower pointed to America's own record of tolerance toward

---

[27] Gerges, *Far Enemy.*

Muslim minorities, including his own role in attending the dedication of the Washington Islamic Center.[28]

Unfortunately, though, Americans have increasingly come to view the religion of Islam with deep suspicion and fear, especially after the September 11 attacks. Though Muslims comprise only 1 percent of the population, American Muslim communities have quickly become America's most hated religious group and the constant targets of harassment, intimidation and discrimination, seen in the mass protests against the so-called ground zero mosque in New York City to efforts in state legislatures to ban sharia. In the lead-up to the 2016 presidential election, several Republican candidates attempted to outdo each other in their incendiary remarks about Islam and Muslims. Neurosurgeon-turned-politician Ben Carson declared that a Muslim could not serve as president unless first renouncing Islam, implicitly rejecting the Constitution's First Amendment. Donald Trump, the candidate who would go on to capture the presidency, called for the intensive monitoring of Muslim Americans, proposed barring Muslims from immigrating to the United States, suggested that Muslims should be forced to register with the government and spoke admiringly of leaders abroad who were closing down mosques. These views about Islam are not isolated opinions held by a handful of extremist politicians but rather seem to hold serious sway in some portions of the American population. For example, a September 2015 poll by Public Policy Polling found that 72 percent of North Carolinians believed that a Muslim should not be allowed to be president of the United States and that 40 percent believed that Islam should be banned completely.[29] In short, the United States has experienced a worrying trend with respect to religious liberty at home, which will certainly complicate efforts at promoting it abroad. It must therefore defend its "first freedom" as both a moral and strategic imperative.

These ten proposals flow naturally from the findings and arguments contained in this book. The promotion of international religious freedom is an invaluable but underutilized instrument of soft power. Such an approach will no doubt have its skeptics who will quickly identify the difficulties that will accompany some of these suggestions. Yet the reality persists that religious freedom conditions remain under assault across much of the world, especially in countries from where the greatest threats to American national security stem. In such contexts, religious freedom is not merely a desirable privilege; it is a foundational human right with a distinct public dimension – one that is absolutely necessary for the success of states. This is doubly true for highly religious countries, where religious freedom is being increasingly demanded by marginalized and persecuted communities. International religious

---

[28] William Inboden, "Responding to Religious Freedom and Presidential Leadership: An Historical Approach," Berkley Center for Religion, Peace and World Affairs, February 19, 2015, http://berkley center.georgetown.edu/responses/promoting-religious-freedom-from-the-oval-office.

[29] Public Policy Polling, "Trump Steady in North Carolina; Biden Polls Well," last modified September 29, 2015, http://www.publicpolicypolling.com/pdf/2015/PPP_Release_NC_92915.pdf.

freedom policy may well have its problems, but the risks of not taking religious liberty seriously as an instrument of policy far exceed the dangers of doing so, as seen so vividly in recent events around the world. While many have debated the merits of Immanuel Kant's famous "democratic peace" for well over 100 years, it appears that in the twenty-first century the best hope in the struggle against violent religious extremism lies more in a "religious freedom peace."[30]

Finally, note that while these proposals have focused on American foreign policy specifically, the fight against global religious extremism does not belong to the United States exclusively. This is a transnational challenge that affects the community of nations. The United States must support the work of its counterparts at the United Nations, the Organization for Security and Cooperation in Europe, the European Union and the International Panel of Parliamentarians for Freedom of Religion or Belief and within countries like Norway and Canada, both of which have created special envoys for freedom of religion and belief. These organizations and countries must work in concert through multinational efforts to effectively combat the threat posed by modern religious terrorism. The recent creation of an International Contact Group to foster increased collaboration among these different entities represents an important step in the right direction.

THE CRITICS OF RELIGIOUS LIBERTY

Not everyone supports the idea that the United States should advance religious liberty abroad as part of its foreign policy. Not only has religious liberty come under assault by authoritarian regimes and extremist movements, a new cadre of Western academics has called into question its very desirability.[31] They make three interconnected arguments: (1) the principle referred to as "religious liberty" is not universal as its advocates maintain; (2) its invocation simply serves as a cover for Western cultural imperialism; and (3) its promotion reinforces and exacerbates religious divides in society. Importantly, against the argument of this book, these scholars would argue that religious liberty *promotes* religious extremism and terrorism, rather than combating it.

First, skeptics argue that contrary to assertions of universality, religious liberty is a product of the West, rooted in a particular understanding of religion and state unique to European Protestantism and based on the ideals of the Enlightenment and Reformation. According to this narrative, the very concept of religion is a modern construct that cannot be applied across cultures or time periods, but is

---

[30] Nilay Saiya, "The Religious Freedom Peace," *International Journal of Human Rights* 19, no. 3 (2015): 369–382.

[31] Elizabeth Shakman Hurd, *Beyond Religious Freedom: The New Global Politics of Religion* (Princeton, NJ: Princeton University Press, 2015); Saba Mahmood, *Religious Difference in a Secular Age: A Minority Report* (Princeton, NJ: Princeton University Press, 2015); Winnifred Fallers Sullivan, Elizabeth Shakman Hurd, Saba Mahmood and Peter G. Danchin, *Politics of Religious Freedom* (Chicago, IL: University of Chicago Press, 2015).

instead distinctive to the Protestant countries of the Western world. This modern understanding of religion traces its roots to the Peace of Westphalia in 1648, where it was agreed that religion had a largely divisive, discordant and pernicious influence on politics and that it should be excluded from politics and subordinated to state control.[32] According to the skeptics of religious freedom, this state of affairs birthed a new concept of religion best understood as creedal, inward, private and highly individualistic, rather than a set of practices experienced in community. Political scientist Elizabeth Shakman Hurd draws a distinction between the "governed religion" of those in power and the "lived religion" of ordinary civilians, arguing that those who get to determine what does and does not constitute religion place themselves in positions of authority to protect those expressions of religiosity that fit with their view of religion while ignoring others.[33] In her view, because religious liberty is highly variable across time and space and culturally relative, it is a principle devoid of any normative value.

Is the right to religious liberty universal, or is it simply a product of a context particular to the West? The historical record suggests that a transcultural and transhistorical conception of religious liberty has, in fact, existed for millennia. In ancient Persia, an edict by Cyrus the Great allowed Jews to practice their religion freely or return to their homeland. Edicts proclaiming religious liberty existed in India under the Buddhist emperor Ashoka. Early Christian church fathers like Tertullian, Irenaeus and Lactantius developed theologies of religious liberty nearly akin to that which appears in international human rights covenants today. The Bible – a book considered sacred by Protestants as well as a plethora of other religious groups – contains numerous passages supporting the idea of free religious belief *and* expression.[34] Similarly, in Islam one finds the oft-cited injunction in Quran 2:256 that there is "no compulsion in religion." As noted throughout this book, those who make arguments in support of a just claim to religious freedom today can be found in every religious tradition – Christian or not. Conversely, Protestantism itself has been marred by some of the most serious violations of religious freedom, stemming back to the Reformation itself and its most seminal figure, Martin Luther, who turned out to be no friend of religious freedom. As political scientists Daniel Philpott and Timothy Samuel Shah aver, "[r]eligious freedom has never been consistently, much less irrevocably, intertwined with the Protestant religion."[35] Philpott and Shah further note that the remarkably wide array of international conventions dealing with religious freedom – most notably the United Nations Declaration on Human Rights, the International Covenant on Civil and Political Rights, and the

---

[32]   Elizabeth Shakman Hurd, *The Politics of Secularism in International Relations* (Princeton, NJ: Princeton University Press, 2007).
[33]   Hurd, *Beyond Religious Freedom*, 30.
[34]   For example, see Romans 14:5 and 1 Corinthians 10:29.
[35]   Daniel Philpott and Timothy Samuel Shah, "In Defense of Religious Freedom: New Critics of a Beleaguered Human Right," *Journal of Law and Religion* 31, no. 3 (2016): 392.

Declaration on the Elimination of All Forms of Intolerance and Discrimination Based on Religion or Belief – do not reduce religion to beliefs but instead protect "a remarkably wide array of dimensions of religion."[36]

Second, the critics of religious liberty assert that because religious liberty lacks universalism, attempts to export it by the West constitute a form of neo-imperialism aimed at serving the interests of those who wield power, seeking to advance their political ends. It is thus a vehicle of control imposed by dominant countries on less powerful states. In these countries, ordinary people are forced to conform to a particular model of religion, marked by belief, separation of religion and state and Reformation/Enlightenment ideals. This argument is nearly identical to the one made by those who reject the idea of inherent and inalienable human rights as Western cultural imperialism foisted upon indigenous, non-Western cultures.[37]

Again, the empirical record raises serious problems with this perspective. In fact, the reality is quite the opposite. As detailed in this book, religion, and by extension religious liberty, has historically been seen as a *threat* to those who wield power, and, for this reason, authoritarians seek not the free exercise of religion but rather its subjugation. Even in early modern Europe, repression of religion and not religious freedom was the weapon of choice to consolidate power. Contrariwise, religious liberty has been advocated most forcefully by those most removed from the centers of power. When Tertullian and Lactantius articulated their ideas about religious liberty, they did so during a time when the church experienced its greatest persecution. Persecuted groups in the Anabaptist tradition proved to be the most vocal and persistent advocates of religious liberty in Europe after the Reformation. Individuals like Roger Williams were sometimes banished from their own communities precisely because they advocated for religious liberty.

The most powerful states today do not believe that promoting freedom of religion strengthens their power positions and therefore generally ignore religion and religious freedom considerations in their foreign policies. On the contrary, those in the foreign policy establishment tasked with promoting religious freedom abroad have documented in great detail the difficulty they have encountered in attempting to persuade senior leaders to take religion and religious freedom considerations seriously.[38] Ironically, this negligence of religion, what former diplomat Thomas Farr attributes to a "religion avoidance syndrome" pervasive throughout the foreign policy establishment, owes to the very historical factors – the Protestant Reformation and the Enlightenment – that the critics of religious freedom argue gave rise to policies of religious liberty in the first place. "American diplomacy is distinctly uncomfortable with the whole topic of

---

[36] Philpott and Shah, "In Defense of Religious Freedom," 392.

[37] For a powerful critique of this position, see Reza Afghari, *Human Rights in Iran: The Abuse of Cultural Relativism* (Philadelphia, PA: University of Pennsylvania Press, 2001).

[38] Farr, *World of Faith and Freedom.*

religion," Farr explains.[39] Another diplomat, former secretary of state Madeline Albright, lamented the fact that "[d]iplomats of my era were taught not to invite trouble, and no subject seemed more inherently treacherous than religion."[40] On the rare occasion that states advocate for religious freedom, it is usually on behalf of those individuals and religious communities that are most isolated and perse- cuted. If the countries of the West are guilty of exporting any religion-related policy, it is surely not religious liberty but religious *repression* in the forms of both anti-religious ideologies – Marxism, fascism, anti-clericalism, secular nationalism – and material aid used to support local oppression. If religious liberty is really a path to power, why has it not been embraced by every country in the world?

A third argument made by skeptics is that Western promotion of religious liberty is likely to backfire, and may even create or exacerbate religious divisions and conflict. Hurd, in particular, argues that this is likely to happen because policymakers in the West put themselves in the position of deciding both what counts as a religion and who benefits from their freedom policies. These policy elites, so goes the argument, will naturally favor groups whose religion looks like theirs, marked by a focus on beliefs and privatization, as opposed to the "lived religion" practiced by much of the world, thus codifying religious difference, excluding other ways of belonging and leading to societal conflict along religious lines. In one provocative article, Hurd warned that an "international 'religious freedom' agenda will only embolden ISIS" by reinforcing the "political salience of sectarian divisions and empowering some leaders and orthodoxies over others." She did not equivocate in her conclusion that "religious freedom advocacy is not the answer to the violence and oppression plaguing the contemporary Middle East."[41]

Have polices of religious freedom promulgated by the West led to these negative outcomes in the non-Christian world? In one sense, it is indisputable that religious freedom policies in general have not been successful either at combating religious repression or in stemming the rising tide of violent religious extremism, both of which are trending in the wrong direction. To acknowledge this fact, however, is very different from claiming that religious freedom is *responsible* for these negative developments. The reality is that none of the major approaches to American foreign policy – *realpolitik*, neoconservatism and liberal interventionism – takes religious subject matter, including religious freedom, seriously. Because these approaches do not believe that religion is a primary motivator of state behavior in international relations, they tend to engage with religious subject matter superficially or neglect it

---

[39] Thomas Farr, "International Religious Freedom and Moral Responsibility," in *Challenges to Religious Liberty in the Twenty-First Century*, ed. Gerard V. Bradley (Cambridge: Cambridge University Press, 2012), 194.

[40] Madeline Albright, *The Mighty and the Almighty: Reflections on America, God, and World Affairs* (New York, NY: Harper Collins Publishers, 2006), 8.

[41] Elizabeth Shakman Hurd, "International 'Religious Freedom' Agenda Will Only Embolden ISIS," *Religion Dispatches*, November 10, 2014, http://religiondispatches.org/international-religious-free dom-agenda-will-only-embolden-isis/.

altogether. The problem is not that religious freedom has been coopted by those in the halls of power, but rather that it has been almost entirely superseded by hard power issues.

In Iraq, for example, had religious liberty been taken seriously by policy elites, the result would not have been the reinforcing of religious divisions, as Hurd claims, but rather the preservation of the country's religious diversity – the very thing that ISIS worked so relentlessly to destroy. True, religious liberty would have sought the emancipation of religious minorities like Yazidis and Chaldean Christians whom ISIS targeted ruthlessly on the basis of their faith. At the same time it would have also empowered those who suffered the most at the hands of ISIS, namely majority Muslims. As argued in Chapter 4, the rise of ISIS can be directly traced to Saddam Hussein's brutal treatment of Iraq's Shia population that stirred up a longing for revenge that was ultimately uncorked after Saddam was removed from power. The sudden empowerment of Iraq's Shias expectedly gave way to a "religious persecution paradox" in which the persecuted suddenly took on the role of persecutors themselves, creating the conditions ripe for the inception of ISIS. It was the utter *restriction* of religious liberty, first by Saddam then by Nouri al-Maliki and finally by ISIS, that led to heightened sectarianism and civil war. In the end, it is virtually impossible to point to any real-world cases where a genuine commitment to religious liberty in policy praxis can be causally linked to outcomes of marginalization, exclusion and social conflict as the critics of religious freedom claim. A far more convincing case can be made that many of the policy failures described by these scholars in Egypt, Burma, Turkey and elsewhere are the *product* of religious liberty being denied, rather than it being pursued too zealously.

CONCLUDING THOUGHTS

Today, billions of people around the world are either denied their basic rights to seek transcendent truth, or they do so in the face of stiff legal penalties, societal intimidation or both. To make matters worse, the global trend in religious freedom continues to deteriorate in both depth and breadth of violations. Some might see religious restrictions as an inopportune situation for people of faith but necessary given the contemporary realities of violent religious extremism and the security threat that it poses. This position is on the surface logical: if religion poses a threat to a country's security, then the natural response (and the default position of many governments) is to restrict its expression. This view ignores the point, however, that these restrictions themselves are often the cause of such violence to begin with. In a world where the vast majority of people holds religious beliefs, the suppression of religious freedom often leads to extremism and violence. Unfortunately, until this immensely important dimension of statecraft is internalized, a perceived tradeoff between security interests and the promotion of religious liberty will continue to guide the thinking of policymakers. Yet as this project has shown, religious liberty constitutes an important weapon in the fight against terrorism and a cornerstone of sustainable security.

How might the world look different today had extremists like Osama bin Laden or Abu Bakr al-Baghdadi been raised in climates of religious tolerance where they would have been exposed to competing interpretations of Islam, minority religious beliefs and nonreligious conceptions of a good society instead of being inculcated exclusively into the radical traditions of Ibn Taymiyyah and Muhammad ibn Abd al-Wahhab? Would al Qaeda and ISIS have come into existence? Would Saudi Arabia still be one of the world's leading exporters of extremism? Would Iraq have descended into a horrific cauldron of sectarian violence? How might Pakistan look different today had President Muhammad Zia ul-Haq invited freedom of thought instead of pushing his country toward an intolerant rendering of religion and reviving a fundamentalist brand of Islam in an attempt to secure support from the religious establishment? Would it still be one of the world's most terror-prone countries? Would Egypt have faced a prolonged Islamist insurgency in the 1990s had Islamists not been banned, imprisoned and tortured under the repressive reigns of Gamal Nasser and Anwar Sadat? Would Egyptian doctor Ayman al-Zawahiri have been drawn to radicalism and eventually become the leader of al Qaeda after the assassination of Osama bin Laden? What if after the collapse of the Soviet Union, Russia had refused to align itself with the Orthodox Church and control minority groups? Would it be facing the same militant challenge on its southern tier that it does today? How might Turkey, Tunisia, Iran and Malaysia look different today had they embraced, rather than repressed, the ideas of Muslim reformers like Fethullah Gulen, Rached Ghannouchi and Abdolkarim Soroush? And what would have happened if the United States had put greater pressure on its allies to embrace religious liberty as a way to root out extremist ideas and promote tolerance? Would 9/11 still have occurred?

"Those who cannot remember the past are doomed to repeat it," twentieth-century philosopher George Santayana famously quipped. Yet when it comes to the struggle against religious extremism, the lessons of history constantly repeat themselves. The argument set forth in this book is not necessarily intuitive in today's world, but neither is it new. Similar claims were made by prominent intellectuals like John Locke, Adam Smith, James Madison, David Hume and Roger Williams hundreds of years ago. Yet, despite the long intellectual tradition supporting religious freedom, many today fear the implications of increased religious liberty, particularly in the aftermath of the Arab Spring.

As global religious repression increases, so too do extremist theologies and religious terrorism. This does not, of course, justify the violence of religious militants in any faith tradition. Nevertheless, we must attempt to understand the roots of faith-based violence if we are serious about developing policy initiatives aimed at combating its onset. If American foreign policy since the horrific terrorist attacks of September 11, 2001 has taught us anything, it is that repression leads to violence not only against the authoritarian regimes that directly repress their people but also against external powers that support those regimes in the name of preserving stability and security. This is not to suggest that the road to genuine freedom will be free of roadblocks and violent backlash, especially in the short term. But over the long haul, the evidence is clear: the denial of religious freedom increases the likelihood of violent religious forms of political engagement; paradoxically, the best way to combat religious terrorism is not by restricting religious beliefs and practices but rather by safeguarding their legitimate manifestations. The effective promotion of religious liberty by the United States will not only help protect a foundational and indispensable human right, it will also promote stability and ultimately its own national security.

The question for the United States and its allies remains how best to counter the forces of extremism regardless of where they appear. To be sure, terrorism is a complex phenomenon that requires a comprehensive approach to effectively deal with it. For years, the answer has been to employ a wide array of tools, from intelligence gathering to police work to military action. But if the fight against terrorism is to succeed, it also must include efforts to promote freedom of religion. The struggle against violent religious extremism is a war of ideas as much as a battle of brawn, and environments that promote freedom of thought and belief empower moderate ideas and voices to denounce extremist hatred and violence and de-legitimate the narrative of extremists in their countries that their faith is under attack and that America is partially to blame.

The international community faces an enormous challenge with respect to global religious freedom conditions and violent religious extremism. One of the key ways the United States can foster climates conducive to American security interests is by integrating religious freedom into its foreign policy. Advancing the cause of religious freedom is the right thing to do, and it is the strategically smart choice. Not only will genuine freedom empower religious moderates and reformers; it will also deprive extremists of the opportunity to win the battle of ideas by default. It is time for policymakers around the world to take religious freedom seriously, if not for moral reasons, then at least for the sake of peace and stability. Religious freedom is not a panacea, but it is a crucial and all too often overlooked weapon of peace.

Appendix

This appendix presents a statistical analysis for the arguments given in Chapter 1 of this book. The purpose is threefold. The first is to show that the relationship between religious restrictions and terrorism is "statistically significant" – that is, the findings do not come about by chance. The second is to demonstrate that they are also substantively important. Just because a finding is more or less certain does not necessarily mean that it is interesting. Whereas statistical significance concerns measurement precision, substantive importance concerns the size of the effect. The third is to compare the religious freedom explanation for terrorism against alternative explanations that past scholarship has found important.

The main argument of this book is that restrictions on religion increase the likelihood of a country experiencing faith-based terrorist attacks. In the opening chapter, I discussed two ways in which the impeding of religious liberty commonly gives rise to religious terrorism: minority religious discrimination and majority religious cooptation. In the case of minority restrictions, members of religious communities may choose to react violently to their disadvantaged position vis-à-vis the group(s) favored by the state, resulting in aggression against either the state and/or the group(s) with which the state has aligned itself. These kinds of integrated states may also foster bloodshed by emboldening extremists associated with the majority religion to attack minorities, sometimes even with the support of the political leadership. States restricting religious majorities, by contrast, do not engage in such collaborative partnerships, but rather promote terrorism by suppressing religious freedom and limiting avenues for peaceful dissent across the board, even if this entails some degree of outward support for a nonthreatening form of the dominant faith tradition. Religious terrorists see such states as justifiable targets of violence because they believe them to be corrupt, secular and, consequently, illegitimate. These two dynamics not only result in domestic terrorist attacks but can also spawn terrorism against other states apart from where the militancy was birthed (incubation) or invite it from abroad (solicitation).

Data for the outcome variable of interest – religious terrorist attacks – are derived and coded from the Global Terrorism Database (GTD) hosted at the National

Consortium for the Study of Terrorism and Responses to Terrorism (START), an open-source database of terrorist attacks, which includes descriptions of more than 150,000 terrorist incidents between 1970 and 2016 – making it by far the largest public data collection of terrorist attacks. The Global Terrorism Database is widely considered the "gold standard" in empirical terrorism research, though, as discussed in what follows, it is not completely unproblematic.

An attack was coded as "religious" if the following conditions were met: (1) it was carried out by a group or individual that conceives of itself as a predominantly religious actor; (2) the attacker frames its mission in religious terms, though it may have other goals as well; and (3) the actor, though perhaps involved in a communitarian conflict that politicized religious symbols, holds a discernible religious ideology or motivation, apart from its religious identity, which serves to animate its strategies and goals apart from or in addition to the mere utilization of religious objects or rhetoric.[1] This study uses the Global Terrorism Database's strictest terrorism criteria for an attack to be included in the dataset: (1) the act must be aimed at attaining a political, economic, religious or social goal; (2) there must be evidence of an intention to coerce, intimidate or convey some message to a larger audience (or audiences) other than the immediate victims; and (3) the action must be outside the context of legitimate warfare activities, i.e., the parameters permitted by international humanitarian law (particularly the admonition against deliberately targeting civilians or noncombatants). Because the goal of this book is to ascertain which kinds of countries are most susceptible to terrorist antipathy, unsuccessful attacks are also included insofar as they demonstrate aggressive *intention*.

There are no perfect terrorism datasets, and this is true of the Global Terrorism Database. The major drawback of the dataset is its large number of "unknown attacks" – those incidents in which the perpetrator was not identified in the description of the attack. For this reason, I do not include in the analysis attacks in which the perpetrator could not be identified. Dropping unknown attacks from the study almost certainly has the effect of *understating* the findings, however, since the vast number of unknown attacks occurred in religiously repressive settings and were probably carried out by religious actors in the majority of cases. Another factor that unfortunately downplays the findings is the reporting practices of authoritarian states, which tend to underreport the actual number of terrorist incidents their countries experience.[2] In short, for these reasons, the findings I report here are in all likelihood not as strong as they might otherwise be.

Religious restriction scores are taken from three sources: the International Religious Freedom Data compiled by Brian Grim and Roger Finke (2001–2008), the Pew Research Center's Religious Freedom Reports (2009–2013) and the Religion

[1] Hoffman, *Inside Terrorism*, 88–89.
[2] Konstantinos Drakos and Andreas Gofas, "Evidence for the Existence of Under-Reporting Bias in Observed Terrorist Activity: The Message in Press Freedom Status Transitions," *Democracy and Security* 3, no. 2 (2006): 139–155.

and State Project run by Jonathan Fox of Bar Ilan University (1990–2008). All three sources measure the restrictions placed on the practice, profession or selection of religion by the official laws, policies or administrative actions of the state.[3] The scores for the first two religious restriction measures – the International Religious Freedom Data and the Pew Research Center's Religious Freedom Reports – range from 0 to 10, with 10 representing the most egregious offenders of religious freedom in each category. These sources provide information on the general level of religious restrictions present in a country.

To examine state-level religious restrictions in its two component forms – minority religious discrimination and majority religious cooptation – I turn to the Religion and State Project. This study uses two categories of variables found in the dataset: religious discrimination against minority religions ("religious discrimination") and religious discrimination against majority or all religions ("religious restrictions").

The first set of variables – religious discrimination – examines thirty specific types of restrictions placed by the state on the practice of religion by some or all minority religious groups that are *not* placed on the majority group. This category of restrictions attempts to gauge if, and to what extent, governments single out some or all minorities for unequal treatment vis-à-vis the majority group. These policies include restrictions on minority practices, restrictions on minority institutions, restrictions on conversions and missionary activity and other forms of restrictions. For each year, the scores for all thirty components of minority regulation were combined to create a composite measure of minority religious discrimination that theoretically ranges from 0 to 90, though, in reality, no country scores higher than 56 on this measure in a single year. The second set of variables – majority religious restriction – examines twenty-nine specific types of restrictions placed by the state on the majority religion or all religions. This category of restriction attempts to gauge if and to what extent the government restricts, regulates or controls religion in general, rather than looking at government treatment of minority communities. These policies include restrictions on religion's political role, restrictions on religious institutions and clergy, restrictions on religious practices, and other forms of regulation, control and restrictions. For each year, the scores for all twenty-nine components of majority regulation were combined to create a composite measure of majority religious discrimination that theoretically ranges from 0 to 87, though, in reality, no country scores higher than 71 on this measure in a single year.

Each item in both categories is coded on the following scale:

0. Not significantly restricted
1. The activity is slightly restricted
2. The activity is slightly restricted for most/all or sharply restricted for some
3. The activity is prohibited or sharply restricted for most/all.

---

[3] Brian J. Grim and Roger Finke, "International Regulation Indexes: Government Regulation, Government Favoritism, and Social Regulation of Religion," *Interdisciplinary Journal of Research on Religion* 2, no. 1 (2006): 7.

Finally, I include several variables that take into account the unique social, religious and political dynamics of individual countries that past scholarship has found to be related to the onset of terrorism:

- The analysis incorporates a measure of procedural democracy taken from the Polity IV database (*"Polity"*) to assess the effect of electoral politics on terrorism.[4] The Polity project codes the authority characteristics of states using a scale that ranges from −10 (strongly autocratic) to +10 (strongly democratic). Using the Polity measure of democracy allows for the inclusion of a democracy index not covariant with measures of human rights and/or civil liberties, thus separating a country's institutional structures from its government's behavior.

- I also include measures for a country's wealth (measured as *GDP/capita*), *population* and *geographical area* (all logged). These measures control for the possibility that poor, populous and geographically large countries theoretically make it more difficult for states to effectively preempt terrorist activity. These data are all derived from the World Bank's Development Indicators.[5]

- I include a measure of *"foreign occupation"* to account for the finding that foreign military occupation is the key determinant of (suicide) terrorism.[6] Data for this variable are drawn from the list of foreign occupations compiled by Simon Collard-Wexler, Costantino Pischedda and Michael G. Smith.[7] A country under foreign occupation was coded with a "1" or "0" otherwise.

- In addition, the statistical models also incorporate data on *state fragility* taken from the State Fragility Index hosted at the Center for Systemic Peace. The Fragility Index scores each country on both "effectiveness" and "legitimacy" in four performance dimensions: security, political, economic and social. The Index then combines scores on these indicators to produce a continuum that ranges from 0 "no fragility" to 25 "extreme fragility."[8]

- Taken from the Minorities at Risk Dataset, the number of *Minority Religions* measures the number of minority religious groups in a country with at least 5 percent overall population.[9] This variable is included to test

---

4 Monty G. Marshall and Ted R. Gurr, "Polity IV Project: Political Regime Characteristics and Transitions, 1800–2015," 2015, www.systemicpeace.org/polity/polity4.htm.

5 World Bank, *World Development Indicators 2017*.   6 Pape, *Dying to Win*.

7 Simon Collard-Wexler, Costantino Pischedda and Michael G. Smith, "Do Foreign Occupations Cause Suicide Attacks?" *Journal of Conflict Resolution* 58, no. 4 (2014): 625–657.

8 Center for Systemic Peace, "State Fragility Index and Matrix, Time-Series Data, 1995–2016," June 15, 2017, www.systemicpeace.org/inscrdata.html.

9 Minorities at Risk Project, "MAR Data," June 8, 2016, www.mar.umd.edu/.

for the possibility that having more minority religious groups in a country makes religious conflict more likely.

- Two measures of violence are incorporated to control for the effect of other forms of conflict on terrorism. The first is a measure of *Religious Civil War*, taken from political scientist Monica Toft's data on civil wars. These are wars explicitly rooted in religious or ethnic identity.[10] The second measure, *Militarized Interstate Disputes*, accounts for countries involved in international disputes with other countries in which some military force is used short of full-scale war.[11] The variable is taken from the Correlates of War Database. Countries involved in either a religious civil war or a militarized interstate dispute were coded with a "1" or "0" otherwise. Summary statistics are presented in Table A.1.

Three different analyses were performed covering two different timeframes based on the data availability for the different religious restriction indexes. The first analysis examines the effect of general religious repression by states using data from the International Religious Freedom Data and Pew Research Center's Religious Freedom Reports. In this analysis, the data for all variables are arranged into a longitudinal panel setup for 151 countries over the period 2001–2013, as this timeframe corresponds to available data for the theoretically central independent variable –

TABLE A.1 *Summary statistics*

Variable	Observations	Mean	Standard Deviation	Min	Max
Terrorism Incidents	3,829	2.72	21.88	0.00	649.00
General Government Regulation	2,235	3.22	3.10	0.00	10.00
Minority Discrimination	3,276	8.26	10.48	0.00	56.00
Majority Regulation	3,274	10.76	13.24	0.00	71.00
State Fragility	2,106	8.94	6.46	0.00	25.00
Population (logged)	2,233	9.02	1.75	3.49	14.11
Area (logged)	2,235	11.83	2.14	5.07	16.61
GDP/Cap. (logged)	1,965	8.04	1.65	4.38	11.82
Polity	1,904	3.61	6.44	−10.00	10.00
Foreign Occupation	2,275	0.06	0.24	0.00	1.00
Minority Groups	3,909	1.62	1.81	0.00	11.00
Religious Civil War	4,025	0.06	0.23	0.00	1.00
Militarized Interstate Disputes	3,330	0.30	0.45	0.00	1.00

[10] Monica Duffy Toft, *Securing the Peace: The Durable Settlement of Civil Wars* (Princeton, NJ: Princeton University Press, 2009).

[11] Glen Palmer, Vito D'Orazio, Michael Kenwick and Matthew Lane, "The MID4 Data Set: Procedures, Coding Rules, and Description," *Conflict Management and Peace Science* 32, no. 2 (2015): 222–242. Data available from the Correlates of War Project, "The Correlates of War Project," 2018, www.correlatesofwar.org/data-sets/folder_listing.

TABLE A.2 *Religious freedom and terrorism*

	Model 1	Model 2	Model 3
General Government Restrictions	0.58***		
	(0.14)		
Minority Religious Discrimination		0.03*	
Majority Religious Restriction			0.03**
State Fragility	0.34***	0.33***	0.38***
	(0.05)	(0.06)	(0.03)
Population (logged)	1.42***	1.09***	1.35***
	(0.25)	(0.27)	(0.12)
Area (logged)	0.39**	0.26	0.36**
	(0.21)	(0.22)	(0.09)
GDP/capita (logged)	0.88***	0.66***	0.71***
	(0.15)	(0.20)	(0.13)
Religious Minorities	0.07	0.05	0.07
	(0.71)	(0.34)	(0.44)
Polity	0.20***	0.09***	0.14***
	(0.07)	(0.05)	(0.03)
Foreign Occupation	1.44	0.12	0.78
	(0.71)	(0.83)	(0.47)
Minority Religious Groups	0.02	0.07	0.02
	(0.24)	(0.36)	(0.89)
Religious Civil War	1.88***	1.96***	2.14***
	(0.66)	(0.56)	(0.58)
Militarized Interstate Disputes	1.38***	1.33***	1.34***
	(0.10)	(0.37)	(0.36)
Constant	22.42***	18.82***	19.08***
	(2.50)	(2.44)	(1.77)
Observations	1,462	2,203	2,170

$^{*}p < 0.05$, $^{**}p < 0.01$, $^{***}p < 0.001$. Robust standard errors in parentheses.

government restrictions on religion. The second analysis looks at the impact of the first specific way that states can restrict religion – minority religious discrimination – on terrorism. The third analysis does the same, this time examining the impact of majority religious cooptation in the form of majority religious regulation. The latter two models cover the period 1991–2009 based on the availability of the data.

In all three analyses, the country-year is the unit of observation. Because the dependent variable, number of terrorist attacks, is an event count that does not include negative values and is unevenly distributed, negative binomial regression (with robust standard errors clustered on countries) is the most appropriate statistical technique to gauge the relative importance of the independent and control variables on terrorism. The dependent variable, religious terrorist attacks, is lagged one year within country cases to help in determining the direction of causality.

Table A.2 presents the results of the statistical analysis. It is divided into three different models. Model 1 examines the impact of general governmental religious restrictions on terrorism along with the other variables. Model 2 looks at the effect of minority religious discrimination. Model 3 considers religious restrictions placed on the religious majority.

The statistical analysis strongly supports the major arguments of this book. It reveals that, by and large, countries that restrict religion, both generally and in specific ways, tend to experience higher levels of religious terrorism than countries that do not. The variables for general governmental restrictions, minority religious discrimination and majority religious regulation rise to the level of significance in every model in which they appear and are signed in the expected positive direction.

The table also reveals other interesting results. The coefficient for a country's landmass is *negatively* correlated with terrorism; larger countries do not experience more attacks. In two of the models (1 and 3), this finding reaches the level of significance. Also interesting is that poorer countries are not more susceptible to terrorism as the poverty hypothesis would predict. In all three models, the GDP/capita variable rises to the level of significance, and it is in the *positive* direction; richer countries consistently experience *higher* levels of terrorism. Finally, electoral democracy exhibits a *positive* and significant relationship with terrorism in each model. Electoral democracies are *more* likely to suffer religious terrorist attacks. This is an important finding insofar as it supports the contention of this book that religious freedom and democracy are not coterminous and that otherwise democratic states can take steps to curtail religious freedom specifically. Accordingly, this finding suggests that states should shift priorities away from democracy promotion and toward the promotion of religious liberty. Finally, foreign military occupation does not appear to be a consistent predictor of terrorist attacks.

Using post-estimation margins statistics for predicted probabilities of terrorist incidence, Figure A.1 shows the substantive effects of general government religious restrictions on religious terrorism when controlling for other variables. Figures A.2 and A.3 display the effects of the two components of government religious restrictions examined in this book: Figure A.2 shows the effects of minority religious restrictions; Figure A.3 does the same for majority religious restrictions. As expected, as each measure increases, so too does the number of terrorist attacks a country can expect to witness.

A number of tests were also performed to gauge the robustness of these findings. The first examines the effect of all three measures of religious restriction on international religious terrorism, rather than domestic attacks. Here again all variables of interest emerge as statistically significant, signed in the expected positive direction and substantively important. Restrictions on religion are important predictors of both domestic and transnational faith-based terrorism. The second robustness test examines the impact of different majority religious traditions within countries. Some have suggested, for example, that Islam breeds more violence than other religions. After including a dummy variable for Muslim-majority countries, the key

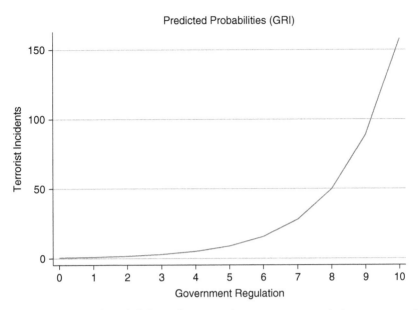

FIGURE A.1 Predicted probabilities for general government restrictions on terrorist incidents

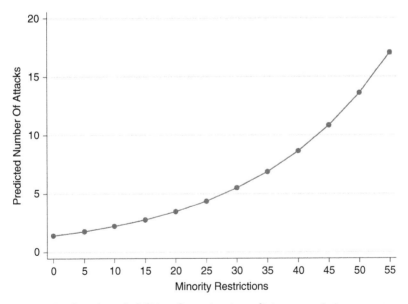

FIGURE A.2 Predicted probabilities for minority religious restrictions on terrorist incidents

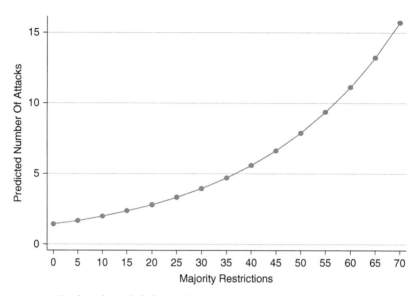

FIGURE A.3 Predicted probabilities for majority religious restrictions on terrorist incidents

variables remain significant, as does the newly added dummy variable for Muslim-majority states. Importantly, though, this finding also shows that the deleterious effects of religious restrictions on terrorism are not being channeled through Islamic-majority countries. A third test looked at the effect of world region to investigate the possibility that specific regions are more likely to give rise to religious terrorism. After assigning dummy variables for European, North American, South American, sub-Saharan African, Middle Eastern and North African and Asian countries, the basic findings remain unchanged, though, unsurprisingly, the regions of the Middle East/North Africa and Asia rise to the level of significance. A final robustness test attempted to see if religious freedom was simply functioning as a proxy for human rights in general. This test included a measure for "physical integrity rights" taken from the Cingranelli–Richards dataset, which research has found to be related to terrorism.[12] After including this variable in Models 1–3, the results for religious restrictions remain the same while the physical integrity measure also rises to the level of significance, indicating that religious rights represent a unique and important category of rights restrictions.

In sum, the findings are statistically significant, substantively important, robust to alternative model specifications and strongly supportive of the argument put forth in this book: where governments impede the expression of faith, religious terrorism increases as does the likelihood that these states will export terrorism to other countries.

[12]   James I. Walsh and James A. Piazza, "Why Respecting Physical Integrity Rights Reduces Terrorism," *Comparative Political Studies* 43, no. 5 (2009): 551–577; James A. Piazza and James I. Walsh, "Transnational Terror and Human Rights," *International Studies Quarterly* 53, no. 1 (2010): 125–148.

LIST OF TERRORIST GROUPS USED IN ANALYSIS

1920 Revolution Brigades

313 Brigade

Abdullah Azzam Brigades

Abu Hafs al-Masri Brigades

Abu Hafs Katibatul al-Ghurba al-Mujahideen

Abu Nidal Organization

Abu Sayyaf

Achwan-I-Mushbani

Adan Abyan Islamic Army

Afghan Mujahideen

Ahrar Al-Jalil

Ahrar al-Sham

Al Barq

Al Furqan Brigades

Al Hadid

Al Jihad

Al-Adl Wal Ihsane

Al-Ahwaz Arab People's Democratic Front

Al-Almi

Al-Aqsa Martyrs Brigade

Al-Arifeen

Al-Badr

Al-Bakazim

Al-Fajr

Al-Fatah

Al-Gama'at al-Islamiyya (IG)

Al-Hamas Mujahideen

Al-Haramayn Brigades

Al-Intiqami al-Pakistani

Al-Ittihaad al-Islami

Al-Khobar

Al-Mansoorian

Al-Nadir

Al-Naqshabandiya Army

Al-Nasireen Group

Al-Nusra Front

(*Continued*)

(Continued)

Al Qaeda

Al Qaeda in Iraq

Al Qaeda in Levant and Egypt

Al Qaeda in the Arabian Peninsula

Al Qaeda in the Lands of the Islamic Maghreb

Al Qaeda in Yemen

Al Qaeda Organization for Jihad in Sweden

Al Qaeda in Lebanon

Al Qaeda Network for Southwestern Khulna Division

Al-Shababb

Al-Shuda Brigade

Al-Sunni Muslim Sect

Al-Umar Mujahideen

Algerian Mujahideen for Moslems

Amr Bil Maroof Wa Nahi Anil Munkir

Ansar Al Sunnah

Ansar al-Din

Ansar al-Islam

Ansar al-Jihad

Ansar al-Sharia

Ansar al-Sunna

Ansar Allah

Ansar Jerusalem

Ansaru (Jama'atu Ansarul Muslimina Fi Biladis Sudan)

Ansarul Islam

Anti-Apostate Movement Alliance

Anti-Balaka Militia

Anti-Communist Command

Anti-Zionist Movement

Arbav Martyrs of Khuzestan

Armed Forces of the Chechen Republic of Ichkeria

Armed Islamic Group (GIA)

Armed Renaissance Group of Ahvaz

Armed Vanguards of a Second Mohammed Army

Army of God

Army of Islam

(Continued)

(Continued)

Army of the Nation

Asa'ib Ahl al-Haqq

Asbat al-Ansar

Aum Shinri Kyo

Avengers of the Infants

Babbar Khalsa International

Bangsamoro Islamic Freedom Movement

Barisan Revolusi Nasional

Bersatu

Bharatiya Janata Party

Bhinderanwale Tiger Force of Khalistan

Bihar People's Party

Black Widows

Boko Haram

Brigade of al-Mukhtar al-Thaqafi

Brigades of Imprisoned Sheikh Omar Abdel-Rahman

Caucasus Emirate

Christian Liberation Army

Dagestani Shari'ah Jamaat

David's Sword

Deccan Mujahideen

Democratic Karen Buddhist Army

Diraa al-Shahbaa Rebel Brigade

Diyala Salvation Council

Eastern Turkistan Islamic Movement

Farzandan-e-Millat

Forbid the Evil Group

Free Aceh Movement

Free People of the Galilee

Fulani Militants

Global Intifada

God's Army

God's Oppressed Army

Great Eastern Islamic Raiders Front

Gulbuddin Hekmatyar Group

Hamas

(*Continued*)

(Continued)

Haqqani Network
Harakat ul-Mujahidin
Harakat-i-Inqilahi-i-Islami
Harkat ul Ansar
Harkatul Jihad-e-Islami
Hasmoneans (Jewish Settler Group)
Hezb-e Wahdat-e Islami-yi
Hizb al-Tahrir al-Islami (HT)
Hizb-I-Islami
Hizballah
Hizballah Palestine
Hizbul al Islam
Hizbul Mujahideen (HM)
Holders of the Black Banners
Huria Kristen Batak Protestan
Husayn Ubayyat Martyrs' Brigades
Huthis
Ikhwan-ul-Muslimeen
Ingush Rebels
International Justice Group
Intifada Martyrs
Iraqi Islamic Vanguards for National Salvation
ISIS
Islam Liberation Front
Islambouli Brigades of al-Qa'ida
Islamic Army in Iraq
Islamic Companies
Islamic Courts Union
Islamic Defenders' Front
Islamic Front
Islamic Front for the Liberation of Bahrain
Islamic Golden Army
Islamic International Peacekeeping Brigade
Islamic Jihad
Islamic Jihad Brigades
Islamic Jihad Front

(Continued)

(Continued)

Islamic Jihad Group
Islamic Jihad Organization
Islamic Jihad Union
Islamic Movement for Change
Islamic Movement of Kashmir
Islamic Movement of Martyrs
Islamic Movement of Uzbekistan
Islamic Movement Organization
Islamic Mujahidin
Islamic Party of Kenya
Islamic Renewal Movement
Islamic Revenge Organization
Islamic Revolution to Liberate Palestine
Islamic Revolutionary Command
Islamic Salvation Front
Islamic Salvation Front (Palestine)
Islamic Swords of Justice in the Land of Ribat
Ittehad-i-Islami
Izberbash Gang
Jadid Al-Qa'idah Bangladesh
Jagrata Towhidi Janata
Jaish al-Ta'ifa al-Mansura
Jaish Usama
Jaish-e-Islam
Jaish-e-Mohammad
Jamaa Al-Islamiya Al-Alamiya (World Islamist Group)
Jamaah Ansharut Tauhid
Jamaat-E-Islami
Jama'atul Mujahideen Bangladesh
Jamiat ul-Mujahedin
Jamiat-e Islami-yi
Jamiat-e Islami-yi Afghanistan
Jammu and Kashmir Liberation Front
Janjaweed
Jaysh al-Muslimin
Jemaah Islamiya

(*Continued*)

(Continued)

Jenin Martyrs Brigades
Jewish Fighting Organization
Jihad Islamic League Front
Jihadi Movement of the Sunna People of Iran
Jihadist Soldiers
Jordanian Islamic Resistance
Junaid Jihadist Battalion
Jund al-Islam
Jund al-Khilafa
Jund al-Sahabah Group
Jund al-Sham for Tawhid and Jihad
Jundallah
Just Punishment Brigades
Kach
Kahane Chai
Karabulak Gang
Karen National Union
Kashmiri Hizballah
Katsina Muslim Society
Khalid ibn Walid Brigade
Khalilistan Liberation Force
Kuki Revolutionary Army
Kurdish Islamic Unity Party
Lashkar-e-Islam
Lashkar-e-Jhangvi
Lashkar-e-Omar
Lashkar-e-Taiba
Lashkari-e-Adam
Laskar Jihad
Libya Shield Force
Liwa al-Haqq
Lord's Resistance Army (LRA)
Maccabee Squad and the Shield of David
Mahaz-e-Inquilab
Mahdi Army
Moro Islamic Liberation Front

(Continued)

(Continued)

Moslem Janbaz Force

Mouhajiroune Brigade

Movement for Oneness and Jihad in West Africa

Movement for the Protection of Jerusalem

Mujahideen Corps in Iraq

Mujahideen Shura Council

Mujahideen Shura Council in the Environs of Jerusalem

Mujahideen Islam Pattani

Mujahideen Youth Movement

Mujahideen-I-Khalq

Mujahidin Ambon

Mukhtar Army

Mullah Dadullah Front

Muslim Brotherhood

Muslim Fundamentalists

Muslim United Army

Nahzat e Eslami

National Liberation Front of Tripuria

New Revolutionary Alternative

NVF

Omar Bin Khattab Group

Organization of Soldiers of the Levant

Palestinian Islamic Jihad

Pattani United Liberation Organization

People's Militia of Dagestan

Popular Army Vanguards – Battalions of Return

Popular Resistance Committees

Protectors of Islam Brigade

Punjabi Taliban

Qari Kamran Group

Rajah Solaiman Revolutionary Movement

Ramzi Nahra Martyr Organization

Rashtriya Swayamsevak Sangh

Republican Anticlerical Group

Revolutionary Security Apparatus

Riyadus-Salikhin Reconnaissance and Sabotage Battalion

(Continued)

Appendix

(Continued)

Rizvon Sadirov Group

Runda Kumpulan Kecil

Salafi Abu-Bakr al-Siddiq Army

Salafia Jihadia

Salafist Group for Preaching and Fighting

Secret Organization of al-Qa'ida in Europe

Shahid Khalsa Force

Shiv Sena

Sikh Extremists

Sipah-e-Sahaba

Sipah-I-Mohammed

Somali Islamic Front

Special Purpose Islamic Regiment

Squadrons of Terror

Students Islamic Movement of India (SIMI)

Supreme Council for Islamic Revolution in Iraq

Sympathizers of Al-Qa'ida Organization

Takfir wal-Hijra

Taliban

Tawhid and Jihad

Tehreek-e-Nafaz-e-Shariat-e-Mohammadi

Tehrik al-Mojahedin

Tehrik-i-Taliban Pakistan

Temple Mount Faithful Movement

Turkestan Islamic Party

Turkish Hizballah

Turkish Islamic Jihad

Uganda Democratic Christian Army

Umar al-Mukhtar Martyr Forces

Ummah Liberation Army

Vanguards of the Caliphate

Vishwa Hindu Parishad

Youth of Islamic Awakening

RESTRICTIONS ON MINORITY RELIGIONS

1. Restrictions on public observance of religious services, festivals and/or holidays, including the Sabbath.
2. Restrictions on private observance of religious services, festivals and/or holidays, including the Sabbath.
3. Restrictions on building, leasing, repairing and/or maintaining places of worship.
4. Restrictions on access to existing places of worship.
5. Forced observance of religious laws of another group.
6. Restrictions on formal religious organizations.
7. Restrictions on the running of religious schools and/or religious education in general.
8. Restrictions on the ability to make and/or obtain materials necessary for religious rites, customs and/or ceremonies.
9. Mandatory education in the majority religion.
10. Arrest, continued detention or severe official harassment of religious figures, officials and/or members of religious parties for activities other than proselytizing.
11. State surveillance of minority religious activities not placed on the activities of the majority.
12. Restrictions on the ability to write, publish or disseminate religious publications.
13. Restrictions on the ability to import religious publications.
14. Restrictions on access to religious publications for personal use.
15. Restrictions on the observance of religious laws concerning personal status, including marriage, divorce and burial.
16. Restrictions on the wearing of religious symbols or clothing. This includes presence or absence of facial hair.
17. Restrictions on the ordination of and/or access to clergy.
18. Restrictions on conversion to minority religions.
19. Forced renunciation of faith by recent converts to minority religions.
20. Forced conversions of people who were never members of the majority religion.
21. Efforts or campaigns to convert members of minority religions to the majority religion that fall short of using force.
22. Restrictions on proselytizing by permanent residents of the state to members of the majority religion.
23. Restrictions on proselytizing by permanent residents of the state to members of minority religions.

24. Restrictions on proselytizing by foreign clergy or missionaries. (This includes denial of visas if this denial is specifically aimed at missionaries, but not if it is the same type of denial that would be applied to any foreigner.)
25. Requirement for minority religions (as opposed to all religions) to register in order to be legal or receive special tax status.
26. Custody of children granted to members of majority group solely or in part on the basis of religious affiliation or beliefs.
27. Restricted access of minority clergy to hospitals, jails, military bases and other places a chaplain may be needed in comparison to chaplains of the majority religion.
28. There is a legal provision or policy of declaring some minority religions dangerous or extremist sects.
29. Anti-religious propaganda in official or semiofficial government publications.
30. Restrictions on other types of observance of religious law.

RESTRICTIONS ON MAJORITY RELIGIONS

1. Restrictions on religious political parties.
2. Restrictions on trade associations or other civil associations being affiliated with a religion.
3. Restrictions on clergy holding political office.
4. Arrest, continued detention or severe official harassment of religious figures, officials and/or members of religious parties.
5. The government restricts or harasses members and organizations affiliated with the majority religion but that operate outside of the state-sponsored or recognized ecclesiastical framework.
6. Restrictions on formal religious organizations other than political parties.
7. Restrictions on the public observance of religious practices, including religious holidays and the Sabbath.
8. Restrictions on religious activities outside of recognized religious facilities.
9. Restrictions on public religious speech.
10. Restrictions or monitoring of sermons by clergy.
11. Restrictions on clergy and/or religious organizations engaging in public political speech (other than sermons) or propaganda or on political activity in or by religious institutions.
12. Restrictions on religious-based hate speech.
13. Restrictions on access to places of worship.
14. Restrictions on the publication or dissemination of written religious material.
15. People are arrested for religious activities.
16. Restrictions on religious public gatherings that are not placed on other types of public gathering.

17. Restrictions on the public display by private persons or organizations of religious symbols, including (but not limited to) religious dress, the presence or absence of facial hair, nativity scenes and icons.
18. Restrictions on or regulation of religious education in public schools. (This variable represents direct government control of teachers and or curriculum, not a ban on religious education in public schools.)
19. Restrictions on or regulation of religious education outside of public schools or general government control of religious education.
20. Restrictions on or regulation of religious education at the university level.
21. Foreign religious organizations are required to have a local sponsor or affiliation.
22. Heads of religious organizations (e.g., bishops) must be citizens of the state.
23. All practicing clergy must be citizens of the state.
24. The government appoints or must approve clerical appointments or somehow takes part in the appointment process.
25. Other than appointments, the government legislates or otherwise officially influences the internal workings or organization of religious institutions and organizations.
26. Laws governing the state religion are passed by the government or need the government's approval before being put into effect.
27. State ownership of some religious property or buildings.
28. Conscientious objectors to military service are not given other options for national service and are prosecuted
29. Other religious restrictions.

References

Abadie, Alberto. "Poverty, Political Freedom and the Roots of Terrorism." *American Economic Review* 96, no. 2 (2006): 159–177.

Adeney, Katharine and Andrew Wyatt. *Contemporary India*. New York, NY: Palgrave Macmillan, 2010.

Afghari, Reza. *Human Rights in Iran: The Abuse of Cultural Relativism*. Philadelphia, PA: University of Pennsylvania Press, 2001.

Aitkin, Jonathan. "An Oasis of Tolerance." *American Spectator*, March 2013, 45–46.

Akbaba, Yasemin and Jonathan Fox. "The Religion and State-Minorities Dataset." *Journal of Peace Research* 48, no. 6 (2011): 807–816.

Akbaba, Yasemin and Zeynap Tydas. "Does Religious Discrimination Promote Dissent? A Quantitative Analysis." *Ethnopolitics* 10, no. 3–4 (2011): 271–295.

Al Jazeera. "Full Transcript of Bin Laden's Speech." Last modified November 1, 2004. www.aljazeera.com/archive/2004/11/200849163336457223.html.

Al Khalifa-Manama, Hamad bin Isa. "The Bahrain Declaration on Religious Tolerance." *Simon Wiesenthal Center*. Last modified July 3, 2017. www.wiesenthal.com/site/apps/nlnet/content.aspx?c=lsKWLbPJLnF&b=8776547&ct=15004381.

Albright, Madeline. *The Mighty and the Almighty: Reflections on America, God, and World Affairs*. New York, NY: Harper Collins Publishers, 2006.

"The Allies Case against Bin Laden." *The Guardian*. Last modified October 5, 2001. www.theguardian.com/uk/2001/oct/05/afghanistan.september11.

Almond, Gabriel A., R. Scott Appleby and Emmanuel Sivan. Eds. *Strong Religion: The Rise of Fundamentalisms around the World*. Chicago, IL: University of Chicago Press, 2003.

Amnesty International. "Central African Republic: Ethnic Cleansing and Sectarian Killings." Last Modified February 12, 2014. www.amnesty.org/en/articles/news/2014/02/central-afri can-republic-ethnic-cleansing-sectarian-violence/.

"Tunisia: A Widening Circle of Repression." Last modified June 8, 1997. www.amnesty.org/en/documents/mde30/025/1997/en/.

Amnesty International UK. "Jabeur Mejri, Imprisoned for Facebook Posts in Tunisia." Last modified May 9, 2014. www.amnesty.org.uk/jabeur-mejri-imprisoned-facebook-posts-tuni sia#.VcKFVqO89Kw.

Anderson, Lisa. "Demystifying the Arab Spring: Parsing the Differences between Tunisia, Egypt, and Libya." *Foreign Affairs* 90 (2011): 2–7.

"Fulfilling Prophecies: State Policy and Islamist Radicalism." In *Political Islam: Revolution, Radicalism, or Reform?* edited by John L. Esposito, 17–31. London: Lynne Rienner Publishers.

"Religion and State in Libya: The Politics of Identity." *Annals of the American Academy of Political and Social Science* 483, no. 1 (1986): 61–72.

Appleby, R. Scott. *The Ambivalence of the Sacred: Religion, Violence and Reconciliation.* Lanham, MD: Rowman & Littlefield Publishers, 2000.

Appleby, R. Scott and Richard Cizik. *Engaging Religious Communities Abroad: A New Imperative for US Foreign Policy.* Chicago, IL: Chicago Council on Global Affairs.

Araj, Bader. "Harsh State Repression as a Cause of Suicide Bombing: The Case of the Palestinian–Israeli Conflict." *Studies in Conflict and Terrorism* 31, no. 4 (2008): 284–303.

Asal, Victor and R. Karl Rethemeyer. "The Nature of the Beast: Organizational Structures and the Lethality of Terrorist Attacks." *Journal of Politics* 70, no. 2 (2008): 437–449.

Ashour, Omar. *The De-Radicalization of Jihadists: Transforming Armed Islamist Movements.* New York, NY: Routledge, 2009.

Atran, Scott. "Mishandling Suicide Terrorism." *Washington Quarterly* 27, no. 3 (2004): 65–90.

Ayubi, Nazih N. M. *Political Islam: Religion and Politics in the Arab World.* London: Routledge, 1991.

Bagby, Ihsan. "The American Mosque in Transition: Assimilation, Acculturation and Isolation." *Journal of Ethnic and Migration Studies* 35, no. 3 (2009): 476–490.

Banyan. "Unforgiving History: Why Buddhists and Muslims in Rakhine State Are at Each Other's Throats." *The Economist.* Last modified November 3, 2012. www.economist.com/news/asia/21565638-why-buddhists-and-muslims-rakhine-state-myanmar-are-each-others%E2%80%99-throats-unforgiving.

Barrett, Justin L. *Why Would Anyone Believe in God?.* Lanham, MD: AltaMira Press, 2004.

Barry, John M. *Roger Williams and the Creation of the American Soul: Church, State and the Birth of Liberty.* New York, NY: Viking, 2012.

Basedau, Matthias, Birte Pfeiffer and Johannes Vüllers. "Bad Religion? Religion, Collective Action, and the Onset of Armed Conflict in Developing Countries." *Journal of Conflict Resolution* 60, no. 2 (2016): 226–255.

Basedau, Matthias, Georg Strüver, Johannes Vüllers and Tim Wegenast. "Do Religious Factors Impact Armed Conflict? Empirical Evidence from Sub-Saharan Africa." *Terrorism and Political Violence* 23, no. 5 (2011): 752–779.

Batatu, Hanna. "Shi'i Organizations in Iraq: Al-Da'wa al-Islamiyah and al-Mujahidin." In *Shi'ism and Social Protest*, edited by Juan Cole and Nikki Keddie, 179–200. New Haven, CT: Yale University Press, 1986.

Baxi, Upendra. "The Constitutional Discourse on Secularism." In *Reconstructing the Republic*, edited by Upendra Baxi, Alice Jacob and Tarlok Singh, 211–233. New Delhi: Har-Anand Publications, 1999.

BBC News. "Myanmar: Who Are the Arakan Rohingya Salvation Army?" *BBC News.* Last modified September 6, 2016. www.bbc.com/news/world-asia-41160679.

Beaumont, Peter. "Iraq's 'Failing to Tackle Death Squads.'" *The Guardian.* Last modified September 29, 2006. www.theguardian.com/world/2006/sep/29/iraq.topstories3.

Beech, Hannah. "The Face of Buddhist Terror." *Time.* Last modified July 1, 2013. http://content.time.com/time/magazine/article/0,9171,2146000,00.html.

Behrend, Heike. *Alice Lakwena & Holy Spirits: War in Northern Uganda 1986–97.* Athens, OH: Ohio University Press, 2000.

"Is Alice Lakwena a Witch? The Holy Spirit Movement and Its Fight against Evil in the North." In *Changing Uganda: The Dilemmas of Structural Adjustment and Revolutionary Change*, edited by Michael Twaddle and Holger Bernt Hansen, 162–177. London: James Currey Publishers, 1991.

Ben-Yehuda, Nachman. *Theocratic Democracy: The Social Construction of Religious and Secular Extremism*. New York, NY: Oxford University Press, 2010.

Berger, Peter L. *The Desecularization of the World: Resurgent Religion and World Politics*. Grand Rapids, MI: William B. Eerdmans Publishing Company, 1999.

Bering, Jesse. *The Belief Instinct: The Psychology of Souls, Destiny, and the Meaning of Life*. New York, NY: W. W. Norton, 2011.

Berman, Eli. *Radical, Religious, and Violent: The New Economics of Terrorism*. Cambridge, MA: Massachusetts Institute of Technology, 2009.

Berrebi, Claude. "Evidence about the Link between Education, Poverty and Terrorism among Palestinians." *Peace Economics, Peace Science and Public Policy* 13, no. 1 (2007): 1–36.

Bigelow, Anna. *Sharing the Sacred: Practicing Pluralism in Muslim North India*. Oxford: Oxford University Press, 2010.

Bilefsky, Dan and Maia de la Baume. "Terrorists Strike Charlie Hebdo Newspaper in Paris, Leaving 12 Dead." *New York Times*. Last modified January 7, 2015. www.nytimes.com/2015/01/08/world/europe/charlie-hebdo-paris-shooting.html?_r=1.

Bin Laden, Osama. "Letter to America." *The Guardian*. Last modified November 24, 2002. www.theguardian.com/world/2002/nov/24/theobserver.

Bjornson, Karin Solveig and Kurt Jonassohn. *Genocide and Gross Human Rights Violations in Comparative Perspective*. New Brunswick, NJ: Transaction Publishers, 1998.

Blake, Matthew. "Fearless Pakistani Lawyer Murdered for Continuing to Defend Man Accused of Blasphemy Despite Receiving Death Threats from the Prosecution." *Daily Mail*. Last modified May 9, 2014. www.dailymail.co.uk/news/article-2624073/Fearless-Pakistani-lawyer-murdered-defending-man-accused-blasphemy-despite-death-threats-PROSECUTION.html.

"Blame It on Newton's Law: Modi." *Times of India*. March 3, 2002.

Bleming, Thomas. *War in Karen Country: Armed Struggle for a Free and Independent State in Southeast Asia*. New York, NY: IUniverse, 2007.

Blitt, Robert C. "Springtime for Freedom of Religion or Belief: Will Newly Democratic Arab States Guarantee International Human Rights Norms or Perpetuate Their Violation?" In *State Responses to Minority Religions*, edited by David M. Kirkham, 45–64. Farnham: Ashgate, 2013.

Boraine, Alex. *A Country Unmasked: Inside South Africa's Truth and Reconciliation Commission*. Cape Town: Oxford University Press, 2000.

Borer, Tristan Anne. *Challenging the State: Churches as Political Actors in South Africa, 1980–1994*. Notre Dame, IN: University of Notre Dame Press, 1998.

Bose, Sumantra. "Hindu Nationalism and the Crisis of the Indian State: A Theoretical Perspective." In *Nationalism, Democracy and Development: State and Politics in India*, edited by Sugata Bose and Ayesha Jalal, 104–164. New Delhi: Oxford, 1998.

Boulby, Marion. "The Islamic Challenge: Tunisia since Independence," *Third World Quarterly* 10, no. 2 (1988): 590–614.

Brass, Paul R. "The Punjab Crisis and the Unity of India." In *India's Democracy: An Analysis of Changing State–Society Relations*, edited by Atul Kohli, 169–213. Princeton, NJ: Princeton University Press, 1988.

Brooks, Risa. "Muslim 'Homegrown' Terrorism in the United States: How Serious Is the Threat?." *International Security* 36, no. 2 (2012): 7–47.

Brownlee, Jason, Tarek Masoud and Andrew Reynolds. *The Arab Spring: Pathways of Repression and Reform*. Oxford: Oxford University Press, 2015.

Burgoon, Brian. "On Welfare and Terror." *Journal of Conflict Resolution* 50, no. 2 (2006): 176–203.

Burki, Shahid Javed, Craig Baxter, Robert LaPorte and Azfar Kamal. *Pakistan under the Military: Eleven Years of Zia Ul-Haq*. Boulder, CO: Westview, 1991.

Bush, George W. "President Bush Discusses Freedom in Iraq and Middle East." Last modified November 6, 2003. http://georgewbush-whitehouse.archives.gov/news/releases/2003/11/20031106-2.html.

"Remarks on the 10th Anniversary of the International Religious Freedom Act." Last modified July 14, 2008. http://georgewbush-whitehouse.archives.gov/news/releases/2008/07/20080714-1.html.

Byman, Daniel. *A High Price: The Triumphs and Failures of Israeli Counterterrorism*. Oxford: Oxford University Press, 2011.

Casanova, Josè. *Public Religions in the Modern World*. Chicago, IL: University of Chicago Press, 1994.

Castets, Remi. "The Uyghurs in Xinjiang – The Malaise Grows." *China Perspectives* 49 (2003): 34–84.

Cavanaugh, William T. *The Myth of Religious Violence: Secular Ideology and the Roots of Modern Conflict*. Oxford: Oxford University Press, 2009.

Center for Systemic Peace, "Polity IV Annual Time-Series, 1800–2016." Last modified June 15, 2017. www.systemicpeace.org/inscrdata.html.

"State Fragility Index and Matrix, Time-Series Data, 1995–2016." Last modified June 15, 2017. www.systemicpeace.org/inscrdata.html.

Cesari, Jocelyne. *The Awakening of Muslim Democracy: Religion, Modernity and the State*. Cambridge: Cambridge University Press, 2014.

Chandler, Adam. "The Long Thorny Path to Calling ISIS 'Genocidal.'" *The Atlantic*. Last modified March 17, 2016. http://www.theatlantic.com/politics/archive/2016/03/isis-genocide-obama/474087/.

Chellaney, Brahma. "Fighting Terrorism in Southern Asia: The Lessons of History." *International Security* 26, no. 3 (2002): 94–116.

Christian Solidarity International. "Burma." Last modified January 11, 2018. www.csw.org.uk/our_work_profile_burma.htm.

Cingranelli, David L., David L. Richards and Chad Clay. "The CIRI Human Rights Dataset." Last modified 2014. www.humanrightsdata.org.

Clark, Janine Natalya. "Religious Peace-Building in South Africa: From Potential to Practice." *Ethnopolitics* 10, no. 3/4 (2011): 345–365.

Clinton, Hillary Rodham. "Remarks at the Release of the 2011 International Religious Freedom Report." Last modified July 30, 2012. www.state.gov/secretary/20092013clinton/rm/2012/07/195782.htm.

Clinton, William J. "Remarks Announcing Guidelines on Religious Exercise and Religious Expression in the Federal Workplace." *American Presidency Project*. Last modified August 14, 1997. www.presidency.ucsb.edu/ws/index.php?pid=54535&st=&st1.

Coates, Elaine. "Interreligious Violence in Myanmar: A Security Threat to Southeast Asia." *RSIS Commentaries* 117 (2013): 1–3.

Cochrane, James, John de Gruchy and Stephen Martin. *Facing the Truth: South African Faith Communities and the Truth & Reconciliation Commission*. Athens, OH: Ohio University Press, 1999.

Collard-Wexler, Simon, Costantino Pischedda and Michael G. Smith. "Do Foreign Occupations Cause Suicide Attacks?" *Journal of Conflict Resolution* 58, no. 4 (2014): 625–657.

Constantine, Greg. "Exiled to Nowhere: Burma's Rohingya." Last modified 2016. www.exiled tonowhere.com/.

Cook, Jonathan. *Blood and Religion: The Unmasking of the Jewish and Democratic State.* London: Pluto, 2006.

Correlates of War Project. "The Correlates of War Project." Last modified 2018. www.correla tesofwar.org/data-sets/folder_listing.

Crawford, Jamie and Laura Koran. "U.S. Officials: Foreigners Flock to Fight for ISIS." *CNN.* Last modified February 11, 2015. www.cnn.com/2015/02/10/politics/isis-foreign-fighters-com bat/.

Crenshaw, Martha. "The Causes of Terrorism." *Comparative Politics* 13, no. 4 (1981): 379–399.

Crowley, Michael. "The End of Iraq." *Time.* Last modified June 19, 2014. http://time.com/2899488/the-end-of-iraq/.

Cruise O'Brien, Donal B. "The Senegalese Exception." *Africa* 3 (1996): 458–464.

Cunningham, Erin. "Ahmad Shah Massoud, Assassinated by Al Qaeda but no Friend of the U.S." *The National.* Last modified September 6, 2011. www.thenational.ae/news/world/south-asia/ahmad-shah-massoud-assassinated-by-al-qaeda-but-no-friend-of-the-us.

Dalacoura, Katerina. *Islamist Terrorism and Democracy in the Middle East.* New York, NY: Cambridge University Press, 2011.

Dawisha, Adeed. *Arab Nationalism in the Twentieth Century: From Triumph to Despair.* Princeton, NJ: Princeton University Press, 2005.

Dawkins, Richard. "Religion's Misguided Missiles." *The Guardian.* Last modified September 15, 2001. www.theguardian.com/world/2001/sep/15/september11.politicsphilosophyandsociety1.

de Soysa, Indra and Ragnhild Nordas. "Islam's Bloody Innards: Religion and Political Terror, 1980–2000." *International Studies Quarterly* 51, no. 4 (2007): 927–943.

Deng, Francis M. "Sudan – Civil War and Genocide: Disappearing Christians of the Middle East." *Middle East Quarterly* 8, no. 1 (2001): 13–21.

Deol, Harnik. *Religion and Nationalism in India: The Case of the Punjab.* London: Routledge, 2000.

Derfler, Leslie. *Yitzhak Rabin: A Political Biography.* New York, NY: Palgrave Macmillan, 2014.

Dingley, James and Michael Kirk-Smith. "Symbolism and Sacrifice in Terrorism." *Small Wars and Insurgencies* 13, no. 1 (2002): 102–128.

Diouf, Mamadou. Ed. *Tolerance, Democracy, and Sufis in Senegal.* New York, NY: Columbia University Press, 2012.

Doxtader, Erik. *With Faith in the Work of Words: The Beginnings of Reconciliation in South Africa, 1985–1995.* East Lansing, MI: Michigan State University Press, 2008.

Drakos Konstantinos and Andreas Gofas, "Evidence for the Existence of Under-Reporting Bias in Observed Terrorist Activity: The Message in Press Freedom Status Transitions." *Democracy and Security* 3, no. 2 (2006): 139–155.

Driessen, Michael. *Religion and Democratization: Framing Political and Religious Identities in Muslim and Catholic Societies.* Oxford: Oxford University Press, 2014.

Durham Jr., W. Cole. "Perspectives on Religious Liberty: A Comparative Framework." In *Religious Human Rights in Global Perspective: Legal Perspectives*, edited by Johan D. van der Vyver and John Witte Jr., 1–44. The Hague: Kluwer Law International, 1996.

Durham Jr., W. Cole and Elizabeth A. Clark. "The Place of Religious Freedom in the Structure of Peacebuilding." In *The Oxford Handbook of Religion, Conflict and Peacebuilding*, edited by Atalia Omer, R. Scott Appleby and David Little, 281–306. Oxford: Oxford University Press, 2015.

Durham Jr., W. Cole and Brett G. Scharffs. *Law and Religion: National, International, and Comparative Perspectives*. New York, NY: Aspen Publishers, 2010.

Eck, Diana. *A New Religious America: How a "Christian Country" Has Become the World's Most Religiously Diverse Nation*. New York, NY: Harper Collins, 2001.

Editorial Board. "Stop U.S. Support for the Repressive Regime in Egypt." *Washington Post*. Last modified October 28, 2014. www.washingtonpost.com/opinions/stop-us-support-for-the-repressive-regime-in-egypt/2014/10/28/0c871dca-5ebd-11e4-8b9e-2ccdac31a031_story.html.

Ergil, Dogo. "The Kurdish Question in Turkey." *Journal of Democracy* 11, no. 3 (2000): 122–135.

Eskander, Wael. "In Search of a New Prayer: An Eye Witness Account of the Cathedral Attack." *Atlantic Council*. Last modified April 8, 2013. www.atlanticcouncil.org/blogs/egyptsource/in-search-of-a-new-prayer-an-eye-witness-account-of-the-cathedral-attack.

Fair, Christine C. *Fighting to the End: The Pakistan Army's Way of War*. Oxford: Oxford University Press, 2014.

Farr, Thomas F. "International Religious Freedom and Moral Responsibility." In *Challenges to Religious Liberty in the Twenty-First Century*, edited by Gerard V. Bradley, 193–207. Cambridge: Cambridge University Press, 2012.

"International Religious Freedom Policy and American National Security." *The Witherspoon Institute*. Last modified September 19, 2014. www.thepublicdiscourse.com/2014/09/13818/.

World of Faith and Freedom: Why International Religious Liberty Is Vital to American National Security. Oxford: Oxford University Press, 2008.

Felter, Joseph and Brian Fishman. *Al-Qa'ida's Foreign Fighters in Iraq: A First Look at the Sinjar Records*. New York, NY: Combating Terrorism Center at West Point, 2007.

Fine, Jonathan. "Contrasting Secular and Religious Terrorism." *Middle East Quarterly* 15, no. 1 (2008): 59–71.

Finke, Roger and Jaime D. Harris. "Wars and Rumors of Wars: Explaining Religiously Motivated Violence." In *Religion, Politics, Society, and the State*, edited by Jonathan Fox, 53–71. New York, NY: Oxford University Press, 2012.

Fisch, M. Steven. *Are Muslims Distinctive? A Look at the Evidence*. Oxford: Oxford University Press, 2011.

Fox, Jonathan. "The Effects of Religious Discrimination on Ethno-Religious Protest and Rebellion." *Journal of Conflict Studies* 20, no. 2 (2000), https://journals.lib.unb.ca/index.php/jcs/article/view/4310/4922.

"Equal Opportunity Oppression: Religious Persecution Is a Global Problem." *Foreign Affairs*. Last modified August 31, 2015. www.foreignaffairs.com/articles/2015–08-31/equal-opportunity-oppression.

Ethnoreligious Conflict in the Late 20th Century: A General Theory. Lanham, MD: Rowman & Littlefield Publishers, 2002.

"Ethnoreligious Conflict in the Third World: The Role of Religion as a Cause of Conflict." *Nationalism and Ethnic Politics* 9, no. 1 (2003): 101–125.

"The Influence of Religious Legitimacy on Grievance Formation by Ethno-Religious Minorities." *Journal of Peace Research* 36, no. 3 (1999): 289–307.

Political Secularism, Religion, and the State: A Time Series Analysis of Worldwide Data. Cambridge: Cambridge University Press, 2015.

Religion, Civilization and Civil War: 1945 through the New Millennium. Lanham, MD: Lexington Books, 2004.

A World Survey of Religion and the State. Cambridge: Cambridge University Press, 2008.

Fox, Jonathan and Jonathan Rynhold. "A Jewish and Democratic State? Comparing Government Involvement in Religion in Israel with Other Democracies." *Totalitarian Movements and Political Religions* 9, no. 4 (2008): 507–531.

Gall, Carlotta. "Show of Power by Libya Militia in Kidnapping." *New York Times*. Last modified October 10, 2013. www.nytimes.com/2013/10/11/world/africa/libya.html?_r=0.

Gambill, Gary. "The Libyan Islamic Fighting Group (LIFG)." *Terrorism Monitor* 3, no. 6 (2005). Last modified May 5, 2005. www.jamestown.org/single/?tx_ttnews[tt_news]=308#.VaBxe6OwXXs.

Gandhi, Mahatma. *The Collected Works of Mahatma Gandhi: Volume 10*. New Delhi: Government of India, Ministry of Information and Broadcasting, 1963.

Gartenstein-Ross, Daveed and Laura Grossman. *Homegrown Terrorists in the U.S. and the U.K.: An Empirical Study of the Radicalization Process*. Washington, DC: FDD Press, 2009.

Gates, Robert M. "Helping Others Defend Themselves: The Future of U.S. Security Assistance." *Foreign Affairs* 98 (2010): 2–6.

Gause III, F. Gregory. "Why Middle East Studies Missed the Arab Spring: The Myth of Authoritarian Stability." *Foreign Affairs* 4 (2011): 81–90.

Gellar, Sheldon. *Democracy in Senegal: Tocquevillian Analytics in Africa*. New York, NY: Palgrave Macmillan, 2005.

Gerges, Fawaz A. *The Far Enemy: Why Jihad Went Global*. Cambridge: Cambridge University Press, 2005.

Gill, Anthony. *The Political Origins of Religious Liberty*. New York, NY: Cambridge University Press, 2008.

Gopal, Sarvepalli. *Anatomy of a Confrontation: The Babri Masjid-Ram Janmabhumi Issue*. New Delhi: Viking, 1991.

Gravers, Mikael. "Anti-Muslim Buddhist Nationalism in Burma and Sri Lanka, Religious Violence and Globalized Imaginaries of Endangered Identities." *Contemporary Buddhism* 16, no. 1 (2015): 1–27.

"Spiritual Politics, Political Religion, and Religious Freedom in Burma." *Review of Faith & International Affairs* 11, no. 2 (2013): 46–54.

Gregg, Heather S. "Three Theories of Religious Activism and Violence: Social Movements, Fundamentalists, and Apocalyptic Warriors." *Terrorism and Political Violence* 28, no. 2 (2016): 338–360.

Grewal, Jagtar S. *The Sikhs of the Punjab. Vol. 2*. Cambridge: Cambridge University Press, 1998.

Grim, Brian J. "Religious Freedom: Good for What Ails Us?" *Review of Faith & International Affairs* 6, no. 2 (2010): 3–7.

Grim, Brian J. and Roger Finke. "International Regulation Indexes: Government Regulation, Government Favoritism, and Social Regulation of Religion." *Interdisciplinary Journal of Research on Religion* 2 (2006): 1–40.

The Price of Freedom Denied: Religious Persecution and Conflict in the 21st Century. New York, NY: Cambridge University Press, 2011.

"Religious Persecution in Cross-National Context: Clashing Civilizations or Regulated Religious Economies?" *American Sociological Review* 72, no. 4 (2007): 633–658.

Griswold, Eliza. "Is This the End of Christianity in the Middle East?" *New York Times Magazine*. Last modified July 22, 2015. www.nytimes.com/2015/07/26/magazine/is-this-the-end-of-christianity-in-the-middle-east.html?_r=0.

Guerin, Orla. "Pakistan Minorities Minister Shahbaz Bhatti Shot Dead." *BBC News*. Last modified March 2, 2011. www.bbc.com/news/world-south-asia-12617562.

Guha, Ramachandra. *India after Gandhi: The History of the World's Largest Democracy*. New York, NY: Ecco, 2007.

Gunning, Jeroen and Richard Jackson. "What's so 'Religious' about 'Religious Terrorism'?" *Critical Studies on Terrorism* 4, no. 3 (2011): 369–388.

Gurr, Ted R. *Why Men Rebel*. Princeton, NJ: Princeton University Press, 1970.

Hafez, Kai. *Radicalism and Political Reform in the Islamic and Western Worlds*. Cambridge: Cambridge University Press, 2010.

Hafez, Mohammed. *Why Muslims Rebel: Repression and Resistance in the Islamic World*. Boulder, CO: Lynne Rienner Publishers, 2003.

Haider, Ziad. *The Ideological Struggle for Pakistan*. Stanford, CA: Hoover Institute Press, 2010.

Hamid, Shadi. *The Islamist Response to Repression: Are Mainstream Islamists Radicalizing?* Washington, DC: Brookings Institution, 2010.

"Rethinking the U.S.–Egypt Relationship: How Repression Is Undermining Egyptian Stability and What the United States Can Do." Prepared Testimony for the Tom Lantos Human Rights Commission. November 3, 2015.

Temptations of Power: Islamists and Liberal Democracy in a New Middle East. Oxford: Oxford University Press, 2014.

Haqqani, Husain. *Pakistan: Between Mosque and Military*. Washington, DC: Carnegie Endowment for International Peace, 2005.

Hassner, Ron E. "Blasphemy and Violence." *International Studies Quarterly* 55, no. 1 (2011): 23–45.

Hemming, John and Dominic Evans. "Defiant Gaddafi Vows to Die as Martyr, Fight Revolt." *Reuters*. Last modified February 22, 2011. www.reuters.com/article/us-libya-protests-idUSTRE71G0A620110222.

Hendrix, Cullen S. and Idean Salehyan. "A House Divided: Threat Perception, Military Factionalism, and Repression in Africa." *Journal of Conflict Resolution* 61, no. 8 (2007): 1653–1681.

Henne, Peter S. "The Ancient Fire: Religion and Suicide Terrorism." *Terrorism and Political Violence* 24, no. 1 (2012): 38–60.

Henne, Peter S., Sarabrynn Hudgins and Timothy Samuel Shah. *Religious Freedom and Violent Religious Extremism: A Sourcebook of Modern Cases and Analysis*. Washington, DC: Berkley Center for Religion, Peace and World Affairs, 2012.

Henne, Peter S. and Jason Klocek. "Taming the Gods: How Religious Conflict Shapes State Repression," *Journal of Conflict Resolution*, doi:10.1177/0022002717728104.

Henry, Clement, Jang Ji-Hyang and Robert P. Parks. "Introduction." In *The Arab Spring: Will It Lead to Democratic Transitions?*, edited by Clement Henry and Jang Ji-Hyang, 12–26. New York, NY: Palgrave Macmillan, 2013.

Hertzke, Allen. *Freeing God's Children: The Unlikely Alliance for Global Human Rights*. Lanham, MD: Rowman & Littlefield Publishers, 2004.

ed. *The Future of Religious Freedom*. New York, NY: Oxford University Press, 2013.

Hibbard, Scott W. *Religious Politics and Secular States: Egypt, India, and the United States*. Baltimore, MD: Johns Hopkins University Press, 2010.

Hitchens, Christopher. *God Is Not Great: How Religion Poisons Everything*. New York, NY: Twelve, 2009.

Hoffman, Bruce. "'Holy Terror': The Implications of Terrorism Motivated By a Religious Imperative." *Studies in Conflict & Terrorism* 18, no. 4 (1995): 271–284.

Inside Terrorism. New York, NY: Columbia University Press, 2006.

Hoffman, Bruce and H. Gordon McCormick. "Terrorism, Signaling, and Suicide Attack." *Studies in Conflict & Terrorism* 27, no. 4 (2004): 243–281.

Human Rights Watch. *All You Can Do Is Pray: Crimes against Humanity and Ethnic Cleansing of Rohingya Muslims in Burma's Arakan State.* New York, NY: Human Rights Watch, 2013.

"Burma: Scrap Proposed Discriminatory Marriage Law." Last modified March 24, 2014. www.hrw.org/news/2014/03/24/burma-scrap-proposed-discriminatory-marriage-law.

"Central African Republic: Muslims Forced to Flee: Christian Militias Unleash Waves of Targeted Violence." Last modified February 12, 2014. www.hrw.org/news/2014/02/12/central-african-republic-muslims-forced-flee.

"Central African Republic: Muslims Trapped in Enclaves." Last modified December 22, 2014. www.hrw.org/news/2014/12/22/central-african-republic-muslims-trapped-enclaves.

Creating Enemies of the State: Religious Persecution in Uzbekistan. New York, NY: Human Rights Watch, 2013.

"Egypt: Rab'a Killings Likely Crimes against Humanity." Last modified August 12, 2014. www.hrw.org/news/2014/08/12/egypt-raba-killings-likely-crimes-against-humanity.

"Egypt: Redress Recurring Sectarian Violence." Last modified April 10, 2013. Accessed August 7, 2015. www.hrw.org/news/2013/04/10/egypt-address-recurring-sectarian-violence/.

Protecting the Killers: A Policy of Impunity in Punjab, India. New York, NY: Human Rights Watch, 2007.

"Tunisia: Let Constitution Herald Human Rights Era." Last modified February 1, 2014. www.hrw.org/news/2014/02/01/tunisia-let-constitution-herald-human-rights-era.

We Have No Orders to Save You: State Participation and Complicity in Communal Violence in Gujarat. New York, NY: Human Rights Watch, 2002.

"World Report 2015: Pakistan." Last modified 2015. www.hrw.org/world-report/2015/country-chapters/pakistan.

Hunt, Katie. "Rohingya Crisis: How We Got Here." CNN. Last modified November 12, 2017. www.cnn.com/2017/11/12/asia/rohingya-crisis-timeline/index.html.

Huntington, Samuel P. "The Clash of Civilizations?" *Foreign Affairs* 72 (1993): 22–49.

The Clash of Civilizations and the Remaking of World Order. New York, NY: Simon and Schuster, 1996.

The Third Wave: Democratization in the Late Twentieth Century. Norman, OK: University of Oklahoma Press, 1991.

Hurd, Elizabeth Shakman. *Beyond Religious Freedom: The New Global Politics of Religion.* Princeton, NJ: Princeton University Press, 2015.

"International 'Religious Freedom' Agenda Will Only Embolden ISIS." *Religion Dispatches.* Last modified November 10, 2014. http://religiondispatches.org/international-religious-freedom-agenda-will-only-embolden-isis/.

The Politics of Secularism in International Relations. Princeton, NJ: Princeton University Press, 2007.

Ibrahim, Saad Eddin. "Anatomy of Egypt's Militant Islamic Groups: Methodological Note and Preliminary Findings." *International Journal of Middle East Studies* 12, no. 4 (1982): 423–453.

Inboden, William. "Responding to Religious Freedom and Presidential Leadership: An Historical Approach." Berkley Center for Religion, Peace and World Affairs. Last modified February 19, 2015. http://berkleycenter.georgetown.edu/responses/promoting-religious-freedom-from-the-oval-office.

International Crisis Group. *Myanmar: A New Muslim Insurgency in Rakhine State.* Brussels: International Crisis Group, 2016.

Islamabad, Aryn. "In Pakistan, Justifying Murder for Those Who Blaspheme." *Time.* Last modified March 21, 2011. http://content.time.com/time/printout/0,8816,2058155,00.html.

Jenkins, Brian Michael. *Would-Be Warriors: Incidents of Jihadist Terrorist Radicalization in the United States since September 11, 2001.* Santa Monica, CA: RAND Corporation, 2010.

Jenkins, Philip. "Mystical Power." *Boston Globe.* January 25, 2009.

Jerryson, Michael K. and Mark Juergensmeyer. Eds. *Buddhist Warfare.* Oxford: Oxford University Press, 2010.

Johnston, Douglas and Brian Cox. "Faith-Based Diplomacy and Preventive Engagement." In *Faith-Based Diplomacy: Trumping Realpolitik,* edited by Douglas Johnston, 11–30. New York, NY: Oxford University Press, 2003.

Jones, Seth G. *Hunting in the Shadows: The Pursuit of al Qa'ida since 9/11.* New York, NY: W. W. Norton, 2013.

Jones, Seth G. and Martin C. Libicki. *How Terrorist Groups End: Lessons for Countering Al Qa'ida.* Santa Monica, CA: RAND Corporation, 2008.

Juergensmeyer, Mark. "The Global Rise of Religious Nationalism." *Australian Journal of International Affairs* 64, no. 3 (2010): 262–273.

The New Cold War? Religious Nationalism Confronts the Secular State. Berkeley, CA: University of California Press, 1993.

Terror in the Mind of God: The Global Rise of Religious Violence. Berkeley, CA: University of California Press, 2003.

"Terror Mandated by God." *Terrorism and Political Violence* 9, no. 2 (1997): 16–23.

Kairos Theologians. *The Kairos Document: Challenge to the Church: A Theological Comment on the Political Crisis in South Africa,* 2nd edn. Grand Rapids, MI: William B. Eerdmans Publishing Company, 1986.

Kalyvas, Stathis N. *The Rise of Christian Democracy in Europe.* Ithaca, NY: Cornell University Press, 1996.

KAM Kah, Henry. "Anti-Balaka/Seleka, 'Religionisation' and Separatism in the History of the Central African Republic." *Conflict Studies Quarterly* 9, no. 4 (2014): 30–48.

Kane, Mouhamadou. "Interreligious Violence in the Central African Republic." *African Security Review* 23, no. 3 (2014): 313–317.

Kathwari, Farooq, Lynne Martin and Christopher B. Whitney. *Strengthening America: The Civic and Political Integration of Muslim Americans: Report of the Task Force on Muslim American Civic and Political Engagement.* Chicago, IL: Chicago Council on Global Affairs, 2007.

Kaur, Jasakaran. *Twenty Years of Impunity: The November 1984 Pogroms of Sikhs in India.* Portland, OR: Ensaaf, 2006.

Kedouri, Elie. *Democracy and Arab Culture.* Washington, DC: Washington Institute for Near East Policy, 1992.

Kepel, Gilles. *Jihad: The Trail of Political Islam.* London I. B. Tauris, 2006.

The Revenge of God: The Resurgence of Islam, Christianity, and Judaism in the Modern World. University Park, PA: Pennsylvania State University Press, 1994.

Kerry, John. "Remarks at the Rollout of the 2014 Report on International Religious Freedom." Last modified October 14, 2015. www.state.gov/secretary/remarks/2015/10/248198.htm.

Khalidi, Rashid. "The Arab Spring." *The Nation.* Last modified March 21, 2011. www.thenation.com/article/arab-spring/.

Khosrokhavar, Farhad and David Macey. *Suicide Bombers: Allah's New Martyrs.* London: Pluto, 2005.

Kipgen, Neghinpao. "Conflict in Rakhine State in Myanmar: Rohingya Muslims' Conundrum." *Journal of Muslim Minority Affairs* 33, no. 2 (2013): 398–410.

Krueger, Alan B. *What Makes a Terrorist: Economics and the Roots of Terrorism.* Princeton, NJ: Princeton University Press, 2007.

Krueger, Alan B. and Jitka Maleckova. *Education, Poverty, Political Violence and Terrorism: Is There a Causal Connection?* Cambridge, MA: National Bureau of Economic Research, 2002.

Kuperman, Alan J. "Obama's Libya Debacle: How a Well-Meaning Intervention Ended in Failure." *Foreign Affairs* 94 (2015): 66–77.

Kurzman, Charles and Ijlal Naqvi. "Do Muslims Vote Islamic?" *Journal of Democracy* 21, no. 2 (2010): 50–63.

Kurzman, Charles, David Schanzer and Ebrahim Moosa. "Muslim American Terrorism since 9/11: Why So Rare?" *Muslim World* 101, no. 3 (2011): 464–483.

Kydd, Andrew H. and Barbara F. Walter. "The Strategies of Terrorism." *International Security* 31, no. 1 (2006): 49–80.

LaFranchi, Howard. "Terrorists in Tunisia Attacks Trained at Islamic Camp in Libya." *Christian Science Monitor*. Last modified July 2, 2015. www.csmonitor.com/USA/Foreign-Policy/2015/0702/Terrorists-in-Tunisia-attacks-trained-at-Islamic-State-camp-in-Libya.

Lagon, Luke and Arch Puddington. "Exploiting Terrorism as a Pretext for Repression." *Wall Street Journal*. January 28, 2015, A15.

Lai, Brian. "Draining the Swamp: An Empirical Examination of the Production of International Terrorism." *Conflict Management and Peace Science* 24, no. 4 (2007): 297–310.

Laqueur, Walter. *The New Terrorism: Fanaticism and the Arms of Mass Destruction.* New York, NY: Oxford University Press, 1999.

Lewis, Bernard. *The Crisis of Islam: Holy War and Unholy Terror.* New York, NY: Modern Library, 2003.

"The Roots of Muslim Rage." *Atlantic Monthly* 266 (1990): 47–60.

Li, Quan and Drew Schaub "Economic Globalization and Transnational Terrorism: A Pooled Time-Series Analysis." *Journal of Conflict Resolution* 48, no. 2 (2004): 230–258.

Li, Xiaorong. "What's in a Headscarf?" *Philosophy & Public Policy Quarterly* 24, no. 1/2 (2004): 14–18.

Locke, John. *A Letter Concerning Toleration.* Indianapolis, IN: Bobbs-Merrill, 1955 [1689].

Loimeier, Roman. "The Secular State and Islam in Senegal." In *Questioning the Secular State: The Worldwide Resurgence of Religion in Politics*, edited by David Westerlund, 183–197. New York, NY: St. Martin's Press, 1996.

Long, Mary Kate. "Dynamics of State, Sangha and Society in Myanmar: A Closer Look at the Rohingya Issue." *Asian Journal of Public Affairs* 6, no. 1 (2013): 79–94.

Lustick, Ian. *For the Land and the Lord: Jewish Fundamentalism in Israel.* New York, NY: Council on Foreign Relations.

Lutz, Ashely. "The New Egyptian President Reportedly Said 'Jihad Is Our Path and Death in the Name of Allah Is Our Goal.'" *Business Insider*. Last modified June 25, 2012. www.businessinsider.com/morsi-says-jihad-is-our-path-and-death-in-the-name-of-allah-is-our-goal-2012-6#ixzz3gT13w97s.

Lynch, Marc. "Islamists in a Changing Middle East." *Foreign Policy*. Last modified July 8, 2012. http://lynch.foreignpolicy.com/posts/2012/07/08/islamists_in_a_changing_middle_east.

Mahmood, Saba. *Religious Difference in a Secular Age: A Minority Report.* Princeton, NJ: Princeton University Press, 2015.

Mamdani, Mahmood. *Good Muslim, Bad Muslim: America, the Cold War and the Roots of Terror.* New York, NY: Random House, 2004.

Mandaville, Peter and Melissa Nozell. *Engaging Religion and Religious Actors in Countering Violent Extremism.* Washington, DC: US Institute of Peace, 2017.

Marshall, Monty G. and Ted R. Gurr. "Polity IV Project: Political Regime Characteristics and Transitions, 1800–2015." Last modified 2015. www.systemicpeace.org/polityproject.html.

Marshall, Paul A. *Religious Freedom in the World*. Lanham, MD: Rowman & Littlefield Publishers, 2008.

Marshall, Paul and Nina Shea. *Silenced: How Apostasy and Blasphemy Codes Are Choking Freedom Worldwide*. Oxford: Oxford University Press, 2011.

Matharu, Hardeep. "Tajikistan Police Shave Beards of 13,000 Men to 'Tackle Radicalism.'" *Independent*. Last modified January 21, 2016. www.independent.co.uk/news/world/asia/tajikistan-police-shave-beards-of-13000-men-to-tackle-radicalism-a6825581.html.

McAdam, Doug, John D. McCarty and Mayer N. Zald. *Comparative Perspectives on Social Movements: Political Opportunities, Mobilizing Structures, and Cultural Framings*. Cambridge: Cambridge University Press, 1996.

McKinley, James C. "Christian Rebels Wage War of Terror in Uganda." *New York Times*. March 5, 1997.

McTighe, Kirsten. "Ex-Egyptian President Morsi's Death Sentence Upheld." *USA Today*. Last modified June 16, 2015. www.usatoday.com/story/news/world/2015/06/16/former-egyptian-president-morsi-sentenced/28796565/.

Migdal, Joel S. *Strong Societies and Weak States: State–Society Relations and State Capabilities in the Third World*. Princeton, NJ: Princeton University Press, 1998.

Miller, Aaron David. "For America, an Arab Winter." *Wilson Quarterly* 35, no. 3 (2011): 36–42.

Miller, Nicholas P. *The Religious Roots of the First Amendment: Dissenting Protestants and the Separation of Church and State*. New York, NY: Oxford University Press, 2012.

Milton-Edwards, Beverly and Stephen Farrell. *Hamas: The Islamic Resistance Movement*. Cambridge: Polity Press, 2010.

Minorities at Risk Project. "MAR Data." Last modified June 8, 2016. www.mar.umd.edu/.

Mircea, Eliade. *The Sacred and the Profane: The Nature of Religion*. New York, NY: Harcourt, 1959.

Mitchell, Richard P. *The Society of the Muslim Brothers*. Oxford: Oxford University Press, 1993.

Mitnick, Joshua. "Israel Moves to Improve Religious Freedom – for Jews." *Christian Science Monitor*. Last modified June 6, 2012. www.csmonitor.com/World/Middle-East/2012/0606/Israel-moves-to-improve-religious-freedom-for-Jews.

Moghadam, Assaf. *The Globalization of Martyrdom: Al Qaeda, Salafi Jihad, and the Diffusion of Suicide Attacks*. Baltimore, MD: Johns Hopkins University Press, 2008.

"Suicide Terrorism, Occupation, and the Globalization of Martyrdom: A Critique of *Dying to Win*." *Studies in Conflict & Terrorism* 29, no. 8 (2006): 707–729.

Montesquieu, Charles Baron De. *Montesquieu: The Spirit of the Laws*, edited by Anne M. Cohler, Basia Carolyn Miler and Harold Samuel Stone. Cambridge: Cambridge University Press, 1989.

Moussalli, Ahmad S. *Radical Islamic Fundamentalism: The Ideological and Political Discourse of Sayyid Qutb*. Beirut: American University of Beirut, 1992.

Mueller, John E. *Overblown: How Politicians and the Terrorism Industry Inflate National Security Threats*. New York, NY: Free Trade Press, 2006.

Mueller, John E. and Mark G. Stewart. "The Terrorism Delusion: America's Overwrought Response to September 11." *International Security* 37, no. 1 (2012): 81–110.

Myerson, Michael I. *Endowed by Our Creator: The Birth of Religious Freedoms in America*. New Haven, CT: Yale University Press, 2012.

Nardin, Terry. "Review: *Terror in the Mind of God*: The Global Rise of Religious Violence." *Journal of Politics* 63, no. 2 (2001): 683–684.

National Consortium for the Study of Terrorism and Responses to Terrorism (START). "Global Terrorism Database." Last modified 2018. www.start.umd.edu/gtd/.

"GTD in Research." Last modified 2018. www.start.umd.edu/gtd/using-gtd/GTDinResearch.aspx.

National Security Council. "Strategy for Winning the War on Terror." Last modified 2006. www.whitehouse.gov/nsc/nsct/2006/sectionV.html.

Nayar, Kuldip and Khushwant Singh. *Tragedy of Punjab: Operation Bluestar & After*. New Delhi: Vision Books, 1984.

Nelson, Dean. "Pakistani President Asif Zardari Admits Creating Terrorist Groups." *Telegraph*. Last modified July 8, 2009. www.telegraph.co.uk/news/worldnews/asia/pakistan/5779916/Pakistani-president-Asif-Zardari-admits-creating-terrorist-groups.html.

Neuhaus, Richard John. *The Naked Public Square: Religion and Democracy in America*. Grand Rapids, MI: William B. Eerdmans Publishing Company, 1986.

Neumayer, Eric and Thomas Plumper. "Foreign Terror on Americans." *Journal of Peace Research* 48, no. 1 (2011): 3–17.

Nielsen, Richard A. *Deadly Clerics: Blocked Ambition and the Paths to Jihad*. Cambridge: Cambridge University Press, 2017.

Noman, Omar. "Pakistan and General Zia: Era and Legacy." *Third World Quarterly* 11, no. 1 (1989): 28–54.

Norris, Pippa and Ronald F. Inglehart. *Sacred and Secular: Religion and Politics Worldwide*. Cambridge: Cambridge University Press, 2004.

Noueihed, Lin and Alex Warrn. *The Battle for the Arab Spring: Revolution, Counter-Revolution and the Making of a New Era*. New Haven, CT: Yale University Press, 2012.

Novak, David. *In Defense of Religious Liberty*. Wilmington, DE: ISI Books, 2009.

Nussbaum, Martha. *The Clash Within: Democracy, Religious Violence, and India's Future*. Cambridge, MA: Belknap Press, 2009.

Liberty of Conscience: In Defense of America's Traditions of Religious Equality. New York, NY: Basic Books, 2008.

O'Sullivan, Jack. "If You Hate the West, Emigrate to a Western Country." *The Guardian*. Last modified October 8, 2001. www.theguardian.com/world/2001/oct/08/religion.uk.

Obama, Barack. "Remarks by the President at Cairo University." Last modified June 4, 2009. www.whitehouse.gov/the-press-office/remarks-president-cairo-university-6-04-09.

"Remarks by the President at the National Prayer Breakfast." Last modified February 14, 2014. www.whitehouse.gov/the-press-office/2014/02/06/remarks-president-national-prayer-breakfast.

"Remarks by the President at the Summit on Countering Violent Extremism." Last modified February 19, 2015. www.whitehouse.gov/the-press-office/2015/02/19/remarks-president-summit-countering-violent-extremism-february-19-2015.

"Remarks by the President on the Middle East and North Africa." Last modified May 19, 2011. www.whitehouse.gov/the-press-office/2011/05/19/remarks-president-middle-east-and-north-africa.

Oberoi, Harjot. "Sikh Fundamentalism: Translating History into Theory." In *Fundamentalisms and the State: Remaking Polities, Economies, and Militance*, edited by Martin E. Marty and R. Scott Appleby, 256–288. Chicago, IL: University of Chicago, 1993.

"The Official Summation of the Or Commission Report." *Ha'aretz*. September 2, 2003.

Pape, Robert A. *Dying to Win: The Strategic Logic of Suicide Terrorism*. New York, NY: Random House, 2005.

"It's the Occupation, Stupid." *Foreign Policy*. Last modified October 18, 2010. http://foreignpolicy.com/2010/10/18/its-the-occupation-stupid/.

Parliament of the World's Religions. "Alliance of Virtue for the Common Good – The Washington Declaration." Last modified February 5–7, 2018. https://parliamentofreligions.org/publications/alliance-virtue-common-good-washington-declaration.

Patterson, Eric. *Politics in a Religious World: Building a Religiously Informed U.S. Foreign Policy*. New York, NY: Continuum, 2011.

Pedahzur, Ami and Arie Perliger. *Jewish Terrorism in Israel*. New York, NY: Columbia University Press, 2011.

People's Union for Democratic Rights and People's Union for Civil Liberties. *PUCL–PUDR Report: Who Are the Guilty? Report of a Joint Inquiry into the Causes and Impact of the Riots in Delhi from 31 October to 10 November 1984*. Last modified April 1, 2003. www.pucl.org/Topics/Religion-communalism/2003/who-areguilty.htm.

Pettigrew, Joyce J. M. *The Sikhs of the Punjab: Unheard Voices of State and Guerrilla Violence*. London: Zed Books, 1995.

Pew Research Center. *Arab Spring Adds to Global Restrictions on Religion*. Last modified June 20, 2013. www.pewforum.org/2013/06/20/arab-spring-restrictions-on-religion-findings/.

The Global Religious Landscape, last modified December 18, 2012, www.pewforum.org/2012/12/18/global-religious-landscape-exec/.

Global Restrictions on Religion. Last modified December 17, 2009. www.pewforum.org/2009/12/17/global-restrictions-on-religion/.

Latest Trends in Religious Restrictions and Hostilities. Last modified February 26, 2015. www.pewforum.org/files/2015/02/Restrictions2015_fullReport.pdf.

Muslim-Americans Middle Class and Mostly Mainstream. Last modified May 22, 2007. www.pewresearch.org/files/old-assets/pdf/muslim-americans.pdf.

Religious Hostilities Reach Six-Year High. Last modified January 14, 2014. www.pewforum.org/2014/01/14/religious-hostilities-reach-six-year-high/.

Rising Restrictions on Religion – One Third of the World's Population Experiences an Increase. Last modified August 9, 2011. www.pewforum.org/2011/08/09/rising-restrictions-on-religion2/.

Rising Tide of Restrictions on Religion. Last modified September 20, 2012. www.pewforum.org/2012/09/20/rising-tide-of-restrictions-on-religion-findings/

Tolerance and Tension: Islam and Christianity in Sub-Saharan Africa. Last modified April 15, 2010. www.pewforum.org/2010/04/15/executive-summary-islam-and-christianity-in-sub-saharan-africa.

Trends in Global Restrictions on Religion. Last modified June 23, 2016. www.pewforum.org/2016/06/23/trends-in-global-restrictions-on-religion/.

Phillips, Andrew. "The Islamic State's Challenge to International Order." *Australian Journal of International Affairs* 68, no. 5 (2014): 495–498.

Philpott, Daniel. "The Catholic Wave." *Journal of Democracy* 15, no .2 (2004): 32–46.

"Explaining the Political Ambivalence of Religion." *American Political Science Review* 101, no. 3 (2007): 505–525.

"Has the Study of Global Politics Found Religion?" *Annual Review of Political Science* 12 (2009): 183–202.

Just and Unjust Peace: An Ethic of Political Reconciliation. New York, NY: Oxford University Press, 2012.

Religious Freedom in Islam? Intervening in a Culture War. Oxford: Oxford University Press, 2018.

Philpott, Daniel and Timothy Samuel Shah. "In Defense of Religious Freedom: New Critics of a Beleaguered Human Right." *Journal of Law and Religion* 31, no. 3 (2016): 380–395.

Piazza, James A. "Incubators of Terror: Do Failed and Failing States Promote Transnational Terrorism?" *International Studies Quarterly* 52, no. 3 (2008): 469–488.

"Is Islamist Terrorism More Lethal? An Empirical Study of Group Ideology, Organization and Goal Structure." *Terrorism and Political Violence* 21, no. 1 (2009): 62–88.

"Rooted in Poverty? Terrorism, Poor Economic Development, and Social Cleavages." *Terrorism and Political Violence* 18, no. 1 (2006): 159–177.

"Types of Minority Discrimination and Terrorism." *Conflict Management and Peace Science* 29, no. 5 (2012): 521–546.

Piazza, James A. and James I. Walsh. "Transnational Terror and Human Rights." *International Studies Quarterly* 53, no. 1 (2010): 125–148.

Pope Benedict XVI. "Religious Freedom, the Path to Peace." Last modified January 1, 2011. www.vatican.va/holy_father/benedict_xvi/messages/peace/documents/hf_ben-xvi_mes_20101208_xliv-world-day-peace_en.html.

Pope Francis. "Address of His Holiness Pope Francis." Last modified November 30, 2015. https://w2.vatican.va/content/francesco/en/speeches/2015/november/documents/papa-francesco_20151130_repubblica-centrafricana-musulmani.html.

Prakash, Aseem. "Re-Imagination of the State and Gujarat's Electoral Verdict." *Economic and Political Weekly* 38 (2003): 1601–1610.

Public Policy Polling. "Trump Steady in North Carolina; Biden Polls Well." Last modified September 29, 2015. www.publicpolicypolling.com/pdf/2015/PPP_Release_NC_92915.pdf.

Qutb, Sayyid. *Al-Adala al-Ijimaiyya fi-I Islam*. Beirut: Dar al-Kitab al-Arabi, 1979.

Radio Free Europe/Radio Liberty. "Missing Tajik Police Commander Appears on Internet, Says Has Joined IS." *RFE/RL's Tajik Service*. Last modified May 28, 2015. www.rferl.org/a/tajikistan-police-commander-video-says-joined-islamic-state/27041183.html.

Rajagopal, Arvind. "The Gujarat Experiment and Hindu National Realism: Lessons for Secularism." In *The Crisis of Secularism in India*, edited by Anuradha Dingwaney Needham and Rajan Rajeswari Sunder, 208–224. Durham, NC: Duke University Press, 2007.

Ranstorp, Magnus. "Terrorism in the Name of Religion." *Journal of International Affairs* 50 (1996): 41–62.

Rapoport, David. "Fear and Trembling: Terrorism in Three Religious Traditions." *American Political Science Review* 78, no. 3 (1984): 658–677.

"Some General Observations on Religion and Violence." *Terrorism and Political Violence* 3, no. 3 (1991): 118–140.

Rashed, Mohammed Abouelleil and Islam El Azzazi, "The Egyptian Revolution: A Participant's Account from Tahrir Square." *Anthropology Today* 27, no. 2 (2011): 22–27.

Rawls, John. *Political Liberalism*. New York, NY: Columbia University Press, 1993.

Rice, Susan E. *The New National Security Strategy: Focus on Failed States*. Washington, DC: Brookings Institution, 2003.

Richter, William L. "The Political Dynamics of Islamic Resurgence in Pakistan." *Asian Survey* 19, no. 6 (1979): 547–557.

Rodrick, Dani. "The Poverty of Dictatorship." *Project Syndicate*. Last modified February 9, 2011. www.project-syndicate.org/commentary/the-poverty-of-dictatorship.

Ronen, Yehudit. "Radical Islam versus the Nation-State." In *Religion, Politics, Society and the State*, edited by Jonathan Fox, 131–145. Oxford: Oxford University Press, 2012.

Roy, Oliver. *The Failure of Political Islam*. Paris: Esprit/Seuil, 1994.

Rubio, Marco. "Rubio Comments on the Release of the International Religious Freedom Report." October 14, 2015. www.rubio.senate.gov/public/index.cfm/press-releases?ID=6d9c39fb-1df2-4a8a-8915-fa52aeacdfd9.

Ryan, Yasemine. "The Tragic Life of a Street Vendor." *Al Jazeera*. Last modified January 20, 2011. Accessed June 26, 2015. www.aljazeera.com/indepth/features/2011/01/20111684242518839 .html.

Sageman, Marc. *Understanding Terror Networks*. Philadelphia, PA: University of Pennsylvania Press, 2004.

Saiya, Nilay. "Blasphemy and Terrorism in the Muslim World." *Terrorism and Political Violence* 29, no. 6 (2017): 1087–1105.

"Explaining Religious Violence across Countries: An Institutional Perspective." In *Mediating Religion and Government: Political Institutions and the Policy Process*, edited by Kevin R. den Dulk and Elizabeth Oldmixon, 209–240. New York, NY: Palgrave.

"Religion, Democracy and Terrorism." *Perspectives on Terrorism* 9, no. 6 (2015): 51–59.

"The Religious Freedom Peace." *International Journal of Human Rights* 19, no. 3 (2015): 369–382.

"Religion, State and Terrorism: A Global Analysis," *Terrorism and Political Violence*. doi:10.1080/09546553.2016.1211525.

Saiya, Nilay and Anthony Scime. "Explaining Religious Terrorism: A Data-Mined Analysis." *Conflict Management and Peace Science* 32, no. 5 (2015): 487–512.

Sanchez-Cuenca Ignacio and Luis de la Calle. "Domestic Terrorism: The Hidden Side of Political Violence." *Annual Review of Political Science* 12 (2009): 31–49.

Sarkissian, Ani. *The Varieties of Repression: Why Governments Restrict Religion*. New York, NY: Oxford University Press, 2015.

Schbley, Ayla. "Defining Religious Terrorism: A Causal and Anthological Profile." *Studies in Conflict & Terrorism* 26, no. 2 (2003): 105–134.

Schober, Juliane. *Buddhist Conjunctures in Myanmar: Cultural Narratives, Colonial Legacies, and Civil Society*. Honolulu, HI: University of Hawaii Press, 2011.

Schwedler, Jillian. *Faith in Moderation: Islamist Parties in Jordan and Yemen*. New York, NY: Cambridge University Press, 2007.

Sciolino, Elaine. "Spain Struggles to Absorb Worst Terrorist Attack in Its History." *New York Times*. Last modified March 11, 2004. www.nytimes.com/2004/03/11/international/europe/ 11CND-TRAI.html.

Sedgwick, Mark. "Measuring Egyptian Regime Legitimacy." *Middle East Critique* 19, no. 3 (2010): 251–267.

Seiple, Chris and Dennis R. Hoover. "Religious Liberty and Global Security." In *The Future of Religious Liberty: Global Challenges*, edited by Allen D. Hertzke, 315–330. New York, NY: Oxford University Press, 2013.

Shah, Timothy Samuel. *Religious Freedom: Why Now? Defending an Embattled Human Right*. Princeton, NJ: Witherspoon Institute, 2012.

Shahin, Emad Eldin. *Political Ascent: Contemporary Islamic Movements in North Africa*. Boulder, CO: Westview Press, 1997.

Shamseddin, Moataz. "In Translation: April 6's Ahmed Maher on Egypt under Sisi." *Huffington Post Arabi*. Last modified July 29, 2015. https://arabist.net/blog/2015/8/17/in-translation-april-6s- ahmed-maher-on-egypt-undersisi?utm_source=Sailthru&utm_medium=email& utm_campaign=New%20Campaign&utm_term=*Mideast%20Brief .

Sheehan, Michael. "Terrorism: The Current Threat." Last modified February 10, 2000. www.brookings.edu/events/2000/0210terrorism.aspx.

Shuja, Sharif. "Indian Secularism: Image and Reality." *Contemporary Review* 287 (2005): 38–42.

Simon, Steven and Daniel Benjamin. "The Terror." *Survival* 43, no. 4 (2001): 5–18.

Singh, Pritam. *Federalism, Nationalism and Development: India and the Punjab Economy*. London: Routledge, 2008.

"Two Facets of Revivalism." *Punjab Today* (1987): 167–179.

Slater, Jerome. "Zionism, the Jewish State, and an Israeli–Palestinian Settlement: An Opinion Piece." *Political Science Quarterly* 127, no. 4 (2012): 597–625.

Smidt, Corwin. Ed. *Religion as Social Capital: Producing the Common Good*. Waco, TX: Baylor University Press, 2003.

South Asia Terrorism Portal. "Pakistan – Terrorist, Insurgent and Extremist Groups." Last modified December 2017. www.satp.org/featurelist.aspx?countryid=2&featurename=Terrorist%20Groups.

Spencer, Alexander. "Questioning the Concept of 'New Terrorism.'" *Peace, Conflict & Development* 8 (2006): 1–33.

Sprinzak, Ehud. *Brother against Brother: Violence and Extremism in Israeli Politics from Altalena to the Rabin Assassination*. New York, NY: Free Press, 1999.

"Three Models of Religious Violence: The Case of Jewish Fundamentalism in Israel." In *Fundamentalism and the State: Remaking Politics, Economies, and Militance*, edited by Martin E. Marty and R. Scott Appleby, 462–490. Chicago, IL: University of Chicago, 1993.

Stark, Rodney. *The Victory of Reason: How Christianity Led to Freedom, Capitalism and Western Success*. New York, NY: Random House, 2006.

Stepan, Alfred C. "The Multiple Secularisms of Modern Democratic and Non-Democratic Regimes." In *Rethinking Secularism*, edited by Craig Calhoun, Mark Juergensmeyer and Jonathan van Antwerpen, 114–144. New York, NY: Oxford University Press, 2011.

"Religion, Democracy, and the 'Twin Tolerations.'" *Journal of Democracy* 11, no. 4 (2000): 37–57.

"Rituals of Respect: Sufis and Secularists in Senegal in Comparative Perspective." *Comparative Politics* 44, no. 4 (July 2012): 379–401.

"Tunisia's Transition and the Twin Tolerations." *Journal of Democracy* 23, no. 2 (2012): 89–103.

Stepan, Alfred C. and Juan J. Linz. "Democratization Theory and the Arab Spring." *Journal of Democracy* 24, no. 2 (2013): 15–30.

Stephen, Chris. "Fear of Tunisia's Democracy Led ISIS to Launch an Attack on Its Tourist Economy." *The Guardian*. Last modified March 21, 2015. www.theguardian.com/world/2015/mar/22/tunisia-terror-attack-tourists.

Stern, Jessica. "Pakistan's Jihad Culture." *Foreign Affairs* 79, no. 6 (2002): 115–126.

Terror in the Name of God: Why Religious Militants Kill. New York, NY: Harper Perennial, 2003.

Strenski, Ivan. *Why Politics Can't Be Freed from Religion*. Chichester: Wiley-Blackwell, 2011.

Sullivan, Winnifred Fallers, Elizabeth Shakman Hurd, Saba Mahmood and Peter G. Danchin. *Politics of Religious Freedom*. Chicago, IL: University of Chicago Press, 2015.

Svensson, Isak. "Fighting with Faith: Religion and Conflict Resolution in Civil Wars." *Journal of Conflict Resolution* 51, no. 6 (2007): 930–949.

Svensson, Isak and Emily Harding. "How Holy Wars End: Exploring the Termination Patterns of Conflicts With Religious Dimensions in Asia." *Terrorism and Political Violence* 23, no. 2 (2011): 133–149.

Swami, Praveen. "The Well-Tempered Jihad: The Politics and Practice of Post-2002 Islamist Terrorism in India." *Contemporary South Asia* 16, no. 3 (2008): 303–322.

Tagliabu, John. "A Nation Challenged: The Suspects: Arrests in Belgium Highlight Its Role as a Militant's Base." *New York Times*. Last modified December 20, 2001. www.nytimes.com/

2001/12/20/world/nation-challenged-suspects-arrests-belgium-highlight-its-role-militants-base.html.

Taheri, Amir. *Holy Terror: The Inside Story of Islamic Terrorism*. London: Hutchinson, 1987.

Takeyh, Ray and Nikolas Gvosdev. "Do Terrorist Networks Need a Home?" *Washington Quarterly* 25, no. 3 (2002): 97–108.

Thames, Knox. "Defending Religion from Itself." *Foreign Policy*. Last modified July 30, 2015. http://foreignpolicy.com/2015/07/30/defending-religion-from-itself/.

"Pakistan's Dangerous Game with Religious Extremism." *Review of Faith & International Affairs* 12, no. 4 (2014): 40–48.

Theodorou, Angelina E. "Which Countries Still Outlaw Apostasy and Blasphemy?" *Pew Research Center*. Last modified July 29, 2016. www.pewresearch.org/fact-tank/2016/07/29/which-countries-still-outlaw-apostasy-and-blasphemy/.

Thurston, Alexander. "Why Is Militant Islam a Weak Phenomenon in Senegal?" *Working Paper No. 09–005*. Institute for the Study of Islamic Thought in Africa. Bufett Center for International and Comparative Studies, Northwestern University, March 2009.

Toft, Monica D. "Getting Religion? The Puzzling Case of Islam and Civil War." *International Security* 37, no. 4 (2007): 97–131.

Securing the Peace: The Durable Settlement of Civil Wars. Princeton, NJ: Princeton University Press, 2009.

Toft, Monica D., Daniel Philpott and Timothy Samuel Shah. *God's Century: Resurgent Religion and Global Politics*. New York, NY: W. W. Norton, 2011.

Toft, Monica D. and Timothy Samuel Shah. "Why God Is Winning." *Foreign Policy* 155 (2006): 39–43.

Truth and Reconciliation Commission. *Volume Four: Truth and Reconciliation Commission of South Africa Report*. Last modified November 11, 2015. www.justice.gov.za/trc/report/finalreport/Volume%204.pdf.

Tutu, Desmond. *No Future without Forgiveness*. New York, NY: Doubleday, 1999.

US Commission on International Religious Freedom. *Annual Report 2015*. Washington, DC: US Commission on International Religious Freedom, 2015.

Annual Report 2017. Washington, DC: US Commission on International Religious Freedom, 2017.

Burma: Religious Freedom and Related Human Rights Violations Are Hindering Broader Reforms: Findings from a Visit of the U.S. Commission on International Religious Freedom. Washington, DC: US Commission on International Religious Freedom, 2014.

US Department of State. "Country Reports on Terrorism, 2000–2016," last modified 2016, www.state.gov/j/ct/rls/crt/.

US Department of State Bureau of Counterterrorism and Countering Violent Extremism. "Country Reports on Terrorism 2000–2015." Last modified 2016. Accessed January 10, 2017. www.state.gov/j/ct/rls/crt/.

US Department of State Bureau of Democracy, Human Rights and Labor. "Burma," 2015 *International Religious Freedom Report*, 2015, www.state.gov/documents/organization/256305.pdf.

"Central African Republic." 2015 *International Religious Freedom Report*. Last modified 2015. www.state.gov/documents/organization/256217.pdf.

"Egypt." 2013 *International Religious Freedom Report*. Last modified 2013. www.state.gov/j/drl/rls/irf/religiousfreedom/index.htm#wrapper.

"Egypt." 2016 International *Religious Freedom Report*. Last modified 2016. www.state.gov/j/drl/rls/irf/religiousfreedom/index.htm#wrapper.

"India." *2016 International Religious Freedom Report.* Last modified 2016. www.state.gov/j/drl/rls/irf/religiousfreedom/index.htm#wrapper.

"Iraq." *2003 International Religious Freedom Report.* Last modified 2003. http://m.state.gov/md24452.html.

"Iraq." *2015 International Religious Freedom Report.* Last modified 2015. www.state.gov/j/drl/rls/irf/2015religiousfreedom/index.htm#wrapper.

"Israel." *2014 International Religious Freedom Report.* Last modified 2014. www.state.gov/j/drl/rls/irf/religiousfreedom/index.htm#wrapper.

"Israel." *2015 International Religious Freedom Report.* Last modified 2015. www.state.gov/documents/organization/256481.pdf.

"Libya." *2015 International Religious Freedom Report,* Last modified 2015. www.state.gov/j/drl/rls/irf/religiousfreedom/index.htm#wrapper.

"Libya." *2016 International Religious Freedom Report.* Last modified 2016. www.state.gov/j/drl/rls/irf/religiousfreedom/index.htm#wrapper.

"Pakistan." *2016 International Religious Freedom Report.* Last modified 2016. www.state.gov/j/drl/rls/irf/religiousfreedom/index.htm#wrapper.

"Senegal." *2015 International Religious Freedom Report.* Last modified 2015. www.state.gov/j/drl/rls/irf/religiousfreedom/index.htm#wrapper.

"Tunisia." *2013 International Religious Freedom Report.* Last modified 2013. www.state.gov/j/drl/rls/irf/religiousfreedom/index.htm#wrapper.

"Tunisia." *2016 International Religious Freedom Report.* Last modified 2016. www.state.gov/j/drl/rls/irf/religiousfreedom/index.htm#wrapper.

"Yemen." *2013 International Religious Freedom Report.* Last modified 2013. www.state.gov/j/drl/rls/irf/religiousfreedom/index.htm#wrapper.

USAID. "Central African Republic – Complex Emergency: Fact Sheet #10, Fiscal Year (FY) 2015." Last modified March 2, 2015. www.usaid.gov/sites/default/files/documents/1866/car_ce_fs10_03–02-2015.pdf.

Van der Veer, Peter. "Religious Nationalism in India and Global Fundamentalism." In *Globalization and Social Movements: Culture, Power and the Transnational Public Sphere,* edited by John Guidry, Michael D. Kennedy and Mayer Zald, 315–336. Ann Arbor, MI: University of Michigan Press, 2000.

Van der Vyver, Johan D. "The Contours of Religious Liberty in South Africa." *Emory International Law Review* 21 (2007): 77–110.

Van Dyke, Virginia. "The Khalistan Movement in Punjab, India, and the Post-Militancy Era: Structural Change and New Political Compulsions." *Asian Survey* 49, no. 6 (2009): 975–997.

Varadarajan, Siddharth. "A Stench That Is All Too Familiar." *The Hindu.* March 24, 2009.

Villalón, Leonardo A. "Generational Changes, Political Stagnation, and the Evolving Dynamics of Religion and Politics in Senegal." *Africa Today* 46, no. 3 (1999): 129–147.

Islamic Society and State Power in Senegal: Disciples and Citizens in Fatick. Cambridge: Cambridge University Press, 1995.

"Negotiating Islam in the Era of Democracy: Senegal in Comparative Regional Perspective." In *Tolerance, Democracy, and Sufis in Senegal,* edited by Mamadou Diouf, 238–266. New York, NY: Columbia University Press, 2012.

Villa-Vicencio, Charles and Fanie Du Toit. *Truth and Reconciliation in South Africa: 10 Years On.* Cape Town: New Africa Books, 2006.

Villa-Vicencio, Charles and Wilhelm Verwoerd. Eds. *Looking Back, Reaching Forward: Reflections on the Truth and Reconciliation Commission in South Africa.* Cape Town: UCT Press, 2000.

Wach, Jochim. "The Role of Religion in the Social Philosophy of Alex De Tocqueville." *Journal of the History of Ideas* 7 (1946): 74–90.

Walsh, James I. and James A. Piazza. "Why Respecting Physical Integrity Rights Reduces Terrorism." *Comparative Political Studies* 43, no. 5 (2009): 551–577.

Waltz, Susan. "Islamist Appeal in Tunisia." *Middle East Journal* 40, no. 4 (1986): 651–670.

Ware, Lewis B." Ben Ali's Constitutional Coup in Tunisia." *Middle East Journal* 42, no. 4 (1988): 587–601.

Warren, Rick. "Rick Warren on Religious Freedom – A Conversation." Remarks to Georgetown University. Washington, DC, February 12, 2013.

Weaver, Matthew. "Muammar Gaddafi Condemns Tunisia Uprising." *The Guardian*. January 16, 2011.

Welby, Justin. "Archbishop of Canterbury on Religious Freedom. Last modified July 16, 2015. www.archbishopofcanterbury.org/articles.php/5591/archbishop-of-canterbury-on-religious-freedom.

The White House. "Remarks by the President on Egypt." Last modified February 11, 2011. www.whitehouse.gov/the-press-office/2011/02/11/remarks-president-egypt.

Wiarda, Howard J. "Arab Fall or Arab Winter?" *American Foreign Policy Interests* 34, no. 3 (2012): 134–137.

Wickham, Carrie Rosefsky. *Mobilizing Islam: Religion, Activism, and Political Change in Egypt*. New York, NY: Columbia University Press, 2002, 93–118.

Wiktorowicz, Quintan. *Radical Islam Rising: Muslim Extremism in the West*. Lanham, MD: Rowman & Littlefield Publishers, 2005.

Willis, Michael. *Politics and Power in the Maghreb: Algeria, Tunisia and Morocco from Independence to the Arab Spring*. Oxford: Oxford University Press, 2014.

Woodberry, Robert D. "The Missionary Roots of Liberal Democracy." *American Political Science Review* 106, no. 2 (2012): 244–274.

World Bank. *World Development Indicators 2017*. Washington, DC: World Bank, 2017.

Wright, Jonathan. "Uganda Army Marches on Voodoo Priestess." *Glasgow Herald*. October 6, 1987.

Wright, Tom. "Leading Pakistani Politician Killed." *Wall Street Journal*, January 3, 2011, www.wsj.com/articles/SB10001424052748704723104576061371508098218.

Ya, Li. "China Bans Many Muslims from Ramadan Fast." *Voice of America News*. Last modified July 8, 2014. www.voanews.com/a/china-bans-many-uighur-muslims-from-ramadan-fast/1952829.html.

Yadav, Yogendra. "The Patterns and Lessons." *Frontline* 19, no. 26 (2003): 10–16.

Yang, Fenggang. "The Red, Black, and Gray Markets of Religion in China." *Sociological Quarterly* 47, no. 1 (2006): 93–122.

Yuhas, Alan. "How Yemen Spawned the Charlie Hebdo Attacks – the Guardian Briefing." *The Guardian*. Last modified January 14, 2015. www.theguardian.com/world/2015/jan/14/yemen-aqap-civil-war-extremism?CMP=share_btn_tw.

Zaimov, Stoyan. "Christians in India Demand Justice for 2008 Orissa Massacre." *Christian Post*. Last modified January 3, 2012. www.christianpost.com/news/christians-in-india-demand-justice-for-2008-orissa-massacre-66264/.

Zakaria, Fareed. *The Future of Freedom: Illiberal Democracy at Home and Abroad*. New York, NY: W. W. Norton, 2007.

Zald, Mayer N. and John D. McCarthy. *The Dynamics of Social Movements: Resource Mobilization, Social Control and Tactics*. Cambridge, MA: Winthrop Publishers, 1979.

Zarocostas, John. "More than 7,000 Tunisians Said to Have Joined Islamic State." *Mclatchy DC*. Last modified March 17, 2015. www.mcclatchydc.com/news/nation-world/world/middle-east/article24781867.html.

Zauzmer, Julie. "Pence: America Will Prioritize Protecting Christians Abroad." *Washington Post*. Last modified May 11, 2017. www.washingtonpost.com/news/acts-of-faith/wp/2017/05/11/pence-america-will-prioritize-protecting-christians-abroad/?utm_term=.afof98b2e443.

Ziring, Lawrence. *Pakistan in the Twentieth Century: A Political History*. Karachi: Oxford University Press, 1997.

Index